298 4

W9-BWV-092

# How to Say It®

# ONLINE

Everything you Need to Know
to Master the New Language of
Cyberspace

## Kim Baker and Sunny Baker

Prentice
Hall Press

11/01

#45715338

**Library of Congress Cataloging-in-Publication Data**

Baker, Kim,
    How to say it online : everything you need to know to master the new language of cyberspace / Kim Baker and Sunny Baker.
        p.   cm.
    Includes index.
        ISBN 0-7352-0164-1 (pbk.)
        1. Business communication—Data processing.   2. Commercial correspondence—Data processing.
3. Electronic mail messages.   I. Baker, Sunny.   II. Title.

    HF5718 .B346   2001
    808'.06665—dc21                                          00-068681

© 2001 by Prentice Hall

Printed in the United States of America

10 9 8 7 6 5 4 3 2 1

ISBN 0-7352-0164-1 (pbk.)

---

**ATTENTION: CORPORATIONS AND SCHOOLS**

Prentice Hall books are available at quantity discounts with bulk purchase for educational, business, or sales promotional use. For information, please write to: Prentice Hall Special Sales, 240 Frisch Court, Paramus, New Jersey 07652. Please supply: title of book, ISBN, quantity, how the book will be used, date needed.

---

# PRENTICE HALL PRESS
Paramus, NJ 07652
http://www.phdirect.com

# *How* You Say It Online Is More Important than *What* You Say

UNLESS YOU'VE BEEN LIVING IN A CAVE, you've seen enormous changes in communications technology over the past two decades. From orbiting satellites routing long distance phone calls to email to undreamed-of growth of the Internet, the age of communicating online, using computers and networks, is upon us all.

And what could be better news? To keep in touch, there's nothing faster or cheaper than email. To gain access to information and people, the power of online communication expands your reach from the local to the global. To meet new friends and even romance a potential life partner, online venues provide rich opportunities (if you know the right things to say and the best way to say them). At school, the Internet places volumes of knowledge on every subject at your fingertips, and at work, computer networks make business communications more efficient than ever.

In the words of Star Trek's Borg, "Resistance is futile." Even diehard "I'll-never-use-a-computer" types are being swept up in the wave, setting up email accounts and checking out online chat rooms to find new friends or hear expert opinions. Meanwhile, technology marches on, making communication ever more available with intelligent electronic personal assistants, palm-sized hand-held computers, cellphones, and a host of other electronic organizers and instant message devices, including your television. But this brave new world brings with it its own set of challenges.

You know the cliché: "It's not what you say, but *how* you say it…" This sentiment is even more true in the online world, where a message requiring 150 carefully chosen words and a picture can be inappropriately condensed into 15 rather terse words and cryptic abbreviations that can confuse—and even offend—the recipient.

Online communication is more complex than most users realize. It's surprisingly easy to send unintentionally harsh or poorly worded messages via email, gaffs within chat rooms, or accidental insults to favorite Internet pen pals. Equally difficult is interpreting incoming mail and chat responses. What do those symbols and odd abbreviations mean? Why does such a sensitive "e-message" seem so terse? What is the writer implying—if anything? Should the communiqué be accepted at face value or is there something subtle that doesn't initially meet the eye?

These issues become especially crucial if you're communicating with someone who's very important to you—your boss, for example. If he is incompetent or insensitive when it comes to reading email, you could miscommunicate without even knowing it. Your important description of a major corporate priority might be interpreted as irrelevant trivia—just because you used the wrong subject line to describe the contents of the message.

Fortunately, this book can help. You'll learn how to say the right things when you want to and how to avoid barrages of unwanted and unsolicited emails. Transforming yourself from novice communicator to a savvy, electronic orator is easier than you think. We've created *How to Say It Online* as your "friend in the business" reference to flatten the learning curve for you.

We focus on the *content* of online communication: how to say what you want and need to say. Our guidelines include the basics of *netiquette*—which embody the ways to be polite online, but also go beyond simply showing you how to be a nice person. Our advice and guidelines show you how to be more efficient, clear, and effective in all your online communications.

We keep the technical information to a minimum, discussing it only when the topic at hand hinges on the electronic mechanism employed. If setting up for online schmoozing seems alien to you, however, don't be embarrassed. Start by taking the Quiz in Chapter 1 to see how savvy you really are in your online communications. For those with little experience, we've included basic descriptions of email operations in Chapters 2 and 3.

These brief chapters cover the basic online communication issues, but remember: we don't go into detail on all the options, buttons, and commands in the programs. Those totally new to computers should still pick up a book of recent vintage (published within the last two years) that explains how to connect to the Internet and use standard email programs such as Microsoft Outlook, Outlook Express, Eudora, Netscape Communicator, or America Online.

After going through the basics of email and chat, we go on to discuss specific ways to handle all sorts of online communications with aplomb—whether at home, work, or play. Remember that our recommendations are *not* hard and fast rules. Let your own judgment be the final arbiter.

We hope this book will help you examine your assumptions about online communication and maximize your effectiveness in the online world. Once you've reflected on the basic issues and practiced for a while, you'll be able to write online with confidence using your own style and personality.

Our goal for you is the same one we hold for ourselves: to become more effective online communicators in every online venue.

# contents

## The Basics of Communicating Online

# Putting Yourself Across Online

# PART ONE

# The Basics of Communicating Online

CHAPTER ONE

# How Good Are You at Online Communication?

NEITHER RAIN, NOR SNOW, nor sleet, nor gloom of night can stay the Internet from delivering its email, but sometimes you wish _something_ would—especially after you've sent a message that seemed to have exactly the wrong effect on the person at the other end. The ease with which we can put our half-thought-out, easily misunderstood ideas into electronic print for other eyes to read can be a recipe for catastrophe. And to make matters even more complicated, this brave, new world online has developed an entire lingo of its own.

Inept electronic communication has sunk more than one person's career, potential romantic relationship, or online friendship, and for some of us, it may have done all three.

Fortunately, life online doesn't have to be that way. Communicating electronically may demand some skills that are new to you, but they're skills you can easily master.

## Definition: *com.*

Although not in the dictionary (yet) the word "com" (or "comm") replaces the longer winded "communications."

## SELF-TEST: GAUGING YOUR ONLINE COMMUNICATIONS EFFECTIVENESS

To bring you up to speed on the state of your current online communications skills, try taking this 40 question quiz. But remember, it's not a contest. The purpose is not to achieve a high score, but to gauge your current online communications skills realistically, so provide an honest response even if it doesn't appear to be the "right" one.

|  | True | False |
|---|:---:|:---:|
| 1. I communicate online effectively, meaning that people always understand what I mean and intend. | ___ | ___ |
| 2. I compose email messages without much effort. | ___ | ___ |
| 3. I use email frequently because I feel comfortable with the medium. | ___ | ___ |
| 4. My email almost always nets me good responses. | ___ | ___ |
| 5. I know exactly when an email message would be inappropriate. | ___ | ___ |
| 6. I feel confident when I send my thoughts via email. | ___ | ___ |
| 7. In my email, I have no trouble saying what I mean. | ___ | ___ |
| 8. I have no trouble communicating to my peers using email. | ___ | ___ |
| 9. I have no trouble communicating to my subordinates using email. | ___ | ___ |
| 10. I have no trouble communicating to my managers (or superiors) using email. | ___ | ___ |
| 11. I have no trouble communicating to my friends using email. | ___ | ___ |

| | True | False |
|---|---|---|
| **12.** I have no trouble communicating to my family using email. | ____ | ____ |
| **13.** I have online pen pals that I've also met in person. | ____ | ____ |
| **14.** I have pen pals that I have never met other than online. | ____ | ____ |
| **15.** My email messages receive timely responses. | ____ | ____ |
| **16.** My questions sent through email almost always receive clear responses. | ____ | ____ |
| **17.** I can tell the difference in email sent by experienced vs. inexperienced users. | ____ | ____ |
| **18.** When I need to contact someone, I automatically think "phone or email?" | ____ | ____ |
| **19.** I enjoy using chat for fun or for improving my understanding of a subject of interest to me. | ____ | ____ |
| **20.** When using chat, I understand most of the shortcuts and symbols. | ____ | ____ |
| **21.** When using chat, I am comfortable participating. | ____ | ____ |
| **22.** When using chat, I feel comfortable with the banter when it involves me. | ____ | ____ |
| **23.** I consider chat as a recreational choice like attending a movie. | ____ | ____ |
| **24.** I use the World Wide Web for business transactions (i.e. purchasing things or making stock investments). | ____ | ____ |
| **25.** I feel comfortable "surfing" the web for fun and/or education. | ____ | ____ |

Score 1 for each *true* response, 0 for *false*.

**Total 1 – 25** ____

| | True | False |
|---|---|---|
| **26.** Sometimes I put off answering my email for a week or more. | ____ | ____ |
| **27.** I prefer to respond to email by phone or conventional mail. | ____ | ____ |

|  | True | False |
|---|---|---|
| 28. I prefer to write one line responses to email and then answer in detail in person. | ____ | ____ |
| 29. I prefer to write very long email messages to fully explain myself. | ____ | ____ |
| 30. I avoid online meetings or chat room use wherever possible. | ____ | ____ |
| 31. I often use all capital letters in my online email or chat because it's easier to type that way. | ____ | ____ |
| 32. I prefer to write email first in longhand and then key it into the computer. | ____ | ____ |
| 33. I've heard that some people get angry/upset with my email. | ____ | ____ |
| 34. I don't know what parts of the email addresses mean. | ____ | ____ |
| 35. I find that online communication is more work than it's worth. | ____ | ____ |
| 36. I find that online communication is almost always ineffective. | ____ | ____ |
| 37. I find that online communication is slower than other methods. | ____ | ____ |
| 38. I find that I can't get my message across online. | ____ | ____ |
| 39. I find that words fail me in online communication. | ____ | ____ |
| 40. I think that the world is passing me by because I can't effectively communicate online. | ____ | ____ |

Score 1 for each *true* response, 0 for each *false*.

**Total 26 – 40** ____

Total Score (subtract the total for items 25 - 40 from the total of items 1 - 25)

**Your Total Score** ____

## What This Exercise Means to You

This test is a quick way to evaluate your comfort and experience with online communication. Look at your total score. If it is:

**Higher than 30.** You are probably comfortable online and are at least an adequate online communicator.

**20 to 30.** You are reasonably comfortable online and understand how to communicate, but the nuances of effective online communication may be beyond your experience.

**19 and below** (including negative numbers). You neither enjoy online communication nor are very good at it . . . yet. But you're about to be. Just read on.

# CHAPTER TWO

# Getting Started
# with Basic Email

ONCE UPON A TIME, bar-going singles and new business contacts would exchange phone numbers scrawled on the backs of matchbooks in the hope of establishing a relationship. These days, all that has changed. They're far more likely to trade email addresses.

Email, short for electronic mail, travels as fast as a phone call but, like a letter, allows you to take all the time you need in deciding what you want to say. No longer do you have to worry about avoiding embarrassing silences on the phone or wait on the whims of the post office to deliver your paper mail (now known as "snail mail"). And even better, you can enhance your electronic messages with pictures and sound!

So how do you get started? The first thing you'll need is software. (If you're already an experienced user, you'll know all this, so simply skim this chapter to pick up interesting tidbits and proceed to the later, content-specific chapters.)

## The Pieces of the Telecom Puzzle

Online communication of even the simplest kind requires a sophisticated interaction between man and machine. Here are the elements that must be present for successful communication to take place.

1. You, the communicator, who creates the online messages.
2. A computer equipped with the appropriate software programs, including an email program, chat software, and, if you decide to get really hi-tech, video-conferencing software (along with a camera and microphone).
3. Either a modem, which allows you to telephone into the Internet or email network, or a direct Internet or network connection. On some networks, such as those used within a company, you can email directly from your computer to another user in the company without the use of an Internet service.
4. A network infrastructure which includes cables, phone lines, satellites, and/or fiber optic cable for sending and receiving online communications.
5. A remote computer or group of computers on a network that will receive your communication.
6. The recipient(s) who will read, hear, or see the online communication. The recipients, of course, also need the appropriate computer, software, and network connection at their end.

## COMMUNICATIONS SOFTWARE BASICS

One of the most popular email software packages is Microsoft Outlook. Also available as a "lite" package called Outlook Express, this program comes free with most new computers as part of the Microsoft Explorer Internet browser.

The full version of Outlook is sold with Microsoft's Office package and includes added capabilities for handling your personal schedule and scheduling meetings with other people who share the Outlook product on a Microsoft network (if your company is using the Microsoft Exchange networking feature). For email only, however, either Outlook Express or Netscape Messenger is fully capable of doing almost every email function and is simple to use.

## Where to Get Free Email Software

If you have a computer that's already hooked up to the web, you can update your browser and get free email software in the same package.

You can get a free copy of Microsoft Explorer, which comes with Outlook Express, at **http://www.microsoft.com/windows/ie/**

Netscape Communicator, the other major Internet browser, also includes a built-in email program called Netscape Messenger. You can download a free copy of Netscape Communicator at

**http://www.netscape.com/computing/download/index.html**

Most modern email programs (even those programs provided through the free online email services), have several primary functions. The major ones include:

- **A writing, formatting, and spelling tool** set for composing email messages.
- **Send, receive, and forward functions** for sending, receiving, and rerouting your messages.
- **A filing system** for organizing incoming and outgoing messages according to topic, date sent, or other methods you set up.
- **An address book** for storing the electronic addresses and other information about the people, companies, and organizations you write to.
- **A search system** for locating messages in the filing system.
- **The ability to "attach" files** to messages. For example, you might want to send a report of the third-quarter financial results with a brief note explaining what's in it. By attaching the report in its original format, such as an Excel spreadsheet file, to an email, the recipient can open and read the report, using the software that created it.
- **The ability to automatically send and receive email** at times preset by the user.
- **The ability to send an automatic return message** when an email is sent to you. This is useful if you won't be able to respond to your email in a timely fashion, to let people know that you're unavailable, or simply to let people know that you've received the email and will be responding as soon as you have time.

■ **Rerouting capability**, which allows you to send messages you receive to other email addresses automatically. This is convenient if you use multiple email accounts, or if you want to have your email rerouted to your assistant or to a colleague while you are out of the office.

■ **Additional tools** for converting message formats and compressing pictures to save transmission time and disk space. (These tools are often optional or available as free downloads from the Internet.)

## Anatomy of an Email

Email can be formal or informal, simple or complex, but every message sent through cyberspace must contain three basic elements:

1. **The address line** tells the system to whom the message should be sent. You type the address or get it from your online address book. This can be an individual, a small group, or thousands of recipients, depending on what the address contains. Entering nothing will cause your email program to refuse to send the message.

2. **The subject line** typically contains just a few words describing the overall subject of your message. This helps your recipient decide which messages to read first. If you enter nothing in the subject line, your email program may automatically fill in the blank space with the words "no message." Or, the program may refuse to send it altogether and ask you to fill in the line.

3. **The "body" of the message** is the letter portion of your email and may contain just a few words or literally pages of information. Be aware that truly long messages may be refused by the recipient's computer as a way of screening out junk mail and abusive users. If you have only a short note, you can sometimes send only a subject line without including any text in the body, but we don't recommend this. At the very least, repeat the subject line in the body so the communication isn't misinterpreted as an incomplete message.

Whether you choose Outlook or some other software package, you need concern yourself only with the basics of using it. While email programs may look different from each other on the screen, what they do and how they do it is largely the same from a user's (your) point of view.

## YOUR ONLINE ADDRESS

Just as a paper letter needs to have a recipient's address and a return address, so does an email.

Internal and private email systems, like the ones used in company offices, can handle many different kinds of addresses. If your name is John Jones, your email address might also simply be "John Jones." But it could also be something like J12124322/unix/net/serve7b.

The most common email addresses used on the Internet look something like this: karen.smith@cellscorp.com, or jimjones@flyby.edu, or Jacques@bonjour.ca. The words before the @ (at) sign indicate the exact recipient and the letters after the @ signify the computer system (domain name) where the email account is located. Note that only letters, numbers, and "-" and "." are allowed in most addresses, which is why the addresses sometimes look so odd.

There are many users who by accident or choice have unusually cryptic names. But no matter how strange a user name may seem, it always comes down to the same basic elements: the recipient's email name (**karen.smith**@compuserve.com or **rex.pluto.gol.ttt7**@xerxes.net) and the computer where the account is located (**@compuserve.com** or **@planet.pluto.net**).

The last two or three letters at the end of the email or Internet address (for example, .com, .net, .edu, .ca, .ga or others) explain the type of connection that is being used. In the United States .com stands for commercial accounts and businesses; .net stands for companies that operate direct network accounts; and .edu stands for educational institutions. There are also endings for countries. For example, .ca stands for Canadian accounts, .dr represents accounts in Germany, and .gr represents accounts in Greece.

---

**ONLINE LINGO**

**Network system:** A network system—you'll see this phrase frequently in this book—is a group of computers that can talk to each other. It can be as large a network as America Online with its huge list of subscribers, or just a few people who work or play together through their computers.

## What's in a Domain?

### ■ STANDARD US DOMAINS

**COM** US Commercial

**EDU** US Educational

**GOV** US Government

**INT** International

**MIL** US Military

**NET** Network

**ORG** Non-Profit
  Organization

**ARPA** Old style
  Arpanet

**NATO** Nato field

### ■ COUNTRY DOMAINS

**AD** Andorra

**AE** United Arab
  Emirates

**AF** Afghanistan

**AG** Antigua and
  Barbuda

**AI** Anguilla

**AL** Albania

**AM** Armenia

**AN** Netherlands
  Antilles

**AO** Angola

**AQ** Antarctica

**AR** Argentina

**AS** American Samoa

**AT** Austria

**AU** Australia

**AW** Aruba

**AZ** Azerbaijan

**BA** Bosnia and
  Herzegovina

**BB** Barbados

**BD** Bangladesh

**BE** Belgium

**BF** Burkina Faso

**BG** Bulgaria

**BH** Bahrain

**BI** Burundi

**BJ** Benin

**BM** Bermuda

**BN** Brunei Darussalam

**BO** Bolivia

**BR** Brazil

**BS** Bahamas

**BT** Bhutan

**BV** Bouvet Island

**BW** Botswana

**BY** Belarus

**BZ** Belize

**CA** Canada

**CC** Cocos (Keeling)
  Islands

**CF** Central African
  Republic

**CG** Congo

**CH** Switzerland

**CI** Cote D'Ivoire (Ivory
  Coast)

**CK** Cook Islands

**CL** Chile

**CM** Cameroon

**CN** China

**CO** Colombia

**CR** Costa Rica

**CS** Czechoslovakia
  (former)

**CU** Cuba

**CV** Cape Verde

**CX** Christmas Island

**CY** Cyprus

**CZ** Czech Republic

**DE** Germany

**DJ** Djibouti

**DK** Denmark

**DM** Dominica

**DO** Dominican
  Republic

**DZ** Algeria

**EC** Ecuador

**EE** Estonia

**EG** Egypt

**EH** Western Sahara

**ER** Eritrea

**ES** Spain

**ET** Ethiopia

**FI** Finland

**FJ** Fiji

**FK** Falkland Islands
  (Malvinas)

**FM** Micronesia

**FO** Faroe Islands

**FR** France

**FX** France,
  Metropolitan

**GA** Gabon

**GB** Great Britain (UK)

**GD** Grenada

**GE** Georgia

**GF** French Guiana

**GH** Ghana

**GI** Gibraltar

**GL** Greenland

**GM** Gambia

**GN** Guinea

**GP** Guadeloupe

**GQ** Equatorial Guinea

**GR** Greece

**GS** S. Georgia and
  S. Sandwich Isls.

**GT** Guatemala

**GU** Guam

**GW** Guinea-Bissau

**GY** Guyana

**HK** Hong Kong

**HM** Heard and
  McDonald Islands

**HN** Honduras

**HR** Croatia (Hrvatska)

**HT** Haiti

**HU** Hungary

**ID** Indonesia

**IE** Ireland

**IL** Israel

**IN** India

**IO** British Indian
  Ocean Territory

**IQ** Iraq

**IR** Iran

**IS** Iceland

**IT** Italy

**JM** Jamaica

**JO** Jordan

**JP** Japan

**KE** Kenya

**KG** Kyrgyzstan

**KH** Cambodia

**KI** Kiribati

**KM** Comoros

**KN** Saint Kitts and
  Nevis

**KP** Korea (North)

**KR** Korea (South)

**KW** Kuwait

**KY** Cayman Islands

**KZ** Kazakhstan

**LA** Laos

**LB** Lebanon

**LC** Saint Lucia

**LI** Liechtenstein

**LK** Sri Lanka

**LR** Liberia

**LS** Lesotho

**LT** Lithuania

**LU** Luxembourg

**LV** Latvia

**LY** Libya

**MA** Morocco

**MC** Monaco

**MD** Moldova

**MG** Madagascar

*continued*

## What's in a Domain? (continued)

| | | |
|---|---|---|
| **MH** Marshall Islands | **NE** Niger | **PM** St. Pierre and |
| **MK** Macedonia | **NF** Norfolk Island | Miquelon |
| **ML** Mali | **NG** Nigeria | **PN** Pitcairn |
| **MM** Myanmar | **NI** Nicaragua | **PR** Puerto Rico |
| **MN** Mongolia | **NL** Netherlands | **PT** Portugal |
| **MO** Macau | **NO** Norway | **PW** Palau |
| **MP** Northern Mariana | **NP** Nepal | **PY** Paraguay |
| Islands | **NR** Nauru | **QA** Qatar |
| **MQ** Martinique | **NT** Neutral Zone | **RE** Reunion |
| **MR** Mauritania | **NU** Niue | **RO** Romania |
| **MS** Montserrat | **NZ** New Zealand | **RU** Russian Federation |
| **MT** Malta | (Aotearoa) | **RW** Rwanda |
| **MU** Mauritius | **OM** Oman | **SA** Saudi Arabia |
| **MV** Maldives | **PA** Panama | **Sb** Solomon Islands |
| **MW** Malawi | **PE** Peru | **SC** Seychelles |
| **MX** Mexico | **PF** French Polynesia | **SD** Sudan |
| **MY** Malaysia | **PG** Papua New Guinea | **SE** Sweden |
| **MZ** Mozambique | **PH** Philippines | **SG** Singapore |
| **NA** Namibia | **PK** Pakistan | **SH** St. Helena |
| **NC** New Caledonia | **PL** Poland | **SI** Slovenia |

## THE ALIAS

You can also use an email "alias." This displays only your name (John Jones) to those who receive mail from you but automatically turns that name into your full email address when they send mail back to you. You can create this alias (also called a contact name or account name) in the setup or preferences routine in your email program.

You can also create aliases for people you send messages to all the time. Usually, you do this in the address book or contacts area of your email program. (Refer to the email program "help" files or manual to learn how to create aliases; don't forget that they are usually called *contact lists* or *accounts*.) Aliases save you the time and

| | | |
|---|---|---|
| **SJ** Svalbard and Jan Mayen Islands | **TJ** Tajikistan | **VC** Saint Vincent and the Grenadines |
| **SK** Slovak Republic | **TK** Tokelau | **VE** Venezuela |
| **SL** Sierra Leone | **TM** Turkmenistan | **VG** Virgin Islands |
| **SM** San Marino | **TN** Tunisia | (British) |
| **SN** Senegal | **TO** Tonga | **VI** Virgin Islands (U.S.) |
| **SO** Somalia | **TP** East Timor | **VN** Viet Nam |
| **SR** Suriname | **TR** Turkey | **VU** Vanuatu |
| **ST** Sao Tome and Principe | **TT** Trinidad and Tobago | **WF** Wallis and Futuna Islands |
| **SU** USSR (former) | **TV** Tuvalu | **WS** Samoa |
| **SV** El Salvador | **TW** Taiwan | **YE** Yemen |
| **SY** Syria | **TZ** Tanzania | **YT** Mayotte |
| **SZ** Swaziland | **UA** Ukraine | **YU** Yugoslavia |
| **TC** Turks and Caicos Islands | **UG** Uganda | **ZA** South Africa |
| **TD** Chad | **UK** United Kingdom | **ZM** Zambia |
| **TF** French Southern Territories | **UM** US Minor Outlying Islands | **ZR** Zaire |
| **TG** Togo | **US** United States | **ZW** Zimbabwe |
| **TH** Thailand | **UY** Uruguay | |
| | **UZ** Uzbekistan | |
| | **VA** Vatican City State (Holy See) | |

effort of remembering complete email addresses. You have only to type the recipient's name in the "To:" box, and the software does the rest.

## EMAIL NETWORK SERVICES

Among the most popular email services are those that come with a subscription to an online network, such as AOL (America Online). Millions of users pay a relatively low monthly fee for AOL's unique blend of information services, email, and chat rooms. Its mail system works much like Outlook and other mail programs, but is

## Email for Free!

Today, you can sign up for free email on lots of systems, including Yahoo!, Hotmail, and Netzero, to name a few. Depending on the system, you may be required to use an email program, or you may be able to access all of its features right on the World Wide Web. Occasionally, access for sending and receiving messages may be restricted. However, most of the major free email systems (Yahoo! or Hotmail, for example) offer virtually unlimited use of the system for sending and receiving mail.

If you use a free email system, ads may be present. Ignore them if you wish. Or, if something interests you on an ad, click away and see what they have to offer. Of course, don't forget to finish your email session first.

especially easy to use by people who are new to computers. Even addressing is easier when you send to other AOL customers, because you need only the AOL user name without the @aol.com at the end. In addition, senders can receive confirmation of receipt and "unsend" mail to others on AOL.

Other people prefer to subscribe to an Internet Service Provider (ISP), which will provide them with access to the Internet, along with email, chat, and World Wide Web capabilities.

### The Email Message and How It Looks

To: Jerryb@serrin7.com
Subject: Forbin Delivery Problems
From: kenr@serrin7.com
Talked to the Forbin Project people. They're worried about a delay in the next order. Can you do anything?
——————————Headers——————————
Return-Path: ⟨····owner-dmanhand-bradjanetshake7-
test@LISTSERV.BRADJANET.COM····⟩
Received: from lmailbradjanet2.bradjanet.com (lmailbradjanet2.brad-
janet.com [152.163.225.39]) by air-yao4.mail.bradjanet.com (v70.20)

with ESMTP; Wed, 05 Apr 2000 18:36:43 -0400
Received: from LISTSERV.BRADJANET.COM by lmailbradjanet2.brad-
janet.com (LSMTP for Windows NT v1.1b) with SMTP id
❬⋯3.000573B3@lmailbradjanet2.bradjanet.com⋯❭; Wed, 5 Apr 2000
18:35:51 -0400
MIME-Version: 1.0
Content-Type: text/plain; charset="US-ASCII"
Content-Transfer-Encoding: 7bit
X-Mailer: BRADJANET for Dmanhandintosh sub 60
Message-ID: ❬⋯71.20e692f.261d1917@bradjanet.com⋯❭
Date: Wed, 5 Apr 2000 18:32:55 EDT

In the email at the bottom of page 16 and above, we've included the complete "header,"[1] which means all the bric-a-brac that comes before the actual message. We're showing you the header here so you don't panic if you see one in your own email. Whether your email shows headers or not, they're nothing to worry about. Some email programs hide them, some don't, and some give you a choice.

The headers look highly complex, but most of their content is of importance only to a system administrator who can use the information to diagnose email routing problems (sometimes).

**Sample of a Simple Message**

To: Jerryb@serrin7.com
Subject: Forbin Delivery Problems
From kenr@serrin7.com
Talked to the Forbin Project people. They're worried about a delay in
the next order. Can you do anything?
— — — — — — — — — — —Headers— — — — — — — — — — — —

---

[1] The header info is actually from another message. It's included to demonstrate what a message looks like. For the rest of the book, we'll skip the header information since it wastes space and is only important to those debugging problems with messaging systems.

In this message, not even the barest personalization is included. There's no greeting, no signature, no introduction, and if you did not know what the Forbin project was, the message content would be meaningless.

The sender is counting on the recipient to know the background information behind the message. You would use this short form only to say that you're still on watch but have no news. You would _never_ use this form with a customer unless you don't mind giving the account up to a competitor.

The informal message below looks similar. This tone and format is only for friends, family, and co-workers with whom you work closely and who won't take offense at your "shorthand."

---

**Sample Informal Message**

Liz got her new job! I wanted you to be the first to know. I'll call later!
————————————————Headers————————————————

---

The upside of this format is that key information can be conveyed quickly.

## STANDARD EMAIL MESSAGES

Most email has more content than the example above. The message greets the receiving party, relays content with enough detail to make it understandable to anyone, and ends with the name of the sender.

---

**Sample Standard Email**

To: Jerryb@serrin7.com
Subject: Possible Forbin Delivery Problems
From kenr@serrin7.com
cc esterc@serrin7.com (Ester Cervantes), mbond@serrinmain.com
(Mike Bond)
Hi Hal: I spoke with the people at the Forbin Project yesterday. Their brass said they're pleased with our new technology and its speed, relative to what they were already using. Glenn Balmer, one of the

---

> engineers, said the computer is getting so big that they've nicknamed
> it Colossus! His only concern was that the next shipment of triode
> tubes arrive on time for the next phase of development. (It starts
> March 11th.) I assured him that we would meet his deadline. I would
> like a confirmation from you that the date is still okay.
> Ken
> — — — — — — — — — — — —Headers— — — — — — — — — — — — —

This message is comfortably understandable, informative, and requests a response. It acknowledges the recipient's name, and it's signed.

This is the standard format for communicating with co-workers, family, and just about anyone else. Note the length, which makes for a quick read without sacrificing detail. But again, you would have to be familiar with the context of the message to understand it.

## FORMAL MESSAGES

As in any human interaction, the choice of words and tone in an email is paramount to effective and appropriate communication. Sometimes you can be humorous and personal, but at other times, such as when engineering, science, scheduling, or other data or report information is involved, straightforward communication is a *must.*

Certain types of content, such as legal notices, the death of a loved one, or corporate news (especially when it's bad), demand much more formality.

If you're in doubt about the way your message will come across, have another pair of trusted eyes review a printed copy before pressing the "Send" button.

### Raising the Stakes

The following message reaches yet another level of formality and informativeness.

---

**Sample Formal Message**

To: Jerryb@serrin7.com
Subject: Possible Forbin Delivery Problems
From: kenr@serrin7.com

cc esterc@serrin7.com (Ester Cervantes), mbond@serrinmain.com
(Mike Bond)

May 29, 2001

Dear Mr. Bellingham,

Last Tuesday (5/18), I spoke with Jenin Forbes, Jr., Lab director at
Bevery Worthing, and engineers Glenn Balmer, and John George at the
Forbin Project. Ms. Worthing is pleased with our new technology and
its speed relative to the River Technologies product used from May
1999 to January of this year. Mr. Balmer explained that the computer
build-out requires more room than anticipated, which is running up
their budget unexpectedly. They're calling the project "Colossus."

I should mention that I sensed an underlying concern about the next
shipment of 1100 of our hand-built 6L6 vacuum tubes (Serrin part
#1092a). If you remember, these are the ones that use gold and plat-
inum and eat up company cash flow for precious metals buys.

Apparently we have made late deliveries on several occasions now.
This is our biggest order from Forbin. Any delay will directly impact
their project completion dates.

I would like a confirmation from you that the date is still okay.

If "Colossus" becomes as big as Forbin expects, it will be a feather in
our cap to remain their key tube technology supplier.

A physical copy of this message is being sent via interdepartmental
mail in case this email message doesn't arrive because of server problems we've experienced lately.

Your sincerely,

Ken Rosen

Vice-President of Technical Marketing

—————————————Headers———————————————

It's easy to see that as formality and information precision increase, so does message length, so it's important to include only those facts that are necessary. Measure
out your facts carefully so as not to appear to patronize your reader. If your recipient
may already know much of what you must say, acknowledge this in the message.

> **Sample Comment to Recipient**
>
> Dear Mr. Bellingham,
>
> I want to bring you up to date concerning issues with the Forbin account. *You may already be familiar with some of the facts I'll be relating, but I've tried to include as much about the situation as I can, because I don't want to leave anything to chance . . .*

Occasionally, it will appear that not sending anything is more appropriate than sending unpleasant news. But while silence may be golden, failing to keep important people in the communication loop may make them very unhappy, especially if it appears you've ignored them or withheld key information.

## RETURNED MAIL

At some time or other, everyone has seen a film or heard a story about a love letter that gets lost in the mail, then reappears 25 years later. Unfortunately, life often imitates art. A couple of decades ago, the railroad lost two full box cars of mail for two whole years. And while email may have many advantages over "snail mail" as far as speed and ease of use is concerned, it is no more immune from getting lost than your average postcard.

Why? Because a host of gremlins can block your transmission. Your message may never leave your machine simply because on a program like Outlook, you can end up pushing the wrong buttons.

You can also run into problems with networks on your end or the receiving end, or with transmission in between. Technical support from your network or service provider can help, although there may be a generous wait, toll call, or even a fee for its cures.

Network organizations, especially those providing free email (in the interest of avoiding legal correspondence, we won't name names), may lose thousands or even millions of messages without your knowledge. So, for really important mail like, "we're terminating you effective tomorrow for theft of one box of Acme #2 lead pencils," follow up with a second message; verify receipt if your network supports it (AOL mail to other AOL mail users—don't forget to check the Return Receipt box); phone; or if it's *really* important, send a certified letter.

## WRITING YOUR FIRST ONLINE MESSAGE: THE BASICS

Now, finally, we come to the fun part—actually learning to write online messages of your own. To get started, you'll not only need to learn how to use the email software (which you'll do with the help of your program's user guide or other documentation) and the address of the people you want to receive the message, but you'll have to master the fundamental ways to start and end an email message.

### For the Legally Inclined

Test cases, now winding through the courts, are seeking to make email an entity with legal equality to a physical letter, as long as it is signed with a legitimate digital signature. (We'll talk about this later in the chapter.) But at this writing, *the jury's still out*.

Never, never, never send anything critical such as a legal agreement using email without confirming its receipt. Also, until more court decisions hold up precedent, legal documents should not be conveyed via email. It's okay to email draft copies back and forth for review or have preliminary "discussions" using chat, assuming that none of the material transmitted electronically ever appears in court or court-related paperwork. Disappointing, too, since an online dialog between parties and officers of the court produces an instant transcript on everyone's machine.

But, like everything electronic, this is an evolving field. You should keep an eye on decisions as they are made for and against the admissibility of electronically originated media. With advances in digital signatures, security, and the need for speed in the legal system, an electronic legal future looks as inevitable as death and taxes.

## The Subject Line and Body of the Message

After entering the address of the recipient, you'll fill in the subject line. We'll take a closer look at writing effective subject lines in the next chapter, but for now, just know that you must make your subject line short, clear, and meaningful.

Next, you'll write the body of the email, which should include an opening, a message, and a closing.

Every new communication medium develops its own protocols for opening and closing messages. Telephone conversations start with "Hello" and end with "Goodbye." Letters open with "Dear" and end with "Sincerely" or "Very Truly Yours." Because email is so new, there aren't yet any firm rules on how to open and close.

Many people use neither a salutation nor a signature in their email messages. They write only the body of their message. However, that kind of treatment might not convey the proper formality or status cues for your purposes.

We think both greetings and closings are important in online communication.

## Greetings and Salutations

In most cases, the greeting or salutation contains the first words in your email message. Greetings are difficult to do well, especially if you're crossing cultures or languages. In the United States, you can be pretty informal, but you still need to be careful that you aren't making assumptions or using "sensitive" words.

Be aware that the family name comes first in some cultures and last in others. And titles are frequently different for men and women, and you may not be able to tell which you are addressing.

In the United States, it is a bad idea to use "Sir" or "Mr." unless you are absolutely certain that your correspondent is male. Similarly, it is probably safer to use "Ms." instead of "Miss" or "Mrs." when you're writing to a woman, unless you happen to know what her preference is.

Using someone's first name In the United States is *usually* ok. Thus, you can usually get away with a "Dear" and the first name:

**Dear Kim:**

## Do You Really Need a Salutation?

Given that email is a relatively informal mode of communication, dispensing with names and titles in a salutation frequently isn't a problem. Here is an example that works without a name, as the recipient is simply an unknown webmaster:

Hello. I saw your web site and noticed that you incorrectly cited the title of my book. The correct title is "The Complete Idiot's Guide to Project Management, 2nd Edition."

Sunny Baker, Ph.D.

Author

Instead of "hello", we usually use a simple "hi" as an email greeting for people we already know:

While we're on the subject, starting an email with either "Good Morning" or "Good Evening" doesn't make a lot of sense, as you won't know when the person intends to read the message. You may want to avoid the salutation "Greetings" in the United States; it reminds many people of draft notices or poorly written direct mail advertisements.

Again, you must be careful about cultural differences. The East Coast of the United States is more formal than the West Coast. Germans are even more formal; they can work side-by-side for years and never get around to dealing with each other on a first-name basis. Starting a message to anyone in Germany with Dear Werner would be a bad idea.

Here you are covered regardless of whether Kim is male or female. But beware of using a diminutive if you aren't certain your correspondent uses it. It might rankle Elizabeth to be called Liz; Joseph might hate being called Joe.

If you are addressing a group of people, you can say "Dear" plus the unifying attribute. For example:

**Dear Project Managers:**

Or:

**Dear Mesa Weavers Guild:**

Once you know a person pretty well, most experienced emailers just use the first name as a salutation. To some this may seem rude, but in practice, it's the way things are done—so don't attach any meaning to it one way or the other.

---

**Sample with a Name-Only Greeting and Closing**

Sal,

Your idea for lunch sounds great. How about Tuesday?

–Sam

---

If you know the person you're writing to and the status of the relationship is appropriate (i.e. Sal isn't the President of the United States), this type of message is just fine.

### Who Are You?

If you are sending email to someone who doesn't know you yet, you should let them know the answers to these questions in your first message to him or her:

- Who are you?
- How did you learn of your reader?
- What do you want from your reader?
- Why should your reader pay attention to you? (If you can't answer this question, you should wonder if you should even send the email.)

Putting some of that information in a signature is better than putting it nowhere at all, but putting it at the beginning (top) of the body of the message is better for several reasons:

- A lot of people get hundreds of messages per day, and so read them very quickly. If you don't establish immediately who you are, your reader may delete your message before he or she gets to the bottom (where the signature is).
- Your identity is an important clue to the context of the message.
- If there is a problem with the transmission of the email, the end is much more likely to get lost than the beginning.

Good answers to the questions can take several forms.

---

**Sample Answers**

Dear Ms. Baker: I am an editor at Faulkner Gray Publishing. I sat next to your husband on American Airlines last week, and he mentioned that you are interested in publishing an article based on your project management book. I have read your book and would be very interested in receiving a proposal from you.

Or:

My name is Fred Ogleby and I'm the legal counsel for Big Computers Company. We are deeply disturbed at the aspersions you cast upon us and our computers in your project management article. Therefore, we order you to immediately cease and desist using any reference to Big Computers Company in your future articles and to write a formal apology to be printed in the next issue of the magazine. If you do not, we will be forced to file suit against you.

Or perhaps:

Hello, Sunny Baker- I am new to using email and just read your book on online communication. I don't know if you are the right person to ask or not, but do you know what the German word for "Mister" is? If you can tell me, I'll promise to buy your next book.
Thanks for your help.
Fred Newbie

---

### The Closing and the Signature

Closings are simple. For informal email, simply say thanks (if appropriate) and write your name. For more formal email, use the same closings you'd use in a business letter, such as *Sincerely* or *Yours truly*.

You can always type in your signature by hand, but most email programs allow you to set up a default signature to be included at the end of every message. Many people use these signatures as an easy way to give their name and contact information. But be careful. You can easily overdo it.

**Sample Overdone Signature**

Hi Joe. When do you have time for lunch together?

Sal Meyers

Wonka Tools, Inc.

555 Anonymous Land

Redlands, CA 92314

+1 (909) 555-1234 voice

+1 (909) 123-4568 FAX

smeyers@wonkatools.com (work)

sally777@earhlink.net (personal)

Such a long signature in contrast to such a short question (to someone Sally obviously already knows) looks silly. Much of the above signature is extraneous in this context. For this type of message, Joe probably doesn't need Sally's FAX number or street address. (If Joe needs to send a FAX or package, he can ask for addressing information.) He already has one email address in the message Sally sent, so she didn't need to add another.

Including your name is perfectly acceptable, especially if your email messages don't include it in the "From:" line. (You can send yourself email to see if your name is there or not.)

The telephone number is also okay—if you're willing to be interrupted by a phone call. Emotions are easier to convey over the phone, and some people prefer phone to email.

If the message is business-related, including the company name is smart—even if the message is going to someone else in your own company.

One thing that is missing from Sal Meyers' signature, above, is her job title. That may have more influence on the reader than anything else. In most cases, especially in formal email communication or communication with business colleagues, including your title is recommended.

---

**Sample Signature for Short Messages**

Sal Meyers

Western Regional Sales Manager.

+1 (909) 555-1234 voice

---

The signature is still a bit much for something like arranging lunch, of course. In that kind of informal email, you might use an alternate signature line (most email programs will allow you to do this) that includes different or truncated information that is more appropriate for informal correspondence.

After setting up a signature or multiple signatures for automatic inclusion, it is easy to forget about it. After all, your email software might not show it to you, or it

## Is It Clever to Be Clever?

In the past, it was very common for people to put "entertaining" elements in their email signature line: artwork, philosophical sayings, jokes, and/or quotations. This isn't a bad custom, but don't overdo it. Try to keep your signature length down to no more than five lines—at all times and in all types of email contexts.

Many people put ornamental separators — lines, horizontal bars, and so on — around their signatures. For example:

—————————————————————

Sunny J. Baker, Ph.D. | CEO, Bakersquared Consulting, Inc.

+1 (555) 335-5555 Voice | +1 (555) 336-4444 Fax

sunny@bakersquared.com          |

—————————————————————

A box around a signature may or may not be attractive, depending on your taste, but it's becoming more common for people to use the voice capabilities of their computers to read email out loud—so use your common sense. A computer would read lines around an email signature out loud as: "hyphen hyphen hyphen hyphen hyphen hyphen..." So think twice before you make pretty pictures around your signature.

might be so routine that you never look at it again. So whenever a piece of contact information changes, revisit your signature and make sure that it's still up-to-date.

If you have an entertainment piece in your signature, change it every once in a while. Things are only funny the first time people see them.

Further, if you use multiple signatures, remember to choose the correct one for the moment. It's easy to do this in most modern email programs, but you still have to remember to select the one you want to use. It could be a big mistake to send your boss the signature you use with your closest friends.

To avoid this problem, make the default signature the one you send at work, and choose the funny or special occasion signatures manually when you want to use them.

One final note on using signatures: they are a good way to let your correspondent know that the entire message was transmitted. There is no body language to signal that you are "done talking" and, unfortunately, email transmissions sometimes get interrupted. Thus, we recommend always using a signature of some sort (even one line) to let people know that the message is complete.

## THE FIRST SIX STEPS OF WRITING AN EMAIL

Now that you know how to construct an email message, it's time to get up and running. Here are the six steps you need to follow.

### Step 1. Get Connected

You need access to online communication, and there are various ways to get it. You can, of course, connect to other users through the company network if you work in an office. Otherwise, you can use a service like AOL or find an ISP. (Look for ISPs—Internet Service Providers—in the *Yellow Pages* under Internet.) Shop around for the best ISP, meaning one that _never_ has busy signals when you connect by modem and that _always_ has someone on duty to answer the customer service phone.

### Step 2: Acquire the Required Software

Most operating systems come with basic telecommunications packages, but you'll want something better. For company email, your organization will have provided a package in an easy-to-install format. For America Online, just look for a computer magazine with a free AOL disk included. (A friend reports finding an AOL disk in the box of newly purchased shoes!)

To explore the Internet, the two most popular "browsers," Netscape and Microsoft Explorer, are available for free. A version of either or both may have been included with your computer.

### Step 3. Spend Time in Chat Rooms

Chat rooms are easy to find on the Internet and America Online. If you can't find one on your own, go to http://www.chatworld.com, and try one or two for fun.

Chat rooms are simply connections that allow a group of people to "talk" with each other—even though participants may live on the other side of the globe. You'll learn a lot simply watching a busy chat room in action.

### Step 4. Read Your Incoming Email Carefully

Look at the way messages are structured. Notice the physical details. For example, often you'll see text quoted from previous mailings. Each sentence will have a caret (>) in front of it to identify it as a quotation from an earlier writer.

**LO-TECH** TIP

**Best Bet for Improving Your Keyboard Skills:** A perennial favorite for learning "keyboarding" is the CD-based program *Mavis Beacon Teaches Typing*. Once a $50+ product, we've seen a CD-only version in the bargain bins for as little as $10. At that price, it's a steal because, following the computer-based lessons, you really will become a keyboard jockey.

### Step 5. Sit Right Down and Write Yourself an Online Letter

The computer won't care that the sender is also the recipient. Write a message about a topic that's important to you (making sure that no one else can read it, if it's personal), and send it to yourself. Then, after a week or two, look at the "received" letter and consider whether what you wanted to say actually comes across. Where is it too brief or long-winded? Did you make your point?

### Step 6. Hone Your Keyboard Skills

This is a tough one for some. While Sunny is a touch typist, Kim never learned to type despite the best efforts of his mother and the educational system. Your ability to type, assuming you've rarely used a keyboard, will improve with practice.

## SOME OTHER SUGGESTIONS

Online communication, especially in non-verbal formats such as email and text-based chat, depends on the written word. It's no secret that many people—even the most highly educated—can't write effectively.

If you're not comfortable with your writing ability, consider a basic writing class at your local community college—it might even be fun. Also, get yourself a copy of the classic Strunk and White's *Elements of Style*. It's a small, thin, inexpensive paperback, rich with practical writing advice. (Once you're connected to the Internet, you can go to the web and read a copy online for free at http://www.bartleby.com/141/.)

At this point, with email account ready and Internet connection turned on, you're ready to get into some real online communication. So, let's learn how to say it online—the right way!

# CHAPTER THREE

# Writing Email with Style

IN THE LAST CHAPTER, we learned the basics for starting and closing an email message. Now we're going to go into more detail on how to construct your emails appropriately.

In a traditional paper document, it's absolutely essential to make everything completely clear and unambiguous, as your audience may not have the opportunity to ask for clarification. With email documents, because of quick turnaround time, your recipient can ask questions immediately. That's one of the reasons why email tends to be less formal than paper communication and more like conversational speech.

This is not always bad. It makes little sense to slave over a message for hours, making sure that your spelling is faultless, your words are eloquent, and your grammar is beyond reproach, if you only want to tell your co-worker that you're ready to go to lunch.

However, it's not a good idea to get sloppy just because you're using email. For example, if you're making a query for a new job, then all the regular rules of that kind of contact apply: you must make a perfect impression. Thus, your cover letter and your attached resume must be in flawless condition—just like paper-based applications sent via snail mail.

And it's still important to make all of your communications clear and unambiguous (even if other people don't follow this guideline). Email does not convey emotions nearly as well as face-to-face or even telephone conversations. It lacks vocal inflection, gestures, and a shared context for the communication. Your reader may have difficulty telling whether you're serious or kidding, happy or sad, frustrated or silly. Thus, sarcasm is *very* dangerous to use in email.

## THE IMPORTANCE OF CONTEXT

In the last chapter, we talked about the importance of considering context in a business email, but the fact is, context is important to _every_ email you write.

In conversation, there is some minimum of shared context, especially if you're in the same physical location. But even if you're on the phone, you're still talking together in real time and using voice inflection to convey meaning.

## What You See May Not Be What They Get

With love letters, the very paper upon which you pen declarations of your unwavering affection in your own handwriting eventually finds its way into the possession of your beloved to be read, fondled, caressed, and treasured.

Email is an entirely different story. The software and hardware you use to compose, send, store, download, and read messages may be completely different from that of your reader. That means that the way your email looks—the font, the page format, and even the overall size of the message on the screen—can morph into something completely different on someone else's system.

All this adds up to the conclusion that you should think of your email and other online compositions as quite different and distinct from both traditional paper and spoken communications. Never, NEVER, depend on the appearance of your emails to convey meaning or context. You may be conveying nothing at all.

When you generate a paper document, there is often some context embedded in the medium: the text is in the proceedings of a conference, written on a birthday card, handed to your professor with a batch of COMM 101 papers, jotted down quickly on a note to accompany a piece of company promotional material, or something similar.

With email, you can't assume *anything* about a sender's location, time, or frame of mind. And if you don't already know the person you're communicating with, you can't assume anything about the person's profession, interests, or future value to you. This means, among other things, that you need to be careful to give your recipients some level of context.

## MAKE THE SUBJECT LINE CLEAR

Writing a clear subject line is the first rule of creating context in email. The words you put in the subject line should give the recipient a clear idea of what the mail is about. This is especially helpful when people go back to look for messages later ("Subject: The monthly sales report is attached" is much easier to find than "Subject: hi").

Always use a subject line that pertains clearly to the email body. This will help people mentally shift to the proper context before they read your message. Be careful not to use sarcastic or meaningless subject lines—unless you're fooling around with friends who will understand your context.

When you write a subject line, it should be brief (as many mail programs will truncate long subject lines), does not need to be a complete sentence, and should relate the basic contents of the message.

---

**Sample Subject Line and Related Message**

　　Subject: Need 4 Wonka Rollers overnight to Phil.
Ofc

　　Sally – Please send 4 Wonka Rollers to the Philadelphia Office. They need to be sent for overnight delivery for arrival by Thursday. Email me when they ship. Thanks.

---

Here the subject line summarizes succinctly the most important details of the message.

## Subject Line No-No's

Here are some subject lines to avoid because they're either overused or used by spammers (and online pornographers) to get your attention.

Hi Sweetie. (or any related phrase . . .
   be sure the person is known to you
   before you open the mail.)
Here's the data you asked for.
Have you seen this one?
Here are the best.
All new and ready for you.
Are you ready for this?
We met last night in chat, but you left
   before we finished.

Read this now!
Young teens.
An offer you can't refuse.
Special for you.
This is very private . . .
Hi! I'm Julie.
For Adults Only
Click here for something hot.

You get the idea. And if you find that you're receiving email with subject lines similar to these and they take you to offensive web sites, report the situation to your ISP or online service.

## RESPONSES TO OTHER EMAIL MESSAGES

If your message is in response to another email message, your software will probably preface the subject line with Re: or RE: (for REgarding). If your email program doesn't do this, it is both polite and appropriate to put in RE: by hand in the subject line.

### Sample Hand-Written Re:

Subject: Re: Need 4 Wonka Rollers overnight to Phil. Ofc.

Sunny– I've got only 3 Wonka Rollers in stock. Will it be okay to ship only 3? I can ship the other one by Monday. –Sally

## URGENT MESSAGES

For time-critical messages, starting the subject with URGENT: is a good idea (especially if you know the person gets a lot of email).

> **Sample Message Marked "Urgent"**
>
> Subject: URGENT: Need Wonka Roller ASAP
> I've *got* to have another Wonka Roller for the Philadelphia demo office, and I need it by tomorrow afternoon. Sally only has three, and I need one more. If anyone has one in their desk somewhere, I'd really appreciate your sending it along! –Sunny

## REQUESTS FOR ACTION

For requests, starting with REQ: can signal that action is needed.

> **Sample Message Marked "Req"**
>
> Subject: REQ: Turn in Wonka Rollers
> Sunny's call for a Wonka Roller turned up 7 units that were just lying around people's offices unused. Please take a moment to look around your area for Wonka Rollers that you're no longer using, and get them back to Sally. We need them for the demo offices.
> Thanks. –Fred

## INFORMATION ONLY MESSAGES

If you're offering non-urgent information that requires no response from the other person, especially in a business situation, prefacing the subject line with FYI: (For Your Information) is a good idea, as in

> Subject: FYI: Cookies in the conference area.
> Jane's husband has been baking again. There are three dozen of his best efforts in the downstairs conference area. First come, first served!

## The Worst Word to Use in a Subject Line

If there is any single word you should eliminate from your subject lines, and maybe from the body of your messages as well, it's this: INFORMATION. Why? You can't imagine how many overworked webmasters get email that looks like this:

Subject: information

Please send me information about your company.

The webmaster ends up with no clue as to what the sender actually wants. The company's history? Its products? The stock price? The number of employees? The number of buildings? Should the webmaster send paper documents or give Web Site addresses?

Here's how the note should have read:

Subject: Req: IBM history

Are there any Web pages about the history of IBM that you can refer me to?

The more specific you are in your emails, the more likely you are to receive the kinds of replies you're looking for.

## WRITE FOR YOUR AUDIENCE

Always write email and other online communications (chat, for instance) with your audience in mind. An email message sent to a prospective employer should not have spelling errors; and should begin, "Dear Prospective Employer"; and should read like a traditional on-paper letter. (If you need more information on writing traditional paper communications like these, try one of the other books in the How to Say It Series from Prentice Hall.)

Messages sent to friends or colleagues might begin with a simple "Hi" or "Hey," and if you're really in a hurry, they don't need a greeting, good spelling, or full sentences.

### Sample Informal Email

From: kim@zapped.com

To: mark@bongo.com

> Date: Wednesday, July 12, 2000 6:11 PM
> Subject: hasta la vista
> see ya at da party sat at 6. gotta go.

With good friends, you can make up the rules as you go—as long as things are understandable—so this is one place where you can put a little personality into your email style. But never use your personal lingo and shortcuts with employers or formal correspondents. It would be considered rude (and could have negative consequences).

## KNOW YOUR RECIPIENT

Try to understand your recipient's technical and computer limitations. Nothing is more frustrating to email users than a vital message and pix (pictures) sent to a recipient in a format that she can't read or open. Email messages sent as words are always acceptable unless the message is too long or formatted in a character system unreadable to the recipient. (Example: Japanese Kanji to an English-speaking recipient.)

Remember that attached files may be useless if you haven't checked with the reader about his program's capabilities. Sending a Word document to a user of WordPerfect as standardized back in 1994 is not much different than the Kanji to English example.

Similarly, sending pictures in something as common as MIME format (an "encoding" format designed to make files easier to send over the Internet) can be equally frustrating to a recipient with both limited technical knowledge and an archaic mail program that can't deal with MIME formatted files.

**LO-TECH TIP**

**Take Me Off Your Mailing List!:** To forward or not to forward. That is the question... There are plenty of people, who, upon discovering the ease of email, forward all kinds of jokes, messages, "news," and even manipulative chain letters. You can do this too, but at the risk of offending or irritating recipients. Simply be careful of what you send to whom. A negative response is a strong warning to delete them from your FYI list.

## USING PUNCTUATION FOR INTONATION

The most difficult thing to convey in email is emotion. People frequently get in trouble for typing exactly what they would say out loud. Unfortunately, without the tone of voice or a facial expression to signal their emotion, it is easy to misinterpret the intent.

While you cannot make your voice higher or lower, louder or softer to denote emphasis, there are things you can do with text and punctuation to convey vocal inflection and emotion. We cover most of these ways in the next few pages.

### Light Emphasis

If you want to give something mild emphasis, you should enclose it in asterisks. This is equivalent to the use of emphatic italics in a paper document.

Instead of:

> I said that I was going to go last Friday.
> Say:
> I *said* that I was going to go last Friday.
> Or:
> I said that I was going to go last *Friday*.

Which of the two examples you use depends upon whether you're resolute about the commitment you made or adamant that you didn't mean Wednesday. (Restructuring the sentence to remove the ambiguity might be an even better idea.)

Some people capitalize the first letters of words in email to give light emphasis to those words: For example:

> While Sally may say that you should never turn the Wonka Roller past
> nine, this is not Cast In Stone. It will explode if you turn it up to twelve,
> but anything under ten should work just fine.

Other people use initial capitals to refer to things that are dogmatic or reverential. This is probably a cultural holdover from all the capital letters that are used in the English Bible. However, remember that English is a Germanic language, and they still capitalize all the nouns in proper German. Thus, the use of capitalization for either type of emphasis might not translate to other languages or cultures, so the asterisks are probably a better choice.

**Strong Emphasis**

If you want to indicate stronger emphasis, use all capital letters and toss in some extra exclamation marks. Instead of:

> › Should I just boost the power on the Wonka Roller?
> No, if you turn it up to twelve, you'll overheat the relays and it might explode.

Write this instead:

> › Should I just boost the power on the Wonka Roller?
> NO!!!! If you turn it up to twelve, you'll overheat the relays and IT MIGHT EXPLODE!!

Note that you should use capital letters sparingly. Just as loss of sight can lead to improved hearing, the relative lack of cues to emotion in email makes people hyper-sensitive to any cues that might be there. Thus, capital letters will convey the message that you're shouting.

It is totally inappropriate to use all capital letters in a situation where you're calm. Never do this:

> HEY, I JUST WANTED TO SEE IF YOU HAD MADE ANY
> PROGRESS ON THE SCHEDULE FOR THE ANCHOR GROUP ACCOUNT.
> LET ME KNOW WHEN YOU HAVE TIME.

People will either wince when they read this email message or consider you a complete newbie who hasn't taken the time to learn the most basic conventions about writing online communications.

**››EXTREME!!‹‹ Emphasis**

If you *really* want to emphasize something, you can use multiple methods for emphasis:

> If you're late this time, I swear that I will never, *never*, *NEVER*
> !!**NEVER**!! believe your schedules again.

Use this type of emphasis sparingly and only in situations where this type of emotion is absolutely necessary.

## USING EMOTICONS TO HELP TELL YOUR STORY

Because emotions are sometimes difficult to communicate via short email messages, online afficionados often use **emoticons** to help clarify meanings. The emoticons are little icons made from ordinary punctuation marks that express an emotional angle on what you just wrote.

Some people read great meaning into emoticons (if you don't believe us, check out our emoticon chart in Appendix A of this book), but there are three emoticons that are very commonly used and that you should become familiar with (turn your head to the side to see the little smiley faces):

:-) or :) Basic smiley face. This simply expresses smiley-ness and good will.

;-) or ;) Smile-with-wink. This denotes wryness, irony, or that you're joking.

:-( or :( Frowning face. It means your message is unhappy or sad.

### The Three Levels of Emoticons

In practice, there are three levels of emoticons in common usage. These are:

■ Level One - standard emoticons (as shown above) used in everyday communications and widely understood with little chance of unintended misinterpretation.

■ Level Two - standard emoticons with potential double meanings or uncommon usage. These are often used in chat sessions. We've provided an appendix of these common emoticons at the back of this book. Learn these if you'll be using them in chat rooms where emoticons are sometimes the norm of conversational chat.

■ Level Three - emoticons with no standard usage. Not included in this book, they may be employed only by a subset of users, like a local dialect if you will. These are for use only among friends or family or members of the group who agree among themselves about the meanings of the symbols.

**A Simple Emoticon Example**

The most commonly used emoticon is the smiley face, displayed as :) or =) or :–).
Again it's used to:

- indicate that the message preceding it is to be taken lightly.
- mean that it's a joke or that it's meant facetiously.
- to express your happy/friendly mood to the recipient.

Without an emoticon, the phrase "That's it, I'm out of here." seems ominous in
an online message. But with an emoticon "That's it, I'm out of here :)", should come
across to the reader as friendly banter.

---

**Sample Using an Emoticon to Relay That "We're All in This Together."**

I received the sales revenue report this morning, and I can't say that
I'm pleased with the numbers. I know you're all working hard, but management is not going to like this report any better than I do. :-( We've
got to pull together as a team and improve closings within the next 30
days. For my part, I'm going to work with you as a group tomorrow in
conference room 7 before the board meeting and we're going to role
play closing exercises. If we stick this one out and keep our team
spirit, we'll turn these numbers around before next month's report. I'm
counting on you to make next month's report a good one. :-)

---

## Give Your Emoticons a Little Space

When using an emoticon in text, add one or two spaces before and after the
symbol. This helps the reader to immediately identify the element as an emoticon
rather than punctuation gone awry. If the emoticon appears at the end of a sentence or message, consider deleting the punctuation altogether for clarity, lest a
period appear to be part of the symbol instead of the sentence.

## USING ONLINE ACRONYMS

Acronyms are frequently used in online communication to abbreviate a message. However, messages that are filled with acronyms can be confusing and annoying to the reader. Make sure you use acronyms that are generally understood.

We've included an appendix of common acronyms at the back of the book, but we don't recommend using all of these in email messages. It's simply good to have a place to look them up if someone writes a note to you with acronyms you don't understand.

When you use online chat, on the other hand, you'll find that acronyms are the norm—and you'll need to know how to interpret them quickly. If you want to feel comfortable in the informal chat rooms, we recommend memorizing the acronyms.

## The Top 10 Online Acronyms

If you plan to spend any time in chat rooms, here are the acronyms you absolutely MUST know to get through a conversation without seeming like a dunce or a complete newbie:

**BTW** – by the way

**FYI** – for your information

**IMHO** – in my humble (or honest) opinion

**IOW** – in other words

**LOL** – laughing out loud (beware, some people use this in closing for "lots of love" as well—but the context usually makes the meaning clear)

**OTOH** – on the other hand

**BRB** – be right back

**AFK** – away from keyboard

**WB** – welcome back

**WTG** – way to go!!!

## MUTTERING OR SPEAKING "QUIETLY" ONLINE

In person, there are a number of ways that you can indicate that a communication is private and not to be repeated. You can lower your voice, you can glance to your right and to your left, and you can lean closer to the other person. These signals are so ingrained that we use them even when there's nobody around. Unfortunately, lowering your voice and moving your body is hard to do in email.

One way to develop your "muttering" skills is to jot down exactly what you think first, no matter how politically incorrect, and then edit it into a sanitized version in the actual email message (make sure you don't push the send button until you sanitize the message, however).

Some people use double parentheses to denote "true or inner voice", what in the acting world is called an "aside." For example:

> **The VP of Quality Assurance resigned ((got fired)) today**
> **which is going to lead to enhanced**
> **relations between Engineering and Testing ((in**
> **their wildest dreams)).**

Something else that people will sometimes do to denote the "lowering of voice" is to type without any capital letters:

> **psssst!**
> **hey sally!**
> **guess what?**
> **ROBERT GOT THE JOB!!**

We should warn you that many people don't like the shortcuts (emoticons, use of punctuation and capitalization techniques). They argue that if Ernest Hemingway could convey emotion without resorting to such devices, then we should too. Well, if you're not as skilled a writer as Ernest Hemingway, we believe there is a greater danger of angering or offending someone by not using these shortcuts than there is of annoying someone by using them.

## PAUSE EQUIVALENTS

Imagine that you ask someone if you can turn the knob on, say, a nuclear reactor, up to a spot marked "eleven." Then she says, "Well," and pauses for a long time, scratches her head, looks down at the floor, winces, grits her teeth, and says again, "Well," then pauses and says, "It *might* not blow up." You'd get a sense of just how bad a decision it would be to turn the knob up.

On the other hand, the text:

**Well, it might not blow up.**

provides much less essential information.

Experienced emailers often use lots of white space and typed-out vocalizations to convey these types of pauses, as follows:

**Let's think  hem  errr**
**Wellll, it \*might\* not blow up.**

You can also use white space to make clear which words belong to which clause. For example, the following is very difficult to parse:

**Did you want to use a Wonka Roller or a**
**Weeble Roller with a level jimby or a sideways zigwig?**

You could instead remember your high school notes on outlines and write:

**Did you want to use**
    **1. a Wonka Roller**
**or**
    **2. a Weeble Roller**
        **a. level jimby**
        **b. sideways zigwig**

The only problem with using an outline like this is it invites people to send back messages that have nothing in them but the code for the answer they want, such as

2b.

To avoid that, you can use a structure like:

**Did you want to use a**
    **Wonka Roller**
**or**
    **Weeble Roller with a level jimby**
**or**
    **Weeble Roller with a sideways zigwig?**

This encourages people to cut-and-paste the exact, full description of the thing they want:

**> Weeble Roller with a sideways zigwig**

## CREATIVE PUNCTUATION

Experienced emailers tend to use a lot of punctuation in "comic book style." Instead of writing:

**I am very confused and a little mad. Why did**
**you give my report to Kim instead of Sunny?**

Some people might write:

**?!?! Why did you give my report to Kim**
**instead of Sunny?!?**

The question mark used in this way is a kind of shorthand for a "huh?" or a furrowed brow. The exclamation mark is considered shorthand for amazement and possibly a scowl. The two together seem to mean astonishment.

There is a long and honored tradition of using punctuation as a place holder for swearing, e.g.

**That #%&#$(&^%$&^%$&^$%*!**

You will also sometimes see an asterisk in place of important letters, usually the vowel:

**That son of a b****!**

or very rarely

**That s*n of a b*tch!**

In actual practice, this form of self-censorship is rare—except in monitored chat rooms and message board situations; it is more common for people to either use the whole word or omit it completely. We prefer the latter—unless it's among friends who will understand and accept the language.

## QUOTING DOCUMENTS

If you're referring to previous email, you should explicitly quote that document to provide context. Instead of sending an email message that says only:

**yes**

Respond by quoting the relevant question or line from the previous email:

**> Did you get all of the Wonka Rollers**
**> that you needed?**
**yes**

The greater-than sign (>) or double >> are the most conventional ways to quote someone else's email words, although your email software may use a different convention.

Just decide which message portion you want to quote before you select the respond or reply command. Then write your response after the quoted material.

Even if there is a fair number of words in your response, you still might need to quote the previous message. Imagine getting a response on Wednesday to some email that you can't quite remember sending last Friday.

> I talked to them about it the other day, and they want to see
> the demonstration as soon as possible.

Your response would probably be the highly articulate, "Huh???" What demonstration? For who? For What?"

It would be much easier for you to understand the email if it said:

> › I spoke with John Meyers at Oakley about
> › the new Wonka Roller model.
> › They want to see if it will fit in with their
> › Willy Nilly design system.
> › Do you know if they've seen the demonstration yet?

> I talked to them about it the other day, and they
> want to see the demonstration as soon as possible.

This is substantially better, but now errs on the side of too *much* context. Information in the first lines has nothing to do with the question being answered. You should only include enough to provide a context for the message and no more. And make sure your response (as shown below) offers enough context to be clear.

You need only enough context to frame the question being answered:

> › John Meyers at Oakley about
> › the new Wonka Roller model.
> › Do you know if they've seen the demonstration yet?

> I talked to them about it Tuesday (Jun 6), and they want to see the
> demonstration as soon as possible.

## CHANGE PRONOUNS FOR CLARITY

The above example gives a good amount of context, but the response to it still takes a little effort to follow. Who exactly does "they" refer to in the response? A good rule is to look *very* carefully at all pronouns in your sentences. If they don't refer to something explicitly stated in the email, change them to something concrete.

> **I spoke with John Meyer's executive assistant on Tuesday (Jun 6) and she said he wants to see the demonstration as soon as possible.**

Now the answer is very clear and specific. And, since the response contains implicit yet clear references to the original message, less explicitly quoted material is needed. Responses like this, with the context mostly in the body of the message, are the easiest to understand. Unfortunately, they take the longest to compose.

If you want to quote a sentence that is in the middle of a paragraph, or wraps around lines, go ahead and remove everything but the part that you were really interested in, inserting "[. . .]" if you have to take something out in the middle. You can also paraphrase by using square brackets, as above.

If the message isn't important enough to you to warrant the time to strip the original message down, include the whole original message *AFTER* your response, not before. If you put the original message at the end, your readers don't have to look at it unless they don't understand the context of your response.

## NONSTANDARD ENGLISH

First, there is no universally correct set of words for every situation. Figures of speech depend on your audience, although simple, non-dialect words and phrases always work better across a wide range of groups. An unfamiliar dialect is readable only to those who use it:

Nonstandard usage: "hangin with the homeboys"

Or a dialect spelled out as the words sound: "Jamaica. Mi lan an mi country."

Words such as these significantly slow readers who are unfamiliar with the words and sentence constructions. Of course some people may use these words in normal speech and type the King's English online. Complex word constructions or vocabulary may also confuse educated readers, non-English speakers, and those still in the tender school years of K-12. Or in a long message, they may skip reading the material because there are another 223 messages waiting to be waded through.

## Voice Recognition Software

As voice recognition becomes more popular, it will likely be used for email composition. (You can already record voice messages, but that's different from having your voice messages translated into written ones.) The opposite process, voice translation, is already commonly used to "speak" written email to recipients.

If you intend to use voice recognition software to write your email, remember that words-to-type translation technology is not yet perfect. _Be certain to reread your words carefully before sending them_. Otherwise, embarrassing errors will become a part of your message.

## WORDS INTO TYPE

In the communications quiz in Chapter One, questions involved the ways you assemble email. Do you bang it out on the keyboard and hit Send without a second glance or laboriously write it out longhand first? The most common approach is somewhere in between. Sensitive messages undergo careful rewriting, checking, the use of a spelling checker, and another rereading just for safety's sake.

## FORMATTING ISSUES

The underlying rules governing email transmission are generally standardized, but there is a large number of different software programs that can be used to send and read email. It's quite possible that the message you send won't look at all the same when displayed on your reader's screen, so you have to be careful about how you present your text.

### Fancy Text

Some email reading software only understands plain text. Italics, bold, and color changes will show up as what are called "control sequences" in the text. So you might send something like:

Hiya! Hey, I _loved_ the presentation you gave to Jack this morning. **Great Job!**

## The Folly of Fonts

Computers usually include free fonts and typefaces with their operating systems, and you can buy even more for a small charge. Or you can purchase professional quality fonts from companies like Adobe. These fonts may include regular type, elaborate characters, or even symbols or pictures.

While using these non-standard fonts to print out documents in hard copy can be a great idea, using them in online communication is highly risky. Unless your reader has _exactly_ the same typeface, from the same manufacturer, for the same computer platform and often the same version of the operating system, (i.e., Windows 2000), yours will be converted into one that the recipient does have. Chances are it will be common and ugly looking—Courier for example. Or, your cleverly chosen symbols and pictures will turn into meaningless keyboard equivalents. Stick to the common type faces (fonts): Courier, Arial, Helvetica, Times Roman, New Century, School Book, or Bookman.

But if your correspondent's software can't handle formatting, the message could show up as:

> Hiya! Hey, I _loved_ the presentation you gave to
> Jack this morning. **Great Job!**

Web documents are particularly difficult to read with older email programs. You may have a choice of sending the web page as text or as HTML; keep your correspondent's capabilities in mind when you make that choice.

To avoid problems, assume the receiving system to be capable of little more than text handling. That way, your message will arrive as intended, even if it's less decorative than you planned. Basic formatting is, well basic. It includes only:

1. **Characters from the ASCII character set.** In other words, all small and capital letters and basic punctuation for the English language set. Foreign language users can use their special characters if they know that the recipient has the same font available and that the specific character sets (Japanese Kanji for example) are supported by the email software.

**2. A standard typeface with no special characters.** Your PC may include type-faces like Wingdings or your Mac has Zapf Dingbats, but these characters will be converted to the equivalents in a regular typeface. If you absolutely must add a smiley face, use emoticons created with standard characters, such as parentheses, commas, and dashs—like this ;-) and not Windows' built-in happy faces. Since the standards are made of standard keyboard characters and not symbols, they come across correctly on all computers, even old ma-chines that were developed when ASCII was standard.

Don't use tabs for anything. They may look okay for paragraph breaks on your machine but may not materialize the same way on the receiving end. In-stead, use returns (with the Enter key) to put space between paragraphs.

## Extended Character Sets

Back in the dark ages of 1982, when the first email specs were being written, the decision was made to encode email in a way such that only 128 different characters—letters, numbers, punctuation, and so on—could be transmitted from one computer to another. These were called ASCII characters. This system allowed some free space for error correction—something important when com-puters were calling each other with modems.

However, the net is a different place now. Characters like ä, ç, and Ø have be-come important for large numbers of email users. So now there is a way of encoding data so that 256 different characters can be represented, called "quoted-printable."

Unfortunately, the underlying transport is still limited to 128 different charac-ters, so the email gets converted to the more limited set, transmitted, then (hope-fully) converted back on the other end. If the receiving software doesn't know how to do quoted-printable (or if something gets messed up somewhere), the ex-tended characters will show up as an equals-sign and two letter/digit code:

La premi=E8re journe=E9 de nos deux voyageurs fut assez
agr=E9able. Ils=E9=taient

*continued*

## Extended Character Sets (continued)

So why do you care? After all, you might not ever use umlauts.

You care because there are "special" characters that you probably *will* encounter, that are *not* part of the standard extended character set—the trademark symbol, bullet, and "curly" quotation marks, for example. So you have yet another reason to worry about what your correspondent's email software is capable of—and about how you compose your emails.

### Web Links

Some email reading software will recognize URLs (Uniform Resource Locators—a fancy way of saying web addresses) in the text and make them "live" (it will turn them into "links," on which your recipient can double click his mouse pointer to go directly to the web site, if he's connected to the Internet). But whether yours does or doesn't, it's always a good idea to type the entire address, including the "http://" part. While some newer software doesn't need to see this part of the link, older programs still do, so it's safer to include it, if you don't know which kind of software your recipient uses.

You should also be careful about punctuation—especially periods—right after a URL. For example, take the message

> Ken - the URL is http://www.bakersquared.com. See
> if you think our services might meet your needs.

The software on the receiving end may think that the last period after the URL is **part** of the URL. Or, if the software doesn't recognize links, the reader may cut-and-paste the period along with the rest of the address. Either possibility has the potential to lead to a long and wasted email exchange, with your reader insisting that the page doesn't exist and you insisting that it does. It may look inappropriate, but it causes less confusion if there is at least a space after the URL and the period.

> Ken—the URL is http://www.bakersquared.com . See
> if you think our services might meet your needs.

People who are cutting and pasting might also select too little. Since files that come from the web often have either the extension .html or .htm, this can also be a difficult mistake for your reader to catch. To make cut-and-paste mindlessly easy for people, we prefer to always put URLs on a separate line without a period at the end.

> **Sample Message with URL**
>
> Ken – the URL is:
>
>     http://www.bakersquared.com
>
> See if you think our services might meet your needs.

While this *is* technically ungrammatical, we have sometimes found it worthwhile to trade grammatical perfection for unambiguous clarity.

Some URLs are so long that they will get split into two lines.

> **Sample Split URL**
>
> Hi – The URL is
>
>     http://www.sallysdiner.com/italianchoices/menuspecials/lunch/
> diet.html
>
> See if you think you'll like this dish!

If your correspondent's email software makes links live, it is probably not capable of realizing that the second line belongs with the rest of the URL. Also, if your correspondent is cutting and pasting, he or she may not see the last bit. To clarify the URL specification, simply put angle brackets around the URL. Most (but not all) modern email software will recognize that the words or letters inside angle brackets should be kept together.

> **Sample Use of Brackets Around URL**
>
> Hello Reginald! Here is a URL all about comics:
>
>     ‹http://4comics.4anything.com/?%3B&banner=382a&siteid=ll4kg
> Wa8Mss-2FVPasUkKQTz%2FpPwjWOnsg›
>
> ! I think there's lots of great stuff on the site. Give it a try!

## Punctuation and Quotation Marks

American grammar rules say that punctuation belongs *inside* quotation marks, for example the period in the next sentence:

John said, "I need your help."

That's fine when the words in quotes are normal speech, but this convention can cause problems when discussing computer input. For example:

When you get to the password line, type "the password."

Is the period something that goes in the password box or not? To avoid this confusion, many savvy net wizards use the British grammar rules and type the period at the outside of the quotes like this:

**When you get to the password box, type "the password".**

This makes it clear that the period is not part of the password.

If you prefer not to change your deep-rooted habits, modify the sentence so that there isn't punctuation there:

When you get to the password box, type "the password" and hit return.

## Email Attachments

Most email software supports "attachments" where you can specify a document to send along with your email message. This allows people to share almost any file in any format—as long as the people at both ends share the same programs to read the messages.

However, if your reader's email software doesn't understand attachments and you send a non-text file (like a Word document or a picture), be advised that it will appear as lots of garbage. Pages and pages of garbage, usually.

Furthermore, even if your correspondents can receive and view the attachment you send them, if they're low on disk space or dial in from home to get their email, they will *not* be happy to receive a 200MB video of your child's birthday party, no matter how funny it is. (This is less of a problem with newer systems; but be aware that there are still people out there who have precious little disk space for downloading and saving messages.)

It is sometimes better to post large documents on the Web and email the URL instead of the file. If you don't have the option of uploading a large document to the

Web or don't know how, please email your readers first and ask them if they can handle a large attachment of that format. Once you get to know your readers, you'll know what they can handle, and won't need to ask every time.

## Page Layout

Words on a computer screen look different from words on paper, and usually people find it harder to read screen text. (I know several people who even print out their email to read it.) The screen's resolution is not as good as paper's, there is sometimes flicker, the font may be smaller, and/or the font may be ugly. Also, your recipient's email reader may not have the same capabilities as your email software. All of this means that good email page layout is different from good paper document page layout.

## Line Length

If there is a mismatch between your software and your reader's in the way they wrap lines (decide on which word to end one line and go to the next), your correspondent may end up looking at lines that run off the end of the page, making your message nearly indecipherable, as shown here:

> › Sally's help with the Wonka Rollers is greatly appreciated. And
> we think that she should get something to
> › remember that this isn't always the way that we treat such people.

In any case, you should try to keep your lines under seventy characters long. Why seventy and not, say, seventy-six? Because you should leave a little room for the indentation or quote marks your correspondents may want if they need to quote pieces of your message in their replies.

## Terser Prose

How many times when you were in school were you told to write a 10-page paper? Probably a lot, and you got penalized for being terse. So you padded your writing with lots of useless and meaningless words to fill the pages. This approach is definitely not appropriate for email. The rule is: Keep it short. If people want more information, they can ask for it.

If you're sending a report to many people, then you may need to put more detail into the email so that you aren't flooded with questions from everyone on the recipient list. (You should also ask yourself if all the people really need to be on the list.)

Kaitlin Duck Sherwood, at http://www.webfoot.com, explains the rules like this: "The fewer people there are on the recipient list, the shorter the message should be. Books, sold to thousands of people, are tens of thousands of words long. Speeches, which are given in front of large groups, are thousands of words long. But you'd tune out someone at a party who said more than a hundred words at a time.

I try to keep everything on one "page." In most cases, this means twenty-five lines of text. (And yes, that means that [this] document is way, WAY too long for email!) "

## UNDERSTANDING STATUS CUES FROM PEOPLE YOU DON'T KNOW

We've already explained how you'll start out knowing little about a reader's context when you send email. You also won't be able to determine much about their status.

Why? Because you can't see your recipients' car or their clothes, listen to their dialect and rate of speech, consider the timbre of their voice, or see the gleam in their eyes. If you don't know the person, your guesses about your correspondent's age, gender, race, marital status, income level, intelligence, and education will be much less accurate than they might be in a face-to-face or telephone conversation.

Your readers can't tell much about you either. They will probably do the same thing you will catch yourself doing (if you're truly honest with yourself): they'll make assumptions about you on the flimsiest of pretexts.

Although making assumptions about people is really never a good idea, it's important to realize that you and they WILL do it because there are so few status cues to draw upon in email and other online communications. You need to be aware of this, so that you can work on guiding your readers' assumptions if and when you need to.

In general, people will use four criteria to make assumptions about you in your online communications:

■ The language you use
■ Your return address

- Your email signature
- Your facility with email

We're going to discuss each of these in the next few pages to help you put your best image forward in all your online interactions.

**The Language You Use**

Kaitlin Duck Sherwood, in her online guide to email, reminds us that "the biggest status cue is your competence with language. If you have lots of misspellings, your subjects do not agree with your verbs, or you use the wrong words, people may assume that you're uneducated.

From that, they may infer that you're not very clever. It doesn't matter that the correlation between language ability and intelligence is weak (especially among non-native speakers); lots of people will make that inference anyway."

We know that we are personally insulted at times by getting email with errors, especially sloppy typographical errors. The bottom line is this: grammar and spelling really do count (especially in formal email interactions with customers, employers, and professional colleagues).

Spending more time honing your prose can improve the quality of the writing, but it is not possible to spend an hour on each email message if you need to send ten or more messages every day (and most business people do this as a matter of course). Yes, grammar- and spell-checkers can help a bit (and be sure you use them if high status is important to your message). However, there are many errors that grammar- and spell-checkers will not find.

If you really want to boost your language-related status in your online communications, you may have to commit yourself to some significant studying if your language skills are weak. (At the very least, get a copy of the Strunk and White book, *The Elements of Style*, that we mentioned in the Introduction.)

Besides, improving your writing (if need be) will help you in life and work and not just online. The effort is worth it, especially for non-native speakers and those who quit school early to run the farm. Along with cleaning up your ink-on-paper act, your vocabulary will grow. That makes you sound more intelligent and helps you describe events and situations to your peers in clearer language. Using the wrong *its* or *it's,* or *they're, their, there,* can make you look incompetent. It's a good time for a change if your written words suffer from easy-to-fix problems such as these.

### Your Return Address

Your reader will unconsciously derive status cues from your domain name. The domain name is the thing that comes after the at sign (@) in an email address, like *aol.com* or *arc.nasa.gov.* The domain names have different words, separated by periods, that indicate different levels of organization. The size of the organization increases as you go left to right. The domain *arc.nasa.gov,* for example, is for Ames Research Center, which is part of NASA, which is one of innumerous entities of the U.S. government.

If you get email from someone, and there is no '@' sign, then that probably means they have exactly the same domain as you. For example, if *sunnybaker@aol.com* sends email to *kimbaker@aol.com*, Kim will see only *Sunnybaker* in the return address field.

Kaitlin Duck Sherwood clearly states the issues that affect status cues in this way:

"Any stereotype that is held about the organization that gives you your email connection will rub off on you. For example, if your email comes from:

*ibm.com*, people may presume that you're adult, computer literate, and somewhat stuffy.

*aol.com*, some people will presume that you're connecting from home and that your email is not work-related.

*washington.k12.ia.us*, people may think that you're under 18.

*webtv.net*, people will probably assume that you're not terribly computer literate."

Your correspondents will also look at your real name (if visible) and unless your name has cues to the contrary, most people will assume that you're either a male or a female. For ex-

**ONLINE LINGO**

**Thread:** You'll see the word 'thread' used frequently in this book and online. For example, an online service may offer you, for your reading pleasure, the thread of an online event. The thread is simply the conversation flow, in sequence, between participants in a conversation. A celebrity online interview has a thread consisting of the celebrity's words and those of the attendees. A chatroom, in which multiple conversations take place simultaneously has multiple threads: one for each topic during the chat.

ample: *barbara@aol.com* will be female - even though *barbara* could easily be a man named George Barbara.

Or consider our names: is Sunny or Kim the male in the family? (Kim is the boy, and Sunny is the girl.) Unless the name is something like *Smith*, people are likely to assume that the author of any email coming from Singapore is Asian. Unless the screen name is something like *Hamid* or *Mikiko* people will usually assume that authors of email coming from the U.S. are of European descent.

Your user name (also called a log-in ID in some companies) provides even more subtle cues. Having a desirable email name - short and without numbers - can indicate that you were one of the first in your domain to get an email account. Thus, *joe@ibm.com* has probably been using computers longer than *joe4739@ibm.com*.

## The Real You: It's All in the Signature

Since you can't always control your email name or your domain name, you can help adjust people's impressions very easily just by telling them who you are in the signature to your email. It can provide a number of intentional (and, if you're not careful, unintentional) status cues. For example:

> **Reginald Berkmeister**
> **Vice-President of Engineering**
> **Great Big Computer Company, Inc.**

This email signature conveys the status of someone quite important in the engineering world.

On the other hand, the one below gives quite different information:

> **Reggie Berkmeister**
> **Redlands High School**
> **(Age 15)**
> **Check out the German Homepage at http://www.germany.org!**

This signature tells you that Reggie is a young man who is probably of German origin, even if you hadn't already guessed it from his last name.

People may also make assumptions about your maturity and demand for formality in communication. Your reader will probably take *Reginald.Berkmeister.Ph.D.@anchor.com* more seriously than *reggie@anchor.com*.

It can be effective to start off a message with intentional status cues if you don't know your readers:

---

**Sample Openings with Status Cues**

Hi, my name is Reggie and I'm a student at Redlands High School in Southern California. I'm doing a project at school on new innovations in computer design. Could you please send me the latest Great Big Computer Company catalog?

Or:

Hello. – I'm the Vice-President of Engineering at Great Big Computer Company. Could you please send me the latest Wonka Roller catalog? I'm considering purchasing devices similar to these for our new project.

---

Note in the second example that the author not only gives a title and professional affiliation, but also demonstrates language facility by using larger, more formal words: "considering purchasing" instead of "thinking of buying." Overuse of big words can be pretentious, but in short messages can enhance status. Of course, don't use words that are so obscure that your reader won't understand them.

### Your Facility with Email Conventions

Finally, people will consider your skill at using email conventions as an indicator of your status and intelligence. People may simply assume that you're an online newbie if you do not give proper context, type only in capital letters, or use line lengths that run off the edge of the screen. However, they may also assume that you're too ignorant or disinterested to learn the conventions.

## Are Status Cues Really Important?

The importance you should place on the status you convey in your online communications will depend on some basic questions you should ask yourself:

■ **How much do you know about the people you're communicating with?** If you have had lots of contact with your correspondents already, their assumptions about your age, gender, status, and intellect will be established (hopefully in the way you want it to be). Only the most serious abuse of grammar rules and email etiquette (if they notice at all) is likely to affect your status with them.

■ **What results or outcomes depend on your message?** If you're sending email to your boss, you should be careful about your grammar. If you're corresponding with salespeople who want your business, well, they're being paid not to care about your grammar. If you need help, advice, or money, people may be more willing to assist you if you're able to project enough status to make them think that you're worth their time and respect.

■ **Are the people you're communicating with going to care?** High-school English teachers are more likely to care about your grammar than are the members of your camping club. People who send and receive lots of email will probably be more tolerant than people who have an hour to spend on every email message.

■ **If you've seen your correspondent's email already, what does it look like?** If they send you email with incorrect punctuation, poor spelling, and unconscionable grammar, they probably won't care too much if you do the same.

■ **Do incorrect assumptions bother you?** If you're a man named Pat who doesn't mind being mistaken for a woman, then go ahead and use "Pat" instead of "Patrick." If you don't care if people think you're a teenager, go ahead and use the email moniker "InLineSkater."

### Formality

In some ways, you can control to some extent how many responses you get to your email messages by how formal your language is. Because email is so easy to respond to, people naturally tend to use very informal prose. The less formal the email, the more likely people are to respond to you. And vice versa.

This can be a very good thing if you want feedback. However, if your email address is very public, you may well find yourself getting far more email than you're interested in or can respond to (with anything more than an autoresponder which you'll read about in the next chapter).

Therefore, always be cautious about the tone of your messages. If you want people to respond, be chatty and informal. But if you want to discourage people from sending you email, you should write much more formally.

# CHAPTER FOUR

# Email Tools, Techniques, and Words

NOW WE'LL LEARN ABOUT USING THE FORWARD, copying, and alias functions in your email to make sure your communications go to the appropriate people. We'll also review some common words and phrases used in email, as well as some you should avoid.

## CHOOSING YOUR RECIPIENTS

Just as you should be careful about who goes on the distribution lists when writing a company memo (or wedding invitations or anything else), you should choose your email recipients wisely.

Who goes on your 'A' list (your 'send-to' list) and who ends up on your 'B' list (your 'copy to' list) depends upon the content and importance of your message. At work, it's generally best to limit distribution to those who have a "need-to-know."

Annoying the Vice-President of Finance with messages about water cooler overages, for example, is likely to be a career-stalling move.

Friends and family, on the other hand, tend to be far more forgiving about inept emailing. Sending a message inappropriately to a large list of distant or uninterested relatives isn't likely to disturb anybody. Some of them might even enjoy getting mail that has little direct interest for them, because without it they wouldn't get any email at all.

With all that in mind, here are some hints about how to set up your mailing lists and who to put on them.

**Send to:**

Put only the people for whom the message is primarily intended on this line. Do not use it to copy your message to someone from whom you expect neither an action nor a reply. To do so may be insulting.

Here's an example:

> **Yank the damned blocks on rigs 22 and 31 before sunup tomorrow. Tell the crew to work all night if they have to, or I'll have their heads! They never should have worked that strata anyway.**

This note leaves many possible misinterpretations open to inappropriate recipients. Here are just a few:

- They want me to fix a mistake that I didn't even know about, let alone have anything to do with.
- If I'm going to get the blame for something that's not my fault and my job's in jeopardy because of it, maybe I'd better read the riot act to some people.
- What the hell does this mean?
- My department is about to be downsized. This is just flack from the decision.
- I don't know what this means, and I shouldn't be on this list.

Oddly, positive praise or advice works the same way. Let's say you wrote the following to a project team leader:

> **Great job Lewinski and team! You and your people deserve kudos for work well done!**

## Faux Pas Fallout

If you make the mistake of sending an email message inappropriately to a senior manager or other high-ranking company officer, here's what they're likely to think:

1. You made a mistake on your address list.
2. You are new to email and will learn from experience. (Or a similar idea in much less friendly language.)
3. You fail to grasp the complexity of organizational structure and its "dos" and "don'ts." (In a true bureaucracy you may find out too late that messages to any rank above your manager must first be "cleared" by your manager.)
4. You have poor manners online, which may carry over to everything you do, and maybe you should be passed over for key assignments, promotions, etc., should this person receive repeated inappropriate email from you.
5. You have a screw loose somewhere.

Send that message to the wrong people and misinterpretations can abound:

■ Who is Lewinski? I should be up on this person and the project—what should I do?
■ I better call this person and offer congratulations or I'll look bad. But what should I say about a project I know nothing about? I can't ask anyone or I'll really look stupid.
■ Should I have been involved in this project?

Enough said?

**Copy:**

You can copy email to anyone who has an indirect interest in your message's content. Indirect simply means they're not being called to action or receiving "must have" information. Once again, if you copy to people inappropriately, they'll start to question your judgment and skip reading your 'CCs:'.

## Email Defensively

Copying messages is frequently used in business as a "cover your ass" tactic.
That way if something like a project blows up and heads roll, it's more difficult for
those involved on a peripheral level to claim they were unaware of the problem.
So it's just as important to make sure you copy to every single pertinent recipient
as it is to delete anyone who has no need to be on your list.

### Blind Copy or BCC

Blind copy is used to hide additional message recipients from the primary recipient. If you were to reprimand an employee by email and you wanted your boss to receive a copy of the message without the employee becoming aware of it, you would BCC your boss.

Blind copy is also useful for hiding addresses. If you want to send email to several people but don't want to disclose all of the recipients' addresses, you can BCC the ones you want to hide.

## MANAGING INCOMING EMAIL, SPAM, AND OTHER COMM

Controlling which email makes it to your inbox and which doesn't calls for some serious consideration. An incoming message may contain a clickable link that can take you to a site infected with a computer virus, or bring your kids to sites filled with obscene and pornographic pictures and text.

Fortunately, much of today's email software contains useful tools for blocking junk mail, a.k.a. spam. The most basic blocking tools, called filters, allow you to specify only people whom you don't want to hear from. The weakness of this scheme is obvious to anyone with a mailbox crammed with junk from senders they don't know.

Other blocking tools are more sophisticated. Microsoft's Outlook email program, for example, looks for forged addresses—a technique used frequently by spammers—and filters them out. Messages from people listed in your Outlook address book, on the other hand, always get through. AOL also provides a filtering system, although it's pretty brain dead at this writing.

## There's Spam and Then There's Spam . . .

The use of the word spam for junk email is attributed to the English comedians of Monty Python in their BBC Television sketch of a café full of Vikings. The place's menu reads like this: Spam, Spam, Spam, Spam, baked beans, and Spam, Spam with Spam . . . 'Um, sounds delicious.

Reportedly the *real* Spam people—the Hormel Foods Corporation—were initially less than pleased with the entire affair. But with all the free Net publicity they've received, they've regained their sense of humor. You can now visit www.spam.com, join a *Spam fan club* from the site and purchase Spam paraphernalia too.

In many programs—including AOL—you can use a wild card character such as "*" to block mail from an entire domain. Kim, tired of receiving a ton of junk mail from a particular domain name, blocked it with a wild card. The address *.hotmail.com blocked everything with hotmail.com on the end regardless of the first part of the name.

Overnight, a mailbox once crammed with spam was reduced to a normal load of mail. Of course, there was the risk that legitimate mail sent by hotmail users got blocked too. That's a problem with filtering—you're asking your computer to make intelligent decisions when it's not really an intelligent device.

### The Low Profile Approach

The best way to avoid spam is to make your email address invisible. How? To start with, disguise yourself. Use another name when you're participating in a chat room, responding to an outsider's mail, or purchasing anything from the World Wide Web. Avoid taking part in surveys, free contests, and online volunteer services. And just say no to freebies, games, and puzzles.

In short, have less fun. But remember, no matter what you do, nothing works forever. Sooner or later someone will get your email address and sell it to marketers with mailing lists, so you may find yourself changing your email address more often than you'd like to.

## FORWARDING MESSAGES

Most email software has a forward function. Just hit the button and the message you received can be sent on to anyone else.

Forwarding messages is an art. It enables you to send either single messages or long threads to other people for their review. It's a great tool for sending important news to people who need to "be in the know" but weren't included on the original mailing list. However, it can also be used inappropriately to send people information that is really none of their business.

When you forward an email, it will automatically include the original message in its entirety. So make sure the person on the receiving end really needs all that information. If not, edit out the unnecessary parts. Also, to set the context for your reader, you should preface the forwarded message with a brief note of explanation.

Here's an example of a message forwarding sequence with a note added. Note the subject line. Leading with an 'FW:' or 'Forward:' is common practice for this type of email. You'll find the sender's introductory message to you at the beginning of the letter's body, followed by the forwarded message. Some, but not all, email software precedes each line of forwarded text with an >, as with a quoted message.

Here's an example:

> **To: Charley Smith**
> **From: Jan Lipton**
> **Subject: FW: New fiscal year budget cuts; meeting on Tuesday.**
> **Hi Charley:**
> I knew you would want to be copied on this message from my box because most of my cuts must come from your TimesTwo project. See me first thing tomorrow and we'll discuss.
> JAN
> > To: Jan Lipton
> > Date: Jan 14 2002
> > From: Fred Simmons
> > Subject: New fiscal year budget cuts; meeting on Tuesday.
> > Jan—It's a new fiscal year and we're asking all
> > department heads to find ways to chop the budget by 10%
> > during the year. We're looking at personnel changes as a

## What if My Boss Can't Spell?

A small suggestion: Unless you highlight only your own text, your email package's software will spell check the entire document when you're forwarding or replying to a message—whether you want it to or not. To avoid the (small) possibility of offending your sender, don't make or allow changes to his or her message in your reply. And, *never* point out or poke fun at another's writing or spelling ability no matter how illiterate it is.

> › last resort and want you to find projects that can wait
> › for next year. Look also for projects that maybe we don't
> › really need. We're scheduling an all-day meeting on
> › Tuesday, the 5th to review your ideas and proposals. See
> › me personally before the meeting if you can't drop at
> › least 5% of your budget.
> › Fred Simmons, Managing Director

Charley responds to the forwarded email with this message:

Jan, Thanks for forwarding this information. I have always appreciated your honest way of working with me. Although I can't believe this is happening, I trust your judgment and know that you wouldn't agree to anything you didn't believe would have a positive effect for the company. I'll work on some ideas for the budget cuts. Sadly, this may mean the loss of a few key people that my department really needs.
    Charley

## ALIASES

An alias is a single name that represents an entire group of recipients. By mailing to a single alias, you can mail to everyone that alias comprises. So if you often find yourself mass-mailing messages to the same list, using an alias can save you lots of typing.

For example, your immediate family's alias might include:

mom91832@sigh.com
joe@joe.com
bigSIS@earthlink.com
grannysmith@gte.net
sallykempler@halcion.net

Instead of treating these addresses as separate entities, you can add them to an alias called MyFamily. Then, to send a message to all of these people at the same time, just type MyFamily on the 'To:' line.

You can have multiple groups of aliases too. You might use MyFamily for close relatives and then one named SmithClan for relatives outside of your immediate family. To reach all relatives, you would then mail to both aliases, MyFamily and SmithClan. (Sure beats typing all those names and the risk of typos!) Aliases can also be combined with other aliases, individual email addresses, and they can be used with the blind copy function (BCC) in the same way they're used in the address line.

Again, do not overuse the alias function. It's likely that your entire company doesn't need to know about your department's annual picnic. And carefully review your alias list before sending any message that contains sensitive material, in case someone is on the list who should absolutely not receive it.

## WRITING AN AUTORESPONDER MESSAGE

Leaving your home or office for a few days or more? Use your email program—if it supports the function—to create an autoresponder message—an automatic reply to anyone who emails you. You can include information you like, including your return date, the purpose of your trip, emergency contact people and numbers, or even an itinerary. A typical message might look like this:

Hello, you have reached Chuck Carlson's emailbox. I will be away on a
court date January 29th. If you need immediate assistance from my group,

> urgent calls are being taken by Sheila at 619-555-1212. Otherwise, send
> me an email message, and I will check my mail the first day back.
> Chuck (Charles) Carlson

An autoresponder message usually contains the following:

A greeting and simple apology for not being available.

Your name in case there's doubt about the system's integrity about where the
responder message originated.

Why you're not there.

When you'll be back online.

Whom to contact if it's an emergency, with contact info.

You may include a breakout message as well. This is a message for a specific
group of people who may encounter your responder message, and contains additional information just for this group. For example:

> Hello, you have reached Chuck Carlson's emailbox. I will be away
> on a court date January 29th. If you need immediate assistance from
> my group, urgent calls are being taken by Sheila at 619-555-1212.
> Otherwise, send me an email message, and I will check my mail the
> first day back.
>
> If you're looking for more information about the Oceangate issue,
> please call Leon Jerwolsky at 545-555-1212. He will be handling the affair
> in my absence.
> Chuck (Charles) Carlson

## Home and Family Autoresponder Messages

You can use an autoresponder message for home email when you leave on vacation. But, since burglars like knowing about empty houses, this may not be such a
good idea. In theory only trusted family members will receive your message
describing your "gone dates" for a cruise up the Nile. But a junk mailer may
automatically receive it too and pass the responder message on to the black ski
mask people.

## Rain or Shine, the Mail Must Go Through

When you're aware of a scheduled shutdown of the mail system, warn senders with an autoresponder message. That way, they'll know to get word to you in some other way.

Hello: you have reached Chuck Carlson's emailbox. My mailbox will be down from June 11 at 11:00 am (Saturday) until June 14 at 2:00 am (Tuesday) for system upgrade and maintenance. If you're reading this, the temporary system is working. Assume that I will not receive any email correspondence during this period. And, because last time we upgraded, the system was actually down for more than a week, you may want to phone me to confirm receipt of your mail. Really vital messages should come to me by phone or overnight package service. As you know, I can be reached at 416-555-1212 or page me at 416-555-5555.

Sorry about the inconvenience.

Chuck

If autoresponse is impossible, attach a brief version of this advice as a footnote to all outgoing email. That way, at least some of your usual correspondents will get the warning.

### KEEPING MAIL

Briefly, you can save your email automatically by setting up the email program's preferences to do so (you'll have to delete unimportant mail manually). Mail can be saved on the mail system, where it may be auto-deleted after a predetermined number of days, or on your computer for as long as you want.

When you want to reread a message at a later time, you can mark it as Unread so that it will appear as new mail next time you open your mailbox.

### THE DANGERS OF PROOFING

For reasons unclear to us (but certainly borne out by the experience of writing more than 20 books), proofreading on screen misses errors that would be caught in a

## The Basics of Online Proofreading

If you absolutely must proofread your text on-screen, there are some things you can do to make your task easier:

**Make it bigger.** In word processors that support magnification, zoom to 150 percent to improve readability.

**Get better glasses.** Anything that helps create a sharper image onscreen will improve your online experience.

**Use your finger.** Read slowly and carefully using your finger to follow the words (and mess up the screen) if it helps.

**Find a friendly font.** Some character fonts are easier to read than others. Choose one that you find user-friendly.

**Keep characters dark.** Avoid the use of light colors for on-screen type—they're hard enough to read, let alone proof.

print out. Perhaps on screen, it's too easy to keep editing (and adding potential mistakes). Or it may be that type made up of a few dots (pixels)and rendered on a CRT or LCD panel is simply harder to see than printed output.

Whatever the reason, if you want an important message to arrive sans errors, print it and proof the hardcopy. If rewriting is required or the number of typos is found to be high, repeat the process. Note: Spellers and grammar checkers won't catch everything; just look at "there", "their", and "they're"—all perfectly acceptable to a speller. A grammar checker might (or might not) find such errors, but most email programs don't have one.

## EMAIL WORDS AND HOW YOU'RE PERCEIVED

When writing online, you must be especially careful about your phrasing. Your message might sound grand to you but spoil someone else's morning because your tone came across as negative, nasty, or vindictive. Your would-be accolades read like criticisms, and your faintly negative comments seemed devastating.

How could that possibly happen? The online written word is usually so brief that readers are forced to read between the lines.

Study these examples, each pair of which covers the same topic. Note two things: The words in each positive and negative example aren't much different from each other—unless you're the recipient and have tossed and turned all night thinking about their real meaning. Note also that there is a fine line between rude or negative and friendly and approachable.

These examples are not supposed to be severe. Obviously, "I think you are a malevolent toad" is not going to be fixed by simple rephrasing. Instead, they're more like the mistakes everyone makes when they're new to online communication or simply rushed.

> **Neg:** I'm glad to hear that you're finally doing the job we hired you to do.
>
> **Pos:** I'm glad to hear you've worked into meeting our hiring expectations.
>
> **Neg:** You know, you have a funny way of saying things in your email.
>
> **Pos:** Your writing is uniquely you!
>
> **Neg:** You never replied to my email about the Coa Ltd. account. I waited six days etc., etc.
>
> **Pos:** I didn't hear back from you after my Coa Ltd. email. You must be swamped, so I'll call.

### 50 Words to Spruce Up Your Email

This section offers general words you can use in almost any online situation, including email and chat. Some words are online specific (avoid with newbies), but many are commonly used in standard communications. (Note that "good" words aren't always positive. Words like *crash* are useful and endemic to online comm.):

| activity | bookmark | code/coded |
|---|---|---|
| agreed | brainstorm | command |
| answer | build/building | crash |
| associates | chat | cumulative |

| | | |
|---|---|---|
| cyberspace | help/helpful | study |
| dialog | inclusive | surf/surfing |
| dynamic | join us | team |
| enhanced | model | together |
| entropy | mutual | tools |
| evolving | online/offline | useful |
| fast | operational | valuable |
| friends | productive | virtual |
| good listener | run with it | visit |
| good question | site | we agree |
| good to see you | solve | |
|   again | structure | |

## 50 Words Never to Use Online

As you read this list you may want to purvey our sister text, *How to Say It At Work*. The online words are different from the day-to-day words you might use in a written report or even a memo. They're often more expedient, sometimes even juvenile, but avoid them and their ilk just the same.

| | |
|---|---|
| a waste/wasted | forget it |
| anybody want to _____? (this is | get a life |
|   used by people you should avoid) | get off |
| awkward | get off/get out/get outta here |
| busy | hard/hard way to _____ |
| call this number for important | I can't . . . |
|   information . . . | I have pictures . . . (avoid at *all* cost |
| clumsy/klunky |   any reference to this in any chat |
| crisis |   outside of business or someone |
| deleted |   you know and trust online) |
| failure/system glitch | I need employees . . . |
| fix | I won't . . . |

| | |
|---|---|
| idiot savant | shallow |
| impossible | shutdown |
| It's a billion dollar proposition . . . | stupid |
| jerk | take it easy, please! |
| krudge/kludged (slang, proper | unavailable |
|   spellings uncertain) | unfixable |
| learning curve | unlikely |
| lost | unload |
| lost contact | unprofessional |
| make do | useless |
| never | various unprintable swear words |
| newbie (as in "you're obviously a |   used commonly online because of |
|   newbie") |   the lack of online source provider, |
| no way (it's bad enough already, |   legal, or parental retribution. |
|   but never, ever with "Jose") | was' up (reserved for people you |
| odd |   wouldn't want to converse with) |
| panic mode | you _____! you're a _____! |
| patch | you're new to _____? |

**Six Easy Techniques for Improving Text-Only Communication**

It's been said that when he died, assassinated President John F. Kennedy was taking intensive French lessons so that he could effectively communicate with France's then leader, Charles de Gaulle. But, as world news magazine *The Economist* explained, it was a hopeless task because three-quarters of effective French language is gesture *and not words at all*. So, where does that leave you unless you have a video linkup to add nuance to complete the content of the conversation?

Here are six ideas to help users relying on text only systems:

**Say exactly what you mean.** Be precise and complete in your writing, even if that requires more words than you had intended to use. Or in a fast chatroom environment—where the world will have moved onto another topic long before you've finished typing—just skip the thought altogether.

In the following example, there's no way for the reader to know that the tone is intended to be sarcastic.

> "Oh, it's certainly going to be another great day!"

Here's a more complete, clearer rendering:

> "Oh, it's certainly going to be another great day! I've got more than 12 client calls to make and then a speech at the annual meeting that I haven't even started on. I'll be lucky to get to bed before midnight."

**Know your audience.** As mentioned previously, know for a certainty that your recipient understands any electronic shorthand or symbols you use. **Question; don't guess.** There is a longstanding theory that the United States dropped the atomic bomb on Nagasaki only because, following Hiroshima, the Japanese surrender message was misinterpreted. Ask freely for clarification when you fail to understand sentences, words, abbreviations, or even emoticons. This may make you look like a novice in some situations, but that's better than the possibility of outright misunderstanding.

**Keep your cool.** Reserve strong emotions for phone calls or face-to-face communication. Just think about how this would sound to others participating in an online business forum:

> "Jan, you must have no idea what academics think of your position on liberal economics. You're acting both arrogantly and stupidly, as everyone expected you would."

Or in an otherwise mellow family chatroom where an unwanted visitor has appeared:

> "You can take your marriage proposal and . . . you know where to put it! I've flushed your ugly ring down the toilet—if you listen closely, you can hear it cycling down in the background. Never log into our chatroom again, or I'll call the police!"

Neither message will win any popularity contests, either with the recipients or with others online. And to make matters worse, a wounded recipient might take it upon himself to forward your commentary to "interested" parties, possibly costing someone a job or a family relationship.

**Identify yourself as the sender.** If you're using someone else's user ID (email account), make sure you don't send an email under someone else's name. It's surprisingly easy to do. You don't have access to your regular computer so you ask Big Ted if you can use his to send a "quick email message that can't wait." Big Ted jovially agrees, "sure—no problem!"

After he logs you on with his user ID and password, you send your message, forgetting that the recipient will see it came from bigt87. Since the subject line doesn't mention *you're* sending it, it gets deleted as junk mail. If you can't work your identity into the subject line, at least start the message with it:

> **"Ms. Fielding, this is Jackie Arrow. I'm using Big Ted's email since my computer's in the shop after catching fire last week. I just wanted to let you know that . . .", "I have deleted references to this message from Big Ted's machine for security reasons as you would expect . . ."**

**Avoid elaborate formatting.** We've said it before and we'll say it again. What looks good at your end—lines that divide sections, pictures that illustrate your point—may backfire and produce either a garbled looking message or one that the recipient can't even open, much less read. If you feel you must use fancy layout and design, send your message as an attached file in a format your reader can open.

### Phrases to Avoid and Why

Among the zillions of words in all human languages, some (obviously) get used a lot more than others. There are a number of common ones that you should leave out of email, chat, and forums because their meaning is ambivalent. That is to say, the recipient can take them either as intended or as inappropriate. We can't cover all these chameleon-like words and phrases, but we can show you what to watch out for. Keep in mind too that sarcasm does not work well online. You'll see a couple of examples here:

"Where have you been?"
Pos: "We missed you."
Neg: "How come you've been away when we needed you?"

"Don't tell me."
Pos: "Tell me!"
Neg: "Don't tell me."

"Why?"
Pos: "Please explain."
Neg: "I can't believe it!"

"It's too big for us."
Pos: "It's too big for us to handle."
Neg: "It's not important enough to bother with."

"No way!"
Pos: "It's not possible!"
Neg: "That's amazing!"

"You won't believe this . . ."
Pos: "This is so great . . ."
Neg: "Get ready for bad news . . ."

As you can see, it's easy to confuse and confound your reader when you choose the wrong words. The best way to avoid this problem is by making sure that you or someone else has reread your messages—at least the important ones—before sending them.

# CHAPTER FIVE

# The Basics of Chat, Mailing Lists, and Bulletin Boards

THERE ARE TWO BASIC KINDS of communication on the Internet: **asynchronous,** wherein you send some kind of message, such as an email, and your reader responds whenever the mood strikes him; and **synchronous,** wherein the message senders and respondents must be online at the same time and response is immediate. This is also called *realtime* communication—because both participants are interacting in realtime (the techie word for "right now"). Chat communications are synchronous.

## GETTING STARTED WITH CHAT

Chat services allow two or more people anywhere in the world to communicate with each other over the Internet—usually not with their voices, as "chat" would suggest, but by typing messages back and forth to each other in real time.

There are really only two things required for chat other than an Internet connection: two people (or more) to hold a conversation, and chat software. Of course, for multimedia and voice chat, you'll need a microphone and/or web-enabled video camera for each participant.

One of the most important things required of good chatters is patience and understanding. Besides the Internet connection and the software, chatting will be easier and much more pleasant if you also have lots of patience, a common language, basic literacy skills, a good disposition, and a high tolerance for meeting every kind of person imaginable. You'll also find that the accepted practices for chat communication vary based on the type of chat room, the purpose of the chat, and the formality of the chat topic. It's important to adapt to the environment when you are a chat participant.

## CHAT CLIENTS AND PROGRAMS

There is a variety of Internet environments that support chat, including network systems such as AOL Chat, ICQ chat, chat on Yahoo!, and various chat rooms on web sites. Entering a chat room on the web is often just a matter of following the instructions you find on the web site.

Other chat systems require special software. For example, there are many chat rooms on AOL for various interests and topics, but you need to be a member of AOL and use its software to gain access to them. Other chat environments require special chat software, which is usually called a chat client. These programs help users connect to remote servers (the computers on which the back-and-forth is actually taking place).

A variety of these clients is available, and many are free. Chat can be downloaded from various sites on the Internet. Try www.ZDNet.com or www.tucows.com to find chat clients. Just do a search on "chat software" and you'll find many possibilities for general and specific topic chat clients.

## FROM TEXT TO VIDEO CHAT

The original chat programs were simple and text-based, and several pioneers in the field are still popular today, including Internet Relay Chat (IRC) clients available online for free. Among these, mIRC and PIRCH find favor with a great number of users, but fancier clients, such as IRC Toons, which allows you to create animated figures that represent you (avatars) and interact with those created by other people using the same software, have also become popular.

## Avatars

In more advanced chat systems, users are often given a choice of avatars, or iconographs, which are pictures that represent them in three-dimensional chat rooms. Avatars often look like people, with skin tone, hair, and general facial features. Some programs even allow you to use actual photographs. But remember, there is nothing that demands that an avatar actually look like the person behind it, so what you see may be nothing more than an online disguise.

## Using Chat Software

Most chat software is very simple to use. Once you're in a chat room, you're likely to see only two or three elements:

- The window in which the conversation takes place. You will see the words of other participants as well as your own.
- A box or place for you to type your responses before sending them with a Send, Enter, or similar button to submit your message to the conversation window.
- A window showing the user names (or avatars) of others in the room. Not all chat environments show all the users and when this window exists. It can often be turned off to make more room for the conversation window.

In voice-integrated chat rooms, you'll also hear the people as they are given their turns to speak. All this happens while the typing is still going on—which makes it a bit difficult to learn when you first get started.

## Most Chat Is Personal

Most chat rooms on the Internet are strictly for personal interactions among groups of people who share common interests. They are usually open to new members, but beware: some "open" chat rooms "belong" to a specific group of people who have been chatting together for a long time and have formed a sort of clique, with special rules of interaction unique to that group. These people may or may not accept you—presuming, of course, that you want to chat with them after you try out the room.

If a chat room seems "unwelcoming," or "snobbish," then try another. There are plenty of rooms out there where people are open to new participants. You don't need to try to fit in to a chat group that wants to remain elitist.

Recently, with the development of more sophisticated web technology, real-time online communication has moved to the Web's vast and colorful multimedia environment. If you want to see an example of html-based chat, check out the chat opportunities on http://www.ivillage.com/chat/ or chat on http://www.yahoo.com. These offer colorful text chat integrated with a menu of selectable emoticons for placing into your chat messages, and voice chat, which is integrated with the text-based chat program.

In these newer multimedia chat environments, users who can receive audio and video can participate in chat rooms where others are having the same audio and video experiences.

But in spite of all the new technologies that are expanding the opportunities for realtime communication via the Internet, most chat is still performed as text. The main goal for most people using chat programs is to chat—not to make things look pretty. Most "chattees" figure that if the people really want to "talk" to each other, they can always use the old-fashioned phone system.

## ANONYMITY ON THE CHAT CIRCUIT

One of the striking features of personal chat systems is the anonymity that users enjoy. Although this will change as video-based chat becomes more common, for the time being chatters use it to their own personal advantage when they want to. Chatters generally create a "handle" (an alternative identity like those of CB radio users), a "nick" (a nickname), or an "avatar," which is a pictorial representation of the chatter or a chatter's interest.

Chatters are often invited to make public their email address, or their age, sex, and location. (The invitation may simply appear as: A/S/L?) Unless you agree to offer that information, which is not always advisable, your handle or avatar remains the only piece of information that people have to identify you.

And even that can be misleading. If I know that you're owner of a specific handle, I still can't know whether your account has been cleverly hacked (electronically broken into and taken over), or if you've gotten up to get some coffee, leaving an unattended session in the hands of someone else. And, it's not uncommon for people to "share" their handles with friends or devious colleagues.

Chat anonymity also has its advantages. It gives chatters the opportunity to play with their identities. With a simple handle like, say, "spaceman," I portray myself as vastly different from the person my friends, family, and co-workers have grown to know in real life. Online, we may lie about our age, nationality, appearance, income, residence, race, weight, and, of course, gender without repercussions.

## A Question of Gender

Are you M or F? Translation: are you male or female? This is probably the most common question asked in chatrooms. People are always looking for the possibility of romance. But there's always a caveat that comes with the answer: gender misrepresentation is common. So you really won't know who you're chatting with—a real problem when you're trying to set up a romance with someone who seems, from the chat, like your perfect match in the "real" world.

Initially, when fewer women were online (hence the chat-room request, "Won't someone at least pretend to be female?"), it was mostly males posing as females. These days, with so many more women online, could it be the other way around?

## The Virtual Meeting Place

In educational venues, chat technology is becoming increasingly important. In the virtual classrooms of the expanding number of online schools and colleges, it provides a means for delivering lectures and facilitating student interaction.

Using videoconferencing software, which allows the transmission of computer-based images and video as well as text-based and voice-based chat, transcontinental business meetings and slide presentations are happening online at this very moment. Two of the best clients for creating a virtual classroom (or business conference room) are **Microsoft NetMeeting** and **Holodesk Communicator.** You can download both for free from www.tucows.com or www.jumbo.com.

As Dr. Sherry Turkle put it: "There needs to be places just to fantasize and other places where people do take responsibility for who they 'are'. . . I think online life will make room for both."

And it has. There are places in the chat circuit for people with almost any fantasy or emotional need. And there are just as many serious places for important chats about interesting and intellectually stimulating topics. The trick in chatting is to find the place that makes sense for you—real or fantasy.

Eventually, increases in bandwidth will enable us to see and hear each other and even hold real-time video conference calls with large numbers of people. When that happens, anonymity will be a skill, like faking a voice over the phone. For now, though, it's just a matter of clever words to fool people in the text-based chat worlds into believing that you're someone you aren't. So, if you can do it—assume that others will as well.

### WHERE ARE THE CHAT ROOMS?

Chat rooms are everywhere on the Internet and World Wide Web, as well as on pay networks such as AOL. There are general interest chat rooms, chat rooms for people who want to talk about specific topics, special one-time chats (often called "interviews") with invited guests (authors, movie stars, corporate executives, or whoever), and chats about company products on company pages. Go to Yahoo!, or if you belong to AOL, check out the chat rooms there to view the wide range of topics available.

People come and go as they please in these rooms. Often special interest or interview rooms are overseen by a sys-op (the computer term for a person who monitors the chat) or chat leader who helps facilitate the dialog.

Everything from rose gardening to unusual sexual preferences are topics for discussion, so you may want to choose carefully before jumping into a room, especially if it's full of people with tastes and interests that are very different from yours.

Not surprisingly, people who wouldn't step on a sidewalk crack in real life feel free to air their innermost secrets online without a second thought. Shielded by anonymity, they allow themselves a range of emotion and expression they would never dare in the real world. In chat rooms you can find truly competent and compassionate people. But even more easily, perhaps, you can meet disgusting, deranged, and demonic chat fiends. If you do, the solution is simple: go somewhere else.

## Best Times for Chat

On the Internet, it's not at all unusual to click on a chat room button and arrive in a room with no one else in it. On systems like AOL, you can visit chat rooms organized by topic area and many are occupied with one or more visitors almost all of the time. In all chat rooms, the time of your visit is important to finding people there.

Depending on the interests of those who might use the room, it may be busiest late at night or during the business day. Since there are no time zones in electronic communications, entering a chatroom at the seemingly ungodly time of 6:00 AM Pacific Standard Time may reveal a mix of people: those who stay up all night, as well as those on the East Coast where it's already 9:00 AM. Global time consideration enters the picture too, with people on the other side of the world logging on in accordance with their local time zone.

If the chatroom you're in has specifically been arranged around discussing a se-rious topic, and everybody in the room is talking about personal interests and ban-tering about each other's sexual activity, you can do one of two things: you can ei-ther ask the people to stick to the room's intended topic, or you can leave.

However, if this chat room has degraded into a public meat market over time, you may get a negative response from the room's "regulars." If this is the case, simply exit the chat and find a channel or room that is truly intended for discus-sion of the serious topic of interest.

When chatting, the key is to take your turn, especially when mixing voice chat with text chat. Just type as you can—either post a question, make a statement, or respond to someone else's input. That's just about all there is to it. If you watch a chat for a while before venturing into the conversation, you'll get the general idea.

## TAKING IT OFFLINE

Chat is a forum in which social boundaries exist, even if they're not immediately obvious. In business-to-business chat, common social conventions and boundaries of taste are usually the norm, but in more public forums, immaturity is common (though still not acceptable in our view). When someone in a chat room is getting out of line, showing no consideration for others, or acting out rage or resentment in bad language or flame messages, the most important phrase to know is:

**"Take it offline."**

If you feel the general subject of the current chat has gone beyond the bounds of taste, decorum, or decency, ask for a change of subject and explain your reason for making the request. If the other party(ies) insist on continuing the topic, disconnect from the room, and don't feel bad about it.

You must, of course, apply the same standards to your own online behavior. You should take your chat offline when your subject is inappropriate, either because it's too personal or off topic.

If you don't monitor yourself, a sys-op or chat facilitator will probably do it for you. He might simply ask you to "take it offline," or he might banish you from the chat altogether by "kicking" or "banning" you from the room (temporarily or permanently locking out your user name so you can't get in).

If you have something important to say that's not germane to the chat at hand, you can privately invite people to join you in a new room to discuss your issues. However, highly sensitive matters, such as those involving personal, business, or governmental secrets, are too vulnerable for airing anywhere online. Emotionally charged issues are equally risky.

## KNOW THE LINGO

Participation in chat environments runs the gamut from high level academic discussion to highly casual chitchat, which may cross the lower border of good taste. To chat successfully, you need to learn how to control chat room functions, acronyms, and messaging to sound like an experienced participant rather than a novice or outsider. People abbreviate almost everything in some chat rooms, so don't be surprised if the language you see has little to do with standard written English.

At the very least you should know the basic chat acronyms we've presented in Appendix B of this book. Even in the most serious chats, you'll find that people use these acronyms to speed their messages to the screen.

To understand the formality of language used in a room, simply hang out there for a while to determine the level of abbreviation people are using. You might also need to learn some new, basic words or acronyms, as long-standing chat groups often invent their own vocabulary.

### Watch Your Language

Any language, whether spoken or written, only works when the people using it all understand the meanings of its sounds, symbols, and shapes. Speaking fluent Latin to the waitress will probably not get you lunch in most American diners. Likewise online, if you insist on being esoteric and loading up all your comm with emoticons, abbreviations, and words out of *A Clockwork Orange* like *droogs* and *maskies*, best save your conversations for others of your kind.

## THE CHAT FRUSTRATIONS IN A PUBLIC ROOM

Most chat rooms are open to all comers unless it's for a special interest group, club, or professional organization requiring membership. When you join a public chat room, you'll choose a "handle" for yourself, a term derived from the CB-radio lingo. Even after you join, you may be ignored if you're not one of the regulars. You become a regular after repeated visits and through adding complimentary and relevant comments when they seem appropriate. Address comments to individuals when appropriate—chatters like to be treated like individuals in their domains.

Keep in mind that in public chat rooms, you're usually limited to chatting in single sentences of moderate length. If there are a lot of users logged on, your next line in an unfinished sentence may not appear until comments from five others interrupt it, making communication with another user impossible until you join him in a private room.

With regard to public chat among people who've been chatting together for a while, the grammar, spelling, and punctuation aren't perfect and really don't have to be.

We recommend that you always lurk first (that's the Internet lingo for "look around") before you leap into a chat session. A little lurking is not impolite the first

## Interview Chats

Chats with important and interesting people are often scheduled on web sites or chat rooms. These special chat opportunities allow you to interact with people from just about any field, from movie stars to book authors to important medical researchers. You just need to find the time and date for the chat and be there to participate.

The trick to participation in an interview chat is to be courteous and relevant in your interactions with the host of the interview and the guest who is there to answer your questions.

time you visit a chat room, it's just prudent. If you do it too often, however, the sysop may decide to kick you from the room.

## INSTANT MESSAGING

Reasonably new and in mass proliferation is the ability to send a message instantly to others who are signed on to the Internet, America Online, and other services. Instant messaging, or IM, uses simple software available from a variety of places such as AOL, Yahoo!, and MSN (Microsoft Network).

Instant messaging allows two-way communication in real time, just like chat. The difference is that you determine who will be able to interact with you by creating your own list of "instant messaging buddies." Thus, in IM you actually know to whom you're talking—so the anonymity associated with other chat environments is not a factor.

ICQ ("I Seek You"), one of the very first instant messaging programs enables multiple participants to chat together. It is a user-friendly Internet program that notifies you when any of your friends and associates are online and enables you to contact them (providing they also use ICQ). With this program, you can chat, send messages and files, exchange Web page addresses, play games, create your own homepage, surf the Net with your friends, and much more. The newest version of the program, ICQ 2000, even allows voice and text chat to be integrated.

## Fancy Schmancy: Just Type It Up

In IM systems that support color, fonts, and bold or italic face type, keep in mind that none of this may work on the recipient's end. The worst mistake you can make is to choose a type that appears impossibly small or unreadable on remote systems, even though it looks great on your machine. Stick with default fonts for best results, even though they may lack charm. The same goes for color. Pale blue on white is nearly impossible to read.

To use any IM program, you assemble a buddy list of the email addresses of friends or coworkers who use the same IM program as you. When they sign on to the Internet, their names appear in a window and you can write to them. Or, if you're on someone else's buddy list, that person can see that you're available and can immediately strike up a realtime conversation, without invitation. If you don't want your buddies to see you online, you can also turn off your IM program or choose an option in the program to make yourself invisible to other users.

Typically, IM messages are just a way to say "Hi. I see that you're online. How have you been?" to friends and family members.

In instant messaging, a window appears with a box for typing, along with a larger box that shows the entire conversation. Depending on the messaging system, you can either politely invite another user to chat with you or simply bombard him with an uninvited message and hope for a reply. Messages are usually limited in length and the window you type into will ignore further typing if you exceed its character limit. Some systems allow you to assign typefaces, sizes, colors, and even background colors, but that's no guarantee that anything but basic text will appear on the receiving end.

We suggest that you avoid instant-messaging those people you know at work unless they have specifically given you permission to put them on your IM buddy list.

In an example from America Online's version of IM software, an IM session (with you on the receiving end) goes something like this:

You're online writing the great American novel. Suddenly your system chimes and a box pops up with a dialog similar to: "RhondaSue@Wincek.com has sent you an instant message; would you like to accept?" Buttons appear in the window for Accept, Decline, and Help (or similar). Choosing Accept opens the dialog window for an electronic conversation.

Instant messaging is a handy tool for replacing the telephone. Depending on your connection to the Internet, you can message each other all day at the low, low cost of 0¢ per minute.

**Sample IM Session**

Heather456: Hi Jerry! Can you chat now?

Jerdash: Hi Heather, I'm busy on a project for the moment. Can I call you later? What's your phone number? I seem to have misplaced it again.

Heather 456: It's 800-555-1212. Bye Jerry. Hope I didn't interrupt too much.

Jerdash: No, of course not. I'm looking forward to talking to you. It's just that this budget has to get in by noon or my boss will send me to the firing squad. Talk you after 4:00 PST if that's good for you.

Heather456: That's fine. Bye.

Jerdash: Bye

Of course, you can have multiple conversations going at the same time—if you can keep up with it all.

IM does have a pitfall. With more and more people staying logged on all day, you may attempt to contact people who appear logged on but who aren't really near their computer. They will get your IM message later, but by that time you'll be offline.

## Instant Messaging from Hell

Increasingly and unfortunately, the same people who brought you spam have started to use instant messaging. Typically these messages pop up from nowhere and often employ a fictitious or stolen user name. Kim's name on AOL was once stolen and apparently used for pornography messages. (One enraged recipient wrote back, "May you burn in Hell. My child got your message.")

If your name is stolen, let your ISP know as soon as possible so the offender can be located and stopped from using your ID.

## The Person in Charge Isn't You

When you're online, you may see references to the "sys-op" or "channel-op." The sys-op is simply the system operator—the person who runs the computer, computer network, or worldwide system you're using for communication. A channel-op is the person who runs or helps to run the chat in a particular chat room. With the power of a small god, ops can control your email messages and lock out those who transgress the system's written or unwritten rules. They can also be very helpful when problems arise and can hook you into resources for online comm that you won't easily discover by yourself.

Treat the ops well, and they will do the same for you. They can make your technical problems disappear or give you an explanation of electronic paramedic procedures that will get your account up and running in minutes. Treat them badly and you may find your password no longer works.

## THE CHAT WORDS YOU'LL WANT TO USE

Here are the most important words for almost any chat. (You'll notice a pattern here that exemplifies the personal contact associated with chat rooms.)

welcome
good/great/excellent
thanks/thank you
you/your
I/we missed you

## MAILING LISTS

There are two kinds of mailing lists. The first comprises lists that people can join that enable them to get a frequent newsletter or announcement from a company, club, or interest group. These mailing lists are one-way—that is, normally you only receive the mail, you don't respond to it (although you can if you have a mind to).

The other type of mailing list, also called a listserv, allows you to trade messages that will be distributed to an entire group of people. These listservs are more formal than chat, and don't happen in real time. Listservs are often used to discuss important planning ideas or brainstorm an important event or topic of interest.

Listservs can be set up for companies, special topics, large interest groups, or just about anything else. You usually join a listserv by typing your email address in the subject line of a special address provided by the listserv. This email address often begins with majordomo@ or listserv@ and includes the word "subscribe" in the subject line.

Be careful not to address your message to the mailing list itself, or it might be sent to everyone on the list, which annoys people to no end and could start a "flame war" pointed directly at you. In other cases, you will be automatically added to the listserv by the sys-op who oversees the list.

So if you want to subscribe to the "INTERNETNEWS" mailing list (this is a fictitious name, just as an example), the top of your email message might look like this:

From: sunnyb@bakersquared.com
To: majordomo@strange.org
Date: Sat, 23 Aug 2002 09:00:10 -0700
Subject: Subscribe INTERNETNEWS

Or you can send an empty (blank) message to the address. If that doesn't work, you can try typing "help" in the body of your message. That will usually tell the person who maintains the list (the sys-op) that you need help subscribing and getting started. You can try typing "info" in the body, but more than likely that will get you information about the list rather than on how to subscribe.

Mailing lists usually don't stray from their topics. For example, if you join a mailing list that talks about "weird stuff," then all of the messages on the list will discuss ghosts, paranormal events, odd cars that become boats, treasure maps and the hunts that go along with them, and any other strange thing people can think of. Often the messages people send in are collected at the end of the day (or week) and sent out to subscribers in one big email chunk. When checking your weekly mailing list messages, be prepared for your mail to take a little longer than usual to retrieve.

## Problems with a Mailing List

If you have a problem receiving messages or a problem with a difficult participant (someone who flames or spams), send a private message to the sys-op for the mailing list—don't send it to everyone on the listserv. Also, if you have something that is only of interest to one or two people on the listserv, send a private message to these people directly. Don't send it to the entire listserv. Keep your private communications just that—private.

There are many Web indexes of mailing lists and online newsletters, such as http://www.topica.com. Usually these Web indexes will give you all the subscription information that you'll need.

If you decide that you really don't want to get mail about out-of-the-ordinary things after all, you can take yourself off the list. Just follow the same directions you used to sign on, but replace "subscribe" with "unsubscribe" (or sometimes "signoff").

Since many listservs and mailing lists tend to send lots of mail, it may not be very wise to subscribe to several at the same time. Give one or two a try before getting in too deep.

Some mailing lists allow you to add your ideas and comments to the mail that gets sent to everyone, while others simply send you a dispatch that someone else writes. On lists that include the messages sent in, it's a good idea to lurk (read messages without posting anything) for a while before you leap into the fray.

Listservs are almost always monitored. It is, therefore, important that you keep on topic and don't send irrelevant or flaming messages to the listserv for all to see. Respond when you have something important to ask or say. Otherwise, just enjoy the information.

If you simply send a respond message, it will go to the entire mailing list, so keep that in mind when you're writing. And remember: It's not necessary to respond to every listserv message. In particular, _don't_ respond with messages like:

**Hi everyone!**
**I got the message.**

or

**Thanks for the thought.**

These polite-sounding replies will only add clutter to the dialogue. Everyone assumes that the people on the listserv got the message. You can, however, add courtesies if you are also adding some relevant information. For example:

**To: bizplanlist**

**From: SunnyB**

**Topic: Guest Speakers**

*I appreciate the great ideas thus far. I have an additional idea; how about*
*adding a guest speaker from Japan to the agenda for the annual meeting?*
*Any thoughts or ideas in this regard? –Sunny*

## BULLETIN BOARDS AND NEWSGROUPS

Newsgroups and bulletin boards are a lot like listservs, except that you can see past as well as current messages pertaining to a particular topic, question, or thread. You can join newsgroups from the mail program in your Internet browser, where you should be able to find instructions for using it. Be aware that there are THOUSANDS of newsgroups to subscribe to—on almost any topic and in almost any language.

When you respond to a newsgroup message, it will be there for everyone to see—for as long as the sys-op keeps the news on the board. This will vary from newsgroup to newsgroup.

There is a cardinal rule for entering questions, information, and responses to bulletin boards and newsgroups: KEEP IT RELEVANT. If you want to banter with people and simply wile away your boredom, find a chat room instead. Newsgroups are useful because they contain good information on topics of interest to the participants. Make sure your information and questions fit the bill.

So that's the lowdown on chat, mailing lists, and newsgroups. Congratulations! You may not have noticed the transformation, but you are now a techno-savvy online communicator. Now get out there and start discussing, advising, and ranting. It's fun. It's informative. And it's easy.

# CHAPTER SIX

# Netiquette Guidelines

WE'VE ALREADY COVERED MUCH of the fundamental material about saying things correctly in email messages and chat rooms, but to make for easy reference, we've included a list of basic netiquette (Internet etiquette) guidelines in the following few pages.

No matter whom you're writing to, or chatting with, or video-conferencing with, knowing what constitutes good manners in email and chat is important because it helps to eliminate misunderstandings and the bad feelings they can cause. Netiquette involves the proper use of email content (especially when using an employer's computer), special abbreviations and symbols, and email mailing lists. This section will also teach you ways to stay out of trouble :-) by avoiding the accidental use of unacceptable formats.

## RULES OF THE ROAD FOR THE INFORMATION SUPERHIGHWAY

The following guidelines are based on the recommendations listed in the user policy manuals of many organizations and corporations, but as you'll see most are simply from common sense.

**DON'T SHOUT online.** This is one of the most common mistakes made by new email users and chatters, who sometimes prefer to type with the Caps Lock key engaged. All caps means SHOUTING, and using all capitals in online communication is, therefore, considered rude.

*Asterisks* surrounding a word can be used if you want to emphasize a point. Example: Mary, this *June* deadline is very important.

**Whatever you do, DON'T SPAM (shouting intended).** Aptly named after the meat product, spam is net-speak for unsolicited junk email sent to hundreds or thousands of people at one time. Spam congests mailing lists and/or people's mailboxes. It is inconsiderate and makes people angry. If you do it, you will get caught and flamed. (Flamed is the net-speak term for angry responses online.)

Internet spammers love email because it costs next to nothing to send; they can therefore harass the world with limitless solicitations (usually offering smut or get-rich-quick schemes). Spammers will sometimes offer you the option of removing yourself from their emailing list, but more often than not they'll use a non-functioning return address or anonymous remailer, which will make it difficult to stop their assaults. Recent legislation, however, has been passed outlawing this behavior. And you're not helpless: tools like spam-filter programs and a spam-abuse hotline (spam.abuse.net) do provide guidelines for minimizing spam and other junk mail.

## Beware the Spam Police

If you intend to spam, consider this: Under United States law, it is **unlawful** "to use any telephone facsimile machine, computer, or other device to send an unsolicited advertisement" to any "equipment which has the capacity to transcribe text or images (or both) from an electronic signal received over a regular telephone line onto paper." The law allows individuals to sue the sender of such illegal "junk mail" for $500 per copy. Most states will permit such actions to be filed in Small Claims Court—although almost no one ever takes the time to sue a spammer.

**Don't flame.** Flames are scathing messages that express hostility toward someone or something. *Flaming* creates a poor environment for legitimate communication, so most interactive mailing lists, chat rooms, and corporate online policies won't tolerate it. If you do flame someone, chances are you'll just get flamed back. The back-and-forth of flame messages is called a *flame war*.

**Don't post private mail to public places.** If you receive an email message from someone you know, it is very uncool to send it on to other people. Just imagine that you email your best friend a message about how cute your next door neighbor is, and he mass-mails it to everyone in his address book. Get the point?

**Minimize large attachments unless your reader expects a large file.** Attachments allow you to piggyback files onto your email messages. It's best not to use a huge attachment unless you're sure that your recipient will welcome it. It is extremely annoying to waste 5 or 10 minutes downloading an unsolicited photo of somebody's pet snake (especially if you hate snakes). However, *do* use attachments to send important, urgent documents, or long letters that your recipient expects.

**Be careful when using sarcasm and humor.** In the chat world, make sure you've mastered the local lingo before you try any "cute" conversations—they may be inadvertently considered sarcastic, and sarcasm can be taken as cruelty or insensitivity. If you feel you must be humorous, use emoticons to let everyone know you intend a harmless joke. :-) The same goes for email.

**Be concise and clear.** Keep paragraphs and messages short and to the point. When you must make the message longer, attach the bulk of the message as a word processed document or other appropriate file. The art of writing effective email and chat messages is the art of being brief. Most experienced emailers and chatters use some sort of shorthand in their informal messages. Many standard emoticons and acronyms are included in this book. Learn them and learn when to use them.

**When quoting another person in your response, edit out whatever isn't directly applicable to your reply.** Don't let your mailing software automatically quote the entire body of messages you are replying to when it's not necessary. Take the time to edit any quotations down to the minimum necessary to provide context for your reply. Nobody likes reading a long message in quotes for the third or fourth time, only to be followed by a single-line response: "I agree."

**Focus on one subject per message and always include a pertinent subject title.** That allows the user to locate the message quickly.

**Include your signature at the bottom of Email messages.** This is especially important when communicating with people who may not know you personally or when broadcasting to a dynamic group of subscribers, or if your email address does not represent your actual name (i.e., your email address is something like x23@intercom.org).

Your signature should include your name, position, affiliation and email addresses and should not exceed more than 5 lines. Optional information could include your address and phone number or your Web site's URL.

**Limit your line length in email.** Some email systems don't wrap the lines of text. If you're not sure, limit the line length in your sentences to approximately 65-70 characters and avoid control characters (control C, Esc, etc.) in all email messages.

**Never send chain letters through the Internet.** Sending them can cause the loss of your Internet access on company and some commercial online systems (just as sending spam can).

**Use standard formatting of dates.** Because of the international nature of the Internet and the fact that most of the world uses the MM DD YY format for listing dates, please be considerate and avoid misinterpretation by spelling out the month. Example: **04 JUN 02 or JAN 04 02.**

**Follow chain of command procedures for corresponding with superiors.** Don't send a complaint via email directly to the "top" just because you can. If you want to get your point across, send the first email to your immediate superior and send a cc: (copy) of the email to his or her superior. That's enough. Don't send the complaint to every one in the chain of command just because you want to be heard. You will be heard, but you're unlikely to get the positive response you want.

**Be professional and careful about what you say about others.** Email is easily forwarded and easily printed out for all to see. Making uncalled-for remarks about others will reflect more on you than on them.

**Cite all quotes, references, and sources, and respect copyright and license agreements.** Enough said.

**Ask before forwarding.** It is considered extremely rude to forward personal email to anyone else without the original author's permission.

**Never give your email address, user ID, or email password to another person to use.** System administrators who need to access your account for maintenance or to correct problems will have full privileges to your account. In any other case, your email should only come from you.

**Don't interrupt others online.** This guideline applies mostly to chat rooms, message boards, and online email exchanges in real time. Interrupting is rude in casual conventional communication. It's even more rude online, when others are trying to follow and sort through a text-only conversation.

**Communicate at the right time (and in the right format).** Although it's often out of your control, your timing in joining a conversation will make a strong first impression. Arriving on the scene and making your remarks appear contiguous with a thread is a real art. Unfortunately, many online systems post your remarks according to their arrival and the coincidences of the on-line world, some of which can only be explained by theoretical particle physicists.

## The Vagaries of Online Time

You were typing quickly, even though you had to break up your comments to fit the limits of the chat program you were using. Still, the second half of your message didn't appear until eight other people had added their own comments. So how do you avoid this problem in the future?

- Respond quickly without relying on a time-eating spelling-corrector to fix your typos.
- Wait for others to finish typing on instant chat systems that transmit characters as they are typed. Grit your teeth if necessary—but wait until it's really your turn.
- In chat environments, allow others to finish a sentence, even if the program forces them to send long sentences in segments.

**Understand and respect the hierarchy of those with whom you are communicating.** Act and react in accordance with your relative place within the group. Or, break the rules as carefully as you would in a staff meeting at work. For example, a summer intern invited to an online management powwow as an observer would overstep his bounds by monopolizing the conversation. And a senior manager would appear ineffectual in failing to answer high-level questions or in allowing a meeting to run out of control. In informal chat situations, you can pretty much do as you wish.

On the other hand, don't be completely silent. Not speaking might give the impression that you are unwilling, unable, or too snobbish to participate in the proceedings. At work, it won't win you a higher rating in the team player category. With more familiar relationships, you may become isolated as others assume you don't consider them important.

**Always mind your basic manners.** You know the ones; you learned most of them in kindergarten. Avoid vulgar language, strong sexual innuendo, and generally obnoxious behavior online. Not only will you look like a buffoon to other participants, but some public email systems will bump you offline for such behavior (AOL at one time booted people off when certain words were detected in messaging.) Or, other users may report you and your account privileges will be summarily revoked. Bad behavior within a business online meeting could cause your comments to be copied to your boss.

## How to Say, "Howdy!"

Always enter a chat room with a friendly greeting: "Hi gang, it's great to be here!" It's also entirely proper to announce at the start of the session that you are "just listening" if you don't intend to participate. Wait to deploy this message until all key players are present so you, the silent one, won't have to keep repeating yourself. At the same time, respond quickly and relevantly to inquiries directed at you or people you work with or represent. Silence is only golden in an online chat room or message board when it's appropriate.

# PART TWO

# Putting Yourself
# Across Online

# CHAPTER SEVEN

# Putting Yourself Across on the Job

LIKE ALL COMMUNICATION ON THE JOB, what you say online needs to keep everybody happy while delivering an effective message. And, as with conventional communications, there are proven methods for handling nearly any situation online with poise and professionalism. But are you aware of them?

## SELF TEST: YOUR ONLINE COMMUNICATIONS ABILITY AT WORK

Following is a simple diagnostic test. It's not meant to test your business knowledge, but rather to help you gauge how effectively you communicate with coworkers, management, and subordinates through online media.

For the most part, you will find it easy to guess the "right" answer. But getting the right answer is not the point of the test. Respond honestly, even if you feel your response is not the best one possible. This is not a contest. The goal is solely a self-inventory to help you improve your at-work communications.

## Quiz

1. A key customer emails you with an urgent message that needs immediate response. Unfortunately, you won't have an answer to her problem for at least 24 hours. What do you do?
   a. Send an email acknowledging the problem and explaining the need of one-day wait for a solution.
   b. Call the customer and explain the situation.
   c. Fax an acknowledgement with an explanation of the wait and a list of steps you are taking to provide a solution so the problem won't occur again.
   d. Do all of the above.

2. Your boss sends you an angry message criticizing you for a project problem you had nothing to do with. Steam comes out of your ears over her insensitivity and thoughtless accusation. What do you do?
   a. Send a nasty email back telling her how wrong and stupid she is, regardless of the consequences.
   b. Give yourself time to cool down, then write a polite email back explaining that you're sorry about the problem; you were in no way involved with creating it; and now that you're aware of it, you're willing to help in any way you can.
   c. Stomp into the boss' office for immediate resolution of the problem.
   d. Call the boss on the phone.

3. You need to explain to a subordinate about a specific problem you've noticed in his work, but you can reach him only by email for a couple of days because you're out of town. You are moderately upset about the problem. What do you do?
   a. Send an email message that lets your employee know you are angry and also explains how to correct the mistakes he's been making.
   b. Skip the whole issue until you're back in the office, even if it means continued minor product flaws that customers won't notice.

c. Cut your trip short and catch the next Airbus to HQ.

d. Send a polite email explaining how to fix the problem, then wait until you're back in the office to explain your displeasure.

4. In setting up for a video conference, you're the key player in a room full of middle managers. Suddenly you notice that the camera is at the head of the boardroom table, more than 30 feet from your seat. Even with a zoom lens, this will make you look as if you're the size of a mouse to those on the receiving end. What do you do?

a. Politely demand that the camera be placed closer to you.

b. Change seats to get closer to the camera.

c. Accept it.

d. Move the camera over the objections of the cam operator.

5. You have a coworker, boss, or employee who absolutely won't use email. What do you do?

a. Send him some book like The Moron's Guide to Email.

b. Knowing that he won't read his mail, copy him on a major announcement, event, or meeting that he absolutely must attend. Make sure that others don't tell him about the event either.

c. Offer to print out his email.

d. If it's your boss, change jobs.

6. You're in a department meeting held online to accommodate people in remote sales offices. There are so many people chatting that by the time you answer a question, the meeting's moved onto another topic. What do you do?

a. Copy the question in your response so everyone knows what you're responding to. If it's a long question or answer, abbreviate, or use only a portion of the question. Or, make the question part of your answer.

b. Suggest that the meeting be broken up into subgroups.

c. Keep quiet and read a book or yesterday's *Barron's*.

d. Write a response fast, while being especially careful to avoid typos, and let the chips fall where they will in the thread.

## Answers

1. d—Do a, b, c because just responding with email makes it look like you don't care about the customer or the account. It's a fast and easy way to lose business.

2. b—Do b because a nasty response will cost you in the long run, and more direct forms of communication couples you in the boss' mind with the problem. There is also the likelihood of an angry confrontation should you appear in person or reach him on the phone.

3. d—Assuming the employee checks email frequently (this could be a major assumption), you get the problem fixed quickly. And, chances are that your anger will fade before you get back into the office.

4. a—Have the cam operator move the camera. Doing it yourself is a bad idea because the technician needs to fiddle with the focus while you're in your seat. He may not bother to if you irritate him enough. Changing seats is out too, because as a key player you should be at the head of the board table.

5. b—This may come as a painful lesson to the "unconnected one," but his or her job is in jeopardy anyway if the message that email is a vital force in intracompany communication doesn't get through.

6. a—You can only do your best, and including the question will bring the topic back up. Don't keep quiet. You'll look like you logged on and then headed for the restroom.

### What the Quiz Results Mean to You

This test is a quick way to personally evaluate your comfort and experience with online communication in a work environment. If you're really good at online communication at work, you should have correctly answered at least five out of the six. If you scored lower, this chapter will bring you up to speed. You might also want to read *How to Say It At Work* (Prentice Hall) as a companion book.

## 77 WORDS TO USE IN ONLINE COMMUNICATIONS AT WORK

| | | |
|---|---|---|
| accomplished | efficient | opportunity |
| achieved | empowered | package |
| achieved goals | enhance | perspective |
| adjust our priorities | evaluate | plan |
| agree | expedite | pointers |
| alternatives | experienced | positive |
| approval | flexibility | priorities |
| approve | flexible | prioritize |
| asset | fresh | process |
| assist | generous | productive |
| balance | goal | proven |
| best | goodwill | reinvent |
| calculated | gratitude | resolved |
| care | growth | reward (ed) |
| careful | idea | solve |
| commensurate | imagination | strategy |
| commitment | imaginative | strength |
| communicate | improve | structure |
| concept | increase | substantial |
| confident | input | tested |
| consider | judgment | thought |
| contribute | knowledgeable | thoughtful |
| control | loyal | transition |
| cooperative | manage | weigh |
| delight | negotiate | weight |
| easy | objective | |

## PHRASES TO USE IN ONLINE COMMUNICATIONS ON THE JOB

a new perspective

a new way of

a quality perspective

achieve goals

additional consideration

adjusting priorities

an outsider's perspective

assign resources

bankable savings

best case scenario

best for company

best for team

best use of resources

big picture

by the book

careful thinking

clean house

clear thinking

commitment to myself

commitment to quality

commitment to the company

commitment to you

comprehensive package

count on me

cross promotion

cut costs

difficulties to work out

fresh thinking

from the bottom up

given it great thought

good point

I look forward to working with you

improve the bottom line

increase visibility

invaluable experience

knowledge set

make better use of

market analysis

mission critical

need your input

new level of consistency

new possibilities

on time, on budget

problem resolution abilities

process review

quality assurance

reliable figures

run the numbers

starting today

strategic planning

strategic thinking

team player

think it through

think this through

run with it

user friendly

win-win situation

## WORDS TO AVOID IN ONLINE COMMUNICATIONS ON THE JOB

| | | |
|---|---|---|
| afraid | impossible | slowing |
| awkward | lackluster | stalled |
| blame | late | stillborn |
| bored | lesser | stilted |
| brass | loser | stopped |
| can't | mess | stuck |
| cheap | miscue | stupid |
| clumsy | mired | swamped |
| crisis | misjudged | tired |
| dead | mismanagement | unavoidable |
| dicey | missed | undermined |
| disaster | nervous | unlikely |
| dropped | orphaned | unthinking |
| dumb | overloaded | unwilling |
| exploded | quagmire | unworthy |
| fault | questionable | unyielding |
| fear | refuse | useless |
| foggy | reject | won't |
| forgot | risky | worthless |
| ignorant | shaky | |

**PHRASES TO AVOID IN ONLINE COMMUNICATIONS ON THE JOB**

| | |
|---|---|
| afraid to | it's too much trouble/work |
| back burner | long delay |
| beyond me | maybe next year |
| beyond repair | no matter what |
| blew it | not again |
| count me out | not enough time |
| dead in the water | not me |
| dead-end job | not my problem |
| don't attend the online conference | nothing happening |
| don't/won't buy into it | no way |
| don't need your comments | old technology |
| don't support it | screwed it up |
| huge problem | take a chance |
| I don't deserve this | too tired |
| I never read my email | were you even at the e-meeting |
| I only read my email once a week | won't attempt it |
| I'll quit if you | write me a memo instead |
| I'm (you're) too set in my/your ways | you can't |
| I'm fed up | you expect too much |
| I'm only a [. . .] | you must |
| I'm only human | you write at the seventh grade level |
| if you won't | you need more training |
| impossible delay | your chat skills are weak |
| it won't work | your email skills are weak |
| it's not my responsibility | |

## What's an E-Meeting?

An e-meeting is a chat set up between employees and managers in a company, although the format can also be used with customers, the press, and anyone else with access to computers. The unique feature of an e-meeting is that it's held in a private electronic room or chat environment instead of a room in the real world. The advantage of e-meetings is that they allow remotely located personnel to attend without traveling to HQ or suffering through a noisy conference call. Remotely located customers can also participate in problem solving meetings, Q&A sessions, and educational forums.

Online communication with coworkers, managers, and subordinates requires just the right choice of words. It becomes increasingly difficult when the topic is sensitive and you must communicate your message while not bruising your recipient's feelings. In chat meetings especially, you must respond quickly and precisely to questions and comments.

When assembling email, you must communicate your intentions effectively without writing a massive letter that your reader will most likely skim rather than read word for word.

## THE SECRETS OF COMMUNICATING WITH THE ELECTRONICALLY CHALLENGED

While it's true that the computer has penetrated business to an astounding extent, there are still pockets of resistance to using the technology. Among these might be an underpaid line worker who doesn't care much about his job. Or, an aging senior manager who hopes to avoid computers for another year, when he'll reach retirement age. Then there's the boss who still has his administrative assistant print out his email and key responses written on yellow legal pads.

## The 10 Commandments of Online Communication

On the job, your online communications should:

■ Reflect your position in the organization.

■ Be succinct and easy to read and understand.

■ Be of appropriate length, whether in a chat environment or in an email message.

■ Be free of flippant or off-the-cuff remarks that may haunt you down the road.

■ Be timely, whether in a chat environment or responding to email.

■ Avoid humor and sarcasm, which may be misunderstood by other attendees.

■ Remain free of intensely personal matters, which are better handled in person. For example, you would never fire someone by email!

■ Focus on the e-meeting's content so you won't be caught unaware by a question or comment requiring your answer, rebuttal, or clarification.

■ Avoid the use of gimmicky phrases or emoticons, which just don't have a place in most communications on the job.

■ Be addressed to appropriate recipients only.

So how can you help out these folks? Here are some suggestions.

**Try to understand their feelings.** Work with peers and subordinates to learn about their fears or reasons for not using online channels. With probing, you may find that there is a legitimate reason for their reluctance: system throughput problems, ghost mail that never arrives, or a host of other technological problems that can foul up the work flow. Overly complex operation and security systems discourage would-be users as well.

**Make sure that there are enough computer resources.** The days of one computer shared by an entire department are mostly over, but it's still not unheard of for two people to share a machine or a network node. Everyone must have an individual machine and network connection for reasons of productivity and privacy.

**Declare a deadline.** Set a day after which all communication is handled electronically. Enroll those who need it in classes so they understand the system and its operation beforehand. Provide quick reference cards to everyone with tips for email and chat. Then, unplug the photocopier and let paper memos visibly pile up in the inbox. Ask all callers (except customers) to send you an email on the topic of their call because you're "in the middle of something right now."
**Limit your correspondence to electronic media.** That way, others will feel left out if they are reluctant to log on.

If it's your boss or a customer, consider giving in and relying on conventional communications. This may add to your workload because the people to whom you copy will expect your communications electronically. So you will need to produce two versions.

## ASSEMBLING THE PERFECT WORK-RELATED EMAIL MESSAGE IN FIVE EASY STEPS

Assembling an effective email message is easy enough. It's a matter of using these five steps, one at a time, until it becomes natural to you to compose in this way. The steps aren't all that different from those for writing any properly composed business letter. The one difference is that with email too many words make readers skim rather than read. This is especially true of members of senior management who may receive as many as 500 electronic messages a day. Too long, it gets skipped, skimmed, or put aside for later reading (which often never happens). Too short, the message feels blunted or unfriendly and terse.

Here are the steps to take to make sure your business email messages get read:

1. **Decide if email is the correct vehicle for your communication.** If not, choose person-to-person, telephone, letter, etc. If email is the correct choice because of timeliness and the importance of documenting the communication, proceed to the steps below.

2. **After adding a greeting, write a single topic sentence or first line that sums up the content of the message.** If nothing else gets read, this will. An

attention-getting sentence entices the reader to continue reading regardless of the message's good or bad news.

■ For example: We're on schedule! Today we broke ground for the new head-quarters facility.

3. **Take the subject for the message from the topic sentence.**

■ For example: <u>Groundbreaking for New HQ</u> stands out among a list of subject lines such as: <u>Update from Sharon S.</u>

4. **Assemble the body of the message.** It should emphasize and expand on the first sentence. A length of one screen full of text is desirable, but since there are many different screen resolutions in use, this goal is difficult to achieve. As an alternate goal, keep the message to 100 words or less, especially if you're not sure of the screen resolution your reader will be using.

For example, here is an 83-word message:

**After what appeared to be potentially serious delays due to environmental findings at the site, we managed to break ground on schedule. We also have all of our ducks in a row with scheduled contractors moving or ready to move in accordance with the published version of the schedule. Excavation will take the rest of the week, and then it's on to Phase One of the concrete pouring. The team is ready and motivated to keep things on track and so am I.**

5. **Write a conclusion.** Your concluding statement can be a call to action, summation, or thank you, depending on the nature of the message. Length will vary, depending on the subject matter, but it should not exceed three of four sentences. Underline any request for emphasis (if you know that the recipient will be able to see the underlining; most email software will display this).

For example:

**<u>I have one request for you:</u> Please make certain that Finance has the checks ready by Friday for the progress payment to the concrete company. Otherwise, they won't roll their trucks next Monday—and this could mean a delay of an otherwise perfect start!**

Add an electronic or manual signature phrase (example: Thanks, Sharon), and check your message for grammar and typos before you send it.

## A Matter of Privacy

The United States Supreme Court has confirmed the right of any company or corporation you work for to read all of your email correspondence as often as desired. This goes for voicemail and employee telephone communications too. Any file can be intercepted for any reason, and mechanisms are available that can automatically save your mail for later use against you.

Why would a file be intercepted? Lots of reasons. Just the use of certain words can cause a security program to forward a message automatically to the email police.

The only perfect solution to keeping your mail private is to use encryption software, but don't use the one offered by your company. The security people probably have the keys to decode anything that it encrypts.

## EMAILING YOUR BOSS

Almost everyone, even managers, have been forced these days into using email and checking it on a regular basis. The manager who formerly asked an assistant to check his email weekly has either gotten with the program or left the company. The only exception might be a very small company, like a home-based business, that still depends on paper ledgers and index cards. (Tip: Avoid taking a job with someone who doesn't have a late model computer on the desk.) So, assuming that your boss does use email, it's a good idea to look at employee email protocol.

Essentially, there are nine kinds of managers, bosses, and supervisors, and each requires handling that fits his or her particular packaging. Naturally, there is some overlap in categories, but basically, here are the types:

1. The reasonable boss
2. The tyrant
3. The bottomliner
4. The guilt monger
5. The "it's not my fault"-er

**6.** The 15-watt bulb

**7.** The dreamer

**8.** The forgetter

**9.** The volcano

Now here's how to communicate with each type.

### The Reasonable Boss

The best of the bunch is the reasonable boss. He's fair most of the time, keeps his head when he's in difficult situations, and is willing to admit his mistakes. It's easy to like this kind of person. You might even count him among your friends as the years go by and the relationship grows.

Communicating with him begins on a formal note and evolves into a more casual format as the two of you work together and learn more about each other. Because of your regular contact, email is mostly used to pass on FYI information and lists of details, and to schedule meetings and events. More important matters are handled in person, unless either of you works in the field or engages in business trips.

Here's a sample message for when you're new on the job:

> **Hello Mr. Selsnick,**
> I wanted to confirm a few details of our meeting today (12/11) just to make sure I have them right . . .

Here's a sample message after six months on the job:

> **Bob: Went ahead and ordered the materials we discussed today. The Acme Company is quoting a six-week wait. I'll see what I can do to speed things up. Also . . .**

### The Tyrant

Tyrants can be found in most organizations because upper management often confuses tyranny with strong guidance. The tyrant is never to be questioned because (in his opinion) his judgment and pronouncements are set in stone like the Ten Commandments.

If you must work for a tyrant, document everything and always acknowledge an understanding of the commands you are given. That way, you are protected when he makes a mistake that catches the eye of others.

Phrases tyrants use in email include:

1. "You'd better . . ."
2. "Don't you dare . . ."
3. "I'm very disappointed in you . . ."
4. "When I was a [ ], we used to . . ."
5. "If you can't . . ." / "If you won't . . ."

Tyrants are especially fond of quoting clichés from outdated management books, no matter how stupid or inappropriate the quotes may be. Expect also to hear about levels of consistency, winners and losers, whacks on the side of the head, how you're either part of the problem or a part of the solution, etc.

> **Sample Email Message to a Tyrant:**
>
> Hello Mr. Selsnick: Based on our staff meeting today, I want to confirm that you want 10 orders of supplies delivered by Monday. I have checked with the Acme Company and placed the order. It should be in the warehouse about two days early. If you have any change of plan, please contact me before tomorrow when they plan to ship.

## The Bottomliner

Bottomliners are found in two places: In small companies where the boss is the owner and worried constantly about cashflow, and in large companies overly focused on performance bonuses and cash saving. Bottomliners are just that: they look at resources (you) and capital equipment costs, and they fret about how much is spent on office coffee supplies.

Phrases bottomliners use in email include:

1. "A penny saved . . ."
2. "We can't afford that!"

**3.** "Do you have any idea how much it costs us . . ."

**4.** "Filmore in accounting will scream when she sees this!"

**5.** "You know I want this as much as you do, but . . ."

**6.** "I just want a [. . .], not a [. . .]"

Bottomliners are often quiet managers because they spend much of their time with Excel spreadsheets and searching the Internet for an extra nickel's savings.

Writing to these people is a snap. All you have to do is justify everything in terms they relate to.

---

### Sample Email Message to a Bottomliner

Mr. Selsnick: Based on our staff meeting today, I researched the pricing for the Alpha switch. After calling several vendors, I found that Qualigy has the best price. Plus, if we buy 11 switches and pay net within 10 days, they'll knock an additional 12 percent off per switch. Please let me know if I should proceed with the order. If so, I'll notify Finance so we can take advantage of the net 10 discount.

---

### The Guilt Monger

Guilt peddlers are people who make you feel bad about most everything you do. You can never satisfy this kind of manager, but you can protect yourself by the way you communicate with them. Keeping in mind that you can never do enough, measure carefully what you do and quantify it in accordance with common sense.

Phrases guilt mongers use in email include:

**1.** "We're late on the project. I wish there was something someone could do about it."

**2.** "Now, there's Phyllis. She puts in so many extra hours for the good of the company. If only she was *an example to everyone else*."

**3.** "This is a tough time for the company. Without extra, extra effort, we may have to close our doors next year. You know how I hate cutting into family time and vacations, but . . ."

**4.** "Since you're taking sick time, this vitally important task will just have to languish until you get back. Oh, did I mention our new quarterly performance reviews? Yours is scheduled for next Monday at 8:00 am."

**5.** "Oh, we'll get it done without you, (*sniff, sniff*) somehow . . ."

This kind of manager is tough to take. No matter how well you accommodate his essentially outrageous demands for free work, including the donation of your nights and weekends, it will never be enough. The guilt monger is never satisfied, and there's little you can do to please him, so accept it.

You can, however, make sure he knows how much you are contributing, especially when it's above and beyond the call of duty.

---

**Sample Email Message to a Guilt Monger**

Mr. Selsnick: I have completed the Duey account project by working at home over the weekend. I'm now studying the workload left from Trissia to see how it can best be apportioned out to the remaining employees of our group. If you need to reach me this weekend, my home phone—in case you misplaced it—is 555-1019. [In the last line, you are suggesting that you'll be working at home, even if you're spending the day swimming and barbecuing. Give out a cell phone number if you plan to travel.]

---

**The "It's Not My Fault"-er**

The "it's not my fault"-er is a manager who refuses to accept responsibility for his mistakes. Instead, he either sidesteps it or shifts the blame to other departments or some hapless employee. Because you can be terminated for repeated screw-ups, you must protect yourself wherever possible.

Phrases they use in email include:

**1.** "I know it wasn't your project, but I expect you to use common sense and catch these mistakes."

**2.** "Somewhere there's a written policy about how to handle this . . ."

**3.** "It's not my fault that you didn't know enough to check the micrometer settings twice with the factory."

**4.** "I had no idea that you would . . ."

**5.** "You should have seen this coming."

This kind of manager is also tough to take. If you get the blame for small stuff, try to forget about it. But if your continued employment is compromised, then you must take action. The best way to do this is to document events by using email, and then save copies of everything off-site, which you can later send to the human resource department or your boss' boss.

If you find yourself blamed unjustly for some problem and you've decided to confront your boss about it, you can copy others on your correspondence and build a case file should you need it. Confrontation must, at least initially, take a soft but unarguable approach. Leave the scene if possible. Apologize if possible and suggest the two of you get together later to discuss the matter after a cooling-down period.

---

**Sample Email Message to a "It's Not My Fault"-er**

Mr. Selsnick: I have spent my weekend studying the problems with Project Alpha and, contrary to your report, I found that I took the correct actions during the lifecycle of the project based on the training I currently possess. It is my intention on our next project to work more closely with you so that I can better learn from your experience. Also, I would like to take additional company training so that I better understand the established procedures and protocols.

---

**The 15-Watt Bulb**

There are two kinds of 15-watters, although both seem dim when you work with them. There are those managers who aren't very bright, and those who simply aren't with the program because they lack training or expertise, or because of simple laziness. Neither is difficult to work with. Both tend to get in your way more than anything.

Phrases 15-watt bulbs use in email include:

**1.** "Great job, swell work, keep it up!" [From a manager who hasn't a clue about what you do and how you do it.]

**2.** "Explain to me again why we need this."

3. "Have a look at Project Alpha and give me a detailed report on your take of what it's about."

4. "The manual says to do it this way, and in this company we always follow procedure to the letter."

5. "This is something to work out among yourselves."

The best way to work with this kind of boss is to take care of your work without his being aware of it. Education is the key here: train your boss how to do the job or at least to stay out of your way.

---

**Sample Email Message to a 15-Watt Bulb**

Mr. Selsnick: As you know, it's nearly time to create the quarterly update to the shareholders. It's this department's job to take care of the design, layout, and printing of the quarterly results. We're ready to go. All we need is for you to get the final numbers from finance by no later than June 12. Then, we'll take care of the rest.

---

**The Dreamer**

A dreamer boss is usually someone who once had a vision for the company but somehow lost it along the way. A dreamer can be worked around unless he is the principal officer of a small company, in which case you should update your resume and get your interview outfit pressed.

Dreamers will send you email on:

1. Their next big idea.

2. The big picture from their point of view.

3. New management styles to put in place immediately. (Get a copy of the book they stumbled upon if possible so you know what to expect.)

4. What should be important in the organization according to the *Harvard Business Review.*

5. Requirements for preliminary studies of almost anything.

The best way to work with a dreamer is to keep doing what you know must be done. A dreamer will assume that there is infinite time to research and implement

## The cc-you-cc-me Boss

Much like managers of old (pre-1980), some bosses still want to approve all of your outgoing correspondence for "quality." Today's version of this megalomaniac insists that you copy to him or her all correspondence sent via conventional letter, memo, and email.

Do just that. Copy your boss on everything, especially if you write hundreds of email messages a week and swamp the inbox. Then any really personal material should be sent using channels outside the company's watchful eye: face to face, letter from home to home, microdots . . . well, you get the idea.

new ideas. Should you go along with that way of thinking, your work will suffer as your time is vacuumed into one hopeless new project after another.

> ### Sample Message to a Dreamer
>
> Mr. Selsnick: I think your new idea for the Alpha Project is a great one. Unfortunately, my work day is too fully booked with "must do" tasks vital to the company. I suggest you look for someone to implement the idea who can better juggle a work load to make time for it. Keep me posted on how everything works out.

### The Volcano

Possibly the worst kind of boss to work for is the volcano. You'll have to learn just how to approach him to avert yelling, ranting, and finger pointing episodes. In common with the "it's not my fault"-er, volcanoes tend to blame everything on others, but when they blame, they become explosive, so workers learn to tiptoe around them and to avoid confrontation.

Volcanoes write email messages that include phrases like:

■ "In all my days as a [. . .] I've never seen such a . . ."
■ "This is garbage, absolute garbage . . ."
■ "Don't let me see your face around here again until you have . . ."

■ You're so stupid. I don't know who hired you."

■ "What does it take to get anything done around here!"

Email is a good tool for working with the volcano boss. It keeps you physically away from him and his tantrums, which allows you to think and work without raging interruptions. When you do set him off, ignore what he says in rage and quietly respond to the problem with email. Never get sucked into a verbal argument with a volcano. You can only lose. Instead, remove yourself from the situation physically.

---

**Sample Email Message to a Volcano**

Mr. Selsnick: I've looked into the problem you brought up today and I have found a way to speed up Project Alpha. Granted, it is a little risky, but I understand that timely completion is very important to you. Here are my suggestions and a revised schedule to go along with them . . .

---

## Talking it Out with HR

At one time or another, we've all been beguiled by those magic words invented by managers to seduce us into trusting them: the open door policy. Got a problem you can't resolve? Just go to your boss or the boss's boss, and solutions await you.

Unfortunately, in most companies, this is a myth, but most of us have become savvy to that fact. Online communications have created an interesting variant that some people might not yet be aware of.

If you have a problem with your boss and approach, say, the Human Resources Department for help, it may instruct you to copy it on all email correspondence with him or her.

Beware! This approach will backfire. HR will end up talking to your boss, who will then likely hold a grudge, or at least dislike you, forever and make every effort to undermine you.

## EMAILING PEERS

Communicating with peers is usually easier than with the Big Cheese, because (in theory) you are equals. Peers divide neatly into categories:

- Those you know and work with on a daily or near-daily basis.
- Those you know but don't usually work with closely.
- Those you know only as a name on an org chart.

In addition, each member of the three groups above falls into one of these three categories:

**Easy to get along with.** Efficient. Does a good job. Pleasant to work with. Could become a friend outside the workplace.

**Difficult to get along with.** Has an agenda tied to department politics, or a cold, combative, or otherwise immature personality.

**Under-skilled or unproductive.** Coworkers resentfully have to take up the slack for this person.

## Test the Water Before Jumping In

New to an organization? Initially keep all email in a friendly but pseudo-formal mode until you get to know the players. Follow the same format in online meetings. Make all comments appear as suggestions. Instead of:

"I've worked with Willingsly oiless bearings before and found them to be overpriced junk. They fail almost as fast as you can replace them, and the manufacturer always blames all problems on the user. These things are worthless!"

Instead, try:

"I'm new here so this is just a suggestion: I've worked with Willingsly oiless bearings in the past. My previous company discontinued their use because of repeated reliability problems and an unsuitable attitude on the part of the manufacturer."

**Those You Know and Work with on a Daily or Near-Daily Basis**

The people you work with on a daily basis are not necessarily located in the same office or facility as you. You may work with them by phone or electronically. (We've worked with our literary agent, Mike Snell, for more than ten years, but we've never met him in person.) You probably have more than just a formal working relationship with these people. In fact, you might know them so well that you can often guess their opinions without asking them. (Ask them anyway!)

Here are some sample messages for the three types of people you're likely to work with on a regular basis:

### 1. EASY TO GET ALONG WITH

Working with coworkers can feel as comfortable as a favorite pair of old shoes. You joke, you have fun solving problems, and you know you can rely on them if push comes to shove. Email tends to be very informal, more like correspondence between friends than colleagues:

---

**Sample Email to an Easy-to-Get-Along-With Coworker**

Hey Landstrom,
Where are those pie charts you promised me yesterday? Don't tell me you ran out of transparency film again. Well get on it, or you know who will be down my throat by tomorrow. Lunch at Murphy's at 11:30 to beat the rush?
Jan

---

This message assumes familiarity between sender and recipient, and a kind of shorthand is used to convey information. Sending this kind of email to someone who doesn't know you would be cause of great confusion, since the words assume information not supplied.

### 2. DIFFICULT TO GET ALONG WITH

Close coworkers who make your life hell are best dealt with in a formal manner. Spell out EVERYTHING in detail so that no one can say your communication lacked something significant. That way, your rear is covered should something go wrong. You can (and should) try to improve your working relationship with this person, but if that proves impossible, stick with this kind of message for best results:

---

**Sample Email Message to a Hard-to-Get-Along-With Coworker**

Mr. Landstrom: I'm checking on the status of the Forbin Project pie charts you agreed to provide me by yesterday. Please email me with the status of the charts. If you are having problems with the equipment or need more information to complete the charts, please let me know. I have to present them tomorrow morning to the senior staff, and I would like to have them today to use in rehearsing my presentation.

I know you are feeling under the weather with your cold, and I can probably ask Tammy to assist you with chart production, if that would help.

Thanks again for your help with this task—Jon Kipling, ext 1234

---

In this formal message, all of the requisite facts are spelled out, the tone conveys a friendly, but not too familiar approach, and you diplomatically offer additional help in the interest of pleasing all parties and getting the job done.

### 3. UNDER-SKILLED OR UNPRODUCTIVE

People like those in Scott Adams's *Dilbert* comic strip actually exist and may work for the same company you do. What makes matters even more difficult is that some of these folks may be legitimately likeable and kind. The best way to deal with them is to be encouraging while leading them every step of the way.

> ## Sample Email Message to an Under-Skilled or Unproductive Coworker
>
> Hi Herb,
>
> I've got to pass the buck to you on the Forbin project. We're swamped over here and I need your help. Here is what I need you to do: Get clearance from the military rep on section B's blueprint revision. The rep is Colonial Marvin Asker. You have met him before. His number is 654-555-1923. He needs only to look at the plans and approve the Allocation redesign. I've already faxed him a copy, but we need his initials on the actual prints. Remember this is classified, and we need the sign-off no later than Friday. If there's any problem call me immediately! Home: 555-9865, cell 555-8932. I'm counting on you!
>
> —Jon, ext 1234

In this message, you have successfully spelled out the task, provided explicit directions, and backed up the information provided with an army of phone numbers. Most importantly, you don't sound condescending. That's vital, because while the skill sets may be weaker than those of a lab rat, it doesn't mean that he or she is stupid or insensitive.

## Those You Know but Don't Usually Work with Closely

### 1. EASY TO GET ALONG WITH

You can have a great relationship online with colleagues you don't see everyday or who are far away. Email can fly, chat is almost like being there, and cams make you feel like you're in the same room as the other person. Still, you need to assure that information doesn't get lost because of the almost unnoticeable barriers that can creep into remote relationships.

> **Sample Email to an Easy-to-Get-Along-With Coworker Whom You Don't Know Personally**
>
> Hey Landstrom,
>
> I need those transparency films for tomorrow, or old Melissa will be on my case. These are the ones from the Brunet presentation that we planned to subset for mañana's executive meeting. It should only take you a few minutes to generate the film, but in case you've misplaced the input, I've attached a file with the markups you'll need. Send them FedEx Priority—that should work just fine for the 4:00 meeting.
>
> Let's do lunch next time you come to HQ. I found a great new sushi bar!
>
> Jan

This message isn't much different from the earlier example of email between two people who work close to each other, but it contains more information. This is necessary because if you're not working side by side, some details may get lost or forgotten.

### 2. DIFFICULT TO GET ALONG WITH

People who are both not local and difficult to work with require special attention. If you're developing a critical project together, it may be best to hop a plane and work side by side, because email may not be up to the task.

For lesser activities, here's the tone you might want to use:

> **Sample Email to a Difficult-to-Get-Along-With Coworker Whom You Don't Know Personally**
>
> Mr. Landstrom: I am thanking you in advance for completing the pie charts for us. I will be looking for them tomorrow, assuming you send them FedEx Priority. That will get them here in plenty of time for tomorrow's 4:00 p.m. meeting. Any questions? Just call or email me. Thanks again.
>
> —Jon Kipling, ext 1234

This message accomplishes three things:

■ It reminds the other party that the pie charts are important and you are waiting for them.

■ It thanks the recipient in advance, making it more difficult for him to avoid the task.

■ If the person fails to perform, you have made an appropriate effort to urge completion of the task, so you're covered when the charts don't turn up.

### 3. UNDER-SKILLED OR UNPRODUCTIVE

The best way to work with this kind of person on a remote basis is to mix email and phone calls to make sure the work is getting done. You might suggest that, before completion of 200 ugly and useless pie charts, you be sent a sample for review by "the committee" even if that committee comprises only you.

Have the work done in small batches so that you can check it and offer feedback as needed. Obviously, if a project requires fast turnaround, this is not the person to turn to. Consider outsourcing the task.

### Those You Know Only as a Name on an Org Chart

Since you don't know this person, you can't presume anything about a way to approach him. If you're addressing a critical issue, consider putting out feelers before making contact electronically. You may find useful information in company databases, annual reports, or just through the people you know.

The best approach to communication in these situations is probably to begin with a phone call, wherein you introduce yourself and request whatever assistance you need. After that, you can open an email dialog to nail down the fine points and provide scheduling information. From this interactivity, you will quickly get a reading on exactly what you're dealing with. Then approach the person in the same way as you would those you know but don't usually work closely with.

## EMAILING SUBORDINATES

Communicating electronically with employees can be almost as delicate as writing to a boss who is computer-illiterate. Why? Employees—especially in this day and

## How to Foster a Great Relationship with Subordinates

There is nothing more important in your relationship with your subordinates than a sense, by them, that you respect each one of them as a unique personality with special needs that match each one's special skills.

This sense of being appreciated results from a complex equation of:

■ A friendly environment.

■ An employer who doesn't roll heads frequently. One who does expect the remaining employees to take up the slack as if nothing has happened.

■ Timely interaction. Sending an employee a "must do" message on the same day it must be done is like asking that person to disarm a time bomb that will explode in 45 seconds. It can't be done.

■ Special tasks that demand special personalities. You should respond to each in turn. Don't assume that scientists respond the same way to accolades/criticism as do your swampers (truck loaders/unloaders).

age of downsizing—tend to read between the lines. ("She said this, but did she really mean that?")

To avoid this problem, you need to do four things:

1. (Again) decide if email is the right vehicle for the communication of your message.

2. Write a draft online of your message.

3. Consider the person you are writing to. How will your message be perceived? What works best with this personality?

4. Reread your draft and make changes as necessary.

### Samples of Emails to Subordinates

There are at least as many types of subordinates as there are bosses, so once again, you should try to fit your emails to the personality of the person you're writing to.

Here, for example, are various ways to respond to a query for management direction on a project that is going late:

---

**1. THE EASY-TO-WORK-WITH PERSON:**

Hi Tammy: This project is going late, as you know. Do you have any suggestions that will help us meet—or at least approach—the original date? As you know, my butt is on the line, and as usual, you're my best resource for pulling the rabbit out of the hat.

**2. THE DIFFICULT (EMOTIONALLY REACTIVE) EMPLOYEE:**

Hello Tammy: This project is going late as you know. We both understand that the schedule slip is not your fault. You've done your best to keep things on track, but now I need you to put on your thinking cap and see if you can invent a solution to get us back on schedule. We're counting on you to help us out of this difficult position.

**3. THE INCOMPETENT EMPLOYEE:**

Hello Tammy: This project is going late and I need to do something about it. It's no reflection on you, but I'm adding a couple of people to help us pick up the slack. Please provide them any information they may need. After all, you are the expert on this project and we're adding manpower to take advantage of your skills and get this thing to bed.

**4. THE PRIMADONNA:**

Hello Tammy: You've done a great job with the project so far. I have the opportunity to add extra manpower to make your job easier. Please welcome Ned and Tina—they will be your direct reports to add resources to the project.

---

## THE EMAIL WORKSHOP

Writing email in an effective manner takes practice. Much like your first business letter on paper that probably left something to be desired, composing effective email takes practice too.

Here's how to get started:

1. Decide who you need to write to and who should be copied on the correspondence. Are the people you are writing to all in the same category, i.e., managers, peers, or subordinates? If not, you will need to modify your correspondence for those in each group unless they are only copied on it.

2. Choose a useful subject line: *Priorities for Omega Project* says more than *Letter from Bob.*

3. Set a priority for the mail. If your system supports it, mark email *Urgent* only when it is.

4. Write a single sentence that summarizes the contents of your letter:

   For example: Project Omega is running two weeks late; what can we do to finish on time?

   If you find writing this sentence impossible, you probably have more than one idea and need to write more than one email message.

   For example: Project Omega is running two weeks late and volunteers are needed for the project's lab relocation.

   Look for constructions (like this example) using bridging words (conjunctions) like *and*. Then compose separate messages, including only one important thought per message.

5. Add the body of the message. All topics should follow the idea introduced in the first sentence. Keep your letter to no more than two screens in length so that recipients are more likely to read the entire document.

## Longer Documents

Documents longer than 1000 words are best sent as attachments. That way, your email can introduce readers to the topic and they can print out the attachment to read at their leisure. Adobe's PDF format is great for this, but you must own the encoding software to assemble a .pdf attachment. Microsoft Word works well too, and most recipients will own a copy.

**6.** Add a concluding sentence or two, usually a call to action that reiterates the content of the message and tell readers what to do.

For example: Project Omega is our first priority. We must keep it on track!

**7.** Sign your name, read it for typos, and send your letter. Always keep a copy for yourself.

## COMMUNICATION STYLES FOR EVERY NEED

In a small company in which everyone knows one another, email tends to take on a more personal tone. In a larger organization, there may be hundreds or thousands of people you have never met and know nothing about. Here you must decide how chummy you want to make your communications. Your email can range from the very friendly to the cool and impersonal, depending on what you need to communicate and who the recipient is.

Gauge the level of formality by imagining yourself delivering your message to the other person in a conventional manner. This will help you to determine the type of message it is:

■ Formal
■ Informal
■ "Team player"
■ Rebuttal
■ FYI and "Visible on radar"

The category you choose will determine the tone of the message and possibly its vocabulary and length as well. Here's what to look for.

### Formal

When communicating with the boss of another department, about whom you know little or nothing, it's best to adopt a formal tone. Formality is also useful when conveying bad news. The formal email format does the following:

■ It conveys only information, recommendations, and relevant data.
■ It avoids familiarity, which the receiving party may consider unwarranted or inappropriate.

■ It has some of the format of a conventional business letter, with salutations, possibly even a superfluous date in addition to the ones added by the system. (Showing a date indicates that you are aware of the date if the correspondence is project-related. It also represents the real date, should your message sit in a system queue prior to transmission or reception.)

---

**Sample Message Written in the Formal Style**

To: CNMolnarphd@aol.com
Subject: The Omega Code
May 29, 2001
Dear Dr. Molnar,
Allow me to introduce myself. My name is Kerry Ashtar, and I am the lead engineer on Project Omega. I have a need to work with your department regarding quality control measures that must be in place by the initial manufacturing date (currently projected as Nov 1). I have outlined what we, in my group, see as fundamental procedures, but we would like your group's input and help in establishing those procedures. I have spoken with my manager, Lisa Robbins, and she has given me permission to set up a meeting time with you to discuss this matter. Please contact me regarding your availability or, if you prefer, I can set up a time through your administrative assistant. I will forward the project information to you through internal mail for your preliminary review.
Sincerely,
Kerry Ashtar
Lead Engineer
Project Omega
Tel Ex. 2915

---

## Informal

The informal style is used with people you interact with on a first-name basis. Your recipient should know you well and be comfortable with your style of doing things. You can use this with your immediate boss if the two of you have a friendly working relationship. This approach can contain less information, assuming that the person you're writing to has some familiarity with the topic.

---

**Sample Message Written in an Informal Style**

To: CNMolnarphd@aol.com
Subject: QC Procs on PO?

Hi Charly,
Hope your fishing expedition to the White Mountains went well and you caught some big ones. Did you shoot any pix for us to see?

On a biz note: Project Omega is coming closer to production and it's time we talk about QC procedures before we get much closer to production. I've sent you (via interdepartmental snail mail) the preliminary QC procedures our group hacked out in last week's project meeting. Let me know when you're available. My calendar is pretty open next week. Lunch on Wednesday would be good.

---

**Team Player**

Use the team player approach to exert some friendly persuasion or to build new alliances within an organization. It works best with recipients who are also team motivated. Avoid it when communicating with someone known for an icy personality or for rigid thinking. If you know nothing about your recipient's personality, this approach carries some risk.

---

**Sample Message Written in a Team Player Style**

To: CNMolnarphd@aol.com
Subject: Project Omega & QC Procedures

Mr. Molnar: My name is Kerry Ashtar and I'm the lead engineer on Project Omega. We're very excited about Omega and its potential for the company. As of this week, I think it's time to look at manufacturing quality control, which is, of course, your department. My team would

---

like to work with your team to put the right procedures in place. I've already sent a package of my group's assumptions to you through company mail. Let's set up a meeting ASAP to exchange ideas. Project Omega may be the biggest thing to hit the company for years and we want your support. We're ready when you are!

Kerry Ashtar

Tel Ex. 2915

## Rebuttal

The rebuttal format email is used when you need to argue a point, answer a mildly negative message, or set someone straight. Its purpose is to put the facts on the table and clarify the issue at hand without resorting to an angry response. The format can be either formal or casual, depending on how well you know the other party. However, resorting to a formal tone can sometimes convey a sense of anger, even to someone you know well. Keep this in mind when sending a rebuttal.

### Sample Rebuttal

To: CNMolnarphd@aol.com

Subject: Project Omega Issues

Mr. Molnar: I received your message concerning your group's intended participation in Project Omega. I would like to suggest your participation begin much sooner than November. Here are my reasons for this request:

- An October start for your group won't allow sufficient time to put people and procedures in place by the November ship date.
- Your people may need to make recommendations for changes to the product that we won't have enough time to incorporate before shipping.

> ■ Project Omega is a Class One priority project to the corporation and is expected to count for significant revenue in Fiscal 2002. We don't want to take chances that we ship an inferior or problematic product.
>
> Please reconsider your decision and advise me of your plans for the QC study and procedure establishment.
>
> Kerry Ashtar
> Lead Engineer
> Project Omega
> Tel Ex. 2915

### FYI and *"Visible on Radar"*

FYI (for your information) is just that. It's keeping a person in the loop who should be informed about any given issue. This format keeps you and your efforts on the radar so that others know what you're working on and how busy you are.

You can simply copy this person on mail sent to others, but you may want to write a separate message specifically intended for him or her. For example, you wouldn't copy a senior manager using the informal example above, because the tone might be construed as inappropriate and the recipient wouldn't understand parts of the message. FYI is also CYA (short for *cover your a\*\**). Your message shows what you are doing and demonstrates that you are keeping tabs to the best of your ability. Use it to protect yourself should something go wrong.

## Watch Your Tone

When corresponding with someone familiar to you in a business environment, the tone of email messages tends to creep toward the informal as the exchange goes on. Should you become upset with the other party, reverting suddenly to a formal tone will be noticed and can be misinterpreted. Unless you're trying to make an enemy, always remain aware of your tone, and try not to change it abruptly.

---

**Sample FYI Email**

To: CNMolnarphd@aol.com

Subject: FYI on Omega QC Procedures

Mr. Molnar: This message is to keep you up to date on Project Omega.

As you know from my update last week, we are about to need your group's participation on Project Omega. I am assuming that you've briefed your people on time and resource requirements by now.

I plan on meeting with your team's project leaders next week to bring them up to speed and get their recommendations. Our projected ship date is still set for November, and we will need the QC manufacturing procedures in place and tested before that time.

If you have any questions, please respond to this message or call me at ex. 2915

Kerry Ashtar

Lead Engineer

Project Omega

---

**Broadcast Email**

Broadcast email is a message sent to multiple users. A typical broadcast message might go out to a department, division, or entire company. Usually reserved for information that must reach groups of people ASAP, the broadcast message is less personal and more generic than mail sent from one person to another. It may require additional clarification for subgroups within the mail list. For example, a broadcast message to all departments that announces major spending cutbacks would probably spawn another one with additional details for managers only.

---

**Sample Broadcast Email**

To: All_Employees[1]
Subject: Important Budget Information

　　As you know, last quarter's earnings and profit were down significantly from the previous quarter. As you can imagine, I and the stockholders are very concerned about this development. From this day on, to contain capital expenses and improve the bottom line, all capital expenditures over $100 will require the signature of the originating department's vice-president and all capital expenditures over $1000 will also require my personal signature. Before submitting an expense for signature, I request that the person generating the request attach a one-page justification for the item. Ongoing expenses for items such as building maintenance and drinking water are naturally exempt from this requirement.

　　Thank you for your attention to this matter.

Kurt Simmons
Persimmon Corp.

---

In this example, the email is not addressed to any one person. Instead, it is a blanket message from the president to all staff members. Kurt Simmons might also elect to send a separate email to an alias comprising vice-presidents only to further outline his restrictions and requirements, or he might decide to communicate that info in a staff meeting.

Broadcast email is certainly not just reserved for bad news. It's a powerful tool for congratulating a team or organization for a job well done and for passing on must-know information as quickly as possible. Like all email tools, broadcast messages should not be overused to the degree that recipients start to ignore them.

One step you absolutely must take is to create an effective set of aliases so that broadcast messages are sent only to groups you need to target. In addition to an all-employees alias, separate ones might be assembled for individual departments, two or more related departments, company seniority levels (all-vice-presidents),

---

[1] All_Employees is an alias that automatically sends the message to everyone in the company.

and customers (users of Omega product). This last category might be useful to disseminate timely technical information.

## DEALING WITH "FLAME" EMAIL AT WORK

Sooner or later, every employee and manager receives a nasty email message, also called *flame mail* in the online world. There's one lesson these messages teach clearly: words can and do hurt. But remember, flames are usually composed in anger by the sender, and it's vitally important not to respond in turn. Instead, think the issue through, even if it means a walk around the block to cool off first. Then appraise the situation with a cool head and calm demeanor.

Ask yourself:

**What does the message really mean?** Is the person legitimately angry or just blowing off steam? Is the person mad at you or did you just happen to be at the wrong place at the wrong time?

**Why did the person send it?** What is the reason for sending such a message? Is this person normally a hot head or troublemaker or has something you did legitimately made him angry?

**Are you an innocent victim of a message sent to too many people?** If it was sent to multiple parties, are you really the target of the message or just a name on an overly broad alias list?

After you ask yourself these question, you'll have to decide what to do next. Your options include:

**Writing back calmly** to clarify the situation if the sender was misinformed.

**Apologizing for a problem** you caused or were a part of.

**Ignoring the message** because to respond would dignify its inappropriate content.

**Taking the matter up with your supervisor** for advice or to pass the problem along.

**Calling a meeting** or private chat meeting to work out the problem.

**Copying the sender** on the message and including a reminder about online manners.

Which approach to take is always a tough call, especially when the message is from a boss or manager. It's an overwhelming urge in us humans to respond in kind when someone hurts our feelings. But, in the straitlaced world of business, emotions are not supposed to rule the roost—even when the message sender has already overstepped that boundary.

That's why a cooling down period is so vital. It allows you to respond with rational logic and problem-solving skills and to make the hothead feel juvenile for mishandling the situation.

---

**Sample Flaming Message**

To: JasmineD

Subject: You idiot!!!

I can't believe you screwed up another account. I worked with these people for four years, and they never got angry with me. You, on the account for just a week, already have them pissed off as hell and ready to look for a new vendor. What is it with you? Are you really as stupid as you seem or do you work at it? I'm disgusted with the job you're doing here, and if I were you, I'd get my resume and job hunting skills lined up. You're probably going to need them real soon.

Terry

---

And here is the way to use each possible response. Note that each one calls the sender on the carpet about the message's tone, even when the recipient was at fault:

### Writing Back Calmly to Clarify the Situation if the Sender Was Misinformed

Terry: I must admit the anger in your message upset me greatly. First, I want you to know that while I am a part of the Domino account team, my involvement is strictly internal and not supervisory in any way. I am aware of the problem you wrote about, but neither was I a source of it nor could I have improved the situation by using my role in the organization. I have suggested to Tom, the Domino team's acting supervisor, that we hold a meeting with you, the Domino team, its manager, and myself in order to resolve this problem and hold onto the account. He has agreed to set this up and will contact you. I'll see you there.

Jasmine

*(Include a copy of the original message at the bottom to remind the sender of what he wrote and how inflammatory it was.)*

### Apologizing for a Problem You Caused or Were a Part Of

Terry: I must admit the anger in your message upset me greatly. First, I want you to know I take full responsibility for the problem. I made an error in judgment, and I've learned from my mistake. It won't be repeated. In the interest of holding onto the account, I've scheduled a meeting with myself, Tom, my boss, and the client to go over what we plan to do to remedy the situation. Following that session, they are invited to lunch (on us) at Monty's—the favorite restaurant of Morly and his staff. This effort will, I hope, patch up our differences and let us better serve the account both now and in the future.

Jasmine

*(Include a copy of the original message at the bottom to remind the sender of what he wrote and how inflammatory it was.)*

### Ignoring the Message Because to Respond Would Dignify Its Inappropriate Content

No response to an inappropriate message is a loud response in itself. Assuming the sender is expecting a strong reaction from you, no response means you found the message so offensive that you plan to pretend it was never sent. Silence can be deafening!

### Taking the Matter Up with Your Supervisor for Advice or for Him to Handle the Problem

Terry: I must admit the anger in your message upset me greatly. I have forwarded it to Tom, my boss, with a request that the three of us meet to work this out.

Jasmine

*(Include a copy of the original message at the bottom to remind the sender of what he wrote and how inflammatory it was.)*

The sender may be mortified at the thought that the unsuitable message has taken wing within the organization. This approach also allows your supervisor to work out the problem and let the sender know that such communications are out of place in the company.

### Calling a Meeting or Private Chat Meeting to Work Out the Problem

Terry: I must admit the anger in your message upset me greatly. Let's set up a private chat to discuss this issue and work on solutions to the problem. Let me know by email when you will be available, since I won't be back from San Francisco until late next week. Until then, please contain your angry feelings about me until we've at least had time to talk about the issues.

Jasmine

*(Include a copy of the original message at the bottom to remind the sender of what he wrote and how inflammatory it was.)*

### Copying the Sender on the Message and Reminding Him or Her of Online Manners

(This approach is usually used with a subordinate or peer. It's not suggested for use with your manager or those senior to you, unless you already know you're leaving the organization and don't care about burning bridges.)

Terry: I must admit the anger in your message upset me greatly. I want to remind you that this kind of anger does not belong in company email. If you have a problem with my performance or other issues, focus your letter on the problem, not your personal opinions or your attitudes about me. I will ignore this message for now until you cool down and replace it with one written with a level-headed point of view.

Jasmine

*(Include a copy of the original message at the bottom to remind the sender of what he wrote and how inflammatory it was.)*

## Formal Dress for Email

To make replies more formal, you might consider using your formal name and title. That notifies the sender that you are no longer—at least for the life of the message—on a first name basis. Signing "Jasmine Siong, Director of Product Enhancements" instead of the usual "Jasmine" chills the relationship, if there was one to begin with. Signing "J. Siong, Director of Product Enhancements" is even icier. It implies that you are no longer on a first name basis with the other party. From either of these points, you can begin to rebuild the relationship.

## DEALING WITH "FLAME" CHAT IN A WORK ENVIRONMENT

One of the ugliest scenarios imaginable is that of a colleague who chooses to write a blaming or nasty comment during an online meeting. Here your options are more limited because the words are out there for everyone to see and possibly add to. You don't even have much of a cooling off period available because without an immediate response, the meeting will continue and the thread will move on.

So, what _can_ you do? You can:

1. Reply and explain you were not a part of the problem.
2. Reply and defend yourself.
3. Ignore the comment.
4. Remind the sender of his or her online manners.
5. Announce online that you are requesting a brief private chat with the offender and will be back in a moment.
6. Leave the online meeting.

Again you will note that the first item of business is to declare that the comments are out of place. You will also see that the comments in reply are brief and immediate.

### Reply and Explain You Were Not a Part of the Problem

Terry: Your comment was inappropriate here. But I want you to know that I had nothing to do with this problem. Let's talk about this offline later.

### Reply and Apologize

> Terry: Your comment was inappropriate here. But I have apologized for my actions and learned from my mistake. It's time to put this issue away.

### Ignore the Comment

Pretend like you didn't see the comment by not responding. It's entirely possible that others in the meeting will rally to your support and tell the offender that he or she is out of line.

### Remind the Sender of Appropriate Online Manners

Like the email responses, this is very risky to do to a manager more senior than yourself.

> Terry: Your comment was inappropriate here. Your manners online leave much to be desired. I will ignore your outburst for now.

### Announce Online That You Are Requesting a Brief Private Chat with the Offender and Will Be Back in a Moment

> Terry: Your comment was inappropriate here. Let's go offline briefly to discuss this. Meet me in a private chatroom called terry_jasmine_chat. We will be back in a minute or two.

Should the offender decline or ignore your offer, continue with the meeting if that is your choice. Other participants will see that you tried to resolve the conflict, but your antagonist didn't. Score one point for you.

### Leave the Online Meeting

> Terry: Your comment was inappropriate here. I apologize to everyone else, but I'm leaving the meeting. For now, I'm too upset to participate.

And do leave. Most systems will report to other participants that "JasmineD has left the room." This tactic, while unattractive, puts the offender in the dubious position of receiving criticism from other participants for blowing you offline.

## JOB OFFERINGS ONLINE

Breakfast with the help-wanted section of the Sunday paper pales in comparison when you consider there are *millions* of job offerings online. Equally, if you are an employer with a quick search you might find the perfect candidate there.

Job seeking online is a little like using ads in the personals to look for a mate. There are plenty of "buyers" and "sellers," but it takes some looking to narrow the field effectively.

### For the Job Seeker

If you're currently looking for a new job, you will be amazed at the wealth of opportunities you can find through online services. There are countless sites, message boards, and lists available, ranging from local to international, general to specialized, and free to costly (rare). In addition, headhunters and company personnel departments very often list available jobs on a web site page.

### A Two-Way Street

In addition to searching the web for postings of open job positions, you can also place your resume on various sites for employers to read. The more *visibility* you have, the more you'll make your skills and availability known to people who might want to hire you. Some of the inquiries you get in return may surprise you, such as a message Kim received for a university teaching position on an island near Fiji. (He declined politely.)

### Locality

Job sites generally divide into three categories:

- General with little or no restriction on location or job type.
- Specialized for people with delineated skill sets.
- Restricted to jobs in a particular geographical area.

Most job seekers try to focus their efforts by looking for employment in a particular field and locale. You can, of course, try more of a shotgun approach, placing your ad on every site that accepts it, but this takes extra work and employers may wonder about an aerospace engineer placing his or her ad on a site dedicated to academia. Likewise, finding an ad for aerospace engineers on a site for musicians would appear equally odd.

For job seekers, physical location has become a major issue. Increasingly, companies have become very tightfisted about relocation expenses for all but the most key or hard-to-find employees. Once, an employer might have purchased your existing house, paid your moving expenses, and provided you with first-class airfare to your new location, but now you're more likely to pay for all of this out of your own pocket.

More importantly, employers screening your resume may reject you out of hand if you live in California and the opening is in Boston, because they may assume that you come with relocation expenses which they don't want to pay. For this reason, you may want to state up front (in your online resume) that relocation expenses are negotiable.

On the other hand, sometimes your location doesn't matter, because instead of driving or taking public transportation to work every day, you can ride the online airways instead: you can telecommute. That Boston-based company may hire you enthusiastically if the nature of your work can be done with only infrequent visits to HQ.

For people accustomed to working in a traditional business environment, having no office can take a little getting used to. But for the self-starter, telecommuting can give you freedom like you've never experienced before in a working environment.

## When Info Goes Stale

When searching job listings online, one of the most important things you can do is to check any relevant dates the ads may hold. In general, people are much better about posting material than they are about removing it once it goes stale.

Conscientious employers generally delete out-of-date job listings that have already been filled, but many others don't. Likewise, people who find successful employment may leave their materials on line in case something new and better comes along or just because they're too lazy to remove it.

Some of the problem lies with the sites themselves. While it may be easy to post an opening or resume, for security reasons, it may be more difficult to take it off.

## Using .pdf Format

When saving your resume in .pdf format, consider its size. First of all, you will probably want to save it at screen resolution, not printing resolution. Saving in the 70 dpi range is adequate for a crisp display on the recipient's screen. Saving at higher resolutions (150 dpi and up) makes for a much larger file, a longer download, and frustration on the user's part.

Second, as most resume how-to books will tell you, avoid excessive length. A five-page resume with multiple color pictures again makes for a huge .pdf file. Most readers will simply avoid downloading your resume—because they don't have time to do so—and they'll probably assume you have a screw loose.

### Posting Your Resume

You can place a complete resume online, but keep in mind that it must not consist of a huge file that employers will be loath to download. And use a format that employers can read. The safest bet is text only, although you won't be able to do better than typewriter-level formatting.

Microsoft Word is a popular format because most business computer users own a copy. Consider using Word's RTF format available in the Save As dialog box. This allows users of older versions of Word and other word processors to open your document, complete with formatting.

Perhaps the best format for posting resumes is .pdf, which allows you to save compact, neatly formatted resumes, complete with text and pictures. The downside is that you'll need access to software (Adobe Acrobat) that creates .pdf files. The software is moderately expensive, priced at around $250 on www.adobe.com and from all online mailorder houses, so you might want to encode your resume using a friend's PDF writer.

It's not unusual to place a resume online in more than one format so that readers can choose one for which they have software.

## Sites of Interest

There are thousands of sites offering job opportunities. Some are highly special-ized, like www.colostate.edu/Depts/Entomology/jobs/jobs.html, a site for acad-emic bug hunters. Others are very broad, like www.monster.com, www.job-bankusa.com, www.nationjob.com, and www.ajb.dni.us, to name a few. America Job Bank (www.ajb.dni.us) claims to have more than 2,500,000 applicants available and 13,000,000 openings posted.

To find a posting that will interest you, do a search for *job opportunities & [your field]*. (Or if location is important, *jobs & [your city or state]*). Also, every city and state has one or more sites for job postings, and most local newspapers place their classified ads on line so you can spend the 50¢ for a cup of coffee instead of for a copy of the paper.

You may get blown out of the water with the sheer volume of resources, but careful narrowing of your search pays dividends. For example, you may find that a broad location such as AOL's classified doesn't work as well as a site that only handles city maintenance openings for your metropolis.

## Answering an Ad

When replying to an online ad, read and reread the details carefully. It will usually tell you what format is necessary for submission and may describe other hoops to jump through. You might need only to paste your resume into an email. On the other hand, for jobs in the visual arts and multimedia, a full-blown color resume might be your ticket. Failing to follow the prescribed format usually results in an automatic rejection.

## Give Your Resume a Personal Touch

Since the copy machine made it possible to send resumes to thousands of em-ployers, you should rightly assume that your submission faces tens or hundreds of competing applicants. For that reason, you'll want to customize each submis-sion for the particular opening you're after. Again, get a book or two on creating resumes and follow the advice. Remember, the devil is in the details.

### Headhunters

As you surely know, headhunters are paid to find you. There are two kinds: The ones that charge you to find a job and the ones whose fee is paid by the searching company. (Avoid the first at all costs if possible. They only handle entry level jobs, which you could find yourself.)

When working with a headhunter, you must be up front and honest about which companies and other headhunters you have already contacted. It's only fair. Most headhunters will want an exclusive relationship, by the way, so make sure you feel comfortable with whomever you decide to go with.

Should your headhunter fail to deliver useful results within 30 days, terminate the relationship and look elsewhere. But make sure you keep the split on friendly terms. It's very common for a HH to come up empty within the 30-day period and then call six months later with a hot opportunity.

### Temps and Contact Jobs

If full-time, permanent employment isn't what you're looking for, consider contacting a temp agency. Searching on temp job opportunities brings up pages and pages of site listings. Everyone from ditch digger to highly trained professional is in great demand.

The employer pays the temp agency for your time. The temp agency in turn pays you your share of the loot. Temp jobs have a nice habit of turning into permanent employment, complete with salary and benefits. For that reason, you should use the Net to cast a wider net than the local *Yellow Pages* provides.

Contract work is another area you might want to explore online. Often paying extremely well for the life of a contract, these jobs are difficult to find without the help of a headhunter or an appropriate Web site.

### The Silence of the Lambs

In case you haven't picked up on it yet, the competition among online applications is fierce. Of course, if your talents are highly sought after—if, for example, you're a Cal-Tech trained microprocessor design engineer—a well developed resume will have employers on your doorstep in five minutes. For the rest of us, submissions to multiple openings may bring no acknowledgement whatsoever. This includes headhunter sites too.

Where it once was standard operating procedure to acknowledge your application, the sheer volume of applicants has changed business protocol. Rudeness—ignoring you completely—is now fully acceptable at most companies. But you can't blame them. After all, they may be receiving hundreds of applications a day. So if you're ignored, don't take it personally. Just keep on trying.

### More About You

When answering an ad that requests emailing your resume, you may want to take matters further. Assemble an employment-oriented web page, which brings out more about you than just the emailed resume. You can include additional biographical data about yourself, lists or pictures of your accomplishments, and anything else that an employer might need to know. Naturally, the site must be first rate. You want to "wow" the potential employer, not blow them away with an unattractive or horrifically designed site.

Get professional help if you think it's warranted. For job seekers looking in the $100K+ region or offering highly specialized skills, such a site is a must.

# CHAPTER EIGHT

# Putting Yourself Across to Friends and Family

AMERICAN (AND CANADIAN) FAMILIES[1] are changing location more than ever. According to a study sponsored by Mayflower Van Lines (and they should know!), 20 million Americans will move in the *next three months.* If people keep moving at that rate, we can figure that the average American will change residences about 12 times throughout his or her lifetime.

The consequences for our culture are profound. No longer do the kids take over the family farm or business and stay put. The old neighborhood, where friends and family lived within 20 miles of each other for generations, has gone the way of the hand-operated water pump. Enclaves of traditional extended families still exist, especially in the southeast, but chances are they won't remain immune to the relocation frenzy much longer.

---

[1] "Families" includes both individuals and non-nuclear family structures such as couples living together and unstructured groups of roommates who stick together while changing housing situations.

---

Still, our network of personal relationships is a major component of our lives. The saddest of people must be the person who has no friends or family. For that reason, we need to stay in touch. Online communication offers us an unparalleled opportunity to do so.

## SELF-TEST: YOUR ABILITY TO COMMUNICATE ONLINE WITH FRIENDS AND FAMILY

The following is a simple diagnostic test. Its purpose is not to test your knowledge of online relationships but to help you gauge how effectively you communicate with those close to you. For the most part, you will find it easy to guess the "right" answer. But getting the right answer is not the point of the test. Respond honestly, even if you feel your response is not the best one possible. This is not a contest. The goal is solely self-inventory. (Note: In this chapter when it reads family or friends it means *both* family and friends.)

| | True | False |
|---|---|---|
| **1.** I am comfortable communicating with my family in person and on the phone. | ____ | ____ |
| **2.** I am comfortable communicating with my family using email or chat. | | |
| **3.** I communicate effectively online. | ____ | ____ |
| **4.** I put off answering family email frequently. | ____ | ____ |
| **5.** Most of my family has email, but I don't use it. | ____ | ____ |
| **6.** I use email for most of my family correspondence. | ____ | ____ |
| **7.** I have friends I've never met outside of email. | ____ | ____ |
| **8.** My family has regular get-togethers in private chat rooms. | ____ | ____ |
| **9.** I usually email family members rather than phone them. | ____ | ____ |
| **10.** I get more than five messages a week from family members. | ____ | ____ |

11. I don't send email to family members because I rarely
    get a reply.                                              ____    ____
12. I don't give my email address to anyone—even friends
    and family.                                               ____    ____
13. I exchange family pictures with email.                    ____    ____
14. I have a digital camera and/or scanner.                   ____    ____
15. I look forward to reading my email every day because
    of the messages from friends and family.                  ____    ____

Score one point for each True response and zero for each False response _except_ for questions 4, 5, 11, 12. For these questions only subtract one point for each True response. A total score below 10 shows that you could probably have a much richer relationship with friends and family through electronic means.

## WORDS TO USE ONLINE WITH FRIENDS AND FAMILY

| | | |
|---|---|---|
| affinity | friend | relationship |
| arrival | gorgeous | remorseful |
| beauty | happy | satisfy |
| bond | heart | strength |
| bonding | heartstrings | together |
| brotherhood | heartwood | togetherness |
| build | help | touch |
| capture | hugs | traditional |
| close | invite | visit |
| closeness | invitation | warmth |
| comfort | love | wisdom |
| contact | loyalty | In addition, there |
| elated | mom, dad, brother, | is an unlimited |
| embrace | sister, etc. | number of affec- |
| family | open | tionate names for |
| feelings | pet | friends and family. |

**PHRASES TO USE ONLINE WITH FRIENDS AND FAMILY**

(family, class, etc.) reunion

blood is thicker than water

don't be such a stranger

don't worry about it

family gathering

family tree

get together

hey, let's have a beer (soda, coffee, etc.)

I depend on your support

I feel so lonely

I forgive [. . .]

I love you [in its many permutations]

I need your help

I need your support

I'll always remember the time when you and I . . .

I'm always with you in spirit if not in body

I'm thinking of you

it's something I can't talk about to anyone else but you

it's wonderful sharing with you

just kidding

keep the home fires burning (use this with older generations)

let's spend more time together

let's talk this over

mi casa es su casa

money can't buy you love

a quiet night at home

reach out

the [name] [family, clan, friends, order, etc.] always stick together

we have so much in common

we need to have a talk

we're friends forever!

we're the best of pals

when you get here, we'll have (little Christmas, etc.)

you are the [. . .] person!

you can be one of the family

you mean so much to me

you're always on my mind

you're the best [friend, Dad . . .] in the whole world

## WORDS TO AVOID WITH ONLINE FRIENDS AND FAMILY

| | | |
|---|---|---|
| a pain | greedy | screw off |
| away | grumpy | selfish |
| boring | hanger on | snotty |
| busy | hate | stealing |
| clueless | heartless | stuck up |
| cold | ignore | stupid |
| copy | irritating | ugly |
| distance | mean | unattractive |
| dull | mooch | uncommunicative |
| dumb | outsider | unforgiven |
| fat | overbearing | unfriendly |

## PHRASES TO AVOID WITH ONLINE FRIENDS AND FAMILY

| | |
|---|---|
| bad taste | no way |
| don't darken my doorstep | stay out of my way |
| get out of my life | that was a dumb decision |
| I am changing my phone number/email address | there's no friendship here |
| | this isn't a relationship |
| I don't have a family | We don't want you on our team |
| I don't need you | we're not close |
| I don't understand you | we're not on speaking terms |
| I don't want to hear from you | you always take |
| ignore her, she's got a screw loose | you presume on a nonexistent friendship |
| keep your distance | |
| leave me alone | you're mean |
| my friends don't like you | you're so [. . .] |
| no love lost | you're too weird |

## THE ELECTRONIC NETWORK

Fortunately for us "movers and shakers," electronics have helped us keep our precious networks of family and friends together. Thanks to the teletype and the telephone, and now the Internet, it has become easier than ever to make and keep new friends. It's even possible to locate long lost family members, school friends, and old so-and-so from whom you have not heard in twenty years.

Better yet, maintaining contact over the Internet with Sheila Brown, who moved to Australia five years ago with her family, costs essentially nothing. You can chat on the Net till you are blue in the face, exchange email, or use the Net's pseudo telephone software to talk it up. There are no by-the-second charges or scary telephone bills at month's end.

## BUILDING YOUR NETWORK

It's easy enough to collect email addresses from friends and family, but, naturally, there will be some holdouts who aren't hooked in—usually older people who want nothing to do with computers, or the occasional anti-technology zealot. You can still send these folks a printed copy of your email if you wish. (There are services that will print and mail email for you, but they're used for large corporate mailings.)

As you build your list of contacts and begin exchanging email, you'll want to build aliases for messages that you want to send to more than one person simultaneously. The alias can be used like broadcast email to announce an important event in your life, to provide a chatty update on what's new, and for mailing to groups of friends or family members.

Those with extended families and/or groups of friends will want to update various clusters with separate news. Not every group will want to hear the same stories.

When sending out "newsy" letters, don't expect a reply. Some people will respond, especially if they haven't heard from you in a long time. Others will wait until they have their own newsy letter to send to you. (As one correspondent put it, "One good broadcast email deserves another.")

## FINDING LOST PEOPLE BY USING THE NET

We speculate that two-thirds of Americans and Canadians have at least one email address. Even if grossly exaggerated, this number will be reached and exceeded soon as more and more people hook in. With so many users online, the Web has become an ideal environment for locating individuals, families, and long lost relatives.

Basic people searching is, well, basic. Try finding people first by using major search engines or AOL. If you come up empty-handed, try more than one engine. And don't be afraid to contact people who sound like possibilities.

---

**Sample Standard and Inoffensive Email Query**

Hi, my name is John Wells and I am looking for my high school sweetheart, Maureen Weber. I found your name while searching for her on the Internet and was wondering if you are she. If you are, let me refresh your memory a little about me. I played football for the Tigers at Weldon High School in Palm Beach, Florida. We went to school there from 1965 to 1969 and dated starting in 1968. We attended the senior prom together and had a blast. I lost touch with you when you moved to LA to attend UCLA in 1970.

Today, I live in Ft. Lauderdale, have two grown children, and I'm single. I would very much like to hear from you.

If you are the wrong Maureen, forgive my intrusion. You don't need to respond to my message. If you are the right Maureen, please write. If you don't wish to correspond with me for any reason, write me a brief note to that effect and I will respect your privacy.

Looking forward to hearing from "Morry,"

"Big" John Wells

---

Looking for family members takes a slightly different tone, but one that's similar in structure and content.

> ### Sample Query When Locating Family Members
>
> Hi, my name is Carry Wendt (maiden name Malden) and I am looking for my niece Marsha Lenta. I found your name while searching for her on the Internet and was wondering if you are she. If you are the right Marsha, you'll know that we grew up in the Seattle, WA, area and your parents are Bill and Mary Lenta. You lived across the lake from me in Seattle, and we had many days of fun hiking the woods and trails of what is now greater Bellevue.
>
> I would like to contact you to rediscover old times and invite you to the big family reunion next year.
>
> If you are the wrong Marsha, forgive my intrusion. You don't need to respond to my message. If you are the right Marsha, please write. If you don't wish to correspond with me for any reason, write me a brief note to that effect and I will respect your privacy.
>
> Looking forward to hearing from you!
>
> Carry

## MORE ON THE SEARCH TOOLS

Sometimes simple searches don't work. AOL, for example, won't show your name or reveal that you're a member unless you have created a profile. Also, for searches that look for email names only, John Smith may use the screen name of Gandalf the Dragon Slayer. There are other ways to find people, either for free or for a fee:

**Search membership directories.** The most useful are those of major online services such as Yahoo or any large online sites that offer free email.

**Search the Internet using relevant information.** A name changed in marriage may kill your search, but if you can find any relatives, then chances are you can find the person.

**Search the various online *White Pages*-type sites.** This is more or less like browsing through every phonebook in America at the speed of light.

## Should You Pay a Fee to Find a Friend?

You'll stumble across many banner ads on online services and the Web that offer to find long lost friends for you. With most, you will get one free simple search (a quick look at the most accessible databases). Anything else costs. The price depends on the thoroughness of the search. There may be more than one price, which escalates when nothing is found and you want to try a more advanced search with better tools. Is it worth the money? Yes, it can be. But before paying, take a little time to do your own searches on the net. The results you get for free may surprise you.

**Build your search around a profession or occupation.** A trip to Amazon.com or any of the large online book retailers will find someone in the blink of an eye. Of course, you may still have to send a letter through the organization in the hope that it will forward it for you because many organizations will not give out personal information directly.

**Use a search engine to find search tools.** Try using the phrase *finding people*. There are many more options available than we can discuss here.

**Use a people-finding engine.** Many companies have ties to large Internet providers that help you locate people.

**Use a people-finding engine that charges a fee.** For a nominal fee, the same companies mentioned previously will do a more expert search. Obviously the more current/correct data you can provide them, the better your chances of success.

**Use a people-finding service.** Priced higher than the above, these services will search all kinds of databases for your target. Even if the person does not use the Internet, you can still score a hit. Some offer a partial guarantee of success. Consider rates and service and warrantees before shelling out for this work.

## ASSEMBLING EMAIL MESSAGES FOR FAMILY AND FRIENDS

Assembling an email for people you know and trust is much easier than creating one in the pressure cooker that is the modern workplace. Generally you can say what you really mean, not worry too much about typos and grammar, and write either a brief or long letter. You don't have to look perfect as you do in business. Instead, most recipients will be glad to hear from you and will usually respond in kind.

The quality of keyboarding varies more among an informal crowd; yours may not be so good either. One aging relative we know spells every other word incorrectly because he types with two fingers and suffers from arthritis in his hands. Does it matter to us? No, we're pleased that he writes at all.

In addition to typing abilities, the knack for putting words in the right order depends upon education, native language, dialog, and many other factors. Your uncle Wilber from Louisiana may have quit school after the sixth grade in order to help with the family's fishing business. His writing may require significant deciphering to comprehend—as your Boston prep school English may to him.

## Getting Started

Writing to a friend or family member is relatively easy. Start by asking yourself these questions:

*What have I written in previous letters or otherwise communicated?*
No one wants to receive the same "news" twice. For example: You realize that you haven't written Gene in Denver recently, but was that before or after your promotion? Look it up on saved email or "read mail." (If you haven't already done so, remember to turn on the automatic save function!)
*What's important to this person?*
Aunt Beth who lives in Appalachia and believes in a back-to-nature approach to life (even though she has a computer and phone) may not be very interested in your purchase of a massive sports utility vehicle complete with onboard video for the kids and satellite communications.
*Does this person know the individual or events you're writing about?*
You're all excited about Alicia getting married and that you will be in the wedding. You plan to write to Gene since it's been too long since you answered his email. But, because Gene has never met or even heard of Alicia, you probably should keep your wedding news to a minimum.

*Would this email be better sent to an entire family group through an alias?*
You have some fresh news on the McCoys that Maynard Hatfield will surely want to know about. But, while writing the email, you realize that the information is pertinent to all of the Hatfields, not just Maynard. So use the family alias to better spread the word.

After you've done the "homework" described above, start to organize your thoughts into a list, like this one, for a letter to brother Gene:

1. My new job promotion
2. How we coped with the big storm and power outage
3. I really miss Grandma and think about her all the time
4. I really liked the jams
5. I think Gene should celebrate the holidays with our family this year
6. With the warm–so–far winter, I'm planning next year's garden. It's tomatoes or bust!
7. Look over Gene's last email and apologize for being slow to write

Once this step is done, write your letter, expanding on your outline. Essentially, you can pretty much write in any format with no restrictions on length, content, or anything else.

## A Sample Letter to Parents

Hi Mom and Dad,

Sorry it's been a while since I wrote, but my new job responsibilities are keeping me later at work these days. The routine is usually to drive home, feed the kids, watch something dull on TV, and then to bed. I haven't heard from Terrance much since our split, but his lawyer seems to be offering an amicable settlement. I just worry what the kids will think. I know this whole thing is hard on

*continued*

## A Sample Letter to Parents (continued)

them, and I feel guilty not spending more time at home. Jerry, being the youngest, seems to be having a tough time understanding where Papa is.

I'm hoping for some child support and alimony from T. so I can cut my workload to part-time. My boss, Ms. Buxley, seems amenable to the idea. I can stay in touch with the office by computer while keeping tabs on the kids. I'm using a new email program that beeps every time I get a new email message and with the ADSL line, I can stay online all the time while my phone still works for regular phone calls.

## Sample Email Between Teenage Friends

Hi Jennifer,

Check out the download on MP3.com for the latest *Sad Lovers and Giant's* release. It's amazing how these guys pack so much music into a single song. The download is free of course, but I went and paid for the whole disk. It was well worth it. I listen to it at home, in the car, and at work, and I'm still not getting tired of it. I can't understand how these guys are so popular in England but we hardly hear them over here except on U of R's station.

I bought the new Rio player. It works great with my Macintosh. Now I'm saving my Taco Bell money for a memory upgrade because I can't fit enough music on just one Smart Card. Anyway, check it out and let me know what you think.

D.

## A Formal Invitation Sent via Email

Dearest Jennifer,

It was so nice to receive your email. Still, I miss the beauty of your handwriting across the peach stationery you used to use. Today I'm writing on behalf of the local Alzheimer's Association. We in the Association are planning a fundraising ball in a private room at Leopold's on September 15 at 7:00 p.m. It will be a gala event and will include the fundraising auction of 90 donated Dali prints. It will be black tie, and a seven-course dinner will be served, with cuisine from the south of France. Please RSVP by August 31. I look forward to enjoying your gracious company again.

Diana Von Below

Chair, West Palm Beach Alzheimer's Benefit Association

## An Email Between Adult Friends

Thanks for sending the business cards. I may still need them, even though I recently started a full-time job at a downtown agency. It's been stressful, but I'm getting used to it. Today I finally got my own office and computer. I'm still waiting for a direct phone line.

My window looks down on a busy one-way street, and my view is filled with big buildings. If I lean over to my left, I can see a bit of the mountains.

Jerry and I are still an "item" as they say in the tabloids. He made dinner for me last night—chicken almondine. I was only an hour late for dinner. (Bad girl!)

How's the AA program going for you? I've lost my home group because I can't get to the noon meetings any more. I miss the group, and am having trouble getting to my usual 3-4 meetings a week. Yesterday I went to a noon group that meets at a church about six blocks away. They seem okay, but not my homies.

Love, Janis

If you're answering questions from a previous email, you can either do this as you would in a paper letter or use quoting, as introduced in an earlier chapter.

---

**Sample Reply**

Hi Alice,

It seems like we never get together anymore. With me in Denver and you in the Big Apple, our paths haven't crossed in FIVE YEARS. Do you believe it?! I'd like to come out to New York for the holidays, but it looks like Debbie's parents want us to come for Christmas and New Years again. As you know, I get a week off at Christmas and I was kind of hoping that Debbie and I could drop in to see you, then head south to Jamaica and get some sun. But, like last year, no such luck.

It's been a warm winter here by Denver standards. Most of the snow melted within an hour or so of falling. At least you don't have to shovel it! I talked to Mom last week. Sounds like her leg problems are getting better. I just wish she wasn't so stoic about taking pain medication. My doc told me that the vein work she had done hurts like you know what. I think she's getting up there in years to still be taking 10 mile walks everyday, but her doctor told her it was okay and would even help her legs heal.

Maybe next year we can all meet at Mom's for the holidays. To make it easy on her, we should book the Hyatt—it's only about two miles from her house. Maybe we can cook the big dinner too so that it's not too much work for her. Her email has hinted several times about coming up, but Debbie, being an only child, has parents with no other kids to spend it with. So off we go again to Houston. I just hope it doesn't pour all week like last year.

Well, it's getting late and I still have a few messages from work to respond to.

Love, Gene

---

If you use the quoting method in your reply, you can answer questions and comment on any sentences of the letter that require a response. Quoting is a powerful tool because it refreshes issues in the minds of both parties. Quoting in a personal letter is a bit different from doing it in business letters because a personal letter is much more free in form.

To use quoting:

- Select all or part of Gene's letter.
- Click reply in your email program. Gene's letter will appear in quoting style, as shown earlier in this book.
- Delete parts of the letter that do not need a response as you write.

---

**Sample Reply Using Quoting**

Hi Gene,

It's good to hear from you. Sorry I'm a little late writing, but my promotion (Yes, I finally got it!) has kept me immensely busy.

> It's been a warm winter here by Denver standards. Most of the
> snow has melted within an hour or so. At least you don't have to
> shovel it!

We've had a much warmer winter too. So far there's been few of those windy days with the cold blowing through the canyons downtown. I must say I like this more early spring kind of winter but this news of Greenland's icesheet melting has me more worried about global warming than ever.

> I talked to Mom last week. Sounds like her leg problems are
> getting better. I just wish she wasn't so stoic about taking pain
> medication. My doc told me that the vein work she had done hurts
> like you know what.

I don't think there's anything any of us can do to help Mom. She's as stubborn as ever and we just have to accept that. I talked to her too a couple of weeks ago and she told me that she's learned to ignore the pain. I don't know, maybe she has.

> ❯ Maybe next year we can all meet at Mom's for the holidays.
>
> Yes, next year sounds like we should do it. Debbie should prepare her parents for the idea early. Has she considered asking her parents to join us at Mom's place? That would be a real get-together. If it happens, I think we should provide all the meals. Either we should cook or take everyone out dutch (except for Mom). Maybe she can do breakfast so she feels like she's still in control of the kitchen and taking care of her guests.
>
> I'm off to do some preparatory gardening by cleaning out last year's clutter. It gets my mind off work. I'm going to try every New Yorker's dream: ripe tomatoes by July 4th. I know it's hopeless, but I have to try. I will start the plants indoors this year. Right now, I'm just going to turn the soil since there's no snow and the ground's softer than usual. It's funny how the weeds seem to grow even in the winter.
>
> Say hi to Debbie and Ted for me.
>
> Love & XXX, Alice

Add attachments, if any, to the message. You can attach pictures, articles, web site addresses (URLs), and clippings from online news sources. The only restriction is that the recipient must be able to open the attachment as described in Chapter 3.

When you are all done creating your message, proofread it and send it on its way. As you would expect, some people will respond almost instantly. Others might take weeks because they are (a) very busy, or (b) don't like letter writing and/or computers.

## THE BROADCAST EMAIL MESSAGE

Broadcast messages are a little different from regular email. There are two kinds of broadcast email for friends and family: messages created for broadcast and messages forwarded as broadcast mail with or without annotation.

A newsy broadcast message is just that: It contains important (or not so important news) that a group of friends and family will like to receive. Much like

## Keeping Your Broadcast on Target

When rereading your broadcast email for errors, make sure it contains no information inappropriate to any recipients. For example, you wouldn't want to insert
the following in the middle of a general family broadcast message:

"Oh, and John, I've got the fishing lures we talked about. I've used all kinds of
lures and jigs and had some luck with them, but nothing comes close to the
Gramme lures. Sometimes simple is better. I've used them for snook, redfish,
cobia, trout, pompano, jacks, ladyfish, bluefish, mackerel, king mackerel, grouper
and snapper."

This aside should be sent separately so as not to confuse readers. Most, with
the exception of John, would stop reading the message at this point.

those Christmas letters that some people love to hate, most broadcast messages
contain good news, although they can also be used to pass on information about
the condition of someone in the hospital. (*Never* use one to announce someone's
death!)

Like all friends and family email, the broadcast message can be as brief or as
long as you like. People, especially shut-ins or those who receive little mail, often
like broadcast letters because it helps them to feel less lonely.

Another kind of broadcast email is the much dreaded chain letter, mentioned
earlier. There is also a segment of the e-world that forwards jokes that have been
forwarded to them. All too often you'll discover that several of your friends
or family are addicted to these and will jam your mailbox with humor
that wouldn't make a second grader giggle. Since the sender usually means
well, it's hard to explain that you don't want to receive any more of these
thigh-slappers.

But if the "laffs" are coming from a sender whom you don't know, use your
email program's blocking mechanism to zap the jokes before you ever see them. Or
write a polite note to the sender asking to be removed from his or her mailing list.

## Online Relationships, Warm and Cool

Even among friends and family, the tone of email messages changes with various sets of correspondents. With some, an intimate exploration of feelings is fun and time well spent. With others, messages may seem more like form letters than personal notes. This can happen for several reasons:

- Your pen pal may be (rightly) paranoid about a significant other or employer reading the mail. Most companies allow the sending and receipt of personal email at work, but that doesn't guarantee against someone in Security reading and filing your messages. Or a bored sy-sop may read the flotsam and jetsam that crosses his electronic port and find something you'd rather he didn't see.

- Some people lack writing skills. If you know this to be the case, you might want to lend them a copy of this book.

- Some pen pals are very busy and writing only a few cursory lines to you may take all the time they have. This may leave you feeling that the person doesn't really care about you, but try the telephone before jumping to any conclusions.

- Some people are more emotional than others. You may find that while one person communicates on an intimate basis, another may not simply because she's more reserved or less verbal than you are.

- Some pen pals simply aren't that attached to you. They may not want to write a three-page letter in response to your emotional twenty-pager.

Don't take it as a brush-off should you receive no response at all from someone. Give the person a second chance. If after a few weeks, you still do not hear, copy your message into a new email and preface it with something like the following:

Dear Biggles, I haven't heard back from you on my last letter. Assuming that you are either busy or simply never received my correspondence, I have enclosed it below. I look forward to continuing our online letters.

Laura

[Insert copy of previous letter here]

# CHAPTER NINE

# Putting Yourself Across Romantically

FEEL LIKE A NINETY-POUND WEAKLING who can't pick up "chicks"? Bitterly divorced and unable to trust men? Live in snowy Cleveland and looking for a date in sunny California? Say goodbye to singles bars, lonely hearts clubs, and blind dates arranged by your Aunt Agatha. This section will help you find that special someone in the place where technology and romance meet: online.

## SELF-TEST: YOUR ONLINE SKILLS AT ROMANCE

The following is a simple diagnostic test. Its purpose is help you gauge how effectively you communicate with prospective partners through the online medium. For the most part, you will find it easy to guess the "right" answer. But getting the right answer is not the point of the test. Respond honestly, even if you feel your response is not the best one possible. This is not a contest. The goal is solely self-inventory:

|  | True | False |
|---|---|---|
| 1. I communicate effectively online. | ___ | ___ |
| 2. I compose email messages without much effort. | ___ | ___ |
| 3. I use email frequently because I feel comfortable with the medium. | ___ | ___ |
| 4. I feel comfortable in a chatroom environment. | ___ | ___ |
| 5. I feel comfortable discussing personal matters online. | ___ | ___ |
| 6. I have online friends whom I never met in person. | ___ | ___ |
| 7. In my email, I have no trouble saying what I mean. | ___ | ___ |
| 8. I am comfortable flirting online. | ___ | ___ |
| 9. I keep an electronic address book with notes with people I meet online. | ___ | ___ |
| 10. I know how to do Internet searches and choose the best keywords. | ___ | ___ |
| 11. I know what to say when someone instant messages me. | ___ | ___ |
| 12. I know how to make my electronic communication more personal than I'd use at work. | ___ | ___ |
| 13. I have fast communications access (better than 56K bps). | ___ | ___ |
| 14. I use a different screen name or user ID when in chatrooms. | ___ | ___ |
| 15. My personal user profile is posted on the services/sites I use. | ___ | ___ |
| 16. I regularly update my personal user profile to reflect changes in my life. | ___ | ___ |
| 17. When online, I protect my physical address and my intimate personal information. | ___ | ___ |
| 18. I am comfortable chatting or emailing people who can't write as well as I can. | ___ | ___ |
| 19. I am comfortable chatting or emailing people who are better writers than I am. | ___ | ___ |
| 20. I'm a fast "keyboardist." | ___ | ___ |
| 21. When using chat, I am comfortable participating. | ___ | ___ |

**22.** When using chat, I feel comfortable with the banter
when it involves me.  ____  ____

**23.** I consider chat as a recreational choice, like attending
a movie.  ____  ____

**24.** I use the World Wide Web for business and/or pleasure.  ____  ____

**25.** I feel comfortable and experienced using the web.  ____  ____

Score 1 for each *true* response, 0 for *false.*

Total 1 – 25 ____

## What It Means to You

This test is a quick way to personally evaluate your comfort and experience with online communication. Look at your total score. If it is:

**18 or higher.** you are probably comfortable online up close, and personal.

**17 or lower.** you are not fully comfortable with romance online and this chapter can help you.

**WORDS TO USE FOR ONLINE ROMANCE**

| | | |
|---|---|---|
| attraction | hope | rose |
| attractive | hug | smooth |
| caress | ingratiating | soft |
| care | invite | softly |
| caring | inviting | subtle |
| charm | kiss | sweet |
| charmed | lasting | think |
| clarity | likes | thinking |
| clear | love | thought |
| commitment | loving | thoughtful |
| complete | me | touch |
| consider | mine | trust |
| dedication | move | understand |
| delicate | movement | understanding |
| desire | moving | undying |
| devote | my | want |
| devoted | need | wanted |
| devotee | needs | warm |
| devotion | notion | warmth |
| elegant | passion | whisper |
| fancy | passionate | wish |
| flower | petal | you |
| fond | precious | your |
| fondness | pretty | yours |
| forever | quiet | youth |
| fresh | reach | youthful |
| glow | realize | |
| grace | rewarding | |

## PHRASES FOR ONLINE ROMANCE

a commitment

a soft place in cyberspace

can we be alone

cherish you

come together

excite me

I love you

I would love to

I've never felt so

it's so romantic

just for now

let's not forget

missed you

missing you

more than just words

my feelings

my passion

my world

quality time

sincerely feel that

special place

thanks for

thinking of you

this will be fun

throughout time

time alone

want you

warm my

warmth and comfort

when I see you

when I'm near you

when we're together

would you like to

you make me so

you're my

you're so different

you're so special

you're so wonderful

your feelings

your passion

your insight

your words are

your world

your space

**WORDS TO AVOID FOR ONLINE ROMANCE**

| | | |
|---|---|---|
| cheat | insensitive | sick |
| cheated | jerk | split |
| clod | lesson | stupid |
| cold | lie | thoughtless |
| dumb | line | tough |
| experiment | luck | trapped |
| fast | mess | ugly |
| fault | miserable | unappreciated |
| fear | never | undecided |
| final | no | unloved |
| gone | nope | useless |
| harsh | non-negotiable | waiting |
| heavy | pick-up | won't |
| hopeless | quick | worthless |
| ignored | quit | wrong |
| impotent | rough | |
| inadequate | scratchy | |

## PHRASES TO AVOID FOR ONLINE ROMANCE

absolutely not

at no time

can't be fixed

doesn't thrill me

I demand

I don't deserve this

I insist

it's too bad

never will I

no way

not my problem

not ready

nothing in common

save your compliments

take a chance

that's final

there's a problem

tired of it

what the hell

where I'm coming from

won't work

you can't

you don't appreciate me

you must

you should

you won't

you're full of

you're insensitive

## First Impressions

As on any first date, the first impression you make online can be lasting. Here's some succinct and sage advice on how to make sure that you make a good one.

**Men:** Be direct and don't pretend that you can financially support a family of 40 progeny.

**Women:** honestly describe your physical characteristics.

"BUT . . ." you object, "what if he or she doesn't like my looks or my bank account?" Well, that's good information to have. If your would-be partner considers money and looks as prerequisites for a relationship, look elsewhere for a more mature mate. Looks can fade and money can disappear. You don't want a partner who will disappear with them.

## IS ONLINE ROMANCE FOR YOU?

Online romance has been around since the first modems brought computers together. Today there are millions of people online, a sizable percentage of whom are looking for significant others or just a date. Many, barely computer literate, log on every night (and day) looking for that elusive Romeo or Juliet. In fact, according to

## The Online Masquerade Ball

People who have a huge amount of time to spend in chatrooms lack either a) a life, or b) a reasonable expectation of meeting someone in a more personal manner. There may be good reasons for *b*, which you will have the potentially difficult task of discovering before moving into a more serious phase. All kinds of subterfuge are possible and common. A recent newspaper article on Internet addiction introduced a 54-year-old woman who pretends to be any sex or age in order to chat nasty online. Her husband allows her to continue the 18+ hours a day because, even though he intensely misses her companionship, no one knows what to do about it. Bottom line: BE CAREFUL!

## Taking Little Steps

Making contact is just the first phase of romance, like you didn't know that! That first meeting may be little more than a casual chat, which may or may not turn into instant messaging between just the two of you. The next step is usually email. Letters give you a chance to stretch comfortably and really get to know the person on the other end. What was important but left out of your initial contact through chat or an ad can be added to the picture here.

National Public Radio, America Online, with its millions of users, is like an online meat market for picking up more than just a flank steak. The Internet is an even broader arena, although learning the chat routine and finding useful URLs (addresses) takes more work than AOL's easy interface does.

Seeking romance online is just as dicey as finding a mate through conventional channels. You're dealing with an unknown quantity who might be (and we hate typing this phrase as much as you dislike reading it) *your soul mate*. Or an axe murderer. The other party has equally meager information about you.

To make matters even more difficult, chatting or exchanging email is less personal than a phone call. And the words you type could push the wrong buttons and terminate a relationship before you even realized anything had happened.

It's also possible that your would-be date has problems keeping up with you. He or she may rely on a 9600 bps modem or be limited by hunt-and-peck typing. Any unintended slowness can strangle intimate talks or make you question your intended's competency.

In the interest of a possible match made in heaven, you have to work within these limitations. Otherwise, log off and try your luck with last week's singles ads.

## KEEPING THE COMPUTER OUT OF THE RELATIONSHIP

If you're an observant reader (and of course you are), you have noticed that this section's "How to Say It" lists contain absolutely no computer jargon. That's because the language of love is *never* technical. Unless you are looking for relationships with

> ## A Hot Tip for Hot Romance
>
> Should your intended be suffering from obvious comm problems or lack of technical knowledge, this is a great opportunity to ask for a phone number so you can assist in a more "one-on-one" fashion. But if he or she doesn't want to give out a number, don't push the issue. Once again, trust online can take a long time to develop.

computer programmers or engineers, techie boorishness will lose your sweetheart's interest as fast as a supercomputer. Chat or email with phrases like "I got you in my relational database *baby*!" annoys even the computer literate. Just because your would-be amour uses a computer doesn't mean he or she wants to go out with the motherboard.

## THE TWO PHASES OF ONLINE CHATROOM COURTSHIP

There are two phases to online courtship, just like real-world relationships. First you have to find someone and then you have to do the wooing. Finding someone can be as simple as spending time in chatrooms trying to separate the wheat from the chaff. Or it may take considerable time, especially if you're new to dating (again) or looking in the wrong places.

### Finding People in Chatrooms

When you first start looking for a love connection, the first option that occurs to most people is the chatroom. Be prepared for a variety of chat styles and the fact that many rooms are useless for anything but idle chatter. Read the real thread below (names have been changed). Frankly, you might have better luck with a message in a bottle:

| | |
|---|---|
| user1: | *where da ladies at* |
| user2: | <~ fine azz lady |
| user3: | It's so quiet in here . . . |
| user1: | ami awake? |

| user4: | *hey what's up cutie* |
| user1: | can any woman wake me up? |
| user3: | why is everyone so quiet? |
| user2: | chillin |
| user5: | *that's cool* |
| user6: | ygm |
| user4: | *so do u have a pic* |
| user7: | NE GUYS WANNA CHAT WITH A HOT GIRL |
| user2: | trying to talk to ya |
| user3: | what's going on cutie |
| user2: | check mail cutie |
| user4: | *cutie u rrrrrrrr damn prettyyyyyyyyyyyyy* |
| user8: | sorry bigbubba |
| user7: | i only accept pics from hott guys |

Pretty exciting? As you get better at locating chatrooms containing more interesting people, however, you'll learn how to avoid getting stuck in a room like this.

Once you've located a chatroom you like, it's usually best to watch the proceedings to see who's saying what. If you're lucky enough to own a large monitor, you may want to have more than one chat open at a time, though this can get awkward and confusing.

## Wooing People in Chatrooms

When you decide it's time to jump into the fray, try the following:

### 1. Introduce yourself briefly:

"Hi everybody! I'm Jan from Toledo."

You may or may not get a bunch of "hi Jans." In a very busy room, you may get little or no response at all.

If you're especially bold, you can try a more up-front approach:

"Hi I'm Jan from Ft. Lauderdale. I'm 42 and a divorced mother of two looking for a permanent relationship. Anyone here interested in a long term, committed relationship with a warm, attractive woman from Florida?"

The second approach works better in some chat environments than others. But it does work sometimes. It opens the door for shy males who may not know how to approach a woman. If males attempt this, it may put off the wallflowers, but other women appreciate a no BS attitude.

Another approach is to look for people with common interests:

"Hi! I'm Jan from Ft. Lauderdale. I'm looking for a special guy to go on treasure hunting trips with me in the waters off Florida. Anyone here interested?"

In chat, what's most important is to make yourself available, visible, and desirable (in some form) without giving away the farm. You want to find romance but not have some emotional basket case latch onto you and your email address.

For this reason, many romance chatrooms allow you to use multiple IDs, and they don't check to see whether Sally is really Joe. This protects you somewhat because you can take on a new name as needed since you are allowed to employ a pseudonym separate from your regular email address.

2. **Watch for a while to see who is there and who sounds intriguing.** Most chatrooms have the names of participants on screen in a separate window. You may be able to look up a brief profile for anyone who sounds interesting to find out more information. (Never assume that profile information is true.)

3. **Respond to questions if possible.** Pay special attention to those posed by people whose profiles sound interesting or who chat well on screen. This begins a dialog that can lead to more in-depth conversation, possibly separate from the chatroom.

## Jo? Would That Be Joseph or Josephine?

If you are looking for romance, it helps to use a screen name that appropriately represents your sex. "Janice" says more than just "Jan" and chatroomies will have to inquire as to the gender of Lk2e2228—if they bother to at all.

## Invitation to the Chat

Private chat is one of the best ways to get to know someone, but sometimes people are hesitant about doing it. Show sensitivity in your request, and accept "no" for an answer, if that's the other person's choice. To increase your chances of getting a "yes," learn from this sample IM script, in which Ken invites Elizabeth to a private chat:

[While still in the chatroom and with others messaging interlaced but not shown.]

Kenb: Elizabeth, I'd like to know more about you. Can we chat privately so that there aren't so many messages interrupting our conversation?

Elizabeth12: I guess so, but I'm not sure how to do it.

Kenb: It's easy. Just click the Private Chat button. I'll open a room called ken-sroom. In the box that appears, type that name and click OK. Okay?

Elizabeth12: Okay.

[Using instant messaging or communicating in a private room.]

Kenb: Are you there, Elizabeth?

Elizabeth: Hi, Ken. This is easier than I thought.

Kenb: So you went to my alma mater. When did you graduate?

4. **If you get a dialog started, consider going to instant message mode.** Or, better still, he or she may ask you to do the same. In IM mode, you can have a private conversation away from the chatroom.

   Note: Someone who requests Hot Chat wants to discuss sex explicitly, *not* romance. You can accept or decline, but assume that little in the way of real romance will come your way.

5. **Exchange email addresses.** If after a long and rewarding IM session you're still interested in the person, and geography or other factors don't preclude a relationship, you'll want to correspond. You should also request a picture to be sent electronically and offer one in return. *But don't give out your physical address until you know a lot more about the person!*

## OTHER ONLINE HOT SPOTS

Romance chatrooms are not the only place to meet people online. Public forums are also good bets. You can choose a forum discussion common to your interests. Other participants will then have at least something in common with you and the "quality" of people will be several cuts above the chatroom variety. Many are people who never visit chatrooms.

"I saw your posting on [subject] and I wanted to respond personally because it appears that we have a common interest."

Assuming your target doesn't log off, repeat your query in about three minutes, in case it was missed for whatever reason. If there's no response or a negative one, try someone else, or, better still, move on to another forum.

In addition to forums, there are many online clubs. AOL, for example, has dozens catering to almost every interest. While many of these club chat areas don't look much better than regular chatroom chatter, some are populated by serious-minded individuals looking for help with a problem, offering advice, or seeking camaraderie.

Another possibility is to respond to threads in newsgroups or bulletin boards. This may be a waste of time, because postings are often ignored for months, but you can try writing directly to the person, since email addresses are usually visible in these venues. Keep your email message brief, enough to intrigue but not so much as to saturate your target with too much information:

"I saw your posting on snakes and I wanted to respond personally because it appears that we have a common interest in herpetology. I've presented several papers on the subject and I'm interested in your research in the field also . . ."

## More Love than You're Looking For

When responding to an address that sounds promising, i.e., chatrooms for singles, be prepared to receive more than you bargained for. Some links will take you to pornographic sites or to people looking for activities you have no interest in. Don't give up. Instead, keep looking for quality sites. You can even ask other people online for site recommendations.

"I saw your posting on [subject] and I wanted to respond personally because it appears that we have a common interest in mountain biking. I plan to participate in the all-state finals this year and I assume you will be there too . . ."

## THE WEB: A FINE PLACE FOR A RENDEZVOUS

Yet another option for finding romance is the World Wide Web itself. Some sites offer listings, descriptions, and even pictures of people. Some are free, some charge a fee. On many sites, you can find fairly complete, even honest information on each romance seeker.

The best sites are often those that charge a fee. Additional depth and richness of personality, likes and dislikes will appear along with a picture, and applicants are more closely scrutinized before being allowed to post their info.

Last, there are online matchmakers. These services tend to be the most expensive, and we suggest you check recommendations carefully before handing over a large enrollment fee and signing any kind of monthly contract charge. Be especially careful of any site that automatically debits your credit card each month.

One final caution about web sites: look for sites that are updated regularly or you may find yourself talking to the new spouse of someone whose ad went up in 1997.

## WRITING YOUR OWN PERSONALS AD

Creating a personals ad of your own to post on a web site is a tough task. How do you make your ad stand out from the others without sounding like an oddball, or in the case of sites that charge by the word, sounding like someone worth contacting without breaking the bank? Fortunately, unlike newspaper singles ads, net ad space providers tend to be more generous about length and the inclusion of a photo, and there's no extra charge for a bold headline. The abbreviations that dominate newspaper ads can be done away with, although most ads still begin with DWF or similar.

Before writing your ad, study the sites and choose the ones that look good for your particular needs and interests. Sites that have no obvious recent updating are out, as are those created for seniors if you're in your twenties.

## TIPS ON WRITING ADS

Demonstrate your assets: For example, it is much more effective to use humor in your ad rather than just to say, "I have a sense of humor." Use interesting word choice, clear ad structure, and colorful and creative descriptions. Here are some other tips that can help.

**Make yourself look your best.** If writing isn't your strongest skill but the ads on the site tend to be well written, ask a friend who can write to help. At the least, run your ad by a friend of the sex you are pursuing to get another take on it as well.

**Be creative.** A well-written ad should be succinct and convey a feeling of your personality. But that doesn't mean it should be straightforward and dull. Use strong, romantic terms to describe yourself. Or consider writing the ad as a poem or sonnet. Just don't overdo it.

**Tell them what they want to know.** What's important to you when reading someone else's ad—i.e. the person's age, employment status and field, kids, interests, etc.—is useful in composing your own ad.

**Be specific, but reasonable.** If you must give ranges for age, for example, don't make it unlikely that anyone will fit your stated requirements. "I'm 42 and looking for someone 35 to 50" will probably net more responses than "I'm 42 and looking for someone from 41 to 43." Too broad doesn't work either. "I'm 42 and looking for someone 18 to 60" sounds as if you're either desperate or completely undiscriminating.

**Let them know more about you.** Generally, the person placing the ad describes himself or herself so that readers can look for a match. Creating an ad that is little more than a list of your demands for the other person puts readers off. Don't sound overly picky or conceited.

**Add richness to your ad.** A personal ad that states, "I like long walks, movies, and dining out" describes millions of people. Instead, add detail to make your ad more intriguing and unique. "I enjoy walking in the woods after a summer rain, the excitement of lining up to be the first to see a hot new movie, and the zest of the cuisine of southern Spain" makes your ad stand out from the crowd.

**Avoid abbreviations if possible.** Unless space is severely limited (i.e., you are charged by the word) avoid abbreviations. They slow down readers. Also, while everyone can figure out that *SWF* is an abbreviation for *single white female,* not everyone knows that *ISF* means *is searching for.*

**Be honest about yourself and your wants.** Describe yourself as others see you, and explain what you are looking for in a relationship.

Personal ads are, well, personal. You can make almost any demand and misrepresent yourself as much as you feel comfortable with. Study ads on various sites for word choice and to determine which ads sound compelling. Keep in mind that men's ads often focus on different things from those of women. This is also true of gay ads and those seeking friendship. It's said that women often misrepresent their weight and men tend to make themselves taller in personal ads. Men also tend to be a bit flakier in real life than they seem in the ads they write.

Being up front about yourself and the characteristics of the person you seek helps avoid disappointments down the road.

## WHERE SHOULD YOU ADVERTISE?

You should carefully choose not only which words you use but also where you post them. Some singles' sites are exclusively sexual or for "special interests," such as one we uncovered for men in search of wives who will put up with polygamy. Placing an ad on these kinds of sites in a shotgun approach to marketing yourself may net responses from people you'd rather not hear from.

When choosing a site for an ad, look for:

- Ads placed by people with whom you seem compatible.
- Requirements for placement, including fees and membership.
- Special interest placement. There are, for example, sites that cater by geographic location, religious preference, sexual orientation, etc. All you have to do is hunt them down with a search engine.
- Additional services: In addition to ad placement, some sites offer special services. These include everything from professional (or amateur) matchmaking to members only chatrooms.
- Traffic volume. If you must pay more than a nominal fee to post or browse on a site, you'll want some guarantee by the site's owners that it's seen by the kind of people you're looking for. You're within your rights querying the sy-sop with its Contact Us button.

## What Price Romance?

It's common for both pay and free sites to sell demographic (personal) information they collect from you. A long membership application that asks for questions like income level is often a giveaway. Some sites say they will never sell your name, but still do. So beware: the price of love may end up being a mailbox so full of spam that you'll have to change your email address.

You will likely want to place your ad on more than one site to increase visibility. Keep in mind that some rewriting may be necessary for space reasons or because a site caters to a specialty market. Your ad can also be placed on message boards, usually for free.

## HOW LONG SHOULD YOUR AD BE?

You can make your ad as long as the allowable length where you post it. But even on sites that allow long ads, it's better to get to the point succinctly rather than being verbose.

---

### Sample Brief Personal Ad

**SBM Looking for a Commitment**

SBM, (widowed) 40 something and financially secure, looking for someone who enjoys the ocean, vacations to tropical islands, and is free to travel. Any age/weight. Looking for someone with poise, intelligence, and charm. Reply to matchmaker@home.com/personals/kevinc. All queries responded to.

---

## Sample Longer Personal Ad

### Widowed Guy Looking for New Relationship

Widowed black male (SBM) 44, alone for one year, looking for permanent relationship (including possible marriage) with SBF age 40 to 50. Me: mature, balding, nonsmoker who loves to travel and relax on tropical beaches in the middle of nowhere. Financially secure with job in the government sector. Looking for someone with like interests to share my life. Send photo. Nonsmoker preferred. All replies answered. Reply to matchmaker@home.com/personals/kevinc.

## Sample Long-Format Personal Ad

### Desperately Seeking Ms. Right After One Year of Widowhood

Widowed black male (SBM) 44, alone for one year, looking for permanent relationship (including possible marriage) with SBF age 40 to 50. You: Mature, likes nights on the town as much as those spent at home in front of the fireplace with a book. I have two grown kids so yours won't be a problem for me as I miss my family life. You'll be my best friend for life, and I will be yours. I am looking for a best friend to spoil and be spoiled by. I want to meet someone who enjoys life to its fullest. Me: mature, balding, nonsmoker who loves to travel and relax on tropical beaches in the middle of nowhere. Other hobbies include snorkeling, photography, and enjoying old movies. Financially secure with job in the government sector. Looking for someone with like interests to share my life. Send photo. I prefer a slim or petite body shape but you don't have to be a "ten" on the outside. You should, however, be a "ten" on the inside. Nonsmoker preferred. All replies answered. Reply to matchmaker@home.com/personals/kevinc.

## THE PHOTO

If you're allowed to include a photo, by all means do so. This takes some of the "blind" out of blind dates. Consider having the photo shot professionally, with you looking casual, but neatly dressed and hair done/trimmed appropriately. An overly formal or extremely stylized image may detract from the real you. The photo should stand out a little from the others on the ad site, but not like a sore thumb. Never use an old picture of yourself. Your suitor may be markedly put off when he or she meets you and you look 25 years older than the picture you used.

Convert the photo into the format and size requested by the site. If you don't know how to do this, ask your photographer, the site operator, or a friend for help. You'll want your picture to show you off rather than appearing too light or dark, out of focus, or poorly posed.

## HOW TO ASSEMBLE THE PERFECTLY ROMANTIC AD

Your ad must accomplish two things: Define you in a manner that motivates a reader to respond, and specify the kind of person you're looking for so fewer inappropriate people contact you. Your ad should contain:

- A headline (Looking for love in Madison, WI).
- A key description of yourself, if appropriate, to get your ad into the right place in the listings. (DWF 28, blond, blue eyes.)
- A description of yourself and key interests. (I'm 45, enjoy walking in the woods after a summer rain, the excitement of lining up to be the first one to see a hot new movie, and the zest of the cuisine of southern France.)
- A description of what you're looking for. (You should be 35 to 50 years old, a college-educated professional who likes to laugh out loud, and have no dependents. Prefer someone who is a nonsmoker/non-drinker.)
- Contact information which varies according to where you place your ad. Interested parties may email you directly or you may receive blind responses handled by a site's mail system.
- A list of your characteristics and another of those you desire from ad respondents. This exercise will help you choose what's important and separate it

from secondary considerations. Cross out everything that you don't consider primary about you and the person you seek.

■ A place for your ad noting any length or content requirements.

After you've done that much, write answers to the following questions based on your lists:

■ What makes me different from other people?
*Example:* I like quiet time alone.
■ What makes me the same as other people?
*Example:* I'm a Lakers fan and must see every game.
■ What am I looking for in a person who is the same as me?
*Example:* I want someone who appreciates my time alone and doesn't hassle me about it.
■ What am I looking for in a person who's different from me?
*Example:* I want someone who's bright and cheery to keep me up on down days.

Now, assemble a headline for your ad from your answers. Make it positive and intriguing.

*Example:* Lakers Lady Looking for Love

On paper, draw three large boxes to divide your ad into three parts. Add the headline to the top of the page and contact information under the third box. Then:

■ From your answers write about yourself in box #1.
*Example:* I currently have a rich, full life, and am interested in finding a partner with whom to share it. I have a career that I love which is continually interesting and brings me joy. I tend to be curious and love to learn, and am passionate about environmental causes and human rights. I also require quiet time alone for thinking and meditation.
■ Write about who you're looking for in box #2.
*Example:* I am looking for someone who has a life: friends, a satisfying career, varied interests, and a good sense of himself. My wish list also includes someone who is a good communicator, is silly & playful, and who enjoys sharing himself—his thoughts, feelings, dreams and wants.

■ Write a conclusion about yourself and what you want from the relationship. Add any key points not covered earlier in the ad. (One ad of a female looking for a male ominously ends, "No job? Then don't bother to write.")
*Example:* I'm drawn toward color in my life, literally as well as figuratively, and live with a bold, rich palette of colors in my home. If this sounds like you, I'd love to hear from you! I have an active social life with a varied circle of friends, and am now wanting to add a special partner to my life.

Review your ad before submission. You should rewrite it a couple of times to improve readability and adjust its length if necessary. Then put the ad away for a day or two and reread all three versions of it. Choose the one that reads best and describes your attributes and your desires adequately. Consider having a friend read it too. Last, proof it carefully for typos before sending it off.

## A WEB SITE FOR MORE INFORMATION

One other tool available to you is your own web site. Having a site up and running can expand an interested party's knowledge quickly. All you need provide is the address, which can be passed on in ads, email, newsnets, other sites, and during chat sessions. You can use the site to make a personal impression with information and pictures about yourself. Or you can refer people to a professional page on another site, should you have one. A bio page on the site of an impressive company or institution makes you stand out among the crowd.

## GETTING MORE PERSONAL

Whether you've met someone through a chat room, newsgroup, or personals ad on a web site, the next obvious step to take is getting to know someone in more depth.

That usually involves multiple private chat sessions and email flying back and forth. Even for someone located geographically close to you, you'll want to learn more about that person before you arrange a physical meeting. Repeated chat sessions are a good way to do this. The content of these sessions can go in any direction, and they provide an ideal way to explore someone's interests and thoughts.

Beyond chat, or along with it, is electronic messaging. Email is a useful tool for getting to know the other party in depth. You can exchange details on interests, family, employment, likes and dislikes, etc. You can ask personal questions about the other party's previous relationships and provide information on your own.

## ASSEMBLING YOUR FIRST ROMANTIC EMAIL

Your first email message to your intended should be newsy about yourself and answer any outstanding questions the other person may still have about you.

A long letter is okay, but you should be confident that the recipient wants to know that much about you before sending along 1000+ words. Save your own questions until the end of the letter, so the reader doesn't lose them within the text. It's best to send this message on a day when your recipient is away from work or school. That way, it might be read at his or her leisure, instead of chancing a quick scan on the fly.

Here's how to create your letter in five easy steps:

1. **Reintroduce yourself.** Your message should remind the other person of where you met, your name, and any other curiosities that will make you stand out in case someone else has his or her ear too:
   *Example:* Hi Toby,
   We met last night in the Apollo site chat room. I just wanted to tell you a little more about myself. I'm the one who lives in Boston with the animation studio.
2. **Make a list of important points about yourself.** Consider what's important to you about yourself that you would like to share with your new friend. If you disclosed much of this information in an ad or long online chats, repeat only the key points.
   *Example:* My 1984 back injury that keeps me out of most sports.
3. **Make a list of what you know about the other person.** List out what you know about the other person that's important to you (that you find favorable).
   *Example:* We're both of the same religion.
4. **From that process, make a (hopefully) shorter list about what you don't like.**
   *Example:* When we were chatting, he mentioned he had an ex-wife.

**5. Assemble your message from your lists.** Here's how:

- Add the "reintroduction," address the message, and add a simple subject line like, "Message from SheilaB."
- Write about yourself, filling in the gaps in the information you have already provided. Expand if necessary on key points the other person has already been made aware of.
- Write about what you both have in common.
- Add questions about the other person to learn more about him or her and to clarify points that sound like potential negatives for a relationship.
- End your message with an encouragement to write back as soon as possible.

Reread your message before sending it off. You should rewrite it a couple of times to improve readability and adjust its length if necessary. Consider having a friend read it too. Last, proof it carefully for typos before sending it off. Print it if possible so it's easier to proof.

## REMEMBER, TALK IS CHEAP . . .

Online romance demands a mix of strategically good timing, your great personality, and the luck of the draw. The good news is that, as mentioned before, a huge number of global users are looking for love—certainly more than you'd ever meet in Des Moines joining church groups. And with what you know now, finding the person you're looking for should be a snap. So good luck in your search! Remember, as the Beatles used to sing, "All you need is love."

# CHAPTER TEN

# Putting Yourself Across to Clients and Customers

IF YOU'RE A SUCCESSFUL BUSINESSPERSON, you know the old rule that says "it's easier to keep an existing customer than to find a new one." In online customer relationships, this rule is just as important. When using online communications with customers, your goal should be not only to get new customers, but to cultivate your customer base to yield repeat sales and referrals from satisfied purchasers.

Besides a good product or service, there are only three things you need for successful online customer interactions: strong communication, common courtesy, and exemplary customer service. Unfortunately, these old-fashioned values are often missing in many companies' online promotional communications.

## A QUIZ ON YOUR ONLINE CUSTOMER HANDLING STYLE

Here's a little quiz to see how good you are already at online customer and client communications:

1. *When someone responds to "info@yourcompany.com," how soon do you answer with a personal-sounding email (not an automated response)?*
   Same business day, 3 points
   Next business day, 2 points
   Anything longer or never, 0 points

2. *How do you address your customers in your emails?*
   Not at all ("The price is..."), 0 points
   Informally ("Dear Jane"), 1 point
   Generically ("Greetings"), 2 points
   Formally ("Dear Ms. Smith"), 3 points

   Not including any salutation is cold. Using a first name, while acceptable to some, risks turning off others who don't like such presumed familiarity. A safe middle ground, especially if you don't know the gender of the recipient, is a simple "Greetings." (Remember the examples earlier in the book, where Kim, for example, can be both a female's name and a male's. Don't offend if you don't know for sure.) If you are sure of the gender, however, most people prefer a traditional greeting like "Dear Mr. Jones" when hearing from a company. Do the best you can with the information you have on the customer and send a salutation that won't offend.

3. *How do you sign your email to customers?*
   Anonymously (Wonka Roller Service Department), 1 point
   With a real person's name, 2 points
   With a real person's name and a toll-free phone number, 3 points

   People don't want to do business with WonkaRoller.com, they want to do business with Jack Johnson at WonkaRoller.com. When you give someone a name and phone number, you are establishing a human relationship, and that's what business is all about.

**4.** *What percent of your company's emails to customers and prospects is totally free of spelling, punctuation and capitalization errors before they're sent?*
100 percent, 3 points
Anything less, 0 points

   The quality of your grammar reflects on the quality and intelligence of your company, and no one wants to do business with low quality companies (or stupid ones, for that matter).

**5.** *When was the last time you updated a page on your Web site?*
This week, 3 points
Last month, 1 point
Anything longer, 0 points

   If you're not posting and updating dynamic information on your Web site (for example, feature articles, press releases, information directories, event listings, product or business tips, newsletters, and relevant trade show and seminar schedules) you're not giving customers reasons to return to your site. (You'll learn more about ways to get repeat web site visitors later in this chapter.)

**6.** *Where does your company's address and phone number appear on your Web site?*
On the home page and a contact page, 3 points
Just on a contact page, 2 points
It doesn't, 0 points

   The company address should be easy to find. If it isn't, you're missing interactions from both media representatives who could write about your company and customers who simply want to know where you're located.

**7.** *If you require Web visitors or email customers to fill out a form to get general information, how many fields must they fill out?*
Five or fewer (name, title, organization, email), 3 points
Six or seven (also phone number and home address), 1 point
Anything more, 0 points

**8.** *How much visual noise is on your customer web site?*

Give yourself 3 points if you have none of the following

2 points for one or two

0 points for anything more.

- Links to affiliate programs that have no relationship to your business.
- Banner ads
- Site awards
- News, stock or weather tickers
- Hit counter
- Non-stop music or animation
- Cute decorative (not meaningful) images
- Links to browser downloads
- Links to media player downloads

Many people, especially less experienced Web surfers, find it intimidating—even paralyzing—to land on a page overloaded with miscellaneous icons, images and sidebars. Some newbies feel like they have to examine everything on a page. They're afraid there might actually be something important among all that stuff. Clear the clutter: it gets in the way of action. Include only information that's important to promoting your site and your business. Some of that information may be fun, such as trivia games about the industry, or useful pages on related technologies. Just don't add junk that people can get from anywhere.

**9.** *How soon after a sale do you send customers an email thanking them for their business and asking them if they were satisfied with the experience?*

Add a point if the email includes a contact name and toll-free phone number.

Within one week, 3 points

Within two weeks, 2 points

Within one month, 1 point

Anything else, 0 points

## An Exception to the Clutter Rule

If you are producing what is now called a "web portal," a sort of super web site that provides information links to all sorts of relevant web places for people with a special interest in the subject of your portal, many links to other sites are not only useful, but are necessary to the success of the portal.

There are portals being developed for almost every subject area and product category you can imagine. WebMD (http://www.webmd.com) is an example of a portal that provides information for doctors and ordinary people with an interest in all sorts of medical information. But note that the best portals still don't provide cluttered information and wasted images; they provide only relevant and useful stuff.

10. *Do you maintain an opt-in email alert program (they choose to get the email) or newsletter to inform customers and contacts about new developments in your business and industry, and if so, how often do you issue one?*

   Yes, about once every month, 3 points

   Yes, about two times to six times a year, 2 points

   Yes, about two or three times a month, 1 point

   Yes, about once a week or more, 0 points

   No, 0 points

   Giving people valuable and informative news about your industry helps build customer loyalty; sending alerts about limited-time sales opportunities is also appreciated if not overdone. But if you send email alerts more than once a month you risk being perceived as a pest and a spammer—even if the customer did choose to get the information from you.

11. *Do any of your standard customer email messages end with the line, "Please do not respond to this email"?*

   No, 0 points

   Yes, minus 3 points

   Don't ever do this. It's like asking people to be disinterested in your product or service. You might as well say, "Please don't buy our product!"

Scoring:

**25-30 points:** Congratulations, you're an online customer communication guru.

**20-24 points:** You're doing a good job online. Keep working for perfection.

**10-19 points:** You've got potential, but need to focus on the important things, like response times, courtesy, and relevant information.

**0-9 points:** Your online business acumen needs some serious refocusing on customer priorities.

If your score wasn't high, you need to remember that people expect a response to their email inquiries immediately. If you don't have an answer at hand, respond by telling them you're working on the request or problem and you'll get back to them by a specified date. (And make sure you actually <u>do</u> get back to them on that date—even if you don't yet have an answer.)

Remembering to thank people for their purchases and their helpful comments is another important point. People like to be appreciated. And it's even better if you use their name in the email message. (Even if you do use autoresponder software, you can program the message to look personal by using the person's name and email address in the reply.)

If you have a web site to promote your business (and you should), remember that time and privacy are the two most valued commodities among Web surfers. The more you ask your Web visitors to part with either, the more you risk losing potential customers. Thus, keep information request forms down to the minimum information you need.

And make sure it's easy to find ways to contact you, via online and traditional methods (i.e. the telephone). It has always amazed us to see how many companies don't include basic contact information on their Web sites. The thinking must be that they don't want to be bothered by phone calls or email. That's not the kind of thinking that leads to more business.

## WAYS TO USE ONLINE SERVICES TO PROMOTE YOUR PRODUCTS

There are many ways to communicate with customers online. The first is through your web site, which we cover in Chapter 12. You can also make use of newsgroups, chat services, and general information sites that contain shareware software and "free" reports (which can really be demos of your full-featured products and services).

Best of all, online marketing beyond the Web represents some of the most effective and least expensive (often free) ways to market your products. You can use classified online advertising (often free), direct email promotions, and simple word-of-mouth ads on newsgroups and chat programs to communicate with customers.

### Using Newsgroups as Promotional Channels

As we mentioned in Chapter 5, newsgroups, also known as Usenet groups, are bulletin board areas that draw people with similar interests to discuss their opinions. The newsgroups are topic-specific places (which still work mostly in text-only mode at this writing) where information is shared, ads are placed, and questions are answered.

Some newsgroups allow outright advertising on the group for relevant products; some groups don't. However, if you become an information resource on a newsgroup and casually sign your name in the mail with a reference to your web site, you can do a lot to promote your wares without alienating the news readers.

How do you participate in newsgroups? There are thousands of them, so be selective before you get involved. Most Internet Service Providers (ISPs) and browsers include news service software in their package. If your ISP doesn't provide the software, consider buying something like Forte Free Agent that allows you to access the groups, read messages, and post them to the groups of interest to you.

### Special Interest Promotions

SIGs (special interest groups) are similar to newsgroups, except that they're available only to subscribers of commercial online services (such as America Online or Microsoft Network). These groups cater to chat discussions and often support bulletin boards and interest areas, which can be used for relevant advertising. If you have special expertise, you can offer to become an expert on a SIG that can provide special chat sessions or other support services (such as mentoring) for members.

We promote our book *From Book Idea to Best Seller* (Prima, 1997) by acting as mentors to new writers on the Writers SIG on iUniverse and America Online. We sell at least a couple of books every day by offering our advice services for free to the SIG. We estimate that each of these online book "sales" results in 5 to 10 additional sales of the book—and we also provide a valuable service to people who want to get into writing books. Either way, it's a relatively low-involvement way to promote our writing and our expertise.

### Permission-Based Email Promotions

Email marketing is not all bad and not all email marketers are spammers. Did you know that "permission" e-mail marketing typically yields more than five times the response rates of banner ads (that usually cost much more)? Permission email is a smart, spam-free way to promote your business, product, or service.

Permission email lists (which we'll talk about later) are developed by you as a database of marketing contacts from information you gather from your web site, or through the permissions gained by email list vendors who only develop "permission obtained" mailing lists. (Yes, there are actually a lot of people out there who like to get email from companies that have products they might actually purchase!)

Permission email can consist of newsletters that go out periodically or simply announcements of new products and special offers. Promotional newsletters—also called e-zines—can be products in their own right, complete with ads from other vendors which you'll learn about later.

One company that can help you promote your spam-free email is DigitalWork. You can reach it at http://www.digitalwork.com. Of course, there are many other companies that provide similar marketing services for business emailers. Do an Internet search on *email marketing* and you'll get many more companies to choose from.

Permission-based email promotions should follow all the established rules of netiquette and formal email communications. Address the customer formally by name and title and sign the email.

The most important rule is to market to those people most likely to buy your product. Don't just send email to everyone in the world—even though there are programs that will enable you to do this with relative ease. The most important thing you'll need to assemble is a good mailing list and a well-written email campaign to get good responses.

Just "spamming" the readers with UCE (unsolicited commercial email) will gain you little—unless you have an irresistible product. There are many sources of email addresses you may want to look up: one is PostMaster Direct Response (*www.PostmasterDirect.com*) and Targ-it.com (*www.targ-it.com*), which offer opt-in email lists of people who have indicated that they actually like to receive commercial email on topics of interest to them. There are others that offer this service as well. Just do a search on "email lists" on a major search engine to see some of the others.

## WRITING SALES EMAIL

Marketing via email is direct marketing—even if it's permission-based email addresses that you're using—so all the rules of direct marketing apply. (In fact, if you haven't procured a good book on direct marketing, now is the time to do so if you want to succeed in selling your wares or services via the online channel.) Here are some basic rules you should follow when using email as your sales channel when you're writing a sales letter.

## Anatomy of an Email

Ever wonder what first grabs the attention of an email reader? Knowing that can be a huge help to you in presenting your offer. Here's the order in which readers tend to review the parts of messages they receive:

1. The Headline
2. Any Captions for Photos or Drawings
3. Any Large Text Subheads
4. The Post Script (PS) message
5. The Order Section, if one is included in the message
6. (Finally!), the Text of the email

Customers actually place orders for products without ever reading the text. This means that attention must be paid to all of the elements listed above.

1. **Break the copy up into short copy paragraphs.** A single-sentence paragraph can make a striking point.

2. **Use as many headlines and sub-headlines as you can.** Just be careful not to overdo it and make the message look silly.

3. **Use bullets, numbers, and dashes (-) to break up copy.** Also, allow plenty of white space to make reading your message even easier for the recipient.

4. **Use arrows (->), boxes, color or shading, graphics, indentations, bold lettering, CAPITAL LETTERS, italics, and punctuation!!** However, use a light hand here. Don't beat the readers over the head with too many elements or colors. Use style and finesse instead of a hammer.

5. **Give customers premiums if this is appropriate for your product or service.** Over-deliver on the offer that first interested your prospective customer. Expert sales writer Marlon Sanders calls this the "dollars for dimes" approach - you give your customers far more perceived value than they actually pay for. Premiums also add value to your offer without substantially increasing your cost.

6. **Emphasize the word FREE wherever it applies**. We've all heard it a million times: "free" is the most powerful word you can use in direct marketing.

7. **If you do choose to use an HTMP (graphic)-based letter instead of text-only, remember to use fast-loading graphics that actively support your message.** Avoid generic clip-art graphics—they look tacky and detract from your message.

8. **Provide testimonials.** If you don't have them, get some from satisfied customers (even if they do happen to be your in-laws).

9. **Urge "Immediate action."** Have a time limit on your offer. Many companies offer premiums only if prospective customers buy within a window of a few days.

10. **Appeal to the customer's needs and wants.** The better you know your target audience the more sales you will make. The key is to give them something they really need—or think they need.

### Online Classified Ads

There are thousands of commercial and private online classified areas where you can place an ad or product announcement for free. Some sites charge for these ads

Here's an example of an online classified ad for a bulletin board or online classified web site:

**SUPERIOR KONA COFFEE AT UNBELIEVABLE PRICE**

**Fresh and Available Now!**

**Only $39** For a case!

Superior Royal Kona Coffee

Each case contains 64 - 1.5oz bags of Superior Royal Kona Coffee.

This coffee if purchased from a Gourmet Coffee House would cost $70.00 or more.

We have purchased a large quantity of this superior coffee so we can sell a case for only $39.00.

Shipping by UPS within the U.S. is included in this low price.

All orders will be shipped within 1 business day.

We accept VISA.

Satisfaction guaranteed or we will refund your money less shipping charges.

Email us at: KonaQQQcoffee.com

Call us at: 1-800-555-1234

if the site is highly visible or otherwise in a premium location. Look in the marketplace areas of the commercial online services for their (mostly) free classified areas.

Like most things, you pretty much get what you pay for—but the more you get mentioned the better responses you can expect to gain from online classified ads. Keep your ads up-to-date if you want to get the best results. Old classified ads will not pay off over the long haul.

Some sites keep their ads up for a long time—so be sure to make a list of all the sites where you place your ads and update them on a regular basis.

## PLACING ADS IN E-ZINES

You can also communicate with prospective customers online by placing ads in e-zines. The process is simple enough. You have a product or service (or an affiliate program of which you are a member) and you also have a small classified ad promoting the benefits of your product or service. You pay to advertise in e-zines that have a circulation comprised of the audience you wish to target.

---

**Sample Basic E-zine Ad from the RedHerring Ezine.**

ADVERTISEMENT

FORRESTER, OBJECTSPACE & WEB SERVICES.

So what's the connection? Join ObjectSpace and leading Forrester Research analyst Frank Gillette for a LIVE webcast September 14 at 11:00 a.m. CDT: "Powering the Networked Economy with B2B Web Service." Sign up at: http://www.objectspace.com/cod

---

E-zine advertising sounds easy enough. The problem is that it has become so competitive that a smart online marketer needs to use a more sophisticated e-zine advertising strategy. This is necessary in order to stand apart from the competition, reach an audience of targeted customers, and continue to reap the overwhelming benefits resulting from this highly effective medium.

One of the greatest problems with today's e-zine advertising is the fact that your ad gets sandwiched in between 5-15 others of similar content. Naturally, this dramatically decreases the effectiveness of your ad. Further, there are so many affiliate programs in existence that competition between them has escalated to new heights. Many affiliates of the same program now saturate a once responsive market through their e-zine advertising campaigns.

The result has been decreased revenues for the affiliates and public apathy for the product/service. Not only once but on several occasions we have seen e-zines publish the exact ad for an affiliate program (with different affiliate I.D.'s) all in the very same issue. How can this possibly benefit those advertisers?

This is not the fault of the e-zine publisher. The main purpose of an e-zine (for many, but not all publishers) is to sell advertising. A publisher who is approached by someone with advertising dollars cannot be faulted for taking the money, running the ad and simply making an honest living (we hope).

Still, there are some ingenious methods you can employ to get your ad in front of a responsive target market by utilizing e-zine advertising. For starters, if you run an affiliate program, provide your affiliates with several different, tested classified ads that they place in different e-zines. Remember, your affiliates are your salespeople—you want them to make as much money as possible so that you too make as much money as possible. It's in your best interest to help them as much as you can.

If you are an affiliate, try your hand at writing some great classified ads of your own to stand out from the competition. If you are not a great writer, we highly recommend picking up David Garfinkel's course, *Killer Copy Tactics* at http://www.killercopytactics.com/ and putting the ideas to use.

Next, spend a little more money for a sponsor ad or a solo mailing in an online newsletter that offers these services. A sponsor ad is the ad at the very top or very bottom of an e-zine. Since they are closer to the top or bottom they stand apart from the other ads, and so draw a more favorable response from subscribers.

A solo mailing is a 3-7 paragraph ad, which an e-zine sends to its mailing list at a time different from its regular mailing. The size of these ads varies from one newsletter to another, but they have proven, by far, to be an effective, profitable way to invest your advertising e-zine money.

Here's an example solo ad:

NEVER RUN OUT OF HOT WATER AGAIN!

REPLACE YOUR CONVENTIONAL WATER HEATER WITH THE REMARKABLE S.E.T.S. WHOLE HOUSE TANKLESS WATER HEATER WITH THE NASA DESIGNED FLOW SWITCH.

Tired of running out of hot water?

Fed up with high utility bills?

Ever had a hot water tank leak and ruin your floor?

The new SETS Tankless Water Heater instantly heats up the hot water in your home only when you use it—not 24/7 like your conventional tank water heater

*continued*

does. This small 12 inch by 17 inch by 3 inch unit is UL listed, CSA, CEC, and HUD certified. This unit eliminates the possibility of scalding injuries. The critical component used in this system is a flow switch designed by NASA and each unit is covered by a 100% Lifetime Parts Replacement Warranty.

AS SEEN ON THE DISCOVERY CHANNEL'S 'YOUR NEW HOUSE' AND HOME & GARDEN TV'S 'DREAMBUILDERS.'

To see a picture of one of these remarkable units visit http://www.homeideas.com/tankless.htm

For complete information and pricing send an email to: sarahQQQxyzmarketing.net Subject = TANKLESS

Call Mr. Smith now at 555-NON-TANK (877-555-1234) for immediate information.

These advertising methods are powerful tools in an e-zine advertiser's arsenal. There is only one problem: how do you find out which e-zines offer these advertising opportunities?

First you will need to find a comprehensive list of e-zine titles, then spend some time combing through the e-zines themselves to find those that meet your demographic requirements. When that is done you are ready to further narrow the list by sifting through to find the ones that accept ads (free and paid). Finally, you need to pinpoint those that specifically offer solo and sponsorship ad opportunities and do some price shopping. Naturally, you'd need quite a bit of free time to complete this process, but there are resources to help you.

For any marketer selling a product or service via online methods, the first place to go is the Tope-zineads Online Money Machine Directory, available at http://www.tope-zineads.com/index.html. You will instantly find targeted e-zines that offer the most effective methods of reaching a hungry, paying audience. Some other good sources of e-zines (and bulletin boards) are http://www.infojump.com/; http://www.lifestylespub.com/; and http://beste-zines.com/. You can find many more e-zine directories by submitting a search to a major search engine on "e-zines."

## Online Press Kits

A press kit is like a resume for your company or professional service. It's a collection of company information and articles put together to inspire interest from media, investors, clients, and potential employees. The goal is to create a press kit that grabs readers' attention, creates a killer impression, helps them remember you, and makes them hunger to know more.

It used to be that press kits were cut and dry, but new technologies offer us exciting new ways to present our information. Now you can put together an online press kit on the Web or through email to promote your business or services to the media—who will in turn promote your business or services in other online and traditional print or other media sources. A web-based press kit can help keep visitors abreast of your company's latest news, events and accomplishments. The traditional press kit is a collection of articles and information packaged in a presentation folder and sent via mail. The online press kit can contain the same information and more—but put on a web site. Online press kits have the added advantage of being able to include audio and video clips. They're cheaper to mail as well—all you have to do is send the media to the URL where your press information is located.

## LINKS TO RELATED SITES

You can use a search engine service like Yahoo! (*www.yahoo.com*) or Infoseek (*www.infoseek.com*) to find sites related to your company's products or services. Expect to spend some time looking through the sites for their information links areas (which are available on most quality sites). Then, write an email note to the Webmaster of the relevant sites and ask to list your Web site on the list. In return, offer to link their site to your site. This free and cooperative advertising is a time-consuming yet often very rewarding way to get your site in front of interested Web surfers.

You can also place ads in the major online services, such as America Online, the Microsoft Network, Prodigy and others that emerge in the future. Most online services offer SIGs, classified ads, on-screen ads, and other promotional opportunities—at a cost, of course.

## SPECIFIC ONLINE CUSTOMER COMMUNICATIONS

In addition to promoting your products and services through email and ezines, you can use online communications to handle all sorts of common business situations. These include sending out billing reminders.

Here are some examples of appropriate email for vendor-to-customer communications. Notice that the full contact information is always provided by the person sending the email and that an appropriate salutation, including the customer's name, is used. Remember that all the rules of email netiquette apply, especially when dealing with customers and clients.

One important note about sending email requests to customers: make sure this is the customer's or client's preferred method of communication before you assume that the customer reads her email every day. If you make this assumption without asking the customer, you could cause problems because the customer doesn't get the message as quickly as you think she will.

---

**Sample Standard Customer Billing Reminder**

To: Joe Customer
From: Wonka Widgets
Topic: Just a reminder of this month's invoice
Date: July 31, 2002

Dear Joe Customer,

   We were just going through our billing records and noticed that we haven't yet received this month's payment of $127.56, which was billed on Invoice #23456 on July 8. According to our terms, this payment was due on July 15. If you haven't received this invoice or have a problem with it, please give us a call at (123) 555-1234. If the check is already in the mail, please accept our thanks. We'll be looking forward to receiving it.

Sincerely yours,

Ed

Account Representative

Wonka Widgets

1277 Forward Way

Wonkaville, TX 99933

(123) 555-1234

## Sample Request for More Information on an Order from a Long-Term Customer

*In this example, the customer's first name is used in the salutation because of the long, personal relationship. The closing is also on a first-name basis, although the complete company contact information is still provided in the signature.*

To: Joe Customer

From: Wonka Widgets

Topic: Just a reminder of this month's invoice

Date: July 11, 2002

Dear Joe,

We received your order yesterday for 7 Wonka Widgets. Thank you for the order. However, we have two questions before we can ship the Widgets:

1. Do you want blue or purple widgets?
2. Would you like us to ship the order via UPS or regular mail?

> As soon as we get a response, we'll send the order to your Phoenix address as requested.
>
> Regards,
> Ed
> Wonka Widgets
> 1277 Forward Way
> Wonkaville, TX 99933
>
> (123) 555-1234

## THE TRICK TO SUCCESSFUL ONLINE COMMUNICATIONS AND PROMOTIONS

As in all promotions and communications with customers, the real key to making online promotions successful is targeted marketing, courtesy, and responsiveness. Find people interested in your products, whether online or on ground, who want to buy your services and you'll sell your wares. If you are courteous and succinct in your email, you'll get better responses.

Although this sounds easy, the trick to online success with customers and clients is consistent, quality promotions and communications that reach those people who really want your product. This trick is true of all your promotions—so never give up after the first ad or first emailing. And if you have problems with customers, check out the chapter on handling difficult situations online (Chapter 11).

# CHAPTER ELEVEN

# Putting Yourself Across in Difficult Situations

WHEN EMOTIONS RUN HIGH, communication can turn into miscommunication—or even deliberate distortion—especially when those emotions are anger or hurt. Online communication is especially tricky under these circumstances, because it's such an impersonal medium to begin with.

For that reason, we must take extra care in how we communicate electronically, and we should have a protocol in place for resolving problems. This chapter will offer ways to deal with these especially hard-to-handle situations and show you how to work with the subtleties involved.

## QUIZ: HOW WELL DO YOU COPE?

The following is a simple diagnostic test. Its purpose is not to test your knowledge but to help you gauge how effectively you can resolve difficult situations through the online medium. For the most part, you will find it easy to guess the "right" answer. But getting the right answer is not the point of the test. Respond honestly, even if you feel your response is not the best one possible. This is not a contest. The goal is solely self-inventory.

## Quiz

1. When you talk on the telephone and the line is a bit fuzzy, or you and your party have trouble hearing each other, do you:
   **a.** Put up with it, end the "conversation" as quickly as possible without seeming rude?
   **b.** Set up an online chat session?
   **c.** Use email to confirm major points you thought you heard in the "conversation"?

2. You're exchanging email with someone not all that fluent in your language. Nor are you fully fluent in his. Do you:
   **a.** Respond with a clarification like this: "If I understand you correctly, you are asking how duty charges and restrictions will affect your order. Currently…"
   **b.** Choose your words carefully in the hope that the other person will do the same for clarity's sake.
   **c.** Ask a third party knowledgeable in both languages to clarify all questions and answers where necessary.

3. You have disturbing news for someone from a different culture. Do you:
   **a.** Explain it the best way you can, hoping to have communicated with adequate sensitivity?
   **b.** Study that person's culture on the Internet to learn more about how the news you bring should be presented, or ask someone knowledgeable of this culture's intricacies for advice?
   **c.** Just send the stuff. There's nothing you can do about it anyway.

4. You've received a lengthy and critical email and something appears to be missing from the middle of the message. Do you:

   a. Ask the other party to resend it and check it for errors against your copy?

   b. Ignore the whole thing, since you don't want to have to ask someone who is already being difficult to resend trouble?

   c. Since time is short, call the sender on the phone and go over the message? Try to find out what, if anything, is missing and resolve the issue if possible? (Do this in person if proximity makes it an option.)

5. Within a business environment, you accidentally receive a highly personal email meant for someone else. Do you:

   a. Contact the person in person or by phone?

   b. Ignore it and, if asked, pretend you never received the message?

   c. Forward the message to the alias for the entire department or company?

6. There's to be a 10 percent cutback across the board in salaries and hourly wages. It's your task to announce this to the corporate proletariat (lucky you). Do you:

   a. Send out a blanket email announcing the cutback, its effective date, and the reason for it?

   b. Announce the cutback to department heads in person, asking them to pass the word in person to staffers?

   c. Ask one of your subordinates to take care of it?

7. A death in an extended family demands that relatives be notified. This is a large family with many relatives who had a close relationship with the deceased and many who barely knew her. Do you:

   a. Broadcast the bad news with a collection of aliases that reach all family members?

   b. Pass the word in person or by phone to those close to the deceased and email the rest?

   c. Let someone else deal with it?

8. You met a pleasant-sounding woman in a chat room. Going to the next step, you exchange email and get to know each other. The more you get to know her, the less you feel comfortable with her crude ideas about sex and relationships. She, with the sensitivity of a barn door, does not sense your discomfort or simply likes being vulgar. She also has your main email address. What do you do?

   **a.** Tell her your feelings in hopes she'll change her tune?

   **b.** Give up your long-time email address, which everyone uses to contact you?

   **c.** Set up a filter to refuse messages from her?

9. You're leaving for Tahiti tomorrow, hoping to experience at least some of what painter Paul Gauguin saw. You planned the trip for months, and you have nonrefundable tickets. Suddenly your boss comes in and tells you the vacation must be postponed because of a problem with a major account. What do you do?

   **a.** Give up the trip and your dream to fix the problem.

   **b.** Explain to your boss that your tickets are nonrefundable and unless the company wants to reimburse you, you're going anyway.

   **c.** Propose that Holden, who's equally qualified, handle the job, and you'll keep in touch by cell phone.

10. Mom just passed away after a lingering illness. You have a videoconference with your siblings, who live much farther away than you do. It becomes clear that while they miss Mom, no one wants to lift a finger to make the funeral arrangements. And it looks like you're getting stuck with the bill as well. Of course everyone will be present for the reading of the will. What do you do?

    **a.** Graciously take care of everything, even if it empties your bank account.

    **b.** Send a broadcast email to the siblings, telling them that it's their mother too and upon reflection you have neither the time nor the money to take care of everything.

    **c.** Send a broadcast message with a list of tasks and an assignment to each sibling. Divide the tasks as best you can and attach a price tag to each. Offer to be the "project leader" as well as taking on your assigned tasks.

## Answers

1. "b" Why struggle with a bad phone line and possibly end a conversation before everything has been discussed and resolved? Set up a chat session and don't miss anything. Chat sessions are also useful for keeping private conversations private in an open cubicle environment.

2. "a" By paraphrasing the question and then answering it (If I'm understanding you correctly, you think that beryllium—even with its risks—is a superior metal for building the frame components because of its light weight), you make miscommunication less of a problem. It's a double check on message content, vocabulary, and sentence structure.

3. "a" Deliver your message with help from the Net and possibly a coworker from the same culture. Otherwise you may commit a faux pas.

4. "c" Direct contact is the best way to fill in missing information. Emails back and forth will only complicate matters. And, if the topic is especially sensitive, you may dig yourself in deeper with a message that is out of touch with the underlying concern.

5. "a" Direct contact is the best way to put things right again where personal email is concerned. Then let the sender handle damage control if the message went to more than one inappropriate recipient.

6. "b" The middle managers know their staff personally and can address each person with tact regarding cutbacks. Following their announcement, you should send out a blanket email that apologizes for the cutback, the reasons for it, and what steps are being taken to eliminate this problem.

7. "b" Pass the bad news in person or by phone to those closest to the deceased and email the rest. Look in the newspaper for examples of phrasing for an obituary, but make it more personal.

8. Try "a" first. But chances are that this person doesn't realize that she's acting the boor, so your comments will probably land on deaf ears. If so, use "c." Block her name and hang out in other chatrooms. We hope you didn't give out your phone numbers or address!

9. Choose "b" or "c" and stick to your guns. It's your vacation and you earned it. Chances are that either choice won't win you any popularity contests, but maybe it's time to look for another job anyway. No decent company should make such a demand on an employee without offering significant compensation.

10. "c" Assign the tasks for the funeral arrangements, keeping in mind each sibling's ability to pay and time constraints. Should one sibling complain that another seems to be getting off easy, discuss the reason for your decision in person. For example, that person has a new baby to look after and finances are tight. If push comes to shove, sit down round-table style and talk it out.

## WORDS TO USE FOR DIFFICULT SITUATIONS ONLINE

| | | |
|---|---|---|
| aced | cooperation | reasonable |
| actual | doubtless | relationship |
| agree | downhill | responsible |
| agreeable | embrace | secure |
| always | future | simplify |
| apologize | growth | solution |
| best | ingratiate | spirit |
| bind | instant | strong |
| black | ironclad | thoughtful |
| bull | kinship | together |
| caring | mesh | understandable |
| catalyst | missed | viable |
| close | momentum | win-win |
| complete | moving | workable |
| considerate | positive | |

## PHRASES TO USE IN RESOLUTION OF DIFFICULT SITUATIONS ONLINE

100 percent

award winner

complete agreement

complete cycle

cream always rises

everything to gain

fully guaranteed

hand in hand

in this together

lighten the load

make up

maximum leverage

net-net

no risk

talk it through

up to speed

we're right behind you

## WORDS TO AVOID FOR RESOLUTION OF DIFFICULT SITUATIONS ONLINE

awkward

backburner

bear

braindead

bumpy

buried

checkered

condescending

conflict

conflicting

dumb

eclipsed

gone

guestimate

hopeless

hurdle

hype

hypocritical

idiotic

ignored

inconsistent

loser

loss

lost

misguided

misused

odds

outsider

overlooked

read

scattershot

slow

soured

stagnant

strange

stuck

stupid

thoughtless

threat

unknown

unplanned

unprofessional

unquantified

uphill

weird

## PHRASES TO AVOID FOR RESOLUTION OF DIFFICULT SITUATIONS ONLINE

| | |
|---|---|
| a zenith in Mongoloid reasoning | old technology |
| a future upgrade path is planned | out of step |
| big cutbacks are coming! | smoke and mirrors |
| cover up | steep learning curve |
| like it or not | that's just the way it is |
| limited capability | two wrongs don't make a right |
| lost out on | walk that extra mile |
| no win | why bother |
| not a chance | |

## Watch Your Language!

Avoid using swear words no matter how appropriate they may seem to the matter at hand. This rule can be broken only with close friends, family, and *very* close coworkers. Remember, your interpretation of the vernacular may be much more liberal that the one held by the recipient.

Especially avoid obscenities with: older relatives, managers, people whom you don't know very well, friends you've met online, or in chat situations where there are people you know nothing about. There could be people present who are highly religious, but keep it quiet, and might be offended by language not much stronger than a "darn."

## WORDS AND PHRASES FOR CALMING A BAD SITUATION

If used properly, the words and phrases that follow can take the anger out of a situation and leave everyone feeling much more mellow. If you're a manager, head of an organization, or organizer of family chats, keeping the peace may become your responsibility by default, like it or not.

| | |
|---|---|
| after much consideration | calm |
| agree on | common resolution |
| as I lean back in my chair | consensus |

easy

easy does it

easy to [. . .]

if we put our skills together

if we put our heads together

It's a hot idea that requires cool
  thinking

let's sleep on it

make a list of [. . .]

nonconfrontive

one day at a time

one step at a time

patience is a virtue

please

please don't make big waves

quietly

relaxed

slow

softly

solution

take a step back from [. . .]

take it slow

thank you

that's good information

think this through

tranquil/tranquility

use a light touch

walk, don't run

weigh each risk

what are the options

what's your opinion

## CONFRONTATIONAL WORDS AND PHRASES TO AVOID

Just as there are many complimentary and calming words you can use in most situations, there are at least an equal number of insults. Again, the online communication between people can be thought of like a fine silk thread: Durable enough to last, but frail should either side choose to sever it. Here are some words and phrases to avoid if you don't want that strand to break.

[. . .], you're not welcome in this
  chatroom

absolutely not

backstabbing

blunder

fear of God

forget it

get off your high horse

get out

get out of here

get out of my sight

get someone else to type your email
  so I can make sense of it

I demand

I'm keeping an eye on you [I have
  someone there who will report
  back to me]

if you don't . . .

If you won't . . .

it's a political thing

it's NOT in my job description

jealous

like it or not we work as a team

  even if you think the project is a

  bad idea

never again

no

no choice

no more Mr. Nice Guy [can be used

  humorously as well, so clarify its

  intent]

no way

no way, Jose

not your project

paper tiger

tempest in a teacup

that's just the kind of [. . .] I'd expect

  from [. . .]

the idea was stillborn

this is a waste

this is another waste of time

  meeting

this is private

what a dumb idea

what'd you do, come up with that

  on your abacus

what's gotten into your head

WRONG!

you stole my idea

you weasel!

you weren't invited

you'd BETTER get behind it

## COOLING OFF ANGRY CHAT

Because chat is like any other conversation, things can get ugly when disagreement rears its head or tempers flair over inept use of chat protocol. Chat runs off the rails when:

- Adversaries get together in a chat environment with no agreement beforehand to attempt conciliation.
- Bad news is suddenly announced and chat participants are taken aback because they were unaware of the problem. Blaming may become a part of the conversation, turning things from bad to worse to "worser."
- A difficult personality enters the room and struts his ego down main street, six guns at the ready.
- A volcano-style manager participates in the meeting, angering other attendees.

Cooling off angry chat is difficult, to say the least, but it can usually be done, and if you're successful, becoming a peacemaker can add a few feathers to your cap. Here are two different approaches to try:

## Sample Intervention into a Family Argument Online

This is a six-way chat among RonB (you), TammyY, and LarryM. Tammy and Larry are heatedly arguing over an item bequeathed in a will of a dearly departed. Other family members have been silenced by the inappropriateness of the participants' behavior.

It's your opportunity to be a hero and save a formerly robust family relationship, or to sit back quietly and allow an irreparable split to occur:

TammyY: Larry, I just won't put up with this anymore. Granny promised me that sofa more than 11 years ago. The will says your family gets the house and contents, but the sofa is mine. I won't speak to you again if you claim that couch. It's got a lot of memories sitting there!

RonB (you): Tammy and Larry, this is our family's weekly chat where we get together to stay in touch because many of us are thousands of miles distant from each other. This is not the time or place for arguing over a piece of furniture. I respectfully request that you take this discussion offline, or ask Aunt Selma to mediate it for you. I think I speak for everyone here: If you can't drop the topic NOW, please leave the chatroom.

### Plan A

First, evaluate the situation carefully. Scribble an org chart or family tree if necessary so that you can better understand the relationships involved.

Then, if it's a family concern and your clan looks to the wisdom of seniors (or whomever) to settle disputes, by all means call them in. If it's business and one of the non-protagonists is a manager senior to you, ask him or her for help. If neither of these alternatives is available, suggest to the combatants that they take their discussion off line so everyone else can continue with the get-together or meeting.

If the argument continues, discontinue the meeting, or if your chat software supports it, have all other participants "iggy" the offenders. (As mentioned earlier in the book, iggy is used to make people invisible. Once invoked, you won't see their conversation until you "un-iggy" them.)

## Plan B

Not all situations can be ignored or put to bed as described in Plan A. Sometimes, cards on the table is the only way out. This is especially true if you are the senior family member or manager present among the squabblers. Here's how to handle the situation:

1. **Ask each party to describe her beef in 100 words or less.** The rule is that while each party is writing, *no one* interrupt. If either party grossly exceeds the word count or starts to ramble, then interrupt to get things back on track.

2. **Study the two complaints and look for common ground.** Ask questions for clarity if required. (Keep in mind that the original meeting participants will be silently present which helps maintain honesty among the combatants.) Knowing that others are watching, who are of aware of what's true and what's not, will help the combatants to avoid lies and exaggerations.

3. **List the common points between the two protagonists.** After the points are made, you can optionally open up for comments from the other participants who have remained silent until now.

## Quick Tricks for Defusing an Argument Online

Here are a couple of ways you can slow or even stop an argument from exploding disastrously in a chat:

*Change the subject.* You can often use the simple tactic of changing the subject to distract people from their anger. Wait for a brief stall in the battle, address one of the combatants with a message on another topic, and hope that others in the room get the idea and step in.

*Call their hand.* If more drastic measures are in order, you can call for a "cards-on-the-table session" either in the current chat room or in a private room with you as a moderator. Suspend the main the meeting until the problem is resolved.

4. **If everything is agreed upon, have both parties promise not to raise the issue again.** If resolution seems hopeless, set up a face-to-face meeting offline and hammer out an agreement instead of wasting more time online.

## HANDLING HOT, HOT CHAT

As we mentioned in a previous chapter, an invitation to "hot chat" is essentially a request for crude sexual conversation online. You will run into it whether you're male or female.

In email and chat, women will try to sell you pornography and escort services. Men either want an erotic chat (women do this too), or a face-to-face meeting often across state lines.

### Cooling Off Hot Chat with a Bucket of Ice Water

Females often become the victims of overeager males with too much time on their hands. Here's a typical scenario:

You're steaming through an interesting chat session (you finally found one!), in which people are responding to you. It's become an engaging discussion and you're enjoying yourself. You're using a screen name like betty4U and you notice that one person with a male sounding screen name seems to respond to you more often than others. He proposes mild questions about your age, work, and home life:

". . . Betty, that's very interesting. What does your husband do for a living? Do you have kids?"

You, having no hidden agenda, answer 'no, I'm not married.' Suddenly, an Instant Message box or an invitation to a private chat room appears onscreen.

"Hi Betty, you're single and I'm in the process of a divorce. Can we do a hot chat session? I'd love to know more about you." [A real IM message will likely be much stronger and more graphic than anything we can print here.]

It goes downhill from here—or uphill, depending on your point of view. There are many people who enjoy this sort of chat, and if you're one of these, please ignore our warnings. This advice is for those new to online comm, i.e.,

## The Most Important Rule of Chat

What's more important than making new friends, finding romance, or patching up differences online? Your safety and security. And for that reason, this is the most important rule to follow when you're in a chat room with strangers:

*__Never, ever, ever, ever, ever give your ground-based address, phone number, or main email address to anyone online whom you don't know.__*

Otherwise, you may find unusual people sending strange messages, calling your home, or showing up unexpectedly at your door at 3:00 a.m. Note that people have been murdered, yes *murdered* by others they've met online.

readers who may find themselves deep in quicksand before they realize what's happening.

Here are several ways to cool off a hot prospect. Which one you use depends on how offensive the person is, how open you are to the kind of invitation presented, and your willingness to be culled from the chatroom herd that you were enjoying:

- **Leave.** And don't say goodbye, especially in a threatening situation. Just log off and stay off line until the next day. Look for a new chatroom and consider using a different screen name. If you've given out your street address (dumb, very dumb) keep all doors locked and alarms active.

- **Send a notice of chatroom violations to the host.** For example, America Online's chat window has a button that reads: Notify AOL. Clicking this after receiving harassing messages from another user lets you report the incident. AOL will then read their version of the riot act to the bad guy. Most online services have some variation of this tool available, and you should use it if you feel pushed to the edge.

- **Respond honestly.** Tell the person in the Instant Messaging window that you aren't looking for what he has to offer. Then, if the system supports it, block his name.

## WHEN SOMEONE LEAVES THE COMPANY

When someone of rank leaves an organization under unpleasant circumstances, especially when let go, it's sometimes tempting to ignore that fact in the hope that it will be quickly forgotten. However, the departing person may have a significant number of supportive employees and be considered an asset to the organization by other managers and customers.

For these reasons, you must acknowledge the separation and put as pleasant a spin on it as possible. The message should come across positively even though a number of people inside and outside (customers) may have the "down and dirty" on the situation.

The purpose of your announcement is simply factual. Readers will assume that what the company is putting forth is the party line anyway. But, you must do it and sign your name to it as well. If a replacement has been hired for the recently departed Mr. X, this should be included in the announcement as well to help make a smooth transition.

Email is a satisfactory vehicle for inside consumption. A formal press release must be used to notify stockholders. Important customers should get the news before any public announcement, usually in person from their sales reps or from someone in management.

### An Online Departure Press Release for Someone Reasonably Unimportant

When someone is fired from the company, a press release should be sent out. The focus of the release should be positive and/or noncommittal, with no reference to the terms of departure.

In addition to a fax or paper-based release, email can serve as an efficient vehicle for reaching a multitude of employees. The release for a termination can be brief, because most recipients will already know that the person got the ax. Keeping the release short and minimizing the person's accomplishments can help protect the company from a wrongful termination lawsuit.

Any release should come from a senior person. For example, if a senior vice-president leaves, it should come from the CEO. Or, when a line manager leaves, the electronic mailing list can be pared down and the release should come from the division's vice president.

## Sample Termination Release

Here's an online example (which can be identical to a paper-based one) of an email termination release:

> May 28, 2100, For general release
> The Biggles Corporation regretfully announces the departure of long time vice-president of manufacturing, Kathleen Turner. Ms. Turner joined our company in 1990 and assisted in enhancing a number of manufacturing line processes, where her team reduced line overhead by 25 percent. Ms. Turner is leaving to pursue other opportunities, and we wish her the best in her new endeavors. Her departure date will be June 15.
> Stan Baker, Ph.D.
> CEO, Biggles Corporation

If the release will go to customers, the press, or external organizations, add the following:

> Questions should be directed to Alicia Brown at Levit and Brown, Public Relations. Phone 345-234-5678 or online at levitbrown.com. For more information on Biggles Corp., find us on the Web at www.bigglesfabrics.com.

### A Key Player's Departure Announcement

When a key player leaves an organization, more than just a "we will miss him greatly" is in order. We're not talking about the departure of an easy-to-replace cookie cutter CEO or a senior manager of little concern, but someone around whom the company revolves. Examples: Steve Jobs being fired from Apple Computer, Ross Perot's bumpy departure from General Motors, and actress Susanne Summers walking out on the television sitcom *Three's Company*. Each of these people had an enormous loyal following among other employees, not to mention customers and stockholders (and audience members).

This kind of situation requires significant damage control with an army of public relations people attempting to placate the world at large. Online, a corporate web site

## Giving Bad News so They Don't Kill the Messenger

It's a classic maneuver is to launch a minimal attack against the place where the enemy expects an attack in force, then to make the real attack where it it's least expected. In the ensuing confusion, you will meet little resistance. Magicians use the same principle. They call it "misdirection." While they distract you by waving one hand about, they'll use the other to set up a trick.

You can do the same thing with organizational bad news. Send out two releases, one with the bad news and the other with big, bright news on a new product, a brilliant new hire to replace those who have gone before, or solid earning results that are better than expected.

would be employed to "clarify" the news and provide hourly updates on a company's plans for replacing the guy, along with tangential news related to the separation, industry analyst commentary, and placating quotes from the person departing.

### An Electronic Release for a Key Player

The release must be forthright in acknowledging that the departure is a blow to the company's future. Otherwise, those in the know (customers, industry analysts, and the media) will jump all over the attempted soft sell, making for headlines like: "Key player Kathleen Turner departs Biggles Corp.—what next?" or "Stock nosedives on news that Turner is leaving Biggles Corp."

## Saying Goodby to a Key Player

Here is an email announcement for a key player departing a company. You will note that it's relatively long and doesn't try to cover up the company's vulnerability, because important people in the field will be aware of the departure even before it

*continued*

## Saying Goodby to a Key Player (continued)

happens. Instead, it's honest and forthright, acknowledges the person's contribution, and offers (when possible) the company's scheme for covering the loss:

May 28, 2100, For general release:

The Biggles Corporation announced today the departure of long time vice president of manufacturing, Ms. Kathleen Turner. Ms. Turner was a founder of the company and key player in the expansion of domestic manufacturing and distribution. Her loss is expected to make a significant impact on the company's manufacturing operations. In light of her important role, retired founder Marvin Marcian has offered to take over her responsibilities for six months while the search for a permanent replacement continues. CEO Kingsley Brown, Jr., explained in a news conference today, "This company has weathered tough times before and come through unscathed. Granted, the loss of Kathleen was unexpected. But at this time we're going forward with our sails trimmed, a strong balance sheet, and we're technologically ahead of the competition."

Ms. Turner's loss will be felt by this company and the industry. It was her numerous patents on new technology, such as the reverse win-win spin-threader, that brought Biggles to the forefront of the industry as an innovator. For that, the company thanks Ms. Turner.

Kathleen Turner's plans are to seek a position within the federal government. We wish her well in her future endeavors.

The Biggles Corporation has contracted with Manley Executive Search to locate a successor. Contact Angel Smith at 345-029-4829 or www.manleysearch.com.

Questions on Ms. Turner's departure can be directed to Alicia Brown at Levit and Brown, Public Relations. Phone 345-234-5678 or online at levitbrown.com. For more information on Biggles Corp., find us on the Web at www.bigglesfabrics.com

## ADVANCE NOTICE OF LATE PAYMENT

If you must make a late payment, you can take some of the sting out of it by letting the seller know in advance that you won't be on time. The worst thing you can do, on the other hand, is to leave a creditor dangling by not returning his calls or email, and by generally making yourself invisible.

Here's what to do: first, send an email to the supplier. Then, follow up later the same day with a phone call (if the supplier doesn't call you).

---

### Sample Email Bearing Bad Financial News

Hi Ted, I wanted to make you aware of a problem we are experiencing that's affecting our cashflow. Our biggest account is 90 days past due in paying us, and that's making us late paying our bills. We hope to see a check from this customer this week, and I'm applying all the pressure I can to get this matter taken care of. Unfortunately, this means we will be late paying you. I hope to have this matter straightened out within 15 days, and I appreciate your understanding. I will be calling you later today after I have another discussion with our customer. Hopefully, I will have good news, and I'll be able to update you on the situation.

My apologies,
Alex Baldwin, Ph.D.
TechAire Corporation

---

When sending such a message, be as specific as possible about when you can and will pay your bill. In this example, the date is vague because Alex doesn't have hard information about when he will get paid. If you can, offer to pay at least part of the bill immediately. That will demonstrate good faith and make the vendor feel comfortable that payment will indeed by made.

## Heading Them Off at the Pass

Here's a sample message that forewarns the recipient about a late shipment.

Dear Mr. Redlands,

I have disappointing news for you. The new Model 7 Containment housing has not met our engineer's expectations for reliability. There-fore, we are delaying shipping the product until the first quarter of next year. I know this inconvenience will cause enormous problems for your 7-7 launch vehicle customers. To compensate you for this problem, we are prepared to offer you the Model 6 C at 50 percent of our normal price. In addition, we will discount the Model 7 once we've fixed the problem as a further gesture of apology.

I will call you later today or early tomorrow to discuss terms and ex-plain the issues behind the hold-back. We at Acme Technologies ap-preciate your understanding and wanted to let you know, as a highly valued customer, as soon as we knew.

Sincerely, and with apologies,
Alfred Windham
VP of Sales
Acme Technologies

## NOTICE OF A PRODUCT SHIPMENT DELAY

Many new products come to market late. Some come so late that they miss their market window. The reasons are many, from serious technological flaws to poor project management. Since customers may be eagerly anticipating your hot new commodity, or it may be a vital part of a product they sell, your tardiness can af-fect products all the way down the line.

Here's what to do to reassure the customer if your product will be late:

■ Let customers know as early as possible of the product delay, the reason for it, and your game plan for fixing the trouble, providing hard dates if *possible*.

■ Acknowledge the problem and explain how you plan to work around it. If the problem's resolution is likely to be impossible, give people the bad news now instead of surprising them at the last minute, when their own late product, which depends on yours, will then send someone else's sales and marketing plans to the bottom of the sea.

■ Offer an alternative: Offer widgets currently on hand that will fill the bill at a reduced price until the new goods are ready to ship. If your price is low enough, your customer can pass the savings on to his customer, making everybody happy.

## WHEN A FRIEND OR FAMILY MEMBER DIES

The only proper way to announce a death is in person or on the telephone, but for family members who weren't close to the deceased or who are nearly impossible to reach, email will suffice. Your letter should be friendly and empathetic. A family chatroom is _not_ the place to make such announcements, unless the deceased is a _very_ distant relation to those in the room. That means all of them.

An example from a newspaper:

> Nellie Lobikis, Homemaker, 86, of Des Moines died Wednesday, March 26 at her home.
>
> Lobikis a native of Lime Spring, Iowa, lived in Des Moines for 22 years. She was a homemaker for 60 years. She was a member of the First Lutheran Church. She is survived by her son William of Corona, CA and her daughter Christine, of Los Angeles, CA.
>
> Services will be conducted at Montecinto Memorial Chapel in Des Moines. 1325 Blanford st., 765-8765. There will be a sitting at 6:00 p.m. Friday, March 28 and services at 10:00 a.m. Saturday, March 29.

---

**Sample Email Announcement for a Death**

Dear Nancy, I know it's been a long time since you've heard from me, and I'm sorry that on this occasion that I am the bearer of bad news. It concerns Alice's sister-in-law Nellie Lobikis with whom I know you were not too familiar. We all loved Nel, with her passion for home-made preserves and the orchard she kept up all by herself in the big backyard of her house. She died at age 86 at the Des Moines' residence where she lived for 22 years.

I remember when I used to spend summers at Nel's house while I was I going to school at the state college. We went fishing together, and she taught me the basics of the flute. (I must have been an awful student—as I still can't play a scale.)

Nel is survived by her son William of Corona, CA and her daughter Christine, of Los Angeles, CA. Services were conducted at Montecinto Memorial Chapel in Des Moines. She will be buried according to her wishes, next to her late husband, Neil.

Sorry to be the bearer of bad news. Hope we can get together when I move upstate next semester.

Leslie

---

Note that an email obituary is of nearly conventional letter length. This is to make it more personal and assumes that the recipient cares enough to read the announcement. A shorter announcement may come across as cold or distant.

## When Not to Use an Alias

Aliases are a great way to save time and effort in most emailing situations. However, they should _not_ be used to address the announcements of a death. Even the most distant friend or relative deserves to have his name used in the salutation. Of course you can use the alias list(s) to cut and paste names and email addresses.

The example of the online obituary assumes two things:

1. That the addressee and the deceased were not close and your message is more like general family news on a remote relative than a shocking announcement to your sister that your mother just died.
2. That without the email announcement, the recipient would know nothing of Nellie's demise.

It's possible that your correspondent and the deceased were much closer than you're aware of. They may have been close childhood friends years before you were born. If possible, query other relatives to find out how deep the relationships runs before bearing the bad news.

## MAKING UP IS HARD TO DO

Another "toughee" is repairing a soured friendship or family relationship. While the best way to approach this problem would be to have a face-to-face meeting, such as a lunch date, email can provide a good starting point. Why? While the person may not take your phone call, your email will get through (although, it too can be ignored).

Try the options in one of the levels below, keeping in mind that the bigger your transgression (assuming you're willing to take responsibility for the demise of the relationship), the greater the repentance required. Level A is the simplest, Level C the most extreme.

### Level A (not in any order; may be combined)

1. Send a carefully chosen email apology card. Try www.egreetings.com. Cards are free and you can send gifts or gift certificates. There is a variety of companies that offer these and similar services.
2. Make an in-person apology.
3. Send an email apology.
4. Make a telephone apology.

### Level B (not in any order; may be combined)

1. Invite the person for lunch/dinner/cocktails (Cocktails *only* if you know the people involved can consume alcohol safely and enjoy it.)

**2.** Send a gift (*not* a singing-stripping telegram).

**3.** Go to the person's home, and bring something elegant that will be especially appreciated.

### Level C

The most self-deprecating apology is one done in front of the person you have offended and others who are aware of the situation. Start with an announcement something like: "I've worked with Mary for almost seven years now and recently I have done her a major disservice that deserves an apology." Then make your apology in no uncertain terms. Say you're sorry, and say it in as many ways as you feel comfortable with.

If this doesn't restore your relationship, nothing will. Limit the entire talk to less that two minutes, unless you actually need to detail your mistakes because they're that bad.

## DIFFICULT TIMES AND EMOTIONAL TOPICS

Never substitute email for personal contact when personal contact is really required. Sure, it's easy to bang out a paragraph or two of bad news, send it, and be done with it. But until someone does it to you, you won't appreciate the devastating impact that can have on the recipient. The order for delivering negative or emotional news goes as follows, from best to worst.

**1.** In person with a principal delivering the news.

**2.** In person with a second party delivering the news.

**3.** In a video conference, preferably with good sound and optical quality. This requires a phone call in advance, of course.

**4.** On the telephone.

**5.** Using email with sound.

**6.** Using email. (Make sure the person actually uses email regularly before sending this).

**7.** By letter, preferably using an overnight service.

**8.** By telegraph if third world borders complicate communications.

Life is full of difficulties, and you'll certainly experience your share. You can make it more pleasant though, by treating a bad situation with the most courtesy possible and not taking the easy way out, no matter how tempting that may be.

CHAPTER TWELVE

# How to Say It on Your Web Site

THESE DAYS IT SEEMS TO BE COMMON WISDOM that if you're in business, you need to have a Web site. In reality, a Web site will make little or no difference in the overall profitability of many businesses—and the time spent programming the Web Site and keeping it up-to-date may pull time away from other more lucrative marketing efforts.

Think seriously about the needs of your market before you go onto the Web to make more money. It's hard to believe that Fred's Service Station really needs a Web Site to reap new profits. However, for some businesses and professional service firms, the Internet and Web together offer viable marketing and distribution opportunities. Software companies, online magazines, and mail order businesses can do quite well from the Web—if the owners know how to say the right things on their sites.

## The Secrets of a Successful Web Site

Just having a site on the Web will do almost nothing to sell your products or services. To promote your Web site, there are three major things you must do:

1. You must register your Web site with the best search engines.
2. You should consider using the many free and not free advertising opportunities on the Web (which we discussed in Chapter 11).
3. You should search the Web regularly for competitive and related sites, where you can attach a link to your site.

## WHAT ABOUT PRODUCING A WEB PAGE?

If you decide a Web page is a good idea for your business, remember that good Web page design follows the rules of type and visual design (or intentionally breaks them for artistic reasons), but within the framework of a computer screen instead of paper. There are hundreds, maybe thousands, of Web design sites available on the Internet to get you started in creating HTML code (the basic Web programming language), developing page layouts, and publishing images on Web pages. For starters, check the site at http://www.webmonkey.com—this is one among hundreds of such informational sites, for those who want to learn to do a web site on their own.

If you want to know what looks good on the Web, start some serious surfing to see what the best sites look like and get ideas for how the sites work to lure you into their pages for more information. Try sites for some of the major retailers for starters—such as http://www.nordstroms.com or http://www.sears.com—if you plan on selling things on your site. If you're a service firm, such as an ad agency—look at some of the major agencies, such as Chiat Day at http://www.chiatday.com. You get the idea. By the way, just because you're a small company doesn't mean you shouldn't look like a big one. That's one of the marketing advantages of the Web—all companies are equal if they do a good job of presenting themselves.

## HOW TO REGISTER YOUR WEB SITE TO GET NOTICED

If you want people to find your Web site after you develop it, you first need to make your site information available through the major search engines (such as Yahoo!, WebCrawler, Infoseek, and hundreds of others) that help people find the things they're looking for on the net. You can register your site on one search engine at a time, or you can use a search engine registration service, such as Submit It! ®(*http://www.submit-it.com*), to register your site information on hundreds at one time—although it will cost you more. Even so, the registration fees are quite affordable—and we recommend using a quality registration service to do the tedious, redundant work for you.

## Things to Know About Submitting Your URL to a Search Engine

Whether you use Submit It! or another registration service (there are links to a number of services and search engine registration sites on the CD-ROM), or if you submit to services one at a time on your own, here are some basic things to know:

- Every day new directories come into existence and others disappear. While companies like Submit It! try to keep up with all of the changes, the lists provided by the directories may be out of date simply because things change quickly on the Internet and World Wide Web.
- Some directories and search engines charge for listings, but most do not.
- Not all directories and search engines are relevant for all Web sites. For example, some are only for non-U.S. Web sites. Thus, if your site isn't relevant, the directory won't list your URL.
- Some directories and search engines periodically suspend submissions. Therefore, no number of submissions will get your URL into the service on every directory all the time.

*continued*

## Things to Know About Submitting Your URL to a Search Engine (continued)

■ When you submit the URL (Web address) for your Web site, you may find
that it will take from one day to eight weeks or more for your site to appear
in a search attempt on a particular site. This is because search engine sites
are often critical of the information they list in their indexes. If your site isn't
deemed relevant or professional, it won't get listed. Sometimes the waiting
time for indexing your site is simply due to the volume of sites being submitted for review. Be patient and keep testing to see if your site comes up in
a search.

The registration sites typically provide other, more costly products for Webmasters as well, such as consulting services, information monitoring services, and
reports on access to the best sites (best in this case means most frequently visited).
For site registration purposes, Submit-It!, as an example, supports over 400 of the
best, true Internet search engines and directories on the Web. However, the company has over 1200 search engines and reference directories in its database. And,
every day, Submit-It! gets 20 or more new requests from search engines and directories to be included in the Submit It! service.

## STAYING UP-TO-DATE

For those search engine sites that use Excite, Alta Vista, Web Crawler, or some other
robot (also called crawlers and spiders) to categorize the information in a site, here are
some tips on how to keep your site's information up-to-date in the search engine.

**Changing the Title and Content of Your Site.** When you alter the title or content of your site, you don't need to contact each robot automated search engine to point out the changes you've made. Excite and other such programs
will perform automatic updates the next time the program does its update access (often taking the title from the title tag in your document's header—thus

## Manually Updated Search Engines

Some search engine services complete their updating by hand (not through robots). Therefore, you'll have to resubmit information on your site when you make major changes to the content. That's why using an automated submission service (like Submit-It!) is a good idea. The service can help keep references to your site up-to-date without the need to resubmit your basic information to each search engine.

it's a good idea to be creative with your site's title). It may take a week or two for the spider to visit you, but it'll get there eventually.

**Changing the Location of Your Site.** When you change your URL, you'll need to submit a new "add URL" form to the search engine, which the robot can use to index your new site. If the old site remains at the old address, most spider programs will keep indexing your site unless you either remove it or put a robots.txt file on your system. These files point to your new site so the automatic updating programs will find the information in your new location. You can get information on using a robots.txt file in your site at *info.webcrawler.com/mak/projects/robots/faq.html*.

**Changing the Site Summary.** To change the site summary that the various spiders compile, you'll have to change your content. Spider programs typically build a summary of your site by taking sentences that contain the dominant ideas/concepts of your home page directly from the page. The designers of web robots can't tell the spider to use only particular sentences in the summary.

## ADVERTISING ON THE WORLD WIDE WEB

If you have some extra cash in your promotional budget, you may want to consider online advertising on the Web or one of the commercial online services. Advertising on a commercial Web site can range from a simple banner at the top of the site or a simple contact link (that the site charges to provide) for your Web site or a complete feature page of information on your product or services.

Advertising on hot (meaning popular) online sites can be expensive. For example, it costs at least $2000 a year to advertise on the AOL NetFind search engine—and if you want a big ad placed frequently, it will cost a good deal more.

If you want to find out about advertising on a major Web site, simply send some email to the Webmaster and ask about advertising possibilities which will vary by cost, number of contacts made on the site, and reach of the audience. Advertising on the Web is much like advertising in other major media, such as newspapers or magazines. The larger the number of exposures, the more it will cost to have a company-specific advertisement on the Web page.

If your own Web site ever generates enough exposure in your area of expertise, you can also sell advertising space, just as other sites do. In fact, some Web entrepreneurs support themselves entirely through advertising fees. Check out the quality site for movie information at *us.imdb.com*—which supports their effort entirely through advertising fees.

## KEEPING YOUR CUSTOMERS ON YOUR WEB SITE

Retaining your existing Web visitors and customers is just as important as getting people to your Web site in the first place. Consider these Web advertising costs.

One Web site produced by a professional firm: $10,000

A banner advertising campaign on Yahoo!: $15,000

A 1-year web hosting package: $1,200

Retaining your Web site visitors: $0, nada, nothing—just good web site design!

As the number of Web pages on the Internet expands beyond 1 billion, the importance of creating a "satisfying user experience" for Web users is crucial to the success of any Web site. Industry research continues to show that retaining Web site visitors may be the primary challenge in succeeding on the Internet.

A new study reported by Engage Technologies stated that 4 out of 5 visitors to the average Web site never return. Many marketing experts believe that those who expand their number of repeat visitors will prove successful in the on-line arena. On the other hand, these experts warn that acquisition without retention spells long-term disaster.

Retention plays a key role on the Internet as it enables one-to-one relationships, repeat purchases or visits, and a channel for feedback and sharing of ideas about company products, services, and your business practices.

There are many ways to get repeat visitors to a Web site. One example of a company that has taken customer retention on the Web very seriously is Silicon Alley-based Cyber-NY (http://www.cyber-ny.com). According to Damian Bazadona, a partner in Cyber-NY, one way to help expand repeat visitors on your Web site is to create a satisfying user experience. Here is what he recommends.

**Use compression technologies to speed up browsing.** Most Web surfing, at least for personal use, is still done with modems. Someday (maybe soon) everyone will have fast access with DSL lines and cable modems, but most people still use standard dial-up modem connections from their homes. With a 56K modem, which often connects at around 28.8K, most people don't have patience for Web sites that take over a minute to download. To avoid having this problem on your site, compress the graphics. People don't want to wait a day and a half for a 100k home page graphic to load. You should also avoid creating text as graphics when it could simply be created in HTML. This equates to faster download time and more viewers on your site.

**Try using new technologies.** Investigate new technologies, and don't be afraid to use them. Macromedia and other software companies continue to release cutting edge web production tools, which help improve site navigation without hindering download time. Through the use of these tools, you can create content-rich interactive atmospheres that enhance the user experience. Long-term, the user experience will play a large-role in generating repeat visits. Even if you hire a company to produce your Web site for you (a good idea if you don't have great design skills—even though it may cost you a pretty penny), ask it to use the latest technologies and interactive principles.

## BASIC MARKETING PRINCIPLES FOR THE WEB

After you've put up what you think is the perfect Web site for your business (it's fast, looks great, and you regularly promote the Web site via other online venues) you may find that you still have a problem: no one is buying your products.

Now you have to ask yourself if you really used the essential rules in marketing when you created your site. If not, you're in real trouble. Here are the rules that you must follow completely (partial efforts don't count in Web communication and marketing):

**Offer great customer service.** One thing that will drive your customers away faster than anything else is poor customer service. This ranges from taking an eternity to answer your email, to shipping delays. You need to respond quickly, especially when it comes to email. In our "hurry-hurry" society, people will not wait to hear from you for very long before moving on to the next guy. Do you have your email address on every page of your Web site? Nothing irritates people more than having to dig through a site just to find an address to ask a question. Do you offer a toll-free number so they can contact you? This is easy to do and free with http://www.ureach.com.

**Make it clear who you are and what you do.** We can't tell you how many sites never really tell people what they sell. Identify your company and your products on the home page. Don't make people "dig" down into your site for the answer. They won't; they'll just leave. Also, make sure you describe the benefits of your service or product right away. For example, will it save time or money? Make you richer, thinner, or happier? Is it easy-to-use? People don't care about you, they want to know "what's in it for me?" Tell them and tell them fast, or risk losing them.

**Offer the right price!** If you charge too much, no one will buy. If you charge too little, people will think there's no value or that there's something wrong with your product or service. (And they still won't buy.) Before you set your pricing, make sure you do a little research into your competitor's backyard. That way, you'll have a better idea of where to set your pricing. Don't forget about "perceived value." Anything you can add on in the way of free bonuses or free shipping will go a long way in convincing folks to buy.

**Your copy (content) has to sell!** Make sure your text helps motivate your customers to make a purchase. Sprinkle "powerful headlines," "calls to action," and plenty of testimonials from happy customers throughout your pages. Remember that people read differently online: they skim. Make it easy for them to catch the main points and benefits quickly. Also, offer a few different payment options and make it easy to place an order. Simple and easy is the rule.

**Design your site with your target market in mind.** Does the look of your Web site cater to the kind of people who will want to buy your product or service? You need to know the demographics of your intended audience before you even begin the construction process. Know your market's age bracket, income, education, and primary gender composition. If your site is geared towards teenagers, it needs to look fun, trendy, and "cool" (save the sophisticated look for the adults). If your audience is businesspeople, you need a corporate look. Make sure you keep your core audience in mind when choosing your fonts, site colors, and graphics.

**Focus on content and navigation.** Content and ease of navigation are the most important elements in keeping your web visitors. This may sound simplistic, but too many companies put more emphasis on marketing their site than worrying about how and what their web site communicates. Whether it be due to out-dated content or poor navigation or layout, too many web sites are failing to meet the demands of their site visitors. If your site doesn't give the users what they want or the ability to locate what they are looking for quickly, there are thousands of other web sites that probably do.

## Using the Real Time Advantage

How about trying real time communication on your Web site? Take a look at http://www.humanclick.com, which allows you to answer questions from your website guests as they browse your site. The more ways you give people to communicate with you, the better. Many companies fail in their online businesses due to poor customer service, and poor communication is often at the heart of poor service. By offering opportunities for your customers to communicate with you, you'll stand out from the crowd and build better relationships with your contacts, customers, and clients. Remember it's easier to re-sell to an existing customer than it is to find a new one.

You must incorporate these basic marketing principles into your Web site. You'll have a site that looks good and communicates the message of your business. And more importantly, the site will do what you intended it to do: make a sale and keep customers coming back for more.

# Appendices

# Appendix A: Emoticons, Smilies, and Acronyms for Online Communication

## EMOTICONS AND SMILIES: SHOW YOUR EMOTIONS ON THE INTERNET

PEOPLE USE THESE SIMPLE KEYSTROKES, found on any keyboard, to express emotions, thoughts, and actions in online communications. They substitute for the computer user's body language, which can't be seen in text-based interactions. These emoticons (also called smilies) are commonly found in email, usenet postings, newsgroups, chat rooms, and mailing lists. Chatters use the most smilies and acronyms because it saves so much time in a realtime conversation. So, if you want to be a great chatter, you should learn the symbols and the acronyms. For email, limit your use of the emoticons and acronyms to the basic ones shown in the chapters.

| Symbol | Definition | Symbol | Definition |
|---|---|---|---|
| :-) or :) | smile, happy | :-( or :( | unhappy |
| ;-) | wink, jest | I-O | yawning |
| :- )) | very happy | =) | surprised |
| :-D | laughing | :-O | shocked |
| :-< | forlorn | :'-C | crying |
| :-e | disappointed | >:-< | mad |
| >:-( | mad | (:-< | frowning |
| (:-( | frowning | :-> | sarcastic |
| :-p | sticking out tongue | :-* | kiss |
| d:-o | taking their hat off to a great idea | :-8 | talking out of both sides of their mouth |
| :-y | saying it w/ a smile | :-v | is talking |
| :-V | is shouting | :-(0) | is yelling |
| *:-I | day dreaming | :-{ | someone w/mustache |
| =^..^= | cat | :-} | nervous smile |
| :o} | bashful/embarrassed | :o[ | not impressed |
| 8-) | wearing glasses | :-)8 | wearing a bow tie |
| B-) | wearing sunglasses | = : O | WOW |
| =o) | pleasant surprise | :-x | my lips are sealed |
| };-)> | devil | O:-) | angel |
| :q | licking upper lip | :-)} | trying not to laugh |
| :-/ | grim | {{{}}} | lots of hugs |
| :-& | tongue tied | $-) | greedy |
| X-) | I saw nothing | :-I | indifferent |
| (-: | happy left-hander | :-7 | wry comment |
| :-S | confused | :-c | depressed |
| O0o:-) | thinking | :( ) = | can't stop talking |

# Appendix B: Online Abbreviations and Acronyms

HERE'S A LIST OF ACRONYMS AND ABBREVIATIONS you may find in chat rooms or email. In chat, use any of these you think people will understand. In email, limit your use of acronyms to the most basic ones—those we discussed in the chapters. In formal email (such as a job application or a formal product proposal to a customer), don't use these at all.

| | |
|---|---|
| BFN | bye for now |
| BTSOOM | beats the [stuffing] out of me |
| BTW | by the way |
| CUA | commonly used acronym(s) OR common user access |
| FAQ | frequently asked question |
| FU | [fouled] up |

| | |
|---|---|
| FUBAR | [fouled] up beyond all recognition |
| FUD | (spreading) fear, uncertainty, and disinformation |
| FWIW | for what it's worth |
| FYI | for your information |
| GR&D | grinning, running, & ducking |
| HTH | hope this helps |
| IAE | in any event |
| IANAL | I am not a lawyer (also IANAxxx, such as IANAMD or IANACPA) |
| IMCO | in my considered opinion |
| IMHO | in my humble opinion |
| IMNSHO | in my NOT so humble opinion |
| IMO | in my opinion |
| IOW | in other words |
| LOL | lots of luck or laughing out loud or (sometime) lots of love |
| MHOTY | my hat's off to you |
| NFW | no [bleeping] way |
| NRN | no reply necessary |
| OIC | oh, I see! |
| OOTB | out of the box (brand new) |
| OTOH | on the other hand |
| OTTH | on the third hand |
| PITA | pain in the [. . .] |
| PMFJI | pardon me for jumping in |
| ROTFL | roll(ing) on the floor laughing (also, ROF,L, ROFL) |
| RSN | real soon now (which may actually be a long time away) |
| RTFM | read the [full] manual (or message) |
| SITD | still in the dark |
| SNAFU | situation normal, all [fouled] up |
| TANSTAAFL | there ain't no such thing as a free lunch |
| TIA | thanks in advance |
| TIC | tongue in cheek |
| TLA | three-letter acronym (such as this) |
| TTFN | ta ta for now |

| | |
|---|---|
| TTYL | talk to you later |
| TYVM | thank you very much |
| W4W | (WP4W, etc.; all the various products, such as . . .) |
| WYSIWYG | what you see is what you get |
| 7/24 | all day long, seven days a week, 24 hours a day |

# Appendix C: The Ten Commandments for Computer Ethics

THESE TEN COMMANDMENTS FOR COMPUTER ETHICS were created by the Computer Ethics Institute. We think they're worth knowing and practicing to keep the online universe a productive, safe, communicative environment. Here they are:

1. Thou shalt not use a computer to harm other people.
2. Thou shalt not interfere with other people's computer work.
3. Thou shalt not snoop around in other people's files.
4. Thou shalt not use a computer to steal.
5. Thou shalt not use a computer to bear false witness.
6. Thou shalt not use or copy software for which you have not paid.
7. Thou shalt not use other people's computer resources without authorization.

8. Thou shalt not appropriate other people's intellectual output.

9. Thou shalt think about the social consequences of the program you write.

10. Thou shalt use a computer in ways that show consideration and respect.

# Index

# ALL ABOUT VALUE INVESTING

# OTHER TITLES IN THE "ALL ABOUT" FINANCE SERIES

# ALL ABOUT
# VALUE INVESTING

**Esmé Faerber**

New York   Chicago   San Francisco   Athens   London
Madrid   Mexico City   Milan   New Delhi
Singapore   Sydney   Toronto

1 2 3 4 5 6 7 8 9 0    QFR/QFR    1 9 8 7 6 5 4 3

| | |
|---|---|
| ISBN | 978-0-07-181112-5 |
| MHID | 0-07-181112-5 |
| | |
| e-ISBN | 978-0-07-181113-2 |
| e-MHID | 0-07-181113-3 |

This publication is designed to provide accurate and authoritative information in regard to the subject matter covered. It is sold with the understanding that neither the author nor the publisher is engaged in rendering legal, accounting, securities trading, or other professional services. If legal advice or other expert assistance is required, the services of a competent professional person should be sought.

—*From a Declaration of Principles Jointly Adopted by a Committee of the American Bar Association and a Committee of Publishers and Associations*

**Library of Congress Cataloging-in-Publication Data**

Faerber, Esmé.
  All about value investing / by Esmé Faerber.
    pages cm
  ISBN-13: 978-0-07-181112-5 (pbk.)
  ISBN-10: 0-07-181112-5 (pbk.)
  1. Investments.   2. Investment analysis.   3. Value. I. Title.
  HG4521.F274 2014
  332.6--dc23                                                        2013017765

# CONTENTS

# PREFACE

> *Buy and you'll be sorry,*
> *Sell and you'll regret.*
> *Hold and you'll worry,*
> *Do nothing and you'll fret.*
> —The trader's lament

The trader's lament epitomizes the agonies that every investor experiences when making investment decisions. The insight provided by the trader's lament is that hindsight always produces the best results with 20-20 vision. Without clairvoyance into the future, however, investors are open to making investment mistakes. The aim of this book is to reduce the typical investment mistakes made. It is not possible to always be 100 percent correct in the investment decisions made, but knowing when investments are cheap and when they are expensive will decrease the error rate made by investors. Value investing is finding stocks that are trading at bargain prices and then selling them when they have risen in value to their fair or intrinsic values. This could mean waiting a long time, holding these stocks before they are recognized by the majority of investors.

This book illustrates the different value investment styles. Deep value investors look for undervalued stocks that have been temporarily beaten down for one reason or another, but the companies have strong balance sheets and competitive advantages that will restore the stock's value over time. Not all value investors are deep value investors. Growth stocks can come down in price as a result of circumstances and may present value at their lowered prices. Similarly, value investors could look for dividend yielding stocks that present value. If you believe that the business environment is not going to grow significantly, then value stocks that provide dividend yields are the answer. If on the other hand you believe that the economy is geared to growth, then growth stocks are the answer.

This book illustrates the different investment styles. After reading this book, investors should have a better idea of the value investment style that they feel comfortable with in assembling their investment portfolios.

Esmé Faerber

# CHAPTER 1

# Value Investing: What It Is and What It Is Not

There are two sides to every security transaction: a buyer of the security and a seller of the security. So it would seem that one of the two parties must be wrong. Not necessarily; one or both parties could make a profit, depending on the circumstances and the time. On the one hand, either the security has reached a price at which the seller thinks it will not rise any more or at which the seller wants to exit to realize an amount of profit. On the other hand, the buyer of the security thinks the security will rise in price and provide future profit. Consequently, both the buyer and the seller could realize profits over time.

Where or how does the value investor fit in this example? The value investor looks at the underlying aspects of the security to determine whether its price undervalues or overvalues the business to grow its future earnings (profits). The value investor buys the security when the price is less than the underlying value of the business and sells the security when the price is greater than the underlying value of the business.

Value investing can then be defined as looking for companies with strong fundamentals (good earnings, a strong cash flow) that are trading at bargain prices. Value investing is looking for businesses that are incorrectly valued by the market and can increase in value when the market recognizes that mistaken valuation. The astute reader will immediately question the contradiction of this previous statement, which is also negated by the efficient market hypothesis.

## EFFICIENT MARKET HYPOTHESIS

The efficient market hypothesis contends that stocks are always fairly valued, trading at their intrinsic values. According to the efficient market theory, information about companies is conveyed quickly and efficiently by the market, resulting in no underpriced stocks. In other words, when a stock is underpriced, investors will buy the stock, sending it up to its fair value, and when a stock is overpriced, it is sold by holders until it reaches its fair or intrinsic value. Consequently, there are no or very few undervalued or over-valued stocks.

The question to ask is: if the efficient market hypothesis works as stated, how is it possible that there are value investors, such as Warren Buffet, who can outperform the markets? After all, if the efficient market theory is accurate and there are no undervalued stocks, all the financial analysis in the world would not be able to find any profitable stocks. However, the flip side of the coin is that Warren Buffet is real and his returns have beaten the market, which strongly suggests that value investing works.

There are many reasons why the markets are not efficient all the time and stocks trade away from their intrinsic values. History provides many examples of stocks trading away from their intrinsic values. For example, the three-year period of the dot-com (Internet) bubble, when the Nasdaq increased by 317 percent from April 1997 to March 2000, and then declined by more than that increase to end up below the April 1997 base, shows the "irrational exuberance" of the market. Internet stocks were so overvalued in that many of those companies had good ideas, with the promise of revenues, but questionable or no earnings. The prices of those stocks continued their meteoric rise until the bubble burst and the market came to its senses. Many value investors, including Warren Buffet, avoided many of the Internet stocks, and they outperformed the Nasdaq over the five-year period from 1997, while the Nasdaq took years thereafter to recover from the dot-com bubble.

The lesson to be drawn from this example is that value does matter. Following the crowd to buy stocks that are priced at lofty multiples to their earnings might be profitable for nimble investors who trade frequently and who time the markets accurately. However, the odds of timing the market accurately are stacked against investors and day traders. According to a study by T. Rowe Price in 1987, if an investor is correct 50 percent of the time in market timing calls (buy and sell decisions), he would earn less than a buy and hold investor.[1] In another study done by William F. Sharpe, originator of the Sharpe index and the Capital Asset Pricing Model (CAPM), market timers would have to be more accurate more than 70 percent of the time in their market timing decisions of switching between stocks and bonds just to break even with buy and hold investors.[2]

Hindsight provides 20-20 guidance. Investors who bought Internet stocks during the dot-com bubble made money if their timing decisions were 100 percent accurate in that they sold their stocks before the crash in March 2000. However, most investors should not rely on being clairvoyant in investment decision making in order to profit.

When stocks rise in price due to hype or momentum buying, they move away from their intrinsic values, suggesting that the market is not entirely efficient in valuing these stocks. The question is: How efficient is the market in valuing stocks? We know that the market is not 100 percent efficient because there are periods of irrationality when stocks are overbought or oversold. Investors become irrational when they buy stocks that have already gone up considerably in price in order to share in the greed index, and when the market declines, irrational investors sell their stocks for less than they are worth. The major lesson to be learned from this is not to follow the crowd. When stocks have been beaten down in price, they may be selling for less than the intrinsic values in their underlying businesses.

Markets create opportunities for value investors; when the crowd is unloading their stocks, value investors are presented with opportunities to profit. Similarly, when investors are buying stocks and driving them above their intrinsic values, value investors should be selling their stocks to realize profits.

## VALUE INVESTING DEFINED

Value investing has evolved from the work of Benjamin Graham and David Dodd and the premise of finding companies with stock prices trading below their intrinsic worth. This basic definition needs clarification from the following common misconception applied to value investing. A simple example illustrates this misconception. When a stock that was trading at $100 per share is now trading at $50 per share it is a value stock. Not necessarily: whether it is a value stock depends on the underlying worth of the company. Just because the stock has lost half its value does not automatically qualify it as a value stock. When Enron's stock was cut in half, it might have looked like a value stock, but investments at that stock price would have lost money for investors after the stock plummeted to zero at bankruptcy. The price that the stock is trading at does not always reflect the value of the company. For example, Intel stock declined by 20 percent from a yearly high of $23.88 in May 2011 to $19.19 a share on August 10, 2011, even after Intel provided positive future guidance on revenues and earnings, which were above analysts' estimates.

Looking at the fundamentals of the company, you can see why Intel stock was undervalued. Intel is the largest producer of computer chips in the world, and the reason for the decline in the stock price was because the company did not adapt its chips to the lower power needs of mobile processors.[3] Part of the reason for the decline in Intel stock price was that personal computer shipments for the year 2011 rose by only 14.8 percent, whereas by comparison annual shipments for smartphones increased by 63 percent for that year.

Even though the sales of personal computers are expected to be a dying market, Intel is expected to grow its share of the personal computer market due to faster growth in the emerging markets, Brazil and China.[4] Veverka[5] points out that Intel has a four-year lead in manufacturing process technology, which gives Intel an edge in the Ultrabook, tablet, and smartphone markets, which will fuel Intel's future growth in sales and earnings.

According to Todd Lowenstein, the portfolio manager of a value-momentum fund, the upside to Intel's stock price over the next two years is $38–$40 per share, which was 50 percent above the current price of $26 per share on June 12, 2012.[6] Lowenstein's opinion is that Intel's current stock price does not reflect Intel's growth in personal computing in emerging markets, its position in cloud computing, and future growth from its mobile communications business.

Delving further into Intel's financial statements confirms this rosy picture. Revenues have increased every year since 2002 except for two years (2006 and 2009), and estimates for 2012 were for increased revenues over 2011. Gross margins have fluctuated within a range of 50 to 60 percent for the 14-year period from 1995 to 2009. However, in 2010 through 2011 gross margins increased to 65 percent and were expected to remain in this range for 2012. Intel's yearly earnings per share have increased from 2009 to 2011, and future earnings per share are projected to be $2.39 for the year 2012 and $2.51 for 2013. Intel's P/E (price-to-earnings) ratio is currently 11 and for the past five years has traded in a range from a low of 9.27 times in September 2011 to a high of 47.73 times earnings in September 2009. The average P/E ratio for this period for Intel stock was 18. Consequently, Intel stock is trading at the low end of its P/E ratio range, and with increased earnings, the projection is for Intel's stock price to increase due to expansion of its P/E multiple.

Furthermore, Intel pays a dividend of $0.84 per share, which is a 3.1 percent dividend yield. Considering the current low yields of 1.45 percent for a 10-year Treasury bond, owning Intel stock provides a return on capital with upside potential and very little downside risk of loss in the stock price. With this history, investors can assess Intel's current status as a value company.

## Price/Earnings Ratio

Before defining value stocks, it is important to explain the price-to-earnings ratio more fully. The P/E ratio is the most commonly used guide to the relationship between a company's stock price and its earnings. The ratio is computed by dividing the market price of the stock by its earnings per share. The P/E ratio, therefore, indicates the multiple that an investor is willing to pay for a dollar of a company's earnings. In other words, the P/E ratio shows the number of times a stock's price is trading relative to its earnings. Bear in mind that stock prices fluctuate from moment to moment, and so do P/E ratios. Rising P/E ratios are linked to higher stock prices.[7] For example, Intel is currently trading at 11 times earnings, and if it earns $2.51 in 2013, then Intel should trade at $27.61 (11 × $2.51). As Intel's stock price rises, so does its P/E ratio. Consequently, if Intel's multiple expands to 13 and earnings per share grow, the stock price will also increase. Using P/E ratios is one other way to determine whether a stock is undervalued or overvalued.

In general, value stocks have low P/E ratios whereas growth stocks have high P/E ratios. Value investors are bargain hunters, looking for companies with good products or ideas whose stock prices have declined, or companies that have been performing poorly but have good long-term prospects. A good example of another low P/E stock whose prospects look better in the future is Freeport-McMoran Copper & Gold Inc. (ticker symbol FCX). The current P/E ratio of FCX is 8 at a stock price of $32.18 per share. The stock price of FCX has declined because of the economic slowdown in the emerging economies and the developed countries, resulting in less demand for the minerals mined by FCX: copper, molybdenum, and gold. Consequently, FCX stock has the potential to rise in price when the economies of the developed world and emerging markets start to expand, thereby needing more copper, molybdenum, and gold.

Further comparison of the fundamental factors of FCX versus its competitors confirms the rosy outlook for Freeport-McMoran. FCX is one of the largest international mining companies, with an impressive record of returns to its shareholders, despite the decline in its share price from a 52-week high of $56 per share and a low of $28.85.

Return on investment was 19 percent and return on equity was 26 percent. FCX's peers in the mining industry underperformed Freeport on both returns on investment and equity. Investors in FCX stock are paid a 4 percent annual dividend yield while waiting for the price of the stock to rebound when the economies of the world's countries rebound.

The P/E ratio can be calculated using trailing earnings of the past four quarters, or it can use expected earnings based on forecasts of the upcoming year's earnings. This future P/E ratio may be of greater significance to investors looking for value stocks because this is an indication of the expectations for the stock in the future.

However, investors should not base their decisions solely on P/E multiples; the type of industry and capital structure also affect the P/E ratio. Some industries have higher average P/E ratios than others, and it would not necessarily be a meaningful evaluation to compare the P/E ratios across industries. For example, the pharmaceutical and utility companies have much higher P/E multiples than industrial companies, which have been beaten down in price with the talk of the economy entering another recession. Comparing the P/E multiples of Merck with that of Eaton would be meaningless. In addition, some industries require much greater investments in property, plant, and equipment than others, which means that they probably have much more debt on their books. Consequently, a low P/E ratio is a relative measure, and value investors should look at the fundamental characteristics of the company in addition to the P/E ratio before deeming a stock of a company to be a value stock. This note of caution on P/E ratios is further confirmed by the differing P/E ratios within the same sector. The average P/E ratio for the hospital sector for 2013 is 7.9, as compared with P/E ratios of 11.7 for the drug makers and 12.5 for the medical equipment manufacturers.[8]

## Value Stocks Defined

Value investing relies on fundamental analysis to determine when a stock is trading at less than its intrinsic value. This style is the opposite of growth investing, in which investors are willing to chase after stocks with good growth records that have already risen in price. Value investors are bargain hunters looking for stocks that have been performing poorly but have good long-term prospects. A good example of value stocks are the home building companies that declined precipitously in price as a result of the real estate bubble beginning in 2006. Their P/E ratios were around four times their earnings. By 2012 home building companies had risen significantly from their lows, but they are still far from their average price ranges of a decade ago. Value investors are patient investors willing to wait for the home building cycle to move into an expansionary mode.

When a sector of stocks has lagged other sectors over long periods, the gap eventually narrows, and the laggard sectors likely will outperform those other stock sectors in the future. This concept is known as regression to the mean. The flip side of this concept is that stocks that have been outperforming the market likely will revert to the mean and underperform the market at some stage in the future.

Value investors are, therefore, always looking for stocks with P/E multiples that are less than their expected long-term growth rates. A definition of a value stock is one in which the company's P/E ratio is lower than its earnings growth rate. For example, Apple's expected growth rate for 2012 was 69 percent with a P/E multiple of 12, and forecasts for 2013 for Apple's growth is 16 percent with a forward P/E multiple of 10. Consequently, according to this definition, Apple is a value stock. A stock whose P/E ratio exceeds its growth rate is not considered to be a value stock.

There is no unanimous agreement on the definition of value stocks. Some definitions center on low P/E multiples or those that are below the market multiples. Others focus on low multiples of cash flow or low price-to-book (P/B) ratios. The most conservative definition of a value stock is one that has an above-average dividend yield. Out of favor stocks are also classified by some as value stocks. For example, Intel and Cisco were considered to be growth stocks, and when they declined in value in 2006, many fund managers bought them as value stocks. Depending then on how you define value, many investors come up with different sets of value stocks. Some of the bases for determining value stocks are discussed in greater detail throughout this book.

## WHAT VALUE INVESTING IS NOT

Having defined value investing, it is important to understand what it is not, and to look at some of the common misconceptions about value investing.

### Value Traps: Be Aware of Them

Not all stocks that have declined in price are value stocks. For example, the stock price of Nokia, which at one time had the largest share of the world cell phone market, began to fall as it lost market share over the years. When its stock price was cut by two thirds ($7.38 per share on October 27, 2011, to $2.04 on June 18, 2012), many on Wall Street referred to Nokia as a value stock. After Nokia failed to capture market share with its high-end smart phone, the company became a value trap (a company that has no potential growth). It seemed that Nokia had run out of ideas to grow its sales and earnings. Nokia's share of the market was declining and an analysis of its share reveals that it is mainly in lower-end cell phones with low margins. With this type of make-up in the market, Nokia cannot easily boost its earnings (profits).

When a stock has fallen in value, investors need to analyze the business and financial statements of the company to determine whether there is a catalyst that can increase future sales and earnings. If not, it is a typical value trap. Furthermore, Nokia is an unlikely candidate to be bought out by another company; being one of the largest Finnish companies, it is unlikely that the Finnish authorities would allow a foreign company to buy its assets. Consequently, it may take much too long for even value investors to wait to see if Nokia can turn itself around in the long-term future.

## Stock Price Movements May Not Always Reflect the Business of the Company

Stock markets have become more volatile, and when stock prices decline or rise precipitously over a few days, it does not mean that the companies are broken or prospering respectively. In other words, there may be no changes to sales and earnings, and stock prices have gone up or down due to reasons in the market place. There are many reasons other than the fundamental characteristics of companies for volatility in the marketplace. For example, the price of a stock could decline because short-term traders and investors are taking profits (selling) even though the company's fundamental factors are improving. Money managers are sometimes forced to sell to raise needed cash, which can cause the stocks of companies with good earnings to decline in price. Consequently, you need to pay attention to the fundamental earnings of a company to determine whether the long-term prospects are good rather than the stock price alone. Just because the stock is trading at a low price does not in itself make it a value company.

## An MBA or a CPA Is Required to Be a Value Investor

Another misconception is that to be able to pick value stocks successfully, you need years of training in business analysis and finance. Even if you do not understand financial statements, you can still be a value investor by knowing what to look for in the financial statements. The process is the same when you look for bargains when you go shopping, buying something for $5 when it is being sold elsewhere for $10.

You want to be sure that the company whose stock you want to invest in is a financially healthy company. The chapter on financial statements outlines what to look for in them to determine whether a company is financially sound. You can be reassured when you recall the many CEOs of large corporations who have either paid too much to acquire a company or run a company into the ground and bankrupted it. These CEOs more than likely understood the workings of finance and accounting but in the end were clueless. Perhaps these CEOs were sidetracked and lost sight of the company's goals. Value investors want to buy into companies whose stocks are trading below their intrinsic worth. Knowing what to look for in financial statements can assist you in finding value stocks.

### If a Company Is Not Growing, It Appeals to Value Investors

A value stock is not the opposite of a growth stock. A growth stock reflects a company whose sales or earnings are growing rapidly. However, the stock price of such a company is also appreciating rapidly in value to reflect the rapid growth. Value investors would not chase after the price of such a stock. The misconception is that value stocks are the opposite of growth stocks, implying that value stocks reflect companies with no or low growth in sales or earnings.

Value investors are patient investors who are willing to wait until a stock comes back into favor to achieve its potential growth. The key to determining the difference between value stocks and value traps is analysis of the company and the industry it is in.

The discussion between value and growth stock investing is explored further in Chapter 2 so you can determine the investment style with which you are most comfortable.

# Are You a Value Investor?

Understanding the workings of the market and the different investment styles will determine whether you are comfortable being a value investor, and what variation of value investor you are. The first step in the process is to analyze the stock market to see which investment style has been working, as well as the relationships between value and growth stocks. As you will see, studying the performance of the stock market will suggest that there are specific times when it is beneficial to be a value investor.

## STOCK MARKET ANALYSIS

The performance of the stock market during the three-year period from 2009 to 2011 indicates that value stocks underperformed growth stocks, as measured by the Russell 1000 Growth Index versus the Russell 1000 Value Index. These same results were extended into the first six months of 2012: the Russell 1000 Growth Index had an 8.3 percent return as compared with a 4.1 percent return for the Russell 1000 Value Index.[1] Yet, in the first quarter of 2013, small-cap and mid-cap stocks outperformed large-cap stocks, and value stocks outperformed growth stocks among the large-cap and mid-cap stocks.

This disparity in the underperformance of value stocks versus growth stocks bears further analysis. At face value it would seem that cheap stocks got cheaper during this three-and-a-half-year period. Levisohn[2] points out that in 2011 the Russell 1000 Growth Index earned 2.6 percent, which included dividends, as compared with the 0.4 percent performance of the Russell 1000 Value Index. However, removing the financials from the Russell 1000 Value Index resulted in a gain of 7.3 percent for the Value Index. Yet in the first five months of 2012, financials gained 8.6 percent.

The conclusion that can be drawn from this example is that value stocks can underperform growth stocks over a three-to-four-year period every now and again. Over longer periods of time, studies indicate that value stocks largely outperform growth stocks. The Brandes Institute found that value stocks outperformed growth stocks during the period 1980 to 2010 by 575 percent.[3] On a shorter time basis of one year, value stocks outperformed growth stocks in 2008. Similarly, Berkshire Hathaway Inc. (Warren Buffett's company) had three of its worst performance years relative to the market in 1967, 1980, and 1999. Yet in the year following these three, Berkshire Hathaway outperformed the S&P 500 by 49 percent, 102 percent, and 48 percent respectively.[4]

Table 2.1 summarizes the performance of stocks over the 32-year period from 1980 to 2013. There were times when value stocks outperformed growth stocks and when the opposite occurred (growth stocks outperformed value stocks). For the three-and-a-half-year period from 2009 to 2012 growth stocks outperformed value stocks, giving the appearance of growth stocks being overvalued in 2012. Consequently, an investor looking for value might consider buying value stocks over growth stocks because they were trading at a discount multiple to growth stocks.

The question to ask is, should investors continue to choose the leadership stocks in the sectors that have been doing well and ignore the other lagging sectors of the market? It is easier to answer this question for a long investment period, but over the short term, it becomes more of a guessing game. The *momentum investing style* is to invest in those stocks that have been going up in price. However,

**TABLE 2.1**

Performance of U.S. Stocks over the Period 1980–2012

| Value Stocks Outperform Growth Stocks | Growth Stocks Outperform Value Stocks |
|---|---|
| 1981 | 1980 |
| 1983–1984 | 1982 |
| 1986 | 1985 |
| 1987–1988 | 1987 |
| 1992–1993 | 1989–1991 |
| 1995 | 1996–1999 |
| 2000–2008 | |
| | 2009–2011 |
| | 2012 |
| 2013* | |

*first five-months

the main problem with momentum investing is that the turning point can never be predicted accurately. Leadership stocks eventually become laggards and the rotation shifts to other investment styles. Bear in mind that investing in leadership stocks at the top of their price cycles results in negative returns for the period of time until they come back into favor.

Which stocks would have returned more to investors over a long period of time? The answer may be surprising. A study done by David Leineweber and colleagues reported that $1 invested in both value and growth stocks, as followed by the P/B value of S&P 500 Index stocks during the period 1975–1995, would have resulted in $23 for value stocks versus $14 for growth stocks.[5] These results also have been confirmed by studies done on foreign stocks. A study done by Capaul, Rowley and Sharpe[6] determined that value stocks outperformed growth stocks abroad (France, Germany, Switzerland, Japan, and the United Kingdom) during the period January 1981–June 1992. Jeremy Siegel, a professor at the University of Pennsylvania, found that value stocks outperformed growth stocks over the 35-year period between July 1963 and December 1998. Value stocks earned 13.4 percent annually, whereas growth stocks earned 12 percent annually.[7]

This phenomenon of value stocks outperforming growth stocks over long periods should have some significance in the choice of stocks for investment portfolios. However, the evidence shows that winning stocks do not keep their positions over time; they revert to the mean. Similarly, losing stocks do not remain losers over long periods of time because they too rise to the average. In other words, the high-flying growth stocks of today will not be able to sustain their abnormally high returns and will turn into stocks with lower returns, while the low returns of today's value stocks will surprise investors with higher returns. This phenomenon of returns reverting to the mean over time can be applied to small-cap and large-cap stocks, in addition to value and growth stocks. Thus, patient value investors are willing to wait for value stocks to come out of the doghouse. Besides studying the stock market, investors should also analyze the relationship of the economy and the stock market.

## THE STOCK MARKET AND THE ECONOMY

According to Vadim Zlotnikov, chief market strategist at Alliance-Bernstein, the uncertain economic environment has favored growth stocks instead of the typical approach of favoring value stocks.[8] In this uncertain economic environment, investors gravitated toward higher-quality growth companies instead of the cheaper value stocks, which then became even cheaper.

Inflation is another factor to consider. In periods of rising inflation, value stocks tend to outperform growth stocks. During the high-inflation rates during the period 1976–1979, value stocks returned 25 percent versus 9 percent for growth stocks.[9] During rising prices, real assets and equipment also rise in value, accounting for value companies' asset growth and returns. During periods of stable prices and low-interest rates (2008–2012, for example), companies use their resources to pay down debt rather than expanding their assets, which accounts for growth stocks outperforming value stocks.

There is a positive correlation between interest rates and the performance of the stock market. When interest rates increase this has a depressing effect on the market. Similarly, when interest rates fall, the stock markets generally rise. With short-term interest rates held near 0 percent, the stock market has risen as expected. Yet with sustained high unemployment and the uncertainty of higher impending tax rates, more government regulation in the private sector, and low GDP growth, the market has taken a roller-coaster ride, displaying greater volatility. With this volatile trend in the market, investors have gravitated to dividend-paying stocks. Bond investors looking for yield have also moved into dividend-paying stocks. Another reason bond investors have been prompted to move into higher-yielding stocks than the yields currently offered by bonds is that prices of existing bonds move inversely with changes in interest rates. When rates of interest begin to rise from their current near 0 percent, bond prices will decline. Astute bond investors are not going to invest in 10-year bonds paying close to 1.4 percent when they can invest, instead, in blue chip stocks yielding 3 percent on average, such as McDonald's, Home Depot, Conoco Phillips, and Procter & Gamble.

With money market securities earning less than the rate of inflation and bond yields equaling close to the inflation rate, investing in dividend-paying stocks looks more attractive. But the higher-yielding stocks in master limited partnerships and utility companies have risen considerably in price, making them overvalued, and they may not offer as much value as the 3-percent-yielding blue chip stocks.

Studies adapted from Al Frank Asset Management and professors Eugene Fama and Kenneth French indicated that $1,000 invested from June 1927 through 2011 in the top 30-percent dividend-paying stocks (value stocks) would have returned $7.9 million as compared with $800,000 from stocks not paying dividends (growth stocks).[10]

## FIGURE 2.1

Economic Cycles and the Different Types of Stocks

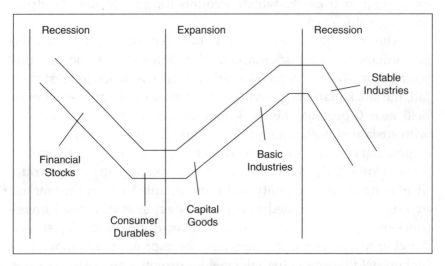

Source: Susan E Kuhn, "Stocks Are Still Your Best Buy," *Fortune,* March 21, 1994, pp. 130–144.

For clarification on which sectors of the economy to invest in, you need to determine where the economy is headed. Figure 2.1 shows when to typically buy different sector stocks in the different stages of the economic cycle. Value investors seeking larger returns might be tempted to buy and sell stocks as market trends and economic factors change. Certain industries are more sensitive to the cycles of the economy than other industries. Those that move in the same direction as the economy are referred to as cyclical industries. In other words, sales and earnings of cyclical industries move with the economic cycle.

The stage in the economic cycle becomes more important to the timing of investments in these cyclical industries and companies. For example, you would not want to invest in auto company stocks, building construction company stocks, and material stocks at the peak of an economic expansionary period because stock prices would be at their upper limits; these companies would face a downturn in earnings when the economy slows down. Because these stocks are sensitive to changes in economic activity, investors should time their purchases of cyclical stocks to the early phases of an economic expansionary period.

Coming out of a recession, financial stocks typically do well because of lower interest rates. This relationship between financial stocks and the economy moving out of recession was not initially confirmed at the end of the 2010 and 2011 recession, but in the first few months of 2012 these stocks outperformed many other sectors, largely due to near 0-percent interest rates.

At the end of a recession, stocks of consumer durable, capital goods, and cyclical companies typically are the ones to buy. During a recession, consumers delay purchases of automobiles, large appliances, and houses. Cyclical stocks fluctuate with the state of the economy, and at the end of a recession, there is pent-up demand in the economy for capital goods, cars, and houses. Into an expansionary cycle, capital goods companies benefit from increased sales in the business sector, which results in an increase in the demand for raw materials and commodities. At the end of an expansionary period, when the economy looks as if it is entering a recession, defensive stocks (stable industries) do well. Stable industries include pharmaceutical companies, health-care stocks, beverage stocks, food companies, consumer services, and household nondurables. Many companies in the defensive sector pay dividends, which also insulates these stocks from some of the market risk when stock prices decline.[11]

This pattern is typical in most economic cycles, but there are always exceptions. During the recession of 2000 to 2002, for example, sales of cars rose significantly because of the sales and marketing programs offered by the auto companies, including 0-percent financing and considerable price discounts. Despite this increase in sales, the auto companies didn't see improved profits. In the recession beginning in 2008, automobile companies performed more typically in that sales of cars declined, despite interest rates declining to near 0 percent. A major reason points to the increasing unemployment rate, with the lowest numbers of Americans employed in the workforce. By timing stock purchases in these industries through different economic cycles, value investors could improve their returns.

## Interest Rates in the Economy

Anticipating changes in interest rates could prompt investors to reallocate the types of investments in their portfolios. When interest rates rise, stock prices typically decline. However, with short-term rates near 0 percent, interest rates would have to increase significantly to impact the stock market. When interest rates reach the point at which stocks are affected, there are a number of different options open to investors. Profits might be taken by selling stocks that have appreciated, or the investor might decide to sell stocks in interest-sensitive industries, such as financial stocks or cyclical sector stocks in the automobile and home-building industries. Some investors might buy stocks in the pharmaceutical and food industries (defensive sector and stable industry stocks), which tend to weather the effects of higher interest rates better than the stocks from other sectors of the economy. Other investors might decide to hold their existing stocks but not invest any new money in the stock market until interest rates start to level off. True market timers might liquidate their entire stock positions and wait on the sidelines for more favorable conditions to get back into the stock market.[12]

Value investors who have investments in bond portfolios also have different strategies available to them when faced with rising interest rates. Bond prices react more predictably than stock prices during rising interest rates. There is an inverse relationship between interest rates and bond prices. When interest rates in the economy rise, prices of existing bonds fall, and the opposite occurs when interest rates decline, with prices of existing bonds rising.

When faced with rising interest rates, there are a number of different strategies that could be pursued. Investors might sell all their bond holdings and invest the proceeds in short-term bonds and money market securities while waiting for interest rates to level off. A less drastic action would be to sell the longer maturity bonds held in their portfolios and invest the proceeds in shorter maturity bonds. Another strategy would be to sell the lowest-yielding bonds held in their portfolios and put the proceeds into higher-yielding bonds. A more passive approach would be to wait to reinvest the proceeds of bonds in their portfolios that mature into higher-yielding bonds when interest rates are perceived to be near their peak.

Investors who have holdings in bond mutual funds will see an erosion of their principal, in that prices of all types of bond mutual funds will decline as interest rates rise. To preserve some of the losses in capital, bond investors could switch their bond mutual fund holdings to higher-yielding bond mutual funds or sell out of their bond mutual funds completely and move their money to money market mutual funds until interest rates near their peak and then go back into bond mutual funds whose yields will have risen.

The distinction between holding individual bonds and bond mutual funds is subtle. Individual bonds mature, but when bonds in mutual funds mature they are replaced by new bonds. Hence, an investor in individual bonds will always receive the principal that was invested, even though the yield will be less than newer bonds in rising interest rates. With bond mutual funds the investor will not get any principal back on bond maturity, so bond mutual fund prices decline steadily when interest rates rise.

## Inflation in the Economy

Inflation hurts all financial investments to some degree or another. Traditionally, however, returns on stocks tend to outperform those of bonds and money market securities during low to moderate growth in inflation. Mining stocks such as gold, platinum, copper, and aluminum companies have been good hedges against inflation.

# GROWTH VERSUS VALUE INVESTING STYLE

Growth and value investing styles are two distinctly different approaches to the selection of investments in stocks and bonds, though they may not be as far apart as they seem. Both value and growth investors are looking for stocks with the potential for good earnings growth, but the difference between the two is whether the stocks are undervalued or fairly valued when purchased by investors. Table 2.2 lists the typical characteristics of growth and value stocks.

Typically, value investors shun high P/E multiple stocks, such as Chipotle Mexican Grill, ticker symbol CMG, which has seen its stock price take off, rising significantly since its split off from McDonald's Corporation. Chipotle is a momentum stock, which is at the opposite end of the continuum of value stocks, as illustrated in Figure 2.2.

**TABLE 2.2**

Characteristics of Growth and Value Stocks

| Value Stocks | Growth Stocks |
|---|---|
| Lower P/E multiple than that of the market | Higher P/E multiple than that of the market |
| Lower P/B ratios than that of the market | Higher P/B ratios than that of the market |
| Stocks of companies that have fallen temporarily out of favor but still have good fundamentals | Higher growth or earnings rates than the market |
| Stock prices of companies that trade below their historic price averages | Stock prices that trade above their average prices |

**FIGURE 2.2**

Value versus Growth Stock Investment Styles Continuum

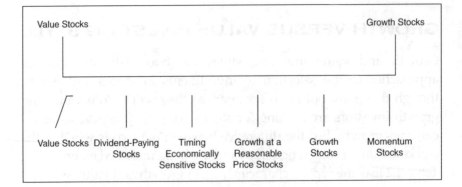

## Momentum Style

Momentum investing is the riskiest of the investing styles. Momentum investors look for stocks that are moving up in price, buy them, and settle in for the ride. The time to sell is when a stock's price peaks (before it begins to fall). This definition implies perfect timing on two accounts. The first is to correctly identify stock prices with an upward trend, and the second is to recognize when the stock is trading at or near its peak price. Many momentum investors will continue to buy a stock at its new high price because that is a sign that the stock has broken through a resistance level and will continue to rise in price.

The momentum style of investing is fraught with risk. Buying a stock at its 52-week high price that then declines in price will result in a loss of principal. To minimize the amount of potential losses, momentum investors need to be nimble traders. This style of investing favors market timing and a short time horizon for holding the stock.

Profits from this style of investing depend on the accuracy of the investor's decisions on when to buy and when to sell. Profits from this style of investing have the potential to be greater than from other styles of investing when these decisions are accurate. Momentum investors are more likely to rely on technical analysis to spot upward price trends.

Figure 2.3 shows the chart pattern of Chipotle Mexican Grill's stock price for the first eight months of 2012 as an example of how the stock price of momentum stocks are priced to perfection. An investor who correctly identified the upward growth trend of the stock price in January 2012 would have been handsomely rewarded by holding the stock until mid-April, when the price reached $440 per share. However, if the investor held the shares until July 20, when the stock price declined from around $400 per share to $300 per share, the investor would have lost money. Even with this precipitous decline in price, on August 24, 2012, the stock price was $295 per share and traded at a lofty P/E multiple of 36. Some of the possible reasons Chipotle lost almost a third of its value on July 20 include: revenues announced missed

**FIGURE 2.3**

Stock Price of Chipotle Mexican Grill

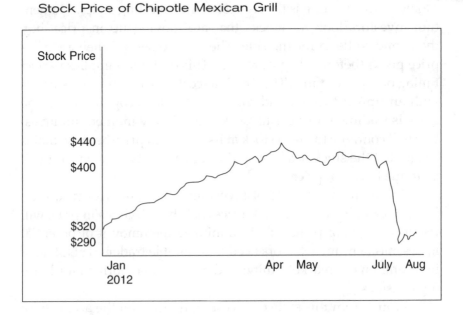

their estimates and same-store sales growth was below the company's past double-digit increases. As food and energy costs rose during 2012, Chipotle might not have been able to raise the prices of its menu items to pass on the increased costs to customers. In addition, Chipotle faced increased competition from its competitors, which also implies that its earnings (profits) will not be able to grow as fast in the future as they did after it was split off from McDonald's. As a value investor, the fundamentals of the stock do not look promising in that the company will likely not be able to support the same pattern of aggressive earnings forecasts as it was able to do in the past. Similarly, Chipotle looks overvalued to a value investor in comparison to its competitors: Chipotle is still trading at a lofty multiple of 36 times earnings when compared with McDonald's at 16 times its earnings, Yum! Brands, Inc., at 20 times its earnings, and Starbucks at 28 times its earnings.

## Growth Stock Investing Style

Growth companies have above average–growth rates of sales and/ or earnings. Growth investors are willing to pay high multiples of earnings for companies with high growth rates, which explains why growth stocks generally have high P/E multiples. Starbucks has a high P/E multiple of 28, and the multiple could expand as the company grows at its expected rate. If growth stocks do not sustain their high growth rates, their stock prices are severely punished, as we saw with momentum stock Chipotle Mexican Grill.

Apple is a good example of a growth stock. It has high sustained growth from sales of its iPad, iPhone, and iPod products, which are dominant in their respective markets, and they still have the ability to increase their market shares. Apple has been more innovative than its competitors, which also underscores its strong management. In addition, Apple paid a 1.57-percent dividend in September 2012, which cushions somewhat a potential fall in the stock price as a result of future disappointing earnings or reduced future estimates of growth.

Apple's stock price for the year from September 2011 to August 2012 in Figure 2.4 shows a better chart pattern than that of Chipotle Mexican Grill in Figure 2.3, illustrating the risk when momentum stocks fall out of favor. From a value investor's perspective, there is more value in Apple stock than in Chipotle Mexican Grill. Apple has a strong balance sheet in that it has $20 billion in cash and has no long-term debt. Its liquidity is good, meaning it can easily convert its current assets into cash to pay off its current liabilities (bills) as they come due. Yet despite paying a 1.57-percent dividend yield, it is still very much a growth stock. The company trades at roughly eight times book value and its P/E multiple is around sixteen times its earnings. As long as Apple delivers on its growth in sales and earnings, its stock price will continue to rise. The downside to growth stocks is that should companies fail to grow as rapidly as expected, their stock prices will be punished more severely than value stocks because expectations for growth stocks are much greater than those for value stocks.

**FIGURE 2.4**

Chart of Growth Stock: Apple Inc.

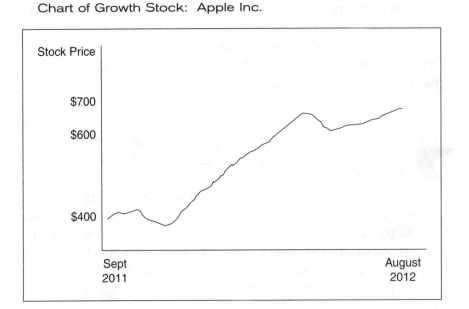

## Growth at a Reasonable Price (GARP) Investing Style

GARP is an investment style that falls somewhere in the middle of the continuum between value and growth. GARP investors look for companies with higher growth rates than their P/E multiples. In other words, they look for companies with relatively low P/E multiples, but the companies are also expected to have high growth characteristics. The PEG ratio (price-to-earnings-growth ratio) measures the valuation or P/E multiple of the company divided by the company's growth rate. GARP investors seek out stocks with a PEG ratio of one or less.

Table 2.3 lists some stocks that have PEG ratios of less than 1. The question to ask is, will these companies continue to grow at the same or greater rates in the future? If the answer is yes, then these companies are trading below their intrinsic values and are worth the investment. If, on the other hand, the growth is questionable or not sustainable into the future, the low PEG ratios become meaningless as to the companies providing value into the future.

**TABLE 2.3**

Growth at a Reasonable Price (GARP) Stocks

| Company | Ticker Symbol | P/E | 5-year NI growth* | PEG ratio |
|---|---|---|---|---|
| Abbott Laboratories | ABT | 21.34 | 22.46% | 0.95 |
| American Tower | AMT | 61.09 | 69.50% | 0.878 |
| CVS Caremark | CVS | 16.06 | 20.84% | 0.77 |
| FLIR Systems | FLIR | 13.26 | 17.15% | 0.77 |
| Intel | INTC | 10.46 | 20.74% | 0.50 |
| National Oilwell Varco | NOV | 14.17 | 23.86 | 0.59 |
| PotashCorp | POT | 14.14 | 37.55 | 0.38 |

*annualized growth rate of net income over a 5-year period; data as of August 29, 2012

## Timing the Purchase of Economically Sensitive Stocks Investment Style

At the outset the title to this section needs clarification in that the author is not advocating that investors resort to the market timing style of actively buying and selling stocks. Rather this section advocates using economic cycles to find undervalued stocks. For example, when an economy enters a recession, cyclical companies' (whose sales and earnings are directly related to the state of the economy) sales and earnings will decline. As a result their P/E multiples will increase as earnings fall, which then impacts the price of the stock in a downward direction. Value investors will use the stages in the business cycle to find value in purchasing stocks that are out of favor. Refer back to Figure 2.1 for the stages at which to time the purchases of the different industries in the economic cycle.

## Investing in Dividend Paying Stocks Investment Style

This investment style looks for the stocks of companies trading below their intrinsic or fair values that also provide a margin of safety through their dividend yields. Dividend investors are rewarded by receiving cash deposits when their stocks pay dividends. Buying a stock for $50 per share that pays a $2 per share dividend has a dividend yield of 4 percent ($2/$50). Dividend investors look for stocks with high dividend yields. However, before rushing to buy stocks with the highest dividend yields, investors should first investigate whether these companies can sustain payment without the risk of the dividend yields being cut in the near future.

To see how safe the dividend is, investors need to determine the dividend coverage of the company, which is the amount of dividends paid out of the company's profits. If, for example, a company has $100 million in profits and pays out $10 million in dividends, its payout ratio is 10 percent ($10 million/$100 million). However, if the company pays out $85 million in dividends, its payout ratio is 85 percent, which does not give shareholders much of a safety cushion for future payouts. Another reason to fear future dividend cuts with a high payout ratio is if profits of the company decline significantly. Investors should be aware of the reasons why a stock pays a high yield. A stock with a high yield that is paying out its earnings to investors may not be earning large profits. Instead, the company could have a high yield because the stock price has declined significantly as a result of poor management or bad news affecting the company. Consequently, it could be facing an imminent dividend cut.

Value dividend investors look for dividend yields that are not the highest but are higher than the yields of U.S. Treasury bonds. It is easy to see why value investors have so enthusiastically gravitated toward dividend stock investing. In the current economic climate, where the yields on money market and bank accounts have dropped to near zero, and 10-year bond yields are as low as 1.5 percent, investors have been pushed into dividend-yielding stocks to replace their lost income. These actions explain the dividend stock bubble, where stock prices of the highest dividend-yielding stocks such as master limited partnerships and utility stocks have been driven to overvalued levels. Consequently, value dividend investors should turn their attention to the lower-yielding traditional dividend-yielding stocks that still present good value.

Studies done by Al Frank Asset Management and professors Eugene Fama and Kenneth French, as reported by Spencer Jakab,[13] contrast the following returns on $1,000 invested from June 1927 through 2011 in baskets of U.S. stocks composed as following:

- $1,000 invested in the top 30 percent dividend payers resulted in $7.9 million

- $1,000 invested in the middle 40 percent dividend payers resulted in $4 million

- $1,000 invested in the lowest 30 percent dividend payers resulted in $1.3 million

- $1,000 invested in nondividend payers resulted in $0.8 million

Even though long-term results from this study point to the greatest advantage from investing in the highest dividend-paying stocks, the current reality of a bubble in these stocks, along with the possibility of a future decline in stock prices, should push value investors into choosing the lower dividend-yielding stocks that are still priced to provide value. The other aspect of this study is that nondividend-paying stocks provided the lowest returns over this long period.

Another approach to dividend-paying stocks is to invest in the companies that are likely to grow their dividends into the future. T. Rowe Price, the mutual fund company, did a study showing the following rates of return in different investments, as reported by Jack Hough in Barron's.[14]

- $100 invested in the Russell 1000 index at the end of 1978 would have increased to $4,055 by July 2012.

- $100 invested in only the dividend-paying stocks in the Russell 1000 index would have grown to $4,573 by July 2012.

- $100 in only the dividend growers would have increased to $5,244 by July 2012.

## Value Stock Investment Style

Value investing is the complete opposite to the growth investing style, which is to make a quick profit. Value investors look for companies whose stock prices are on sale, buy them at depressed prices, and then wait for them to reach their intrinsic or fair values before selling them for a profit. Value investors generally are patient, long-term investors who are willing to wait for the stock price to appreciate to its intrinsic value.

Cliffs Natural Resources, Inc. provides an illustration of a value company whose stock price is depressed due to world economic conditions. Cliffs, ticker symbol CLF, is an international mining and natural resources company. Its main business is the exploration and production of iron ore and metallurgical coal. Its stock price has declined by more than 50 percent from its 52-week high because of the slowdown in China's economic growth, along with the United States and Europe. China, along with other world economies, is a major customer for iron ore and metallurgical coal. When world economies come out of their recessionary cycle, Cliffs stock price will surge. Its stock price was trading at $34 per share as of September 5, 2012, and analysts' expectations are for the stock price to reach $62 per share within a year. Another reason why Cliffs's stock price is depressed and likely to come down further is the price of iron ore, which has been declining steadily and does not seem to have found a bottom.

Even though Cliffs's stock price has the potential to decline further, the company's fundamental strengths look compelling. The current stock price of $34 per share is less than the book value of $40.73 per share. In 2011, sales and income grew by over 60 percent, and the five-year growth rate for sales and net income were equally impressive (revenue growth of 31 percent and net income growth of 101 percent). The current P/E ratio is 2.93 and its forward P/E ratio is 5.14. Its gross profit margin in 2011 was 27.86 percent, its net profit margin 28 percent. Return on invested capital was 21.9 percent. Debt to total assets was 51.5 percent. The company generated a free cash flow of $1.29 billion and its cash flow per share was $16.23. A patient investor willing to buy CLF and wait until the economic environment for iron ore and metallurgical coal improves can expect gains in the stock price. In the meantime, investors in CLF stock are receiving a 7.2-percent dividend yield while they wait for the fundamental economic factors to come back for the company. The payout ratio is 21.7 percent, so there is some room for a decline in earnings that would not threaten the dividend payout. Of course, if the economic environment continues to deteriorate, CLF's stock price will continue to decline. The phenomenon of not being able to pick a bottom in the stock price is always present for value investors.

---

**WHAT IS YOUR INVESTING STYLE?**

- The true value investor focuses on the stocks of companies that are statistically cheap and could become cheaper but also gives the investor the chance of making a good profit by being patient and waiting for the rest of the investment community to realize that the stock represents good value. This style of investing requires the most patience from investors, as well as a steadfastness in not listening to the investment chatter that you should not be buying a stock when others are selling it.

- The growth investor has a shorter time frame and is willing to buy the stocks that everyone else is buying.

- The investment styles in between value and growth investing offer investors the flexibility of choosing the amount of value or growth in the style that offers the most comfort.

# CHAPTER 3

# The History of Value Investing

**W**ith an awareness of the history of value investing, potential value investors will better understand it and appreciate the fact that today there is no magic formula for finding companies that meet the strict requirements of its founder, Benjamin Graham. Graham, who graduated from Columbia University before the Depression and began his career on Wall Street as an analyst, had many successful followers, including Warren Buffett and John Neff, to name a few. Graham co-authored his first book, *Security Analysis*, with David Dodd in 1934, and his second book, *The Intelligent Investor*, was published in 1949. The following are some of his main points.

## RISK TOLERANCE AND TIME

Know the type of investor you are, which is dependent on your level of risk tolerance and the time and effort you are willing to devote to your investments. Your risk tolerance depends on your personal circumstances:

- Marital status
- Number of dependents
- Financial responsibility for dependents

- Secure employment
- Stage in your life cycle
- Financial independence
- The amount of money you can afford to lose on your investments

The answers to these questions outline the level of risk an investor is willing to take with regard to an investing style. For example, a couple who are both professionals at the height of their careers, who are not only high earners in their professions but are both independently wealthy, can take more risk with regard to their investment choices. By contrast, a couple with two small children with only one working spouse and no significant savings would be more risk averse in their investing style.

An investor's financial characteristics outline the acceptable level of risk with which he feels comfortable in achieving financial goals. However, a time frame needs to be stipulated for achieving those goals. Investors with a short time frame—less than two years—should not be investing in stocks. The most suitable investment class for this time frame is money market securities, which preserve capital and produce some level of return. A time frame of five years gives more leeway with regard to investment classes, which could include bonds to bolster the level of returns. A time frame of greater than five years allows an investor to invest in stocks; if the market goes down, the investor has enough time to wait until it recovers before selling his stocks.

Graham believed that investors had two choices in investment styles: active or passive. The choice depends on the investor's time constraints and risk tolerance.

- Active investors earn higher returns by spending time and energy researching the companies in which they are interested in investing. The more time spent researching the underlying strengths and weaknesses of the potential companies to invest in, the greater should be the returns, according to Graham.

- Passive investors do not spend their time and effort researching the fundamental characteristics of companies. They are
  comfortable picking the stocks and bonds of companies that
  are in an index, such as the stocks in the Dow Jones Industrial Average. This type of investor is content with earning a
  return equal to the average earned in the market. However,
  Graham contended that this investor invariably does worse
  than the averages of the market.

Graham also believed that investors needed to differentiate
whether they were investors or speculators. Investors look behind
the stocks to examine the fundamental strengths and weaknesses
of the underlying companies to find ones with value to invest in.
Speculators are more interested in buying the stocks that other
investors are willing to bid up in price. Graham thought it important that people know their investment style.

## MARGIN OF SAFETY

Invest in companies that provide a margin of safety is, the underlying principle of Benjamin Graham's philosophy, which also forms
the basis of value investing. The premise is to find companies or
investments that can be bought at discounts to their intrinsic values.
Graham believed that the key to finding the intrinsic value of a company could be obtained from its balance sheet, along with the margin of
safety provided by the company. Graham looked for stocks of companies whose liquid assets net of debt on their balance sheet were worth
more than the total market capitalization (market price of the stock
multiplied by the number of shares outstanding) of the company.

Assets are classified as current assets and noncurrent assets on
the balance sheet. The distinction between the two classifications is
the time it takes for the assets to be converted into cash. Generally,
current assets can be converted into cash within a year of the operating cycle of the company, whereas noncurrent assets take longer
than a year, which makes them more illiquid than current assets.

Not all current assets are liquid. Marketable securities and
accounts receivable can easily be converted into cash at or near their

reported values. Inventory is often questionable as to its liquidity, depending on its makeup and the number of times it turns over in the year. Some inventory turns over slowly and could become obsolete in the process, making it illiquid. Graham contended that if total liquid assets exceeded the debt of a company, an investment in the company has a margin of safety.

Graham used other measures to find value in a company. One such measure is working capital, or net current asset value, which is determined by subtracting current assets from current liabilities. Accounts receivable and inventory turn into cash, which is then used to purchase or produce more inventory, which is then sold to regenerate a new cycle of cash. Consequently, a company that has strong working capital can generate new sales and earnings. The opposite situation is a company with low or negative working capital, which would struggle to find new sources of sales and earnings because of a shortage of cash. However, the successful management of just-in-time inventory has negated the theory that low working capital does not generate new streams of revenues and earnings.

According to Graham, buying a company for less than its intrinsic value provides a margin of safety by minimizing the downside risk of the investment and increasing the rate of return when the rest of the investment community realizes its value.

## USE VOLATILITY TO GENERATE PROFITS

The markets are volatile, and Benjamin Graham advocated that investors use that volatility to profit from their investments. When there is a sell-off in the market, many investors fear that the world is coming to an end and either sell their existing investments or are paralyzed into inaction. Graham advocated that in such a situation investors should go against their emotions and buy stocks of companies that have been beaten down in price to the point that they are trading below their intrinsic values. Similarly, when the market is rising at a frenetic rate, investors should not be buying with the rest of the herd, but instead should be analyzing which stocks are no longer good value and selling them to realize profits in these overvalued stocks. In other words, Graham thought that the market should not determine investors' emotions with regard to investment decision making.

By diversifying into different classes of assets, investors can mitigate the effects of volatility on the preservation of capital. For example, when investing in both bonds and stocks, an investor has diversified her portfolio from loss. The stock and bond markets do not always go up and down in tandem. There are many occasions when the stock and bond markets diverge from each other. Consequently, an investor could lose principal in the stock market when it goes down while, if the bond market goes up, she could make up some of the losses from the stock market decline.

Another strategy to use during volatile markets to preserve capital and increase profits over time is to use *dollar cost averaging*, which involves investing a fixed dollar amount at regular intervals in the same security regardless of the security's price. One of the obvious advantages of this strategy is that it does away with the need to time the market or the security's market price.

Table 3.1 illustrates this concept using three scenarios: scenario 1 shows a rising market, scenario 2 shows a declining market, and scenario 3 shows a volatile market. Suppose an investor invests $1,000 every month for 12 months into a no-load equity mutual fund.

In scenario 1, with the market price rising over 12 months, the total number of shares purchased at the end of the period is 1,350.01 with a total investment of $12,000. When the share price increases, the investor receives fewer shares for the $1,000 invested; conversely, when the share price declines, the investor receives more shares for the $1,000 invested. The average price per share for scenario 1 is $8.33, but this figure is not as important as the average cost per share, which is $8.89. The average price of the shares indicates the average of 12 months' share price, whereas the average cost of the shares is the average price at which the shares were purchased. In this first scenario, the investor would lose money if the price of the equity fund falls below $8.89 per share but show a gain if the share price of the equity fund moves above $8.89 per share.

In scenario 2, which is a declining market, the average price of the equity fund is $5.88 for the year, and the average cost per share is $5.80 per share. The total number of shares accumulated is greater at the end of the year with the same investment in scenario 2 than in scenario 1 because of the declining market (the lower the share price, the greater the number of shares purchased). The average cost per share is $0.08 less than the average price per share, because when the share price declines, more shares are purchased for the same dollar amount. In a declining market the average cost per share will always be lower than the average price.

In scenario 3, which shows a volatile market, the average price of the equity fund is $7.31 per share, which is greater than the average cost per share of $7.25. Part of the reason for this is that during the months when the share price is low, more shares are purchased for the same dollar amount, and when the share price rises fewer shares are purchased for the same dollar amount.

The total value of the fund in each of the three scenarios is more than likely a surprise to readers in that in a rising market, the total value accumulated in December is not the largest amount. The largest accumulated value comes from a volatile market (scenario 3) because when the price of the fund declines, a purchase with the same investment buys more shares. For example, when the share price declined to $6.25 in September, the lowest price in the 12-month period, 160 shares were purchased, as compared to lower numbers of shares when the price increased. Thus, in a volatile market situation, dollar cost averaging eliminates the need to time the market.

However, in a declining market, scenario 2 is the worst outcome. This example illustrates that even with dollar cost averaging, an investor will lose money in a declining market. Similarly, if the investor sells shares at a depressed price, which is lower than the average cost per share, the investor will lose money.

Dollar cost averaging is good for investors who want to build a position in a security by investing money on a regular basis without having to pick entry points at which to invest and the price at which to invest. This strategy appeals to passive investors. The question that comes to mind is: Should an investor invest a large sum of money immediately or gradually, over time, using dollar cost averaging? The answer depends on the three market scenarios presented in Table 3.1.

**TABLE 3.1**

Dollar Cost Averaging with Three Scenarios

| | Scenario 1 | | Scenario 2 | | Scenario 3 | |
|---|---|---|---|---|---|---|
| | **Rising market** | | **Declining market** | | **Volatile market** | |
| | Price per share | Number of shares | Price per share | Number of shares | Price per share | Number of shares |
| Jan | $7.00 | 142.86 | $7.00 | 142.86 | $7.00 | 142.86 |
| Feb | 7.25 | 137.93 | 6.75 | 148.15 | 7.50 | 133.33 |
| Mar | 7.25 | 137.93 | 6.25 | 160.00 | 7.00 | 142.86 |
| Apr | 7.50 | 133.33 | 6.50 | 153.85 | 6.75 | 148.15 |
| May | 8.00 | 125.00 | 6.20 | 161.29 | 7.25 | 137.93 |
| Jun | 7.75 | 129.03 | 5.75 | 173.91 | 8.00 | 125.00 |
| July | 8.00 | 125.00 | 6.00 | 166.67 | 7.00 | 142.86 |
| Aug | 9.00 | 111.11 | 5.50 | 181.82 | 6.50 | 153.85 |
| Sept. | 9.50 | 105.26 | 5.25 | 190.48 | 6.25 | 160.00 |
| Oct | 9.00 | 111.11 | 5.30 | 188.68 | 7.50 | 133.33 |
| Nov | 9.75 | 102.56 | 5.00 | 200.00 | 8.00 | 125.00 |
| Dec | 10.00 | 100.00 | 5.00 | 200.00 | 9.00 | 111.11 |
| Total # of shares | | 1,350.01 | | 2,067.71 | | 1,656.28 |

Average price per share

$$\frac{100}{12} = \$8.33 \qquad \frac{70.50}{12} = \$5.88 \qquad \frac{87.75}{12} = \$7.31$$

Average cost per share $= \dfrac{\text{total invested}}{\text{total \# of shares}}$

$$= \frac{\$12,000}{1,350.01} \qquad = \frac{\$12,000}{2,067.71} \qquad = \frac{\$12,000}{1,656.28}$$

$$= \$8.89 \qquad\qquad = \$5.80 \qquad\qquad = \$7.25$$

| Total value of fund in Dec. | $13,500.10 | $10,338.55 | $14,906.52 |
|---|---|---|---|

In a rising market investing a lump sum at the beginning of the period results in the greatest accumulation of shares and total dollar appreciation. In a volatile market there is no definitive answer as to which method would be best because it would depend on the actual price of the security and the extent of the volatility. In a down market, investing regularly over a period of time will result in more shares purchased than a lump sum investment at the beginning of the period. However, in a down market dollar cost averaging will not guarantee profits if the market price continues to decline, though, as Graham suggested, diversification and dollar cost averaging will help to mute the negative effects of volatility.

## GRAHAM'S GUIDELINES

Benjamin Graham pioneered the concept of buying the stocks of businesses that were trading at a fraction of their real value. To find these stocks, potential investors need to study the balance sheet (financial statements) of companies to find their intrinsic or real values, which forms the basis of fundamental analysis.

Graham realized that with more fundamental analysis being performed by interested investors, markets would become more efficient, making it harder to find undervalued stocks. According to Graham's model, the greater the number of *yes* answers, the more ideal the stock choice. One of his guidelines was to select low P/E ratio stocks, but bear in mind that stocks were in a bear market during the Depression and thereafter, when Graham formulated his guidelines. It might be difficult to find stocks based on his criteria today, but this is a good model to obtain his perspective on value investing.

According to Graham, if a stock meets seven of the ten guidelines points, it provides value for the investor. Bear in mind that with today's near 0 percent short-term interest rates, many more investors who were previously content to invest their money in certificates of deposit and Treasury bills and notes have been pushed into investing in the stock market and are seeking yields from

## GRAHAM'S GUIDELINES TO INVESTING IN STOCKS

*Rewards*

1. Is the P/E ratio less than half the reciprocal of the AAA corporate bond yield? For example, the current AAA corporate bond yield is 3.48 percent and the reciprocal is 28.74 percent (1/.0348). The P/E ratio of the stock would have to be less than 14.37 (1/2 × .2874) to be bought.

2. Is the P/E ratio less than 40 percent of the average P/E of the stock over the past five years?

3. Is the dividend yield equal to or more than two-thirds the AAA corporate bond yield? Two-thirds of the current AAA corporate bond yield of 3.48 percent is 2.32 percent. In order to rate the stock a buy, the dividend yield should equal or be greater than 2.32 percent.

4. Is the stock price less than two-thirds of the book value of the stock?

5. Is the stock price less than two-thirds of the net current asset value per share (current assets minus total debt)?

*Risks*

1. Is the debt-to-equity ratio less than one? The total debt of the company should be less than the total equity.

2. Is the current ratio equal to two or more? The total current assets divided by the total urrent liabilities should equal two or more.

3. Is the total debt less than twice the net current assets?

4. Is the 10-year average EPS (earnings per share) growth rate greater than 7 percent?

5. Were there no more than two years out of the past 10 with earnings declines of greater than 5 percent?

Source: Paul Sturm, "What If Benjamin Graham Had a PC?" *Smart Money*, March 1994, 32.

dividend-paying stocks. The third guideline in the rewards section provides some guidance for income investors. However, because interest rates are currently so low, investors should not follow these guidelines blindly. An income-oriented investor might set a dividend yield threshold at 3 percent instead of the 2.32 percent suggested in the guidelines for companies in which they are interested in investing. The rest of the guidelines are quite stringent, and probably very few stocks would meet these requirements today. Consequently, they can be changed to include more stocks. For example, by changing the guidelines slightly to the following criteria, an investor would include many more value stocks in their screen:

- P/E ratio of less than 15
- P/B ratio less than 1.5
- Dividend yield greater than 3 percent
- Current ratio over 1.5
- Five years of uninterrupted, increasing dividend payments
- Annual EPS growth for a five-year period of more than 3 percent
- Low debt-to-equity ratio

By changing the criteria slightly, investors can use this model to concentrate on the investment style that is most suitable to their circumstances. For example, a Growth at a Reasonable Price investor would ignore the dividend yield and place more emphasis on the earnings per share growth and the P/E multiple.

Besides these ten guidelines, Graham was most interested in determining the intrinsic value of a stock/company, and he used the following formula:

$$\text{Intrinsic value} = E \times [2g + 8.5] \times 4.4/Y$$
$$\text{where } E = \text{annual EPS}$$
$$g = \text{annual growth rate}$$
$$Y = \text{current interest rate}$$
$$\text{(average AAA bond yield)}$$

Using this formula, the investor can obtain the intrinsic value of Cliffs Natural, which has forward projected EPS of $6.60 with an adjusted conservative growth rate of 2 percent with the economic slowdown, at the current interest rate of 3.48 percent is $104.31 per share:

$$\text{Intrinsic value} = E \times [2g + 8.5] \times 4.4 / Y$$
$$= \$6.60 \times [2(2) + 8.5] \times 4.4/3.48$$
$$= \$104.31$$

Cliffs Natural is currently trading around $40 per share, which suggests that the stock is greatly undervalued and implies tremendous appreciation potential. However, the formula does not adjust for economic slowdowns, which reduces the growth rate, the EPS, and the intrinsic value. By including the AAA bond yield, Graham attempted to balance the effects of interest rates on the cost of capital. When bond yields rise, investors expect higher returns from stocks. If stocks cannot provide these higher returns, investors will invest in bonds. Higher bond yields cause the intrinsic value in Graham's formula to decrease, while lower bond yields cause the intrinsic value to increase.

This formula is not by any means foolproof and investors should not base their decisions to buy stocks solely on it. Graham's formula does not produce a conservative number for the intrinsic value because the growth rate is doubled and then is added to 8.5, which is then multiplied by the EPS. In simplified terms, the PEG ratio used is always greater than 2. Value investors traditionally look for stocks that have PEG ratios of 1 or less.

The next four chapters explore how to obtain financial information about companies and the fundamental aspects of financial statements to give an assessment of the strengths and weaknesses of a company and the effects on the price of the stock. Bear in mind that not all investors will see the same picture presented by quantitative analyses because interpretation of the numbers can produce creative differences. Thus, one value investor might pass on buying a stock or company while another finds that same stock or company very appealing to buy.

# Sources of Information

Investors are reliant on knowledge about the companies in which they are interested in investing. Without this knowledge, a potential investor might as well resort to throwing darts at stock tables to choose which stocks to buy. A value investor goes one step further in that the company information is screened in greater detail to determine which companies will provide the greatest value (meaning they are trading below their intrinsic values).

Publicly traded companies are required by the Securities and Exchange Commission (SEC) to publish complete financial information about themselves. The main source of information about a company is its annual report, or Form 10-K. The company's printed annual report is similar to the 10-K, but because the latter is submitted to the SEC, it provides greater detail minus the glossy photographs.

## THE ANNUAL REPORT

The annual report to shareholders is the principal source of information about a company. Besides the glossy pictures and the easy-to-read text, there is a letter from the CEO (Chief Executive Officer), financial statements, notes to the financial statements, results of continuing operations, an auditor's report or letter, new product plans, market segment information, management's discussion and analysis, and any new developments regarding the company's future. The most important sections to a potential investor are the financial statements, the notes to the financial statements, the auditor's letter or report, and the discussion and analysis by management.

When reading an annual report, you should be aware of the fact that it is written by the company and is also used as a public relations instrument. Companies have the leeway to spin events in their favor. Consequently, you should try to read between the lines and also corroborate events and facts from other sources to get a true and accurate picture of the company.

## 10-K REPORT

The 10-K report is similar to the annual report, but there are differences. Because the 10-K report is submitted to the government, the financial information is much more complete than what is provided on the annual report. The 10-K report includes audited financial statements and a comprehensive view of the company's business and financial condition. The financial statements generally include a greater history (five to ten years) than those on the annual report. The 10-K report must be filed with the SEC within 90 days after the end of the company's fiscal year.

Potential investors can obtain the 10-K filings of public companies in the EDGAR database of the SEC, which can also be downloaded. Similarly, potential investors can obtain a company's annual reports from the specific company's website.

## INFORMATION TO LOOK FOR IN AN ANNUAL OR A 10-K REPORT

As mentioned, the important sections of the annual report are the financial statements, the notes to the financial statements, the auditor's report, and the discussion and analysis by management. There are other sections that provide valuable information for those investors who want to read everything, but the most important information comes from those four sections.

## Highlights

You could start with the highlights section, which summarizes the company's results for a few measures such as sales and earnings for a few years. This section provides a superficial view of the company without providing a complete picture of the financial history. To get a better sense of the accomplishments of the company, an investor should read the letter to shareholders.

## Letter to Shareholders

The letter to shareholders from the CEO gives an overview of the achievements and difficulties facing the company. The letter is often written by the company's public relations or marketing department and puts the best spin on any issues. The phrases used in the letter are chosen with care, presenting an optimistic picture. Bear in mind that if there are any underlying problems that could present a concern for the company, you will not find an in-depth discussion of them here. Value investors should examine this section to get a feel for the honesty, integrity, and willingness of the CEO to discuss important issues frankly. By reading between the lines, investors can pick up on any sensitive issues that are being glossed over. There are a number of key words that can raise red flags:

- Difficulties: This word indicates that something is not going well, and you should look elsewhere in the report to find out what is ailing the company. If you don't find it in the annual report, download the 10-K report from the EDGAR website to get more information about the company's problems or any risks it is facing.

- Restructuring: This word indicates that there were problems facing the company and it has taken corrective action to fix whatever was not working. Look to see what the restructuring cost the company.

## Auditor's Report or Letter

The auditor's report or letter is generally found before or after the financial statements in the annual report. Publicly traded companies have their accountants (CPAs) examine and verify their accounting records, which culminate in an auditor's report or letter. A test of the accounting records does not mean that every financial transaction and document has been examined. Rather auditors (accountants) examine a sample of the financial transactions and documents to determine whether the financial statements reflect fairly the financial condition of the company and that the statements are presented in accordance with generally accepted accounting principles (GAAP). If the auditors find that the financial statements present fairly the financial condition of the company, the auditors will issue an unqualified opinion, which is a clean bill of health for the company.

Value investors look for companies that have had some poor results but are likely to turn around their misfortunes. The auditor's report is the first step to screen out those companies that might not turn around. When an auditor's report indicates that there is a question about the company's ability to be a "going concern," this is really a big issue, and the potential investor should steer away from this company. Similarly, when an auditor gives an adverse opinion, the potential investor should stay away from that company.

The auditors' report or letter uses standard language for an unqualified opinion, which is that the financial statements were prepared using GAAP and the financial statements present fairly the financial condition of the company.

Generally there are three paragraphs in an auditor's report. The first paragraph contains a statement that management is responsible for the financial statements and that the auditors' role is to express an opinion on the financial statements based on their audit.

The second paragraph states how the auditors conducted their audit, namely that they used GAAP standards. These standards are designed to enable the auditors to conclude that the financial statements do not include any material misstatements (errors that could materially affect the company's financial condition).

The third paragraph is where the auditors present their opinion about the financial statements. If no problems are found, the standard language used is: "The financial statements were prepared in conformity with generally accepted accounting principles (GAAP) and present fairly the financial condition of the company."

However, if the auditors find problems in their audit, the opinion issued is qualified, and there may be a fourth paragraph in which the auditors discuss the problems found. Potential investors will need to investigate these problems to see if the company can indeed turn around their problems. The places to look for more information on these problems are in the notes to the financial statements and in the discussion and analysis by management section.

Investors also need to look through several years of annual reports to see whether the company has changed auditing firms frequently. If this is so, it is a warning flag for this company. Companies that disagree with their auditors need to be avoided. For example, when auditors/accountants disagree with management over the presentation of financial transactions and question the company's ability to stay in business over the long term, it is easier for the company to change auditors than to make changes. Frequent changes in a company's auditing firm are not a good sign. Examine the reasons why management has changed their auditing firm. If you can't find answers to your questions from the annual or 10-K report, call the investor relations department of the company before you decide to invest in the company.

## The Financial Statements

The financial statements are usually found in the back half of the annual report. Financial statements include the balance sheet, the income statement, the statement of changes in cash, and the statement of shareholders' equity. Potential investors should pay attention to the financial statements to see that the picture presented by the numbers matches the positive outlook presented by the letter to shareholders. If the company owns subsidiary companies, their financial statements are incorporated in the company's financial statements; together they are called consolidated financial statements, as is the case with Intel Corporation's financial statements, presented in Exhibit 4.1.

**EXHIBIT 4.1**

Intel Corporation Financial Statements from 10-K Report

INTEL CORPORATION
CONSOLIDATED STATEMENTS OF INCOME

| Three Years Ended December 31, 2011 (In Millions, Except Per Share Amounts) | 2011 | 2010 | 2009 |
|---|---|---|---|
| Net revenue | $53,999 | $43,623 | $35,127 |
| Cost of sales | 20,242 | 15,132 | 15,566 |
| Gross margin | 33,757 | 28,491 | 19,561 |
| Research and development | 8,350 | 6,576 | 5,653 |
| Marketing, general and administrative | 7,670 | 6,309 | 7,931 |
| Restructuring and asset impairment charges | — | — | 231 |
| Amortization of acquisition-related intangibles | 260 | 18 | 35 |
| Operating expenses | 16,280 | 12,903 | 13,850 |
| Operating income | 17,477 | 15,588 | 5,711 |
| Gains (losses) on equity investments, net | 112 | 348 | (170) |
| Interest and other, net | 192 | 109 | 163 |
| Income before taxes | 17,781 | 16,045 | 5,704 |
| Provision for taxes | 4,839 | 4,581 | 1,335 |
| Net income | $12,942 | $11,464 | $ 4,369 |
| Basic earnings per common share | $ 2.46 | $ 2.06 | $ 0.79 |
| Diluted earnings per common share | $ 2.39 | $ 2.01 | $ 0.77 |
| Weighted average common shares outstanding: | | | |
| Basic | 5,256 | 5,555 | 5,557 |
| Diluted | 5,411 | 5,696 | 5,645 |

See accompanying notes.

## INTEL CORPORATION
## CONSOLIDATED BALANCE SHEETS

| December 31, 2011, and December 25, 2010 (In Millions, Except Par Value) | 2011 | 2010 |
|---|---|---|
| **Assets** | | |
| Current assets: | | |
| Cash and cash equivalents | $ 5,065 | $ 5,498 |
| Short-term investments | 5,181 | 11,294 |
| Trading assets | 4,591 | 5,093 |
| Accounts receivable, net of allowance for doubtful accounts of $36 ($28 in 2010) | 3,650 | 2,867 |
| Inventories | 4,096 | 3,757 |
| Deferred tax assets | 1,700 | 1,488 |
| Other current assets | 1,589 | 1,614 |
| **Total current assets** | **25,872** | **31,611** |
| **Property, plant and equipment, net** | **23,627** | **17,899** |
| **Marketable equity securities** | **562** | **1,008** |
| **Other long-term investments** | **889** | **3,026** |
| **Goodwill** | **9,254** | **4,531** |
| **Identified intangible assets, net** | **6,267** | **860** |
| **Other long-term assets** | **4,648** | **4,251** |
| **Total assets** | **$71,119** | **$63,186** |
| **Liabilities and stockholders' equity** | | |
| Current liabilities: | | |
| Short-term debt | $ 247 | $ 38 |
| Accounts payable | 2,956 | 2,290 |
| Accrued compensation and benefits | 2,948 | 2,888 |
| Accrued advertising | 1,134 | 1,007 |
| Deferred income | 1,929 | 747 |
| Other accrued liabilities | 2,814 | 2,357 |

(*Continued*)

| | | |
|---|---|---|
| Total current liabilities | 12,028 | 9,327 |
| Long-term debt | 7,084 | 2,077 |
| Long-term deferred tax liabilities | 2,617 | 926 |
| Other long-term liabilities | 3,479 | 1,426 |
| Commitments and contingencies (Notes 23 and 29) | | |
| Stockholders' equity: | | |
| Preferred stock, $0.001 par value, 50 shares authorized; none issued | — | — |
| Common stock, $0.001 par value, 10,000 shares authorized; 5,000 issued and outstanding (5,581 issued and 5,511 outstanding in 2010) and capital in excess of par value | 17,036 | 16,178 |
| Accumulated other comprehensive income (loss) | (781) | 333 |
| Retained earnings | 29,656 | 32,919 |
| Total stockholders' equity | 45,911 | 49,430 |
| Total liabilities and stockholders' equity | $71,119 | $63,186 |

See accompanying notes.

INTEL CORPORATION
CONSOLIDATED STATEMENTS OF CASH FLOWS

| Three Years Ended December 31, 2011 (In Millions) | 2011 | 2010 | 2009 |
|---|---|---|---|
| Cash and cash equivalents, beginning of year | $ 5,498 | $3,987 | $ 3,350 |
| Cash flows provided by (used for) operating activities: | | | |
| Net income | 12,942 | 11,464 | 4,369 |
| Adjustments to reconcile net income to net cash provided by operating activities: | | | |
| Depreciation | 5,141 | 4,398 | 4,744 |

| | | | |
|---|---|---|---|
| Share-based compensation | 1,053 | 917 | 889 |
| Restructuring, asset impairment, and net loss on retirement of assets | 96 | 67 | 368 |
| Excess tax benefit from share-based payment arrangements | (37) | (65) | (9) |
| Amortization of intangibles | 923 | 240 | 308 |
| (Gains) losses on equity investments, net | (112) | (348) | 170 |
| (Gains) losses on divestitures | (164) | — | — |
| Deferred taxes | 790 | (46) | 271 |
| Changes in assets and liabilities: | | | |
|   Trading assets | — | — | 299 |
|   Accounts receivable | (678) | (584) | (535) |
|   Inventories | (243) | (806) | 796 |
|   Accounts payable | 596 | 407 | (506) |
|   Accrued compensation and benefits | (95) | 161 | 247 |
|   Income taxes payable and receivable | 660 | 53 | 110 |
|   Other assets and liabilities | 91 | 834 | (351) |
|     Total adjustments | 8,021 | 5,228 | 6,801 |
| **Net cash provided by operating activities** | **20,963** | **16,692** | **11,170** |
| Cash flows provided by (used for) investing activities: | | | |
|   Additions to property, plant and equipment | (10,764) | (5,207) | (4,515) |
|   Acquisitions, net of cash acquired | (8,721) | (218) | (853) |
|   Purchases of available-for-sale investments | (11,230) | (17,675) | (8,655) |
|   Sales of available-for-sale investments | 9,076 | 506 | 220 |
|   Maturities of available-for-sale investments | 11,029 | 12,627 | 7,536 |
|   Purchases of trading assets | (11,314) | (8,944) | (4,186) |
|   Maturities and sales of trading assets | 11,771 | 8,846 | 2,543 |

*(Continued)*

| | | | |
|---|---:|---:|---:|
| Origination of loans receivable | (206) | (498) | (343) |
| Collection of loans receivable | 134 | — | — |
| Investments in non-marketable equity investments | (693) | (393) | (250) |
| Return of equity method investments | 263 | 199 | 449 |
| Proceeds from divestitures | 50 | — | — |
| Other investing | 304 | 218 | 89 |
| **Net cash used for investing activities** | **(10,301)** | **(10,539)** | **(7,965)** |
| Cash flows provided by (used for) financing activities: | | | |
| Increase (decrease) in short-term debt, net | 209 | 23 | (87) |
| Proceeds from government grants | 124 | 79 | — |
| Excess tax benefit from share-based payment arrangements | 37 | 65 | 9 |
| Issuance of long-term debt | 4,962 | — | 1,980 |
| Repayment of debt | — | (157) | — |
| Proceeds from sales of shares through employee equity incentive plans | 2,045 | 587 | 400 |
| Repurchase of common stock | (14,340) | (1,736) | (1,762) |
| Payment of dividends to stockholders | (4,127) | (3,503) | (3,108) |
| Other financing | (10) | — | — |
| **Net cash used for financing activities** | **(11,100)** | **(4,642)** | **(2,568)** |
| **Effect of exchange rate fluctuations on cash and cash equivalents** | **5** | **—** | **—** |
| **Net increase (decrease) in cash and cash equivalents** | **(433)** | **1,511** | **637** |
| **Cash and cash equivalents, end of year** | **$ 5,065** | **$ 5,498** | **$3,987** |
| Supplemental disclosures of cash flow information: | | | |
| Cash paid during the year for: | | | |
| Interest, net of amounts capitalized | $ — | $ — | $ 4 |
| Income taxes, net of refunds | $ 3,338 | $ 4,627 | $ 943 |

*See accompanying notes.*

## INTEL CORPORATION
### CONSOLIDATED STATEMENTS OF STOCKHOLDERS' EQUITY

| Three Years Ended December 31, 2011 (In Millions, Except Per Share Amounts) | Common Stock and Capital in Excess of Par Value | | Accumulated Other Comprehensive Income (Loss) | Retained Earnings | Total |
| --- | --- | --- | --- | --- | --- |
| | Number of Shares | Amount | | | |
| **Balance as of December 27, 2008** | **5,562** | **$13,402** | **$ (393)** | **$26,537** | **$39,546** |
| Components of comprehensive income, net of tax: | | | | | |
| Net income | — | — | — | 4,369 | 4,369 |
| Other comprehensive income (loss) | — | — | 786 | — | 786 |
| Total comprehensive income | | | | | 5,155 |
| Proceeds from sales of shares through employee equity incentive plans, net tax deficiency, and other | 55 | 381 | — | — | 381 |
| Issuance of convertible debt | — | 603 | — | — | 603 |
| Share-based compensation | — | 889 | — | — | 889 |
| Repurchase of common stock | (94) | (282) | — | (1,480) | (1,762) |
| Cash dividends declared ($0.56 per common share) | — | — | — | (3,108) | (3,108) |
| **Balance as of December 26, 2009** | **5,523** | **14,993** | **393** | **26,318** | **41,704** |
| Components of comprehensive income, net of tax: | | | | | |
| Net income | — | — | — | 11,464 | 11,464 |
| Other comprehensive income (loss) | — | — | (60) | — | (60) |
| Total comprehensive income | | | | | 11,404 |

*(Continued)*

| | | | | |
|---|---:|---:|---:|---:|
| Proceeds from sales of shares through employee equity incentive plans, net excess tax benefit, and other | 68 | 644 | — | — | 644 |
| Share-based compensation | — | 917 | — | — | 917 |
| Repurchase of common stock | (80) | (376) | — | (1,360) | (1,736) |
| Cash dividends declared ($0.63 per common share) | — | — | — | (3,503) | (3,503) |
| **Balance as of December 25, 2010** | **5,511** | **16,178** | **333** | **32,919** | **49,430** |
| Components of comprehensive income, net of tax: | | | | | |
| Net income | — | — | — | 12,942 | 12,942 |
| Other comprehensive income (loss) | — | — | (1,114) | — | (1,114) |
| Total comprehensive income | | | | | 11,828 |
| Proceeds from sales of shares through employee equity incentive plans, net excess tax deficiency, and other | 142 | 2,019 | — | — | 2,019 |
| Assumption of equity awards in connection with acquisitions | — | 48 | — | — | 48 |
| Share-based compensation | — | 1,053 | — | — | 1,053 |
| Repurchase of common stock | (653) | (2,262) | — | (12,078) | (14,340) |
| Cash dividends declared ($0.7824 per common share) | — | — | — | (4,127) | (4,127) |
| **Balance as of December 31, 2011** | **5,000** | **$17,036** | **$ (781)** | **$29,656** | **$45,911** |

*See accompanying notes.*

The financial statements provide the real view of the company's operating and financial position, which explains why the SEC requires companies to file their financial information on a regular basis and in a timely manner. For a value investor the balance sheet, income statement, and statement of changes in cash are essential reading in order to determine whether or not to invest in that company. The balance sheet provides a snapshot view of the company's assets, liabilities, and shareholders' equity at a particular point in time. The income statement shows the operating performance of the company over a period of time (one year, or six or three months). It provides a summary of the company's sales, cost of sales, and expenses. The difference between revenues and expenses are earnings. The statement of changes in cash shows the sources of cash and the uses of cash during the accounting period, usually a year, or six or three months. Cash is not the same as earnings, and companies such as Enron, HealthSouth, and WorldCom manipulated their earnings, but their demise came when they ran out of cash, which does not lend itself to manipulation.

The statement of shareholders' equity is the link between the income statement and the balance sheet. Net income of $12,942 is added to retained earnings, as shown in the Intel changes in stockholders' equity section. Dividends of $0.7824 per common share were paid out to shareholders, and $12,078 was used to buy back its own common stock. In the case of Intel, the ending balance of retained earnings was reduced because the dividends and buy back of common stock was greater than the net income earned. The reduction in retained earnings is shown in the equity section of the balance sheet. From this statement you can see how the earnings retained are used by the company.

The balance sheet, income statement, and statement of changes in cash flows statements are discussed in more detail in chapters 5, 6, and 7.

## Notes to the Financial Statements

Not all information is shown in the balance sheet, income statement, and statement of changes in cash. There is supplemental information in the notes to the financial statements that is new or qualifies or elaborates on the assets, liabilities, revenues, and expenses. For example, loss contingencies that are not recorded in the financial statements are disclosed in the notes. In the contingencies section, look for any guarantees of indebtedness of others; commitments to finance any projects under any circumstances; pending lawsuits with uncertain outcomes (particularly when company lawyers state that the outcome could have a material impact on the company's earnings); guarantees to repurchase accounts receivables that have either been sold or assigned; and disputes over additional taxes owed in prior years.

The notes disclose the methods used to value assets (for example, inventory can be valued on a FIFO—first-in, first-out—, LIFO—last-in, first-out—, or average cost basis) and how costs are allocated (type of depreciation used, straight line or accelerated method). Exhibit 4.2 illustrates how Intel Corporation handles its revenue recognition policies and product warranties.

Investors should also examine the notes for any disclosures of significant contracts or negotiations, such as stock option plans, lease contracts, and pension obligations.

There is generally a time lag between when the financial statements are compiled and when they are issued to the public. During those few months, significant events could occur or change things that have been reported in the balance sheet, meaning changes in estimates need to be made from the originals. Similarly, new conditions could arise that were not apparent at the time the financial statements were compiled.

Just because the notes are often presented in small print and generally are technical in nature does not make them inconsequential to the investor. Rather the notes explain the items listed in the financial statements and provide meaningful information to potential investors in the company.

## EXHIBIT 4.2

Notes to Consolidated Financial Statements from
10-K Report

### INTEL CORPORATION NOTES TO CONSOLIDATED
### FINANCIAL STATEMENTS

*Product Warranty*

The vast majority of our products are sold with a limited warranty on product quality and a limited indemnification for customers against intellectual property rights (IP) infringement claims related to our products. The accrual and the related expense for known product warranty issues were not significant during the periods presented. Due to product testing, the short time typically between product shipment and the detection and correction of product failures, and the historical rate of payments on indemnification claims, the accrual and related expense for estimated incurred but unidentified issues were not significant during the periods presented.

*Revenue Recognition*

We recognize net product revenue when the earnings process is complete, as evidenced by an agreement with the customer, transfer of title, and acceptance, if applicable, as well as fixed pricing and probable collectibility. We record pricing allowances, including discounts based on contractual arrangements with customers, when we recognize revenue as a reduction to both accounts receivable and net revenue. Because of frequent sales price reductions and rapid technology obsolescence in the industry, we defer product revenue and related costs of sales from sales made to distributors under agreements allowing price protection or right of return until the distributors sell the merchandise. The right of return granted generally consists of a stock rotation program in which distributors are able to exchange certain products based on the number of qualified purchases made by the distributor. Under the price protection program, we give distributors credits for the difference between the original price paid and the current price that we offer. We record the net deferred income from product sales to distributors on our balance sheet as deferred income on shipments to distributors. We include shipping charges billed to customers in net revenue, and include the related shipping costs in cost of sales.

Revenue from license agreements with our McAfee business generally includes service and support agreements for which the related revenue is deferred and recognized ratably over the performance period. Revenue derived from online subscription products is deferred and recognized ratably over the performance period. Professional services revenue is recognized as services are performed or, if required, upon customer acceptance. For arrangements with multiple elements, including software licenses, maintenance, and/or services, revenue is allocated across the separately identified deliverables and may be recognized or deferred. When vendor-specific objective evidence (VSOE) does not exist for undelivered elements such as maintenance and support, the entire arrangement fee is recognized ratably over the performance period. Direct costs, such as costs related to revenue-sharing and royalty arrangements associated with license arrangements, as well as component costs associated with product revenue, are deferred and amortized over the same period that the related revenue is recognized.

## Management's Discussion and Analysis

The SEC has mandated that management disclose any significant events and uncertainties with regard to the company's liquidity, results of operations, and capital resources, because management knows more about the company than the users of the financial statements. Exhibit 4.3 illustrates how Best Buy's management discussion highlights the unfavorable sales trends facing the company in its 10-K report for their year ending in 2011.

**EXHIBIT 4.3**

Management Discussion and Analysis from Best Buy Corporation's 10-K Report 2011

Our business, like that of many retailers, is seasonal. Historically, we have realized more of our revenue and earnings in the fiscal fourth quarter, which includes the majority of the holiday shopping season in the U.S., Europe and Canada, than in any other fiscal quarter.

While some of the products and services we offer are viewed by consumers as essential, others continue to be viewed as discretionary purchases. Consequently, our results of operations are susceptible to changes in consumer confidence levels and macroeconomic factors such as unemployment, consumer credit availability and the condition of the housing market.

Recently, consumers have maintained a cautious approach to discretionary spending due to continued economic pressures. Consequently, customer traffic and spending patterns continue to be difficult to predict. Other factors that directly impact our performance are product life-cycle shifts (including the adoption of new technology) and the competitive consumer electronics retail environment. As a result of these factors, predicting our future revenue and net earnings is difficult. Disciplined capital allocation and working capital management and expense control remain key priorities for us as we navigate through the current environment. By providing access to a wide selection of consumer electronics products and accessories; a vast array of service offerings, such as extended warranties, installation and repair; and a knowledgeable sales staff to help our customers select and connect their devices, we believe we offer our customers a differentiated value proposition.

As a value investor, you would want to see how Best Buy could recover from this difficult environment, and you would also want to consider whether there are other factors that are depressing sales and earnings. Consequently, you would want to read the management analysis and discussion very carefully.

Management also provides forward-looking comments about trends that could have a material impact on the company. Management views on the company's products and their quality, their customer base, competitive position, market analysis, and other nonquantitative information not found in the financial statements give a potential investor a more informed view of the company.

## DO YOUR HOMEWORK BEFORE
## YOU INVEST

Not all companies report their numbers in exactly the way they should, and it is the fraudulent companies, such as Enron that give business a bad name. Consequently, investors need to dig through the information in annual and 10-K reports to discover any problems. Starting off with the auditors' report, you can exclude problem companies that have uncertain futures. Look for clues in the letter to shareholders for any carefully veiled words masking difficulties, problems, or challenges. The financial statements provide the financial picture of the company through its numbers. A careful analysis of the numbers can reveal the strengths and weaknesses of the company's financial condition. Bear in mind that companies can manipulate their financial statements to make their numbers look better, known as window dressing, which is discussed in the next chapters. Potential investors will want to read through the notes to the financial statements, which provide supplementary information and the accounting policies used by the company. Finally, the discussion and analysis provided by management discloses any uncertainties, significant events facing the company, and forward-looking comments with regard to any material events facing the company.

Should you still have some issues that need clarification, call the investor relations department of the company for answers. How the investor relations department handles your question will tell you something more about the company.

## CHAPTER 5

# The Balance Sheet

**E**ven if you do not know anything about accounting, after reading this chapter you will understand the basic concepts in a balance sheet and be able to use them to achieve your objectives in finding stocks that present value.

## WHAT A BALANCE SHEET SHOWS

The balance sheet is a snapshot of what a company owns, what it owes, and what is left over after the debts are deducted from what it owns. The balance sheet provides detailed information about the resources of a company (what it owns), also called assets, the company's debts or liabilities (what it owes), and the shareholders' equity or net worth, which is the balance left to the shareholders if the company were to sell all its assets and pay off its liabilities.

The concept underlying the balance sheet is the following equation:

ASSETS = LIABILITIES + SHAREHOLDERS' EQUITY

This equation can also be expressed as:

ASSETS - LIABILITIES = SHAREHOLDERS' EQUITY

The equations above form the basis for all financial transactions and the double entry accounting system used in business. For every dollar added to assets there is a corresponding addition of one dollar to liabilities or shareholders' equity to keep the system in balance. The goal of the balance sheet is to keep the assets in equilibrium with the liabilities and shareholders' equity.

Investors should be aware that a balance sheet portrays a company's financial position as of the date of that balance sheet, often described as a snapshot. Balance sheets are mostly compiled at the end of a company's fiscal quarter or fiscal year. Financial transactions that occur the day after the balance sheet has been reported will change the figures on the balance sheet.

Looked at from another point of view, the balance sheet is a static indicator of the financial position of a company, in that it summarizes the basic types of assets, liabilities, and shareholders' equity on a particular date. The importance of the balance sheet is that it can be compared with prior balance sheets of the same company to establish the trends taking place in the company. Some examples of trends that can be observed are increasing or decreasing inventories, increasing liabilities, and decreasing cash. Another important feature of the balance sheet is the ability to analyze the assets of the company's real value of those assets. For example, a company might have bought significant real estate 50 years ago, which is always recorded at its purchase price on the balance sheet. The market value of those properties could be many multiples of the purchase prices, making the real estate significantly undervalued on the balance sheet.

Assets are resources a company owns that have value. These resources are used to produce products or provide services that can be sold. Assets include cash, accounts receivables (amounts owed by customers), inventory, land, buildings, equipment, long-term investments, and intangibles.

Liabilities are debts or obligations the company owes. Liabilities include accounts payable, taxes payable, wages payable, notes payable, and long-term obligations such as bonds and other long-term debts.

Shareholders' equity is the amount of capital that would be left over if the company sold all its assets to pay off its liabilities. This leftover capital is also referred to as owners' equity, net worth, or book value. Accounts found in the shareholders' equity section are the capital accounts (common and preferred stock), additional paid-in capital accounts, and retained earnings. Net income that is not paid out in dividends is added into the retained earnings account. This account is the link between the income statement and the balance sheet, maintaining the overall balance in the financial statements.

Analysis of the balance sheet is useful to potential investors in that it provides information about the amount and nature of the composition of the assets, liabilities, and owners' equity. Not only does the balance sheet provide a basis for determining the rates of return for a company but also for evaluating the liquidity and financial flexibility of the company, along with the ability to evaluate the capital structure of the company. The major limitation of the balance sheet, as noted earlier, is that it does not reflect current or market value because both assets and liabilities are recorded at their historical costs (purchase prices). Some exceptions to the principal of recording at historical cost are the recording of accounts receivables, marketable securities, and some long-term investments.

## The Format of the Balance Sheet

The basic equation (assets = liabilities + shareholders' equity) is used to show balance sheet items irrespective of which one of the following three formats are used. In the *account format*, the assets are presented in the left column and the liabilities and shareholders' equity are presented in the right column, as shown in Table 5.1.

**TABLE 5.1**

Balance Sheet of Company X as of September 30, XXXX

| Assets | | Liabilities | |
|---|---|---|---|
| Current Assets | $100 | Current Liabilities | $ 50 |
| Investments | 50 | Long-Term Liabilities | 50 |
| Fixed Assets | 100 | **Total Liabilities** | $100 |
| Other Assets | 50 | Shareholders' Equity | 200 |
| **Total Assets** | **$300** | **Total Liabilities & Equity** | **$300** |

The balance sheet can also be presented in the *one-column format* shown in Table 5.2.

**TABLE 5.2**

Balance Sheet of Company X as of September 30, XXXX

| Assets | |
|---|---|
| Current Assets | $100 |
| Investments | 50 |
| Fixed Assets | 100 |
| Other Assets | 50 |
| **Total Assets** | **$300** |
| **Liabilities** | |
| Current Liabilities | $ 50 |
| Long-Term Liabilities | 50 |
| **Total Liabilities** | **$100** |
| Shareholders' Equity | 200 |
| **Total Liabilities & Equity** | **$300** |

Most U.S. companies use the formats shown in Tables 5.1 and 5.2. Foreign companies may use a slightly different format that is illustrated in Table 5.3. You will notice that this one introduces working capital (current assets minus current liabilities) and then adds in all long-term assets and others as noncurrent assets. The last line in the balance sheet is net assets, which is the same as shareholders' equity.

## TABLE 5.3

Balance Sheet of Company X as of September 30, XXXX

| Assets | |
| --- | --- |
| Current assets | $100 |
| Less: Current liabilities | 50 |
| Working capital | $50 |
| Plus: Noncurrent assets | 200 |
| Total assets minus current liabilities | 250 |
| Less: Long-term liabilities | 50 |
| Net Assets | $200 |

## ANALYSIS OF ASSETS

Assets include everything a company owns. Assets are classified into current assets, investments, fixed assets (property, plant, and equipment), intangible assets, and other assets.

### Current Assets

Current assets are actively managed assets that are generally held for a year or less. Besides cash, the other current assets are expected to be converted into cash within a year or the operating cycle, whichever is longer. The operating cycle is the average time it takes between the purchase of materials that are converted into products and then sold and the receipt of cash from sales. If this cycle takes longer than a year, the longer period is used for current assets. The other major point about current assets is that the items are arranged in order of liquidity. Liquidity shows the ability to easily convert an asset into cash without losing very much in the process. The most liquid assets are arranged before the least liquid assets. Exhibit 5.1 shows the consolidated balance sheet of Cliffs Natural Resources, which lists cash, accounts receivables, inventories, and other assets in its current asset section. The five most common current asset accounts are cash, marketable securities, accounts receivables, inventories, and prepaid expenses.

## Cash

Just as individuals need to keep a certain amount in cash for their needs, so do corporations. The question often asked is: How much cash should a corporation keep on hand? Too much means the company is not managing its resources well, since cash does not earn a return, and too little implies a great deal of risk in that there is no safety net in terms of payments for transactions and emergency needs. When a company has too much cash on hand for short-term needs, it invests the surplus cash in *marketable securities*, which generally earn a slightly higher return than savings accounts. The box, Notes to Consolidated Financial Statements (10-K Report), shows the notes to Cliffs Natural, disclosing that the cash balance includes cash equivalents (marketable securities). Marketable securities are considered to be relatively safe because they are in short-term securities (maturities of one year or less) and have a relatively low default rate.

Cliffs Natural had cash and cash equivalents of $521.6 million on December 31, 2011, and three times that amount ($1,566.7 million) on December 31, 2010. Looking through the notes to the company's financial statements, the reason for holding so much in cash was provided: Cliffs Natural acquired Consolidated Thompson for $4,423.5 million in cash.

## NOTES TO CONSOLIDATED FINANCIAL STATEMENTS (10-K REPORT)

*Cash Equivalents*

Cash and cash equivalents include cash on hand and in the bank as well as all short-term securities held for the primary purpose of general liquidity. We consider investments in highly liquid debt instruments with an original maturity of three months or less from the date of acquisition to be cash equivalents. We routinely monitor and evaluate counterparty credit risk related to the financial institutions by which our short-term investment securities are held.

**EXHIBIT 5.1**

The Consolidated Balance Sheet of Cliffs Natural Resources Inc. as of December 31, 2011

*Financial Statements and Supplementary Data.*
**Statements of Consolidated Financial Position**
Cliffs Natural Resources Inc. and Subsidiaries

| | (In Millions) December 31, | |
| --- | --- | --- |
| | 2011 | 2010 |
| ASSETS | | |
| CURRENT ASSETS | | |
| Cash and cash equivalents | $521.6 | $1,566.7 |
| Accounts receivable | 304.2 | 359.1 |
| Inventories | 475.7 | 269.2 |
| Supplies and other inventories | 216.9 | 148.1 |
| Deferred and refundable taxes | 21.9 | 43.2 |
| Derivative assets | 82.1 | 82.6 |
| Other current assets | 168.3 | 114.8 |
| TOTAL CURRENT ASSETS | 1,790.7 | 2,583.7 |

*(Continued)*

| PROPERTY, PLANT AND EQUIPMENT,<br>NET OTHER ASSETS | 10,524.6 | 3,979.2 |
|---|---|---|
| Investments in ventures | 526.6 | 514.8 |
| Goodwill | 1,152.1 | 196.5 |
| Intangible assets, net | 147.0 | 175.8 |
| Deferred income taxes | 209.5 | 140.3 |
| Other non-current assets | 191.2 | 187.9 |
| TOTAL OTHER ASSETS | 2,226.4 | 1,215.3 |
| TOTAL ASSETS | $14,541.7 | $7,778.2 |

**Statements of Consolidated Financial Position**

Cliffs Natural Resources Inc. and Subsidiaries

|  | (In Millions, Except Share Amounts) December 31, | |
|---|---|---|
|  | 2011 | 2010 |
| LIABILITIES | | |
| CURRENT LIABILITIES | | |
| Accounts payable | $ 380.3 | $ 266.5 |
| Accrued employment costs | 144.2 | 129.9 |
| Income taxes payable | 265.4 | 103.4 |
| State and local taxes payable | 59.1 | 38.9 |
| Below-market sales contracts—current | 52.7 | 57.1 |
| Current portion of term loan | 74.8 | — |
| Accrued expenses | 165.0 | 56.5 |
| Accrued royalties | 77.1 | 80.2 |
| Deferred revenue | 126.6 | 215.6 |
| Other current liabilities | 148.1 | 80.6 |
| TOTAL CURRENT LIABILITIES | 1,493.3 | 1,028.7 |
| POSTEMPLOYMENT BENEFIT LIABILITIES | | |
| Pensions | 394.7 | 284.9 |
| Other postretirement benefits | 271.1 | 243.1 |
| TOTAL POSTEMPLOYMENT BENEFIT LIABILITIES | 665.8 | 528.0 |

| | | |
|---|---:|---:|
| ENVIRONMENTAL AND MINE CLOSURE OBLIGATIONS | **222.0** | 184.9 |
| DEFERRED INCOME TAXES | **1,062.4** | 63.7 |
| LONG-TERM DEBT | **3,608.7** | 1,713.1 |
| BELOW-MARKET SALES CONTRACTS | **111.8** | 164.4 |
| OTHER LIABILITIES | **338.0** | 256.7 |
| TOTAL LIABILITIES | **7,502.0** | 3,939.5 |
| COMMITMENTS AND CONTINGENCIES | | |
| EQUITY | | |
| CLIFFS SHAREHOLDERS' EQUITY | | |
| Preferred stock—no par value | | |
| Class A—3,000,000 shares authorized and unissued | | |
| Class B—4,000,000 shares authorized and unissued | | |
| Common Shares—par value $0.125 per share | | |
| Authorized—400,000,000 shares (2010—224,000,000); | | |
| Issued—149,195,469 shares (2010—138,845,469 shares); | | |
| Outstanding—142,021,718 shares (2010—135,456,999 shares) | **18.5** | 17.3 |
| Capital in excess of par value of shares | **1,770.8** | 896.3 |
| Retained earnings | **4,424.3** | 2,924.1 |
| Cost of 7,173,751 common shares in treasury (2010—3,388,470 shares) | **(336.0)** | (37.7) |
| Accumulated other comprehensive income (loss) | **(92.6)** | 45.9 |
| TOTAL CLIFFS SHAREHOLDERS' EQUITY | **5,785.0** | 3,845.9 |
| NONCONTROLLING INTEREST | **1,254.7** | (7.2) |
| TOTAL EQUITY | **7,039.7** | 3,838.7 |
| TOTAL LIABILITIES AND EQUITY | **$14,541.7** | $7,778.2 |

The accompanying notes are an integral part of these consolidated financial statements.

It is important to look through the notes to the financial statements to see if there are any restrictions or commitments on the use of cash. If cash is restricted for current obligations, the amount is separated from regular cash or footnoted in the notes, and in both cases the restricted cash is included under current assets. If, however, cash is restricted for long-term commitments, the restricted cash is recorded in other assets and excluded from current assets.

## Marketable Securities

These securities, also known as cash equivalents, are liquid securities with maturities of a year or less. Marketable securities can also include stocks that are purchased as short-term investments. The important aspect of marketable securities is that they are valued at the lower of cost or market value, which is stipulated in the notes.

## Accounts Receivable

Accounts receivable arise when customers purchase products or services from the company on account. Accounts receivable are recorded at face value, which is the amount owed. There are two issues with accounts receivable: the first is how to classify them and the second is valuation. If receivables are expected to be collected within a year or the operating cycle, they are classified as current assets. If receivables are intended to be collected after a year or the operating cycle, they are classified as noncurrent receivables. Valuation is more complex. Accounts receivable are recorded at their net realizable value, which is the amount the company expects to receive, not the stated value (amount owed). Any accounts receivable that are deemed uncollectible should be reduced from the stated amount. If there are large amounts written off as uncollectible or a large percentage (over 4 percent of accounts receivable) as an allowance for uncollectible accounts, treat this as a warning sign for this company.

To accelerate the receipt of cash from what they are owed, companies can pledge the accounts receivable as security for loans or sell them outright. These actions are disclosed in the notes to the financial statements. Pledging or selling accounts receivable is another warning sign for a company.

*Notes receivable* are like accounts receivable except that they are supported by a written promise to pay the amounts owed at specified dates in the future. Notes receivable are frequently issued to customers who either need extensions on their payment dates or are high-risk customers. If you see notes receivable on the balance sheet, look through the notes to the financial statements to assess the risk of the customers who issued the notes.

Potential investors will want to determine the overall trend in the amount of the accounts receivable relative to sales. If the company's accounts receivable are increasing by greater proportions to sales, the company may be extending itself in its inability to free up cash. You also will want to determine whether the allowance for uncollectible accounts has risen as a percentage of accounts receivable, or whether there is growth in the write-off of bad debts.

## Inventory

Inventory consists of goods either produced or acquired by the company for sale. A retailer purchases merchandise for resale and generally has one inventory account. A production company generally has three inventory accounts: raw materials inventory, work in process inventory, and finished goods inventory. The efficiency of the company in matching its inventory levels with its sales is the key to the company being more successful.

Value investors should examine the inventory balances, along with the size of inventory and the efficiency of its management. In Chapter 8 I discuss inventory turnover, which measures the length of time inventory is held. Slow-moving inventory bears investigation; not only is cash tied up in inventory but there is also an increased risk of obsolescence or a glut of inventory, either of which can result in selling inventory at discounted prices.

How inventory is valued by a company is important for potential investors to understand. Inventory is valued at the lower of cost or market value, which is a slight deviation from the general rule that assets are valued at their historic cost. If inventory falls below its original cost, it is written down to reflect the loss. Market value is the net realizable value or ceiling price for the value of inventory. This rule for valuation prevents inventory from being recorded at an amount in excess of its net selling price.

An examination of Cliffs Natural inventory as stated in its balance sheet (Exhibit 5.1) shows that inventories increased by 76 percent, from $269.2 million in 2010 to $475.7 million in 2011. The major components of inventory at Cliffs Natural consist of 85 percent in iron ore and 11 percent in coal. The notes to the financial statements, in Table 5.4, provide some answers to the valuation of the inventories.

## TABLE 5.4

Notes on Inventories from Statements of Consolidated Financial Statement of Cliffs Natural

**Inventories**

The following table presents the detail of our *Inventories* in the Statements of Consolidated Financial Position at December 31, 2011 and 2010:

| | (In Millions) | | | | | |
|---|---|---|---|---|---|---|
| | 2011 | | | 2010 | | |
| Segment | Finished Goods | Work-in Process | Total Inventory | Finished Goods | Work-in Process | Total Inventory |
| U.S. Iron Ore | $100.2 | $ 8.5 | $108.7 | $101.1 | $ 9.7 | $110.8 |
| Eastern Canadian Iron Ore | 96.2 | 43.0 | 139.2 | 43.5 | 21.2 | 64.7 |
| North American Coal | 19.7 | 110.5 | 130.2 | 16.1 | 19.8 | 35.9 |
| Asia Pacific Iron Ore | 57.2 | 21.6 | 78.8 | 34.7 | 20.4 | 55.1 |
| Other | 18.0 | 0.8 | 18.8 | 2.6 | 0.1 | 2.7 |
| Total | $291.3 | $184.4 | $475.7 | $198.0 | $71.2 | $269.2 |

### *U.S. Iron Ore*

U.S. Iron Ore product inventories are stated at the lower of cost or market. Cost of iron ore inventories is determined using the LIFO method. The excess of current cost over LIFO cost of iron ore inventories was $117.1 million and $112.4 million at December 31, 2011 and 2010, respectively. As of December 31, 2011, the product inventory balance for U.S. Iron Ore declined, resulting in liquidation of LIFO layers in 2011. The effect of the inventory reduction was a decrease in *Cost of goods sold and operating expenses* of $15.2 million in the Statements of Consolidated Operations for the year ended December 31, 2011. As of December 31, 2010, the product inventory balance for U.S. Iron Ore declined, resulting in liquidation of LIFO layers in 2010. The effect of the inventory reduction was a decrease in *Cost of goods sold and operating expenses* of $4.6 in the Statements of Consolidated Operations for the year ended December 31, 2010.

We had approximately 1.2 million tons and 0.8 million tons of finished goods stored at ports and customer facilities on the lower Great Lakes to service customers at December 31, 2011 and 2010, respectively. We maintain ownership of the inventories until title has transferred to the customer, usually when payment is made. Maintaining ownership of the iron ore products at ports on the lower Great Lakes reduces risk of non-payment by customers, as we retain title to the product until payment is received from the customer. We track the movement of the inventory and verify the quantities on hand.

### Eastern Canadian Iron Ore

Iron ore pellet inventories are stated at the lower of cost or market. Similar to U.S. Iron Ore product inventories, the cost is determined using the LIFO method. The excess of current cost over LIFO cost of iron ore inventories was $21.9 million and $2.5 million at December 31, 2011 and 2010, respectively. As of December 31, 2011, the iron ore pellet inventory balance for Eastern Canadian Iron Ore increased to $47.1 million, resulting in an additional LIFO layer being added. As of December 31, 2010, the product inventory balance for Eastern Canadian Iron Ore increased to $43.5 million, resulting in an additional LIFO layer being added during the year. We primarily maintain ownership of these inventories until loading of the product at the port.

Iron ore concentrate inventories are stated at the lower of cost or market. The cost of iron ore concentrate inventories is determined using weighted average cost. As of December 31, 2011, the iron ore concentrate inventory balance for Eastern Canadian Iron Ore was $49.1 million as a result of the Consolidated Thompson acquisition. For the majority of the iron ore concentrate inventories, we maintain ownership of the inventories until title passes on the bill of lading date, which is upon the loading of the product at the port.

### North American Coal

North American Coal product inventories are stated at the lower of cost or market. Cost of coal inventories includes labor, supplies and operating overhead and related costs and is calculated using the average production cost. We maintain ownership until coal is loaded into rail cars at the mine for domestic sales and until loaded in the vessels at the terminal for export sales. We recorded

*(Continued)*

lower-of-cost-or-market inventory charges of $6.6 million and $26.1 million in *Cost of goods sold and operating expenses* in the Statements of Consolidated Operations for the years ended December 31, 2011 and 2010, respectively. These charges were a result of operational and geological issues at our Pinnacle and Oak Grove mines during the periods.

**Asia Pacific Iron Ore**

Asia Pacific Iron Ore product inventories are stated at the lower of cost or market. Costs, including an appropriate portion of fixed and variable overhead expenses, are assigned to the inventory on hand by the method most appropriate to each particular class of inventory, with the majority being valued on a weighted average basis. We maintain ownership of the inventories until title has transferred to the customer at the F.O.B. point, which is generally when the product is loaded into the vessel.

Iron ore inventory and iron ore pellets were written down as the market price of both fell, as indicated by the underlined notes to the financial statements.

Inventory valuation is also affected by the accounting methods chosen to value ending inventory. The accounting methods chosen can be on a FIFO, LIFO, or average cost basis.

Cliffs Natural uses LIFO to value its inventory, which means that the cost of the last goods purchased or manufactured are the first to be matched against revenue. In other words, the goods sold first consist of the most recent goods purchased or the most recently manufactured goods. When prices are rising (inflation), the prices of the goods chosen for sale are the most up to date, which reduces the gross profit and net income. Reduced income results in the tax benefits of lower taxes. However, inventory on the balance sheet consists of lower-cost items, and over time, with rising prices, inventory is understated. Consequently, using LIFO results in a conservative valuation of inventory and income as the highest cost of goods are matched first against sales during rising prices. When prices are falling, as has occurred with iron ore and coal, inventory costs are reduced to the lower of cost or market.

FIFO valuation means that the first goods held in inventory are the first ones to be matched against sales. In other words, the first goods purchased (or manufactured) are the first ones sold. Thus, inventory stated on the balance sheet consists of the more recent purchases (or goods manufactured) and is valued relatively closely to their current costs. The disadvantage of using FIFO valuation is that there is a distortion that overstates gross and net income in that the earliest costs are matched against current revenues when prices are rising.

The accounting method used by companies is always disclosed in the notes to the financial statements. Investors should watch for occurrences when a company changes its method of valuation or when there are periods of high inflation. In addition, when evaluating inventory, look at the amount of inventory relative to the size of sales and how quickly the inventory turns over. These aspects of inventory management are discussed more fully in Chapter 8.

## Prepaid Expenses

Prepaid expenses are those that are paid and recorded ahead of their use. For example, if rent is paid in advance for 18 months, the prepaid rent account is adjusted at the end of the year to reflect the amount that had not been used. Generally, prepaid expenses tend to be a relatively small component of current assets.

## Other Current Assets

*Deferred taxes* occur because of timing differences between estimated taxes that are paid before the actual tax liability is assessed. This item also tends to be a small part of Cliffs Natural's assets.

*Derivative assets* include the costs of hedging prices using futures contracts on iron ore and coal to protect the company's assets from adverse swings in price. The note below explains the use of these futures contracts as insurance against price swings in commodities, foreign exchange, and interest rates.

> **NOTES TO THE FINANCIAL STATEMENTS OF CLIFFS NATURAL (10-K)**
>
> *Derivative Financial Instruments*
>
> We are exposed to certain risks related to the ongoing operations of our business, including those caused by changes in commodity prices, interest rates and foreign currency exchange rates. We have established policies and procedures, including the use of certain derivative instruments, to manage such risks. Refer to NOTE 3—DERIVATIVE INSTRUMENTS AND HEDGING ACTIVITIES for further information.

## Long-Term Assets

Long-term assets include those that are held for longer than a year. These assets consist of investments, property, plant and equipment, intangible assets, and other assets.

## Investments

There are many types of investment assets, which include long-term securities such as stocks and bonds, land and buildings held for speculation, affiliate companies, or setting aside funds in a sinking fund, or pension fund. These investments are held for years and are not purchased to be sold over short periods of time. Investments that are purchased for short-term periods are classified as marketable securities in current assets.

What potential investors want to watch for in a company's 10-K is whether its investments are profitable (fair value is greater than cost) or trading below their cost (fair value is less than the cost of investments). In the latter case, where fair value is less than cost, the company faces large write-downs in their investments. Investors should look at the size of these write-downs in relation to the total assets.

## Property, Plant, and Equipment

The property, plant, and equipment category includes the fixed assets of the company that are used in regular business operations and include land, buildings, equipment, and other productive assets. These assets are recorded at their historical cost and are subject to depreciation over the assets' useful economic lives. Land is the exception in that it is not a depreciable asset. Land is carried at its cost on the balance sheet, and if the land was purchased many years ago, it will be vastly undervalued on the balance sheet.

Depreciation is the systematic method of allocating the cost of the asset over its useful life. In other words, depreciation is the methodic reduction of the cost of the asset over its useful life. The asset is reduced in value and the reduction in value is recorded as an expense on the income statement. When the asset is fully depreciated the asset may be replaced, and the depreciation cycle begins again.

There are a number of acceptable types of depreciation methods. The two basic types are *straight-line* or *accelerated depreciation*. With straight-line, the cost of the asset is expensed in equal amounts over the useful life of the asset. There are a number of different accelerated depreciation methods, which largely result in greater amounts of the asset being depreciated in the early years of the life of the assets and lesser amounts in the later years. Accelerated depreciation increases the expenses in the earlier years of the asset, which then reduces the amount of the reported profit and also reduces the amount of taxes paid in the earlier years. Consequently, potential investors want to pay attention to the methods that are disclosed in the notes to the financial statements so that they can see that the company is not switching its method of depreciation to straight-line in order to expand its income.

Another point about depreciation is that buildings are depreciated over longer periods of time than equipment and computers, so old buildings that were purchased many years ago could represent hidden value on the balance sheet as they may be fully depreciated.

Table 5.5 lists the information on Cliffs Natural's depreciation methods. Cliffs Natural primarily used straight-line depreciation for both 2010 and 2011 for most of their properties, except for the double declining balance for some of their iron ore mines. The significant point in the note is that land increased by more than double, from $3,019 million in 2010 to $7,918 million in 2011.

## TABLE 5.5

Notes to Cliffs Natural 10-K

### Property, Plant and Equipment

*U.S. Iron Ore and Eastern Canadian Iron Ore*
U.S. Iron Ore and Eastern Canadian Iron Ore properties are stated at cost. Depreciation of plant and equipment is computed principally by the straight-line method based on estimated useful lives, not to exceed the mine lives. Northshore, United Taconite, Empire, Tilden and Wabush use the double declining balance method of depreciation for certain mining equipment. Depreciation is provided over the following estimated useful lives:

| Asset Class | Basis | Life |
|---|---|---|
| Buildings | Straight line | 45 Years |
| Mining equipment | Straight line/Double declining balance | 10 to 20 Years |
| Processing equipment | Straight line | 15 to 45 Years |
| Information technology | Straight line | 2 to 7 Years |

### North American Coal

North American Coal properties are stated at cost. Depreciation is provided over the estimated useful lives, not to exceed the mine lives and is calculated by the straight-line method. Depreciation is provided over the following estimated useful lives:

| Asset Class | Basis | Life |
|---|---|---|
| Buildings | Straight line | 30 Years |
| Mining equipment | Straight line | 2 to 22 Years |
| Processing equipment | Straight line | 2 to 30 Years |
| Information technology | Straight line | 2 to 3 Years |

## Asia Pacific Iron Ore

Our Asia Pacific Iron Ore properties are stated at cost. Depreciation is calculated by the straight-line method or production output basis provided over the following estimated useful lives:

| Asset Class | Basis | Life |
|---|---|---|
| Plant and equipment | Straight line | 5–10 Years |
| Plant and equipment and mine assets | Production output | 10 Years |
| Motor vehicles, furniture & equipment | Straight line | 3–5 Years |

The following table indicates the value of each of the major classes of our consolidated depreciable assets as of December 31, 2011 and 2010:

| | (In Millions) | |
|---|---|---|
| | December 31, | |
| | 2011 | 2010 |
| Land rights and mineral rights | $ 7,918.9 | $3,019.9 |
| Office and information technology | 67.0 | 60.4 |
| Buildings | 132.2 | 107.6 |
| Mining equipment | 1,323.8 | 628.5 |
| Processing equipment | 1,441.8 | 658.8 |
| Railroad equipment | 164.3 | 122.9 |
| Electric power facilities | 57.9 | 54.4 |
| Port facilities | 64.1 | 64.0 |
| Interest capitalized during construction | 22.5 | 19.4 |
| Land improvements | 30.4 | 25.0 |
| Other | 43.2 | 36.0 |
| Construction in progress | 615.4 | 140.0 |
| | 11,881.5 | 4,936.9 |
| Allowance for depreciation and depletion | (1,356.9) | (957.7) |
| | $10,524.6 | $3,979.2 |

(*Continued*)

We recorded depreciation expense of $237.8 million, $165.4 million and $120.6 million in the Statements of Consolidated Operations for the years ended December 31, 2011, 2010 and 2009, respectively.

The costs capitalized and classified as *Land rights and mineral rights* represent lands where we own the surface and/or mineral rights. The value of the land rights is split between surface only, surface and minerals, and minerals only.

Our North American Coal operation leases coal mining rights from third parties through lease agreements. The lease agreements are for varying terms and extend through the earlier of their lease termination date or until all merchantable and mineable coal has been extracted. Our interest in coal reserves and resources was valued using a discounted cash flow method. The fair value was estimated based upon the present value of the expected future cash flows from coal operations over the life of the reserves.

Note that property, plant, and equipment is listed at net prices on the balance sheet (Exhibit 5.1). What this means is that the total *accumulated depreciation* is deducted from the cost of the property, plant, and equipment assets to equal the net property, plant, and equipment value. When assets are reported at net values on the balance sheet, a potential investor needs to look at the notes to the financial statements to see how old the assets are, or whether the assets are mostly depreciated, or whether the company is faced with high replacement costs to replace old equipment.

### Intangible Assets

Intangible assets are those that cannot be felt or touched and consist of goodwill, patents, copyrights, and trademarks. Goodwill arises when a company purchases another company and pays a premium price that is higher than the value of the tangible assets of the company. Goodwill is the premium price above the value of the assets. The method for treating goodwill used to be to amortize (write down) the cost over its useful life, but now goodwill is written down when it is impaired. The notes to the financial statements of Cliffs Natural (Table 5.6) show that the relatively large increase in goodwill from 2010 to 2011 arose from the purchase of Consolidated Thompson.

A patent gives a company the right to produce and sell a particular product. A copyright also gives the company that holds the registration the exclusive right to sell the product. Patents, copyrights, and trademarks are all registered with the government. When other companies want to use something that is trademarked, patented, or copyrighted, they must pay the registered owner a fee.

## TABLE 5.6

Notes from Cliffs Natural Resources 10-K

---

**NOTE 5—GOODWILL AND OTHER INTANGIBLE ASSETS AND LIABILITIES**

*Goodwill*

Goodwill represents the excess purchase price paid over the fair value of the net assets of acquired companies and is not subject to amortization. We assign goodwill arising from acquired companies to the reporting units that are expected to benefit from the synergies of the acquisition. Our reporting units are either at the operating segment level or a component one level below our operating segments that constitutes a business for which management generally reviews production and financial results of that component. Decisions are often made as to capital expenditures, investments and production plans at the component level as part of the ongoing management of the related operating segment. We have determined that our Asia Pacific Iron Ore and Ferroalloys operating segments constitute separate reporting units, that our Bloom Lake and Wabush mines within our Eastern Canadian Iron Ore operating segment constitute reporting units, that CLCC within our North American Coal operating segment constitutes a reporting unit and that our Northshore mine within our U.S. Iron Ore operating segment constitutes a reporting unit. Goodwill is allocated among and evaluated for impairment at the reporting unit level in the fourth quarter of each year or as circumstances occur that potentially indicate that the carrying amount of these assets may not be recoverable. There were no such events or changes in circumstances during 2011.

After performing our annual goodwill impairment test in the fourth quarter of 2011, we determined that $27.8 million of goodwill associated with our CLCC reporting unit was impaired as the carrying value with this reporting unit exceeded its fair value. The fair value was determined using a combination of a discounted cash flow model and valuations of comparable businesses. The impairment charge for the CLCC reporting unit was driven by our overall outlook on coal pricing in light of economic conditions, increases in our anticipated costs to bring the Lower War Eagle mine into production and increases in our anticipated sustaining capital cost for the lives of the CLCC mines that are currently operating. No impairment charges were identified in connection with our annual goodwill impairment test with respect to our other identified reporting units. The following table summarizes changes in the carrying amount of goodwill allocated by operating segment during 2011 and 2010:

*(Continued)*

(In Millions)

| | December 31, 2011 | | | | | | December 31, 2010 | | | | | |
|---|---|---|---|---|---|---|---|---|---|---|---|---|
| | U.S. Iron Ore | Eastern Canadian Iron Ore | North American Coal | Asia Pacific Iron Ore | Other | Total | U.S. Iron Ore | Eastern Canadian Iron Ore | North American Coal | Asia Pacific Iron Ore | Other | Total |
| Beginning Balance | $2.0 | $ 3.1 | $27.9 | $82.6 | $80.9 | $196.5 | $2.0 | $— | $ — | $72.6 | $ — | $ 74.6 |
| Arising in business combinations | — | 983.5 | (0.1) | — | — | 983.4 | — | 3.1 | 27.9 | — | 80.9 | 111.9 |
| Impairment | — | — | (27.8) | — | — | (27.8) | — | — | — | — | — | — |
| Impact of foreign currency translation | — | — | — | 0.4 | — | 0.4 | — | — | — | 10.0 | — | 10.0 |
| Other | — | (0.4) | — | — | — | (0.4) | — | — | — | — | — | — |
| Ending Balance | $2.0 | $986.2 | $ — | $83.0 | $80.9 | $1,152.1 | $2.0 | $3.1 | $27.9 | $82.6 | $80.9 | $196.5 |

The increase in the balance of goodwill as of December 31, 2011 is due to the assignment of $983.5 million to *Goodwill* during 2011 based on preliminary purchase price allocation for the acquisition of Consolidated Thompson. The balance of $1,152.1 million and $196.5 million as of December 31, 2011 and 2010, respectively, is presented as *Goodwill* in the Statements of Consolidated Financial Position. Refer to NOTE 4—ACQUISITIONS AND OTHER INVESTMENTS for additional information.

## ANALYSIS OF LIABILITIES

Liabilities are the debts a company owes. If liabilities are to be paid within a year, they are classified as current liabilities. Debts that come due after one year are classified as long-term liabilities. Failure to pay liabilities could force a company into bankruptcy.

### Current Liabilities

Current liabilities include accounts payable, notes payable, taxes payable, accrued liabilities, and the current portion of long-term debt. Accounts payable are the debts owed by the company for products or services bought on account that are to be paid within a year. Accrued liabilities are debts that the company owes but has not paid by the balance sheet date. For example, a company might pay its workers on Fridays, but if the balance sheet is drawn up on a Wednesday, the company needs to record the amount of wages it owes for the unpaid period through Wednesday, which is an accrued liability.

The current portion of long-term debt shows the amount that is to be repaid within the current fiscal or calendar year. Notes to the financial statements include the details of the company's financial obligations.

### How Should You View Current Liabilities?

Current liabilities are considered to be a form of spontaneous credit for a company. When a company buys goods on account and pays thirty days later, it has the use of the goods for that period and the free use of someone else's money for thirty days. Therefore, current liabilities should not be paid down to zero, though current liabilities should not be higher than the company can effectively cope with in the management of its short-term debt.

## Long-Term Liabilities

Long-term liabilities are contractual commitments to pay the amounts borrowed plus interest. These debts come in the form of notes payable, bonds payable, mortgages payable, and capitalized lease obligations. Total liabilities doubled from 2010 to 2011.

## How Much Debt Is Too Much?

This is a question that a value investor should always be concerned with. As pointed out in the current liabilities section, a certain amount of debt can be good for a company because it is using the money of others to invest in the business, also referred to as the concept of *leverage*. Leverage can work to the company's advantage when it earns a greater return on the money borrowed from outsiders than the cost of that money. Returns are then magnified. But the opposite is also true that if the company employs borrowed money and earns a lower rate than the cost of the money, its loss is magnified.

Another aspect of debt financing is that if the company takes on too much debt, it could have difficulty in servicing the debt (paying the interest and paying back the principal at maturity). Debt to total assets ratios are discussed in Chapter 8, along with the use of trend analysis and industry comparisons to determine comfortable levels of debt for companies that might appeal to value investors.

Table 5.7 discloses the nature of Cliffs Natural's liabilities, maturity dates, interest rates, total face amounts, and total long-term debt. Long-term debt increased from $1,713.1 million in 2010 to $3,608.7 million in 2011. This increase resulted from the company taking out a variable $1.25 billion loan at 1.4 percent due in 2016 and a $700 million 4.875 percent fixed note due in 2021.

Cliffs Natural's pension obligations increased by roughly $100 million in 2011, including the deferred pension liabilities it owes its employees for their services under the pension plan.

## TABLE 5.7

Note Disclosing Long-term Liabilities of Cliffs Natural from 10-K Report

### NOTE 7—DEBT AND CREDIT FACILITIES

The following represents a summary of our long-term debt as of December 31, 2011 and 2010:

| | | | | | |
|---|---|---|---|---|---|
| | | | **($ in Millions)** | | |
| | | | **December 31, 2011** | | |
| **Debt Instrument** | **Type** | **Average Annual Interest Rate** | **Final Maturity** | **Total Face Amount** | **Total Long- term Debt** |
| $1.25 Billion Term Loan | Variable | 1.40% | 2016 | $ 972.0 (6) | $ 897.2 (6) |
| $700 Million 4.875% 2021 Senior Notes | Fixed | 4.88% | 2021 | 700.0 | 699.3 (5) |
| $1.3 Billion Senior Notes: | | | | | |
| $500 Million 4.80% 2020 Senior Notes | Fixed | 4.80% | 2020 | 500.0 | 499.1 (4) |
| $800 Million 6.25% 2040 Senior Notes | Fixed | 6.25% | 2040 | 800.0 | 790.1 (3) |
| $400 Million 5.90% 2020 Senior Notes | Fixed | 5.90% | 2020 | 400.0 | 398.0 (2) |
| $325 Million Private Placement Senior Notes: | | | | | |
| Series 2008A—Tranche A | Fixed | 6.31% | 2013 | 270.0 | 270.0 |
| Series 2008A—Tranche B | Fixed | 6.59% | 2015 | 55.0 | 55.0 |
| $1.75 Billion Credit Facility: | | | | | |
| Revolving Loan | Variable | — | 2016 | 1,750.0 | — (1) |
| Total | | | | $5,447.0 | $3,608.7 |

*(Continued)*

| | | December 31, 2010 | | | |
| --- | --- | --- | --- | --- | --- |
| Debt Instrument | Type | Average Annual Interest Rate | Final Maturity | Total Face Amount | Total Long-term Debt |
| $1 Billion Senior Notes: | | | | | |
| $500 Million 4.80% 2020 Senior Notes | Fixed | 4.80% | 2020 | $ 500.0 | $ 499.0 (4) |
| $500 Million 6.25% 2040 Senior Notes | Fixed | 6.25% | 2040 | 500.0 | 491.3 (3) |
| $400 Million 5.90% 2020 Senior Notes | Fixed | 5.90% | 2020 | 400.0 | 397.8 (2) |
| $325 Million Private Placement Senior Notes: | | | | | |
| Series 2008A—Tranche A | Fixed | 6.31% | 2013 | 270.0 | 270.0 |
| Series 2008A—Tranche B | Fixed | 6.59% | 2015 | 55.0 | 55.0 |
| $600 Million Credit Facility: | | | | | |
| Revolving Loan | Variable | — | 2012 | 600.0 | — (1) |
| Total | | | | $2,325.0 | $1,713.1 |

# SHAREHOLDERS' EQUITY

Shareholders' equity is more than merely the difference between assets and liabilities in a company. The creation of many different financial interests in recent years has blurred the distinction between liabilities and equity, making the measurement of income a little more difficult. Liabilities, as we saw in the previous section, include obligations to pay back interest and principal in the future, while equity does not include sacrifices of future economic benefits. Stockholders of a company bear the ultimate risks and uncertainties (losing their entire invested amounts) and receive the benefits when the company's operations are profitable. Stockholders' equity includes net contributions by stockholders plus income that has been retained by the company. In other words, shareholders do not have a claim against specific assets of the company but rather a residual interest against the amount of the net assets (the difference between total assets and total liabilities). When a company is profitable, stockholders' equity increases, but it could disappear entirely when a company is unprofitable. The three major components of shareholders' equity are capital paid by shareholders for the shares, premium accounts consisting of excess amounts paid for shares above the par or stated price, and retained earnings (income retained by the company).

## Capital Stock

Many large corporations issue different classes of stock, but every company must issue one class, which represents the residual interest of the company. This class of stock is called *common stock*. Common stockholders are neither guaranteed the payment of dividends nor the payment of assets on the dissolution of the company. However, common stockholders are the residual owners of the company and generally profit when the company does well financially. Companies can also issue two classes of common stock, Class A and Class B. Each class participates in dividend payments and has the same claim on assets in the case of bankruptcy. The difference occurs in voting: Class A shareholders have voting rights, but Class B do not. The reason for these nonvoting rights is to protect family owners of a company who receive Class A shares.

## Preferred Stock

Companies can create special classes of stock such as preferred stock. Preferred stockholders have preferential rights, generally with regard to dividends. Before a company pays dividends to its common shareholders, it must first pay dividends to its preferred stockholders. Preferred stockholders do not have voting rights. Cliffs Natural has authorized two classes of preferred stock but has not issued any stock. Consequently, you will notice that there are no dollar amounts for preferred stock recorded in the balance sheet in Exhibit 5.1.

## Paid-in Capital

Paid-in capital represents capital paid in excess of par when the company initially sells stock, and then the amounts in excess of par value when subsequent stock is sold. Generally, not much attention is paid to this category.

## Retained Earnings

Retained earnings represent the earned capital of a company, while capital stock and additional paid-in capital represent contributed capital. Retained earnings mostly originate from the operations of a company, which is net income for the current year and income retained from prior years. The sources that could increase retained earnings besides net income are prior period adjustments for errors or changes in accounting principle and adjustments from a reorganization of the company.

Net losses decrease retained earnings, as do the payments of dividends, along with negative prior period adjustments and certain Treasury stock transactions. Treasury stock is the company's own stock that it has repurchased after it has been issued. Treasury stock is not considered to be an asset because a company cannot own part of itself and claim it to be an addition to assets. Treasury stock reduces the company's shareholders' equity.

Value investors want to see retained earnings that are increasing from year to year, meaning that shareholders are benefiting, so to speak. Technically, the higher the retained earnings, the greater the amount that belongs to shareholders. With increased retained earnings, companies can increase their dividend payments to shareholders, which generally exerts upward pressures on the company's stock price.

The opposite side of the coin is declining retained earnings or worse, negative retained earnings, which is a red flag to potential investors.

## SUMMARY

The key points that a balance sheet provides are summarized in Table 5.8.

**TABLE 5.8**

Summary of Balance Sheet Elements

| |
|---|
| Shows a company's financial position at a particular point in time |
| Lists the types and amounts of assets the company owns |
| Lists the current assets of a company (cash, accounts receivable, and inventory) |
| Shows the cost of a company's fixed assets (land, building, and equipment) |
| Shows the accumulated depreciation of fixed assets |
| Lists the current liabilities the company owes to suppliers and others |
| Lists the long-term debts of the company |
| Shows the amount invested by the company's shareholders |
| Shows the earnings retained by the company |

Source: Faerber, Esme. *All About Stock, 3rd ed.*

# The Income Statement

**V**alue investors determine how successful a company is by studying its income statement. In addition, the income statement is used to determine the profitability, credit worthiness, and value of a company. Bear in mind that the measurement of income includes many assumptions and allows for the use of various accounting principles, which could allow for manipulation of income and expenses. Many companies over the years have manipulated fraudulently their income statements to overstate their revenues and profits. Even experienced management personnel have failed to uncover fraudulent financial statements when they have bid to take over those companies. On November 20, 2012, Hewlett-Packard wrote down $8 billion of the $11 billion it paid for Autonomy, a software company, because it allegedly fraudulently overstated their revenues and profits.

Another example of fraud was WorldCom's manipulation of profits by overstating revenue and understating expenses until its final collapse into bankruptcy.

Income is much easier to manipulate than cash, though it still makes the income statement important in that it provides the basis for predicting the amount, timing, and risk of future cash flows.

A profitable company is generally a successful company. You might remember what happened during the dot-com bubble in the early 2000s. Companies with great ideas and promise for the future looked so good that their stock prices took meteoric rises despite the fact that they couldn't rack up any profits. When the Internet bubble burst, many of these companies with revenues but no profits went out of business.

When value investors find balance sheets that indicate an undervalued company, the next step is to analyze the income statement. Should the company not be profitable, the value investor should analyze the income statement and the business to determine whether this is a temporary situation that could reverse itself to generate future profit. If he cannot see a catalyst for turning around such a company from losses into profits, the investor should stay away from investing in that company.

Even for companies that have been profitable, the value investor needs to analyze the income statement to determine whether the profits are from continuing company operations and not from one-time asset sales at greater-than-book values. An analysis of a company's profits should reveal whether the company has competitive advantages that will provide it with increasing future revenues and profits. Apple's stock price fell from a high of $700 to the low $500 range when new versions of the iPhone 5 and iPad mini were introduced because investors felt that they were not significantly different from their predecessor models. However, the stock price presented value when it was trading in the low $500 range because sales would not slow down but rather increase because of greater demand for their products in Europe, Asia, and other emerging markets. Another example is Intel, which is facing great challenges in the future. Intel's stock price has fallen by 23 percent from its yearly high because of uncertainty as to Intel's catalyst for revenue and earnings growth. Intel does not have any of its chips in the fastest-growing tablets (iPads, Nexus 7, and Kindle Fire) or smartphones. To make up for this shortfall in growth, Intel faces a major shift in its strategy: Should it allow its factories to produce chips for other companies, which would produce some growth in its revenues but a drastic reduction in its profit margins? The other strategy for Intel is to pursue the development of its transistor "Tri-gate," which lowers chips' power consumption. Intel is far ahead of its competitors in the development and production of this transistor. If you believed that Intel has an edge in the use of this technology to be the catalyst to future sales and profits, you would buy shares at the depressed price. Many owners of Intel stock would probably hold the stock while waiting to see what happens with this transistor technology. Intel stockholders receive a 4 percent dividend yield while they wait.[1]

## WHAT THE INCOME STATEMENT SHOWS

The income statement shows revenues, cost of goods sold, expenses, gains and losses, and profits or losses for a period of time. The balance sheet is drawn up at one point in time, while the income statement measures revenues and expenses over the period of time stated in the heading of the statement. The income statement does not show either cash receipts or cash disbursements.

The four elements in an income statement are revenues, expenses, gains, and losses. It is important to be able to differentiate between revenues and gains, and expenses and losses. Table 6.1 shows a basic income statement format.

### Revenues

Revenues are inflows of income or cash that result from sales of products or the rendering of services, fees charged, dividends, interest, and rent received. Recording revenues is not a simple matter because they are reduced for discounts and returns, and if the purchaser never pays the company for the goods delivered, the revenues should not be counted. Similarly, revenue recognized does not mean that the company has received the cash for the products or services delivered or rendered. So the question is, when is a sale a sale? The answer cannot be left to management to manipulate revenues recognized to make profits look better than they really are. The accounting profession has formulated rules for recognizing revenue that must be followed. Here are some of the rules,

## TABLE 6.1

Basic Income Statement for the Year Ended
December 31, 20XX

| | |
|---|---:|
| Sales | $20,000 |
| Cost of Goods Sold | 8,000 |
| Gross Profit | 12,000 |
| Operating Expenses | |
| Advertising | $    250 |
| Selling expenses | 750 |
| Depreciation | 200 |
| Salaries | 2,000 |
| Insurance | 500 |
| Total operating expenses | 3,700 |
| Income before Extraordinary items | 8,300 |
| Gain on sale of equipment | 4,000 |
| Loss on sale of truck | (3,500) |
| Net Extraordinary gain | 500 |
| Income before Interest and Taxes | 8,800 |
| Interest expense | 200 |
| Income before Taxes | 8,600 |
| Taxes | 3,400 |
| Net Income | $ 5,200 |

which highlight some of the complexities involved in recognizing
revenues.

- Revenue is recognized when it is realized and it is earned.
  Revenues are realized when goods and services are
  exchanged for cash or on account. Revenue is earned when

the company has accomplished what it must do to be entitled to the revenues.

- If a company sells a product in one year and has an agreement to buy back the product in the next year, revenue is not recognized in the first year because no sale has taken place.

- If a company sells a product that can be returned, a problem is presented, particularly when the return ratio is high. In such a situation, there are several conditions that must be met before revenue can be recognized. In the case of high returns, revenues and cost of sales should be reduced in the income statement to reflect the estimated returns. Unfortunately, most companies do not disclose their returns, showing only net sales (gross sales minus returns).

- If a company sells goods and is obligated to provide further significant services to the buyer, the company cannot count the sale as revenue recognized.

- When a company delivers goods to a retailer who will only pay the company for the goods when the retailer sells them, the company cannot recognize the revenue until the products are sold by the retailer.

- Related party transactions were fraudulently used by Enron and WorldCom to overstate revenues. The rule is, when a company sells products to its subsidiary (and vice versa), the transaction cannot be counted as revenue. It is classified as an asset transfer.

- If a buyer indicates interest in purchasing goods from a seller, the seller cannot include this potential transaction as revenue until a sale is made and the goods are delivered.

- Another problem investors should be aware of is the separation of revenues from receipts. When a company borrows $1,000 from the bank and issues a note payable, the $1,000 received is not revenue; it is a cash receipt.

Similarly, if a company sells an asset, such as land it owns or equipment that is not one of the products the company regularly sells as part of its business operations, the selling price received is not part of its revenues from operations. Instead, receipts received from one-time sales of assets are classified as gains or losses and separated from operating revenues.

- If a company receives a deposit of $10,000 on the last day of its fiscal year for work that will be performed in the next fiscal year, the company should not report the $10,000 received as revenue in the current fiscal year. Instead, the revenue is recognized when the work is completed in the following fiscal year.

- If a company lends money to another company to induce it to buy the company's products, this is a red flag for the investor to stay away. The sales may not be real because the company borrowing the money to purchase the products might never pay the first company back. This was a ploy Lucent Technologies used to boost its sales, which did not materialize into actual sales. Chapter 8 discusses how investors can detect and analyze this situation.

What a value investor would like to see is actual growth in sales from year to year, and/or potential growth in future sales. Attention should be paid to the notes of the financial statements that outline the revenue recognition policies of the company. Exhibit 6.1 shows the Income Statement of Cliffs Natural for the three years from 2009 through 2011. Revenues grew 100 percent from 2009 to 2010, and 45 percent from 2010 to 2011. Revenues were expected to decline in 2012 and 2013 because of declining growth in China, emerging markets, Europe, and the United States.

**EXHIBIT 6.1**

Income Statement of Cliffs Natural from 10-K

| | | | |
|---|---|---|---|
| Cliffs Natural Resources Inc. and Subsidiaries | | | |
| | **(In Millions, Except Per Share Amounts)** | | |
| | **Year Ended December 31,** | | |
| | **2011** | **2010** | **2009** |
| REVENUES FROM PRODUCT SALES AND SERVICES | | | |
| Product | **$6,551.7** | $4,416.8 | $2,216.2 |
| Freight and venture partners' cost reimbursements | **242.6** | 265.3 | 125.8 |
| | **6,794.3** | 4,682.1 | 2,342.0 |
| COST OF GOODS SOLD AND OPERATING EXPENSES | **(4,105.7)** | (3,155.6) | (2,030.3) |
| SALES MARGIN | **2,688.6** | 1,526.5 | 311.7 |
| OTHER OPERATING INCOME (EXPENSE) | | | |
| Selling, general and administrative expenses | **(274.4)** | (202.1) | (117.6) |
| Exploration costs | **(80.5)** | (33.7) | — |
| Impairment of goodwill | **(27.8)** | — | — |
| Consolidated Thompson acquisition costs | **(25.4)** | — | — |
| Miscellaneous—net | **68.1** | (20.5) | 42.0 |
| | **(340.0)** | (256.3) | (75.6) |
| OPERATING INCOME | **2,348.6** | 1,270.2 | 236.1 |
| OTHER INCOME (EXPENSE) | | | |
| Gain on acquisition of controlling interests | — | 40.7 | — |
| Changes in fair value of foreign currency contracts, net | **101.9** | 39.8 | 85.7 |
| Interest income | **9.5** | 9.9 | 10.8 |
| Interest expense | **(216.5)** | (70.1) | (39.0) |
| Other non-operating income (expense) | **(2.0)** | 12.5 | 2.9 |
| | **(107.1)** | 32.8 | 60.4 |

(*Continued*)

| | | | |
|---|---|---|---|
| INCOME FROM CONTINUING OPERATIONS BEFORE INCOME TAXES AND EQUITY INCOME (LOSS) FROM VENTURES | **2,241.5** | 1,303.0 | 296.5 |
| INCOME TAX EXPENSE | **(420.1)** | (293.5) | (22.5) |
| EQUITY INCOME (LOSS) FROM VENTURES | **9.7** | 13.5 | (65.5) |
| INCOME FROM CONTINUING OPERATIONS | **1,831.1** | 1,023.0 | 208.5 |
| LOSS FROM DISCONTINUED OPERATIONS, net of tax | **(18.5)** | (3.1) | (3.4) |
| NET INCOME | **1,812.6** | 1,019.9 | 205.1 |
| LESS: NET INCOME ATTRIBUTABLE TO NONCONTROLLING INTEREST | **193.5** | — | — |
| NET INCOME ATTRIBUTABLE TO CLIFFS SHAREHOLDERS | **$1,619.1** | $1,019.9 | $ 205.1 |
| EARNINGS PER COMMON SHARE ATTRIBUTABLE TO CLIFFS SHAREHOLDERS — BASIC | | | |
| Continuing operations | **$ 11.68** | $ 7.56 | $ 1.67 |
| Discontinued operations | **(0.13)** | (0.02) | 0.03) |
| | **$ 11.55** | $7.54 | $ 1.64 |
| EARNINGS PER COMMON SHARE ATTRIBUTABLE TO CLIFFS SHAREHOLDERS — DILUTED | | | |
| Continuing operations | **$ 11.61** | $ 7.51 | $ 1.66 |
| Discontinued operations | **(0.13)** | (0.02) | (0.03) |
| | **$ 11.48** | $ 7.49 | $ 1.63 |
| AVERAGE NUMBER OF SHARES (IN THOUSANDS) | | | |
| Basic | **140,234** | 135,301 | 124,998 |
| Diluted | **141,012** | 136,138 | 125,751 |
| CASH DIVIDENDS DECLARED PER SHARE | **$0.84** | $ 0.51 | $ 0.26 |

The accompanying notes are an integral part of these consolidated financial statements.

Table 6.2 shows the revenue recognition policies of Cliffs Natural. Revenues for iron ore are recognized when they are realized and when they are earned.

## TABLE 6.2

Note 1 from Cliffs Natural Supplement to Financial Statements

| Revenue Recognition and Cost of Goods Sold and Operating Expenses |
| --- |
| **U.S. Iron Ore** |
| Revenue is recognized on the sale of products when title to the product has transferred to the customer in accordance with the specified provisions of each term supply agreement and all applicable criteria for revenue recognition have been satisfied. Most of our U.S. Iron Ore term supply agreements provide that title and risk of loss transfer to the customer when payment is received. |
| We recognize revenue based on the gross amount billed to a customer as we earn revenue from the sale of the goods or services. Revenue from product sales also includes reimbursement for freight charges paid on behalf of customers in *Freight and venture partners' cost reimbursements* separate from product revenue. |

## Cost of Goods Sold

The cost of goods sold section shows the cost of the goods that were sold to produce the revenues shown in the income statement. Many companies show cost of goods sold as a one-line amount without including the many items that determine the final figure. For a manufacturer, the cost of goods sold includes raw materials used in production, direct labor involved to produce the goods, and the overhead costs allocated to the production of the goods, plus and minus the beginning and ending inventory respectively. A retailer has a more simplified cost of goods sold section in that it includes the cost of the goods purchased plus any shipping costs to the stores.

The way to judge whether a company is doing a good job in managing the costs of production is to analyze the cost of goods sold figures over several years. When the cost of goods sold increases by more than reasonable amounts, it should raise red flags about the caliber of management.

Cliffs Natural muddied the waters by lumping operating expenses into the cost of goods sold amount in Exhibit 6.1. This action makes it impossible to analyze whether cost of goods sold have increased, decreased, or stayed the same over the three-year period.

## Gross Profits

The gross profits section shows revenues minus cost of goods sold (see Table 6.1). Companies can increase their gross profit by increasing prices on their products as long as the company can sell the same number of products as previously sold at lower prices. If the company sells fewer items at higher prices, it could bring in less revenue and lower gross profit. Lowering prices could spur customers to buy more products, which could raise revenues and gross profits. The flip side of the coin is to reduce the cost of goods sold figures by cutting some of the production expenses in order to increase gross profit.

## Analysis of Expenses

Revenues make up the first part of the income statement, with the second part including expenses. Expenses include all payments made for the operation of a business beside the direct expenses related to the production of goods sold. These expenses fall into two major categories: selling expenses and administrative expenses.

## Selling Expenses

Advertising expenses for some companies account for a large percentage of total expenses, primarily because media costs can be quite high. Outlays for television advertising are high even though the cost per thousand is relatively low as a result of the reach of this mass medium. Companies may also spend on promotion to advance the name of the company among its target audience. Research and development expenses appear in the income statements of companies in technologically driven industries. Companies in these fast-changing industries need to develop new or improved products in order to keep ahead of competitors and ensure that they remain in business in the future. Levels of research and development expenditures vary by industry. Industries such as retail or finance, for example, traditionally have small research and development expenditures as a percentage of sales. It is a good idea to study the trend in research and development expenditures in the companies you are analyzing.

## Administrative Expenses

Administrative expenses include wages and salaries, insurance expenses, supplies, and depreciation expenses on property and equipment used to run the company. By examining the selling and administrative expenses of a company over a period of years, you can assess the effectiveness of management in their ability to keep expenses in check.

In Exhibit 6.1, Cliffs Natural's selling and administrative expenses almost doubled from 2009 to 2010, and then increased by 36 percent from 2010 to 2011. Other operating expenses in 2011 for Cliffs Natural were impairment of goodwill, exploration costs, and miscellaneous costs. Impairment of goodwill is an accounting transaction, in that there are no cash payments, but it includes a write-down. The goodwill write-down affects income but not cash flow. Although operating expenses for Cliffs Natural increased in 2011, the company increased its operating profit by almost 100 percent from 2010 to 2011.

## Operating Income

Operating income is determined by subtracting operating expenses from gross profits. Operating expenses are the indirect expenses of obtaining sales and performing administrative duties to operate the business. Operating profits are important in that they show the income generated from the company's business operations. For Cliffs Natural, operating income increased by 85 percent from 2010 to 2011 ($1,270.7 million to $2,348.6 million). Operating profits show the efficiency of management in managing operating activities and how much profits or losses are earned from operations.

## Nonoperating Income and Expenses

This group includes income and expenses from nonoperating sources. When a company sells a building or equipment for a profit, these are nonoperating capital gains and are listed in the nonoperating section. Dividends and interest received from investments in owning other companies' stocks and bonds are also included in this section. It is important to search through these items in the income statement of potential companies that you might want to invest in; some companies can be very creative in slipping some of these gains into the operating section to make operating profits look better than they are.

Interest expense, when it is not commingled with interest income, shows the cost of the company's debt financing. There are other nonoperating costs, such as losses from employee strikes and sale of property, plant, and equipment at a loss. You want to be able to differentiate between ordinary gains and losses and extraordinary gains and losses. Extraordinary gains and losses originate from events that are both unusual in nature and occur infrequently or on a nonrecurring basis, including the discontinuance of business operations, major debt restructuring, or major restatement of earnings as a result of changes in accounting principles. Extraordinary items do not include the write-down of assets or gains and losses from foreign currency changes.

When potential investors in a company look at earnings before taxes that include these gains and losses, they are not getting the true picture of the company's ability to generate income from operations. Profits earned from the company's core business activities might be inadequate, but with the addition of various gains added in, it might appear that the company is able to grow its profits at higher rates than is actually occurring. In addition, investors should be able to differentiate between extraordinary gains and ordinary gains.

Table 6.3 shows the other interest income and interest expenses of Cliffs Natural for 2010 and 2011.

**TABLE 6.3**

Cliffs Natural Notes to the Financial Statements from 10-K Report

| *Other income (expense)* | | | |
|---|---|---|---|
| Following is a summary of other income (expense) for 2011 and 2010: | | | |
| | **(In Millions)** | | |
| | **2011** | **2010** | **VarianceFavorable/ (Unfavorable)** |
| Gain on acquisition of controlling interest | $ — | $40.7 | $ (40.7) |
| Changes in fair value of foreign currency contracts, net | 101.9 | 39.8 | 62.1 |
| Interest income | 9.5 | 9.9 | (0.4) |
| Interest expense | (216.5) | (70.1) | (146.4) |
| Other non-operating income (expense) | (2.0) | 12.5 | (14.5) |
| | $(107.1) | $32.8 | $(139.9) |

As a result of acquiring the remaining ownership interests in Freewest and Wabush during the first quarter of 2010, our 2010 results were impacted by realized gains of $38.6 million primarily related to the increase in fair value of our previous ownership interest in each investment held prior to the business acquisition. The fair value of our previous 12.4 percent interest in Freewest was $27.4 million on January 27, 2010, the date of acquisition, resulting in a gain of $13.6 million being recognized in 2010. The fair value of our previous 26.8 percent equity interest in Wabush was $38.0 million on February 1, 2010, resulting in a gain of $25.0 million also being recognized in 2010. Refer to NOTE 4 — ACQUISITIONS AND OTHER INVESTMENTS for further information.

The favorable changes in the fair value of our foreign-currency exchange contracts held as economic hedges during 2011 in the Statements of Consolidated Operations primarily were a result of hedging a portion of the purchase price for the acquisition of Consolidated Thompson through Canadian dollar foreign-currency exchange forward contracts and an option contract. The favorable changes in fair value of these Canadian dollar foreign currency exchange forward contracts and option contract for the year ended December 31, 2011, were a result of net realized gains of $93.1 million realized upon the maturity of the related contracts during the second quarter

*(Continued)*

of 2011. In addition, favorable changes in the fair value of our Australian dollar foreign currency contracts resulted in net realized gains of $43.0 million for the year ended December 31, 2011, based upon the maturity of $215 million of outstanding contracts during the period. Of these gains, $34.9 million were recognized in previous periods as mark-to-market adjustments as part of the changes in fair value of these instruments. Favorable changes in the fair value of our outstanding Australian dollar foreign-currency contracts resulted in mark-to-market adjustments of $0.7 million for the year ended December 31, 2011, based upon the Australian to U.S. dollar spot rate of 1.02 as of December 31, 2011. The spot rate as of the end of 2011 remained flat when compared to the Australian to U.S. dollar spot rate of 1.02 as of December 31, 2010.

## Net Income

Cliffs Natural's interest expense trebled from 2010 to 2011, primarily as a result of Cliffs taking on more debt in 2011. The gains in foreign currency contracts of $101.9 million partially offset the additional interest expense of $216.5 million, resulting in an overall loss in the total other expenses of $107.1 million. However, in the Cliffs income statement, these other income and expenses are commingled with operating income, which does not present a true picture of income from operations. When taxes and the loss from discontinued operations are deducted, the net income figure arrived at for Cliffs Natural is $1,812.6 million in 2011. Net income increased by 78 percent from the previous year. This increase was primarily as a result of increased sales. Cost of goods sold and operating expenses increased as well, but the increase was proportionately less than the increase in sales, resulting in gross profit growing from $1,565 million in 2010 to $2,658.6 million in 2011. Operating income in 2011 was $2,348.6 million versus $1,270.2 for 2010. The net income figure by itself is not as important as understanding how the figure was arrived at.

Net income is important in that it is used to calculate earnings per share. Net income available to common shareholders is divided by the number of common shares outstanding. Cliffs Natural breaks out its earnings per share figures for both continuing operations and discontinued operations. It calculates basic earnings per share and diluted earnings per share. The number of shares outstanding on a diluted basis is greater than those used for a basic calculation of earnings per share.

## SUMMARY

The key points that an income statement provides are summarized in Table 6.4.

**TABLE 6.4**

Summary of Income Statement Elements

| |
|---|
| Summarizes revenues and expenses over a specified period |
| Measures revenues from customers over a specified period |
| Measures the amounts spent on materials, labor, and overhead |
| Measures the amount of gross profit (sales minus cost of goods sold) |
| Measures the amount spent on selling, general, and administrative expenses |
| Measures operating profit (earnings before interest and taxes) |
| Measures the cost of borrowed funds |
| Summarizes the amount paid in taxes |
| Measures the profitability (net income) over a specified period |

# Statement of Changes in Cash

The income statement and balance sheet do not show the amount of cash that comes into a business or the cash amounts that are paid. The statement of changes in cash shows the sources and uses of cash over the period measured. Net income on the income statement is not the same as cash because of a number of factors, such as timing differences between cash collections and disbursements and deductions of expenses such as depreciation and amortization, which do not require the use of cash. Consequently, although a business might show net income that does not mean it has that amount of cash. Similarly, a company that shows a net loss might in fact be cash positive as a result of noncash items such as depreciation and other noncash expenses. The following discussion of EBITDA illustrates the point that net losses can in fact be turned into positive cash flows for a company.

---

**EBITDA: CASH FLOW VERSUS NET INCOME**

EBITDA stands for earnings before interest, taxes, depreciation, and amortization, and measures the real health of a company. However, as you will see, positive EBITDA over a number of years when a company has constantly racked up net losses cannot be sustained.

To determine EBITDA, the first step is to start with earnings before interest and taxes, or operating income. Depreciation expenses, amortization costs, and other noncash expenses are added back to this figure. If the figure is positive, the company still has cash available to pay off interest expenses and other necessary expenses. A negative EBITDA figure indicates that the company will either have to borrow money or issue more common or preferred stock to raise cash.

Referring to Exhibit 6.1 in Chapter 6, Cliffs Natural had EBITDA of $2,507.1 million, as calculated below:

| | |
|---|---|
| Operating Income | $2,241.5 million |
| Add back noncash items | |
| Goodwill impairment | 27.8 |
| Depreciation | 237.8 |
| EBITDA | $2,507.1 million |

This EBITDA figure for Cliffs Natural for 2011 is not entirely accurate as Cliffs has not presented a clear operating income figure due to the commingling of various expenses. Similarly, deferred charges also do not require the use of cash, and these have not been included in the calculation. The figures for depreciation were disclosed in the notes to Cliffs financial statements, as shown in Table 5.7 in Chapter 5. Although some companies with net losses can turn around and gloat over their positive EBITDA figures, value investors should not be blinded by their success; eventually the company is going to have to replace its buildings and equipment, and then the lack of cash becomes the occasion for a shell game.

## CASH FLOW

Cash flow is the amount of net cash generated by a business over a certain period of time. To compute the cash flow, noncash expenses are added to—or noncash revenues are deducted from—net income.

Noncash items are expenses (depreciation, amortization, and deferred charges) and income that are not paid out or realized in cash. This calculation explains why companies can have negative earnings and still have positive cash flows.

Another more refined measure of cash flow is *free cash flow*, or cash flow minus capital spending (investments in net working capital and long-term assets). Companies that do not generate strong free cash flows have less flexibility, and this is most often recognized in their stock prices.[1]

---

### CASH IS NOT AS EASY TO MANIPULATE AS EARNINGS

Many companies manipulated their earnings during the economic downturn of 2000 to 2003. HealthSouth overstated its earnings by $1.4 billion during the period from 1999 to 2002 according to a guilty plea from its former chief executive officer. WorldCom also overstated its profits by capitalizing expenses. These expenses were amortized over a period of time, rather than deducted as expenses in the period in which they were incurred. The Dutch company, Ahold, also overstated its profits, even though you might think that the supermarket business is more simple and straightforward, and would not lend itself to the manipulation of figures quite like the more complex forms of business, such as the telecommunications industry.

The analysis of cash is a better tool for analyzing a company's strengths and weaknesses, because cash is harder to manipulate than earnings. The *cash flow adequacy ratio* (CFAR) gives a more accurate assessment of the profile of a company.[2]

CFAR (which consists of cash flow after taxes, interest, and capital expenditures) is net-free cash flow, which is compared with the average annual principal debt maturities over the next five-year period. Thomas W. Hoens used this CFAR analysis in the following example, which illustrated Enron's incapability to generate positive cash flows in the years prior to its bankruptcy.

**Enron Corporation**

**CFAR Analysis**

**1998 to 2000**

|  | 2000 | 1999 | 1998 | 1997 | 1996 | Cumulative |
|---|---|---|---|---|---|---|
| Revenues | 100,789 | 40,112 | 31,260 | 20273 | 13,289 | 205,723 |
| Costs | 98,836 | 39,310 | 29,882 | 20,258 | 12,599 | 200,885 |
| EBIT | 1,953 | 802 | 1,378 | 15 | 690 | 4,838 |
| Deprt Amort | 855 | 870 | 827 | 600 | 474 | 3,626 |
| **EBITDA** | **2,808** | **1,672** | **2,205** | **615** | **1,164** | **8,464** |
| Cash Interest | 834 | 678 | 585 | 420 | 290 | 2,807 |
| Cash Taxes | 62 | 51 | 73 | 68 | 89 | 343 |
| Capital Expenses | 2,381 | 2,363 | 1,905 | 1,392 | 864 | 8,905 |
| **NET FREE CASH FLOW** | **(469)** | **(1,420)** | **(358)** | **(1,265)** | **(79)** | **(3,591)** |
| Equity Invest (1) | 933 | 722 | 1,659 | 700 | 619 | |
| | (1,402) | (2,142) | (2,017) | (1,965) | (698) | (8,224) |

Depreciation and amortization, both noncash charges, were added back to earnings before interest and taxes to equal EBITDA, which were positive for Enron for each year in the five-year period shown in the example. However, when interest, taxes, and capital expenses were deducted from EBITDA, Enron had negative free cash flows. This meant that Enron did not have the cash to cover its scheduled debt maturities during the five-year period, the payment of dividends, or the investments in its equity affiliates.[3] Enron had a large number of transactions with affiliate companies, which siphoned off large amounts of cash. From this analysis, you can see why members of Enron upper management went to such great lengths to hide its debt from its balance sheets. Enron's debt and dividend payments are listed below:[4]

| Dividend Analysis: | | | | | | |
|---|---|---|---|---|---|---|
| Common | 368 | 355 | 312 | 243 | 212 | |
| Pfd2 | 17 | 17 | 17 | 17 | 16 | |
| Pfd A&B | 66 | 49 | 0 | 0 | 0 | |
| | 451 | 421 | 329 | 260 | 228 | 1,689 |
| Scheduled Debt Maturities: | | | | | | |
| Year 1 | 2,112 | 670 | 541 | | | |
| Year 2 | 750 | 569 | 413 | | | |
| Year 3 | 852 | 432 | 66 | | | |
| Year 4 | 646 | 494 | 182 | | | |
| Year 5 | 1,592 | 493 | 656 | | | |
| Total | 5,952 | 2,658 | 1,858 | | | |
| **Average** | **1,190** | **532** | **372** | NA | NA | |

Because net-free cash flows were consistently negative in each of the five years, a CFAR for Enron would be meaningless (because the ratios were negative). A company with a negative trend of CFARs certainly raises red flags for potential investors. Companies with CFARs between 0 and 1 indicate that they are not generating sufficient cash to fund their expenditures and would need access to outside sources of cash. A company with a CFAR higher than 1 generates sufficient cash to fund its major cash expenditures. You must look at the trend as opposed to one year's figures in isolation because companies with strong cash flows in some years might have negative CFARs in other years.[5]

This material illustrates the importance of analyzing cash and not relying on the financial statements as presented. A statement of changes in cash position answers three basic questions:

1. Where did the company generate the cash needed for its operations?

2. How much cash did the company spend during the same period?

3. What is the trend of the cash balances shown in the balance sheet for the company over a three-to-five-year period?

## Format of a Statement of Changes in Cash

There are two methods that can be used for compiling a statement of changes in cash. The first is the direct method, which is tedious to use in that each item listed on the income statement is adjusted from accrual accounting to cash accounting. The second method is the indirect method and is more widely used. Net income or net loss is the beginning point, and noncash charges (depreciation, amortization, and deferred charges) are added, and then adjustments are made for the uses and sources of cash as presented in the comparison of the beginning and the ending balance sheet for the period.

There are three sections to the statement of changes in cash:

1. Cash from operating activities.
2. Cash from investing activities.
3. Cash from financing activities.

## Determining Cash from Operating Activities

- Begin with net income and add back all noncash charges— depreciation, amortization, and deferred charges—as these increase the cash balance.

- Compare the current asset accounts from the previous period's balance sheet to the current balance sheet. Any increases in current assets are uses of cash and reduce the cash balance.

- Decreases in current asset accounts over the period in question result in sources of cash and increase the cash balance.

- Compare the current liabilities accounts from the previous balance sheet to the current balance sheet. Any increases in current liabilities are sources of cash and increase the cash balance.

- Decreases in current liability accounts over the period in question result in uses of cash and decrease the cash balance.

In this section, cash flow from day-to-day operations is measured. Net income is the starting figure, and the adjustments listed show whether cash is provided or used by operating activities. For example, when inventory increases from one period to the next, cash has been used to finance the increase in inventory, resulting in a use of cash. Similarly, when an asset decreases from one period to the next, it is a source of cash, as cash has been released by the decrease in the asset. When the total operating adjustments have been netted against net income, the total cash from operating activities is either positive or negative. Why is cash from operating activities important? A positive total cash flow figure from operating activities indicates that the company is able to generate positive cash flows from its everyday business activities. A negative figure (use of cash) is not good, in that the company is unable to support its operating activities and would require raising cash from either its investing activities or its financing activities to bail out its operations. Cash from operating activities shows the cash generated from working capital (net changes in current assets minus current liability accounts). A value investor should avoid companies that cannot consistently generate positive cash flows over a period of time, Enron being a prime example.

## Determining Cash from Investing Activities

This second section of the statement of changes in cash focuses on the purchase and sale of fixed and other long-term assets. You will see the following categories of transactions here:

- Purchases of land, buildings, and major equipment, which is a use of cash
- Sales of land, buildings, and major equipment, which is a source of cash
- Purchases of long-term investments (stocks and bonds of other companies, for example), which is a use of cash

- Sales of long-term investments, which is a source of cash

- Acquisitions and investments in other assets, which is a use of cash

This section shows what the company does to increase or decrease its fixed and other long-term assets. Sales of assets generate cash for a business. Expenditures on land, buildings, and equipment use cash and are often referred to as capital expenditures. Large capital expenditures indicate that the company is investing for the future. For example, investments in property, plant, and equipment indicate that the company expects to increase its sales and grow its operations. In general, for companies that are growing, the investing activities section produces a use of cash rather than a source of cash. When companies indicate positive cash flows from investing activities, they are selling assets they own, which is a situation that cannot be sustained for the foreseeable future.

Value investors want to pay attention to this section of the cash flow statement to see whether the company is investing in or selling assets. If the company is making large investments, you should look for explanations in the notes to the financial statements to see the underlying reasons for the expenditures. If you come away with the impression that the company is making the right investments to grow the business, the company's stock might be a good investment.

## Determining Cash from Financing Activities

Using financing activities allows a company to raise more cash that can be obtained through its daily operations. This section shows where the company has obtained its cash (from debt and/ or equity) to fund operations and expansion. Typical transactions in this section are:

- Payments of debt, a use of cash

- Issuance of debt, a source of cash

- Purchases of Treasury stock (the company's own shares), which is a use of cash

- Issuance of new common and preferred stock issues, which is a source of cash

- Payment of dividends, a use of cash

The sources of cash provided in this section are the issuances of stocks and bonds, and the uses of cash are the payment of dividends, repayment of debt, and the buying back of the company's own stock. When a company has obtained cash for a number of years through issuing debt and equity, this behavior will not be sustainable well into the future; it is an indication that the company has not been able to generate enough cash to fund its operations. One of the many reasons for accumulating cash by issuing debt and equity issues is that the company might be looking to acquire another business.

In this third section of the cash flow statement, companies generally alternate between negative and positive cash flows over the years. A company with excess cash could pay down its debt and/or increase its dividend payments. Alternatively, when a company has a shortfall in cash, it might issue stock and/or bond issues to raise cash.

Companies that cut their dividend payments to shareholders see their stock prices plummet in value. This situation can create an opportunity for value investors who have done their homework on the company and have determined whether the company's stock is trading at a significant discount to its intrinsic (fair) value. When a company cuts its dividend payments, it indicates that it is having problems and is conserving cash. By analyzing the reasons for the cut in dividends and the company's future ability to generate revenues and profits, it can be determined whether this company is a value company or one headed in the wrong direction and so to be avoided.

An additional line appears for companies that operate globally and experience losses and gains from changes in currency exchange rates. Typically, these gains or losses are relatively small.

## The Bottom Line: Increase or Decrease to Cash

To get to the bottom line, the cash sources and uses from the three sections are added to determine whether there is a total increase or decrease to cash. This figure is then added (or subtracted, in the case of a decrease to cash) to the beginning cash balance in the previous period's balance sheet to equal the ending cash balance in the current year's balance sheet. When the cash balance has increased, the company can use this cash on hand to fund operations in the coming year.

## Analysis of Cliffs Natural Statement of Changes in Cash

Refer to Exhibit 7.1, which shows the statement of changes in cash for Cliffs Natural Resources Inc. for the three-year period from 2009 through 2011. This statement is analyzed using the above format to determine the cash inflows and outflows for the company. This statement shows changes to the cash account during the year. This figure is the difference in the cash balances obtained from the balance sheet (Exhibit 5.1):

|                            | 2011     | 2010       | Difference    |
|----------------------------|----------|------------|---------------|
| Cash and cash equivalents  | $521.6   | $1,566.7   | ($1,045.1)    |

This statement shows the changes to the cash account in 2011, which ends up with a decrease of $1,045.1 million to cash and cash equivalents, shown in the third to the last line of the statement of changes in cash flow of Cliffs Natural Resources statement (Exhibit 7.1).

The first section, Cash from Operating Activities, shows the cash inflows and outflows from operations for the year. The noncash expenses, such as depreciation, depletion, amortization, deferred income tax charges, and other adjustments, are added back to net income to provide the company's cash flow. The cash flow is $1,957.3 million for 2011 and $1,373.7 million for 2010. This shows an increasing trend of cash flow, indicating that Cliffs Natural has cash available for investing and financing activities. To these cash flow figures the adjustments in working capital (changes in current assets and current liabilities accounts) are added or subtracted to show the net cash from operating activities: $2,288.8 million in 2011 and $1,320 million in 2010. An analysis of the sources for the positive cash flow from operating activities in 2011 shows that the major portion comes from net income, depreciation, and spontaneous financing of cash from payables and accrued (unrecorded) expenses. For 2010, the major sources of cash from operating activities were produced from net income and depreciation.

Cash was used by Investing Activities in the amounts of $5,304.4 million in 2011 and $1,367.7 million in 2010. The major uses of cash were the acquisition of Consolidated Thompson and property, plant, and equipment purchases in 2011. See below management's discussion of investments by Cliffs Natural in 2011, as reported in the company's 10-K filing.

---

### CLIFFS NATURAL RESOURCES – DISCUSSION BY MANAGEMENT – 10-K FILING

*Growth Strategy and Strategic Transactions*

Throughout 2011, we continued to increase our operating scale and presence as an international mining and natural resources company by maintaining our focus on integration and execution. Our strategy includes the continuing integration of our acquisition of Consolidated Thompson, which was acquired on May 12, 2011.

The acquisition reflects our strategy to build scale by owning expandable and exportable steelmaking raw material assets serving international markets. Through our acquisition of Consolidated Thompson, we now own and operate an iron ore mine and processing facility near Bloom Lake in Quebec, Canada, that produces high quality iron ore concentrate.

WISCO is a 25 percent partner in Bloom Lake. The initial design of Bloom Lake operations is to achieve a production rate of 8.0 million metric tons of iron ore concentrate per year. Additional capital investments were approved by our Board of Directors in January 2012 in order to increase the initial production rate to 16.0 million metric tons of iron ore concentrate per year. We also own two additional development properties, Lamêlée and Peppler Lake, in Quebec. All three of these properties are in proximity to our existing Canadian operations and will allow us to leverage our port facilities and supply this iron ore to the seaborne market. The acquisition also is expected to further diversify our existing customer base.

In addition to the integration of Consolidated Thompson, we have a number of capital projects under way in all of our reportable business segments. We believe these projects will continue to improve our operational performance, diversify our customer base, and extend the reserve life of our portfolio of assets, all of which are necessary to sustain continued growth. Throughout 2012, we also will reinforce our global reorganization, as our leadership moves to an integrated global management structure.

We also expect to achieve growth through early involvement in exploration and development activities by partnering with junior mining companies, which provide us low-cost entry points for potentially significant reserve additions.

If the reasons given for the acquisition of Consolidated Thompson sound compelling to a potential investor, the stock looks as if it is undervalued.

The $2,288.8 million of cash provided by operating activities in 2011 was used to partially fund the uses of cash of $5,304.4 million in investing activities, which means that the balance of cash needed would have to come from either raising cash from Financing Activities and/or drawing down cash on hand. Cash raised from Financing Activities in 2011 was $1,975.1 million, which came primarily from issuing new common stock and new debt (senior notes and a term loan). Some of this cash was used to repay some of the short-term and longer-term debt, assumption of Consolidated Thompson's debt, and payment of dividends. The increase in cash from financing activities was not enough to fund the uses of cash from investing activities, so the cash balance in the 2010 balance sheet was drawn down by $1,045.1 million to equal the 2011 cash balance of $521.6 million.

Cliffs Natural has raised cash from new debt and equity issues for the past three years, and this should add a note of caution to potential investors because this is not a process that can be prolonged for the foreseeable future. In Chapter 8 we will see that the amount of debt Cliffs Natural has taken on presents a question mark in terms of its future as a value company.

## EXHIBIT 7.1

Statements of Consolidated Cash Flows

**Cliffs Natural Resources Inc. and Subsidiaries**

| | (In Millions) | | |
|---|---|---|---|
| | Year Ended December 31, | | |
| | 2011 | 2010 | 2009 |
| CASH FLOW FROM CONTINUING OPERATIONS OPERATING ACTIVITIES | | | |
| Net income | $1,812.6 | $1,019.9 | $205.1 |
| Adjustments to reconcile net income to net cash provided (used) by operating activities: | | | |
| Depreciation, depletion and amortization | 426.9 | 322.3 | 236.6 |
| Goodwill impairment | 27.8 | — | — |
| Derivatives and currency hedges | (69.0) | (39.0) | (204.5) |
| Foreign exchange loss (gains) | (6.2) | 39.1 | (28.1) |

(*Continued*)

| | | | |
|---|---|---|---|
| Share-based compensation | **13.9** | 12.5 | 10.1 |
| Equity (income) loss in ventures (net of tax) | **(9.7)** | (13.5) | 65.5 |
| Pensions and other postretirement benefits | **(26.3)** | 8.7 | 27.3 |
| Deferred income taxes | **(66.6)** | 15.2 | 60.8 |
| Changes in deferred revenue and below-market sales contracts | **(146.0)** | 39.3 | (33.4) |
| Gain on acquisition of controlling interests | — | (40.7) | — |
| Other | **(0.1)** | 9.9 | 3.8 |
| Changes in operating assets and liabilities: | | | |
| Receivables and other assets | **81.4** | (204.6) | (24.2) |
| Product inventories | **(74.5)** | 61.2 | 7.7 |
| Payables and accrued expenses | **324.6** | 89.7 | (141.0) |
| Net cash from operating activities | **2,288.8** | 1,320.0 | 185.7 |
| INVESTING ACTIVITIES | | | |
| Acquisition of Consolidated Thompson, net of cash acquired | **(4,423.5)** | — | — |
| Acquisition of controlling interests, net of cash acquired | — | (994.5) | — |
| Net settlements in Canadian dollar foreign exchange contracts | **93.1** | — | — |
| Investment in Consolidated Thompson senior notes | **(125.0)** | — | — |
| Purchase of property, plant and equipment | **(880.7)** | (266.9) | (116.3) |
| Investments in ventures | **(5.2)** | (191.3) | (81.8) |
| Investment in marketable securities | — | (6.6) | (14.9) |
| Redemption of marketable securities | — | 32.5 | 5.4 |
| Proceeds from sale of assets | **22.4** | 59.1 | 28.3 |
| Other investing activities | **14.5** | — | — |
| Net cash used by investing activities | **(5,304.4)** | (1,367.7) | (179.3) |

## FINANCING ACTIVITIES

| | | | |
|---|---|---|---|
| Net proceeds from issuance of common shares | 853.7 | — | 347.3 |
| Net proceeds from issuance of senior notes | 998.1 | 1,388.1 | — |
| Borrowings on term loan | 1,250.0 | — | — |
| Repayment of term loan | (278.0) | — | — |
| Borrowings on bridge credit facility | 750.0 | — | — |
| Repayment of bridge credit facility | (750.0) | — | — |
| Borrowings under revolving credit facility | 250.0 | 450.0 | 279.7 |
| Repayment under revolving credit facility | (250.0) | (450.0) | (276.4) |
| Debt issuance costs | (54.8) | — | — |
| Repayment of Consolidated Thompson convertible debentures | (337.2) | — | — |
| Repayment of 200 million term loan | — | (200.0) | — |
| Payments under share buyback program | (289.8) | — | — |
| Common stock dividends | (118.9) | (68.9) | (31.9) |
| Repayment of other borrowings | (1.0) | (16.7) | (9.7) |
| Other financing activities | (47.0) | (14.9) | (4.7) |
| Net cash from financing activities | 1,975.1 | 1,087.6 | 304.3 |
| EFFECT OF EXCHANGE RATE CHANGES ON CASH | (4.6) | 24.1 | 13.0 |
| INCREASE (DECREASE) IN CASH AND CASH EQUIVALENTS | (1,045.1) | 1,064.0 | 323.7 |
| CASH AND CASH EQUIVALENTS AT BEGINNING OF YEAR | 1,566.7 | 502.7 | 179.0 |
| CASH AND CASH EQUIVALENTS AT END OF YEAR | $ 521.6 | $1,566.7 | $502.7 |

## SUMMARY

The key points a statement of changes in cash provides are:

**TABLE 7.1**

Features of the Statement of Changes in Cash

| |
|---|
| Summarizes the major categories of sources and uses of cash to show what has happened to the cash account during a period of time |
| Measures the noncash charges within the specified period. |
| Shows cash inflows and outflows from operations |
| Shows the cash amounts spent and received by buying and selling long-term assets |
| Shows cash received from borrowing and cash used to repay debt |
| Shows cash received from issuing common and preferred stock and the cash amounts used to buy back stock |
| Shows the amount of dividends paid |

# CHAPTER 8

# Fundamental Analysis

**W**hy bother with financial statement analysis and number crunching to determine which stocks to invest in? It is easy for investors to follow the published buy, sell, and hold ratings of analysts with regard to which investments to make.

The process isn't quite that simple. The lessons you can learn from the bankruptcies of Enron, WorldCom, and others (in addition to the stock research abuses by analysts) are that investors must look out for themselves. State and federal regulators fined many investment banks and brokerage firms for their analysts' conflicts of interest between their investment banks and their stock research recommendations. Enron and WorldCom showed that investing in the leading companies in their industries was also not foolproof.

Consequently, politicians and regulators created laws and regulations in the hope of making investors feel safe. But even if auditors are more thorough in their examinations of financial statements, greedy executives will still be hired, and boards of directors will still rubber stamp the wishes and deeds of management teams. Laws and regulations will still not insulate investors from poor investments and misdeeds by strategists, analysts, and executives, so investors must scrutinize financial statements, including those of the largest companies. For value investors, finding a company with a strong financial position by analyzing its financial statements goes a longer way than listening to the recommendations of those who have their own motives for generating their investment opinions.

# FINANCIAL STATEMENT ANALYSIS

The basic premise of financial statement analysis, as presented in Chapter 7, is to examine a company's performance to either identify an investment opportunity or avoid an investment disaster. Generally, a company's stock price is influenced primarily by the company's performance. The benefits from financial statement analysis are numerous. You can:

- Analyze a company's historic earnings to project future earnings.

- Compare a company's historic earnings with those of its peer companies in an industry to identify superior or inferior performance.

- Analyze a company's historic earnings over a certain period to identify weaknesses in performance or other problems.

- Use the company's historic data to project future rates of return.

- Assess the likelihood of a company's capability to meet its financial obligations.

## Sources of Corporate Information

You can find much of the information you want to know about a company in its financial statements and filings with the SEC. Public companies with more than $10 million in assets and more than 500 shareholders must file their financial documents electronically with the SEC. You can obtain these filings for free from a company's website, by requesting them from a company's investor relations department, or from the SEC's EDGAR website at www.sec.gov/edgar.

As discussed in Chapter 4, the Form 10-K report provides the most comprehensive information about a company. The report includes the complete set of financial statements (audited three-year comparative income and cash flow statements and comparative year-end balance sheets), along with notes to the financial statements. A careful reading of the notes often provides crucial information that can affect the company's operations. The 10-K is more comprehensive than the annual report, which is sent to shareholders of record. Companies might emphasize pro forma financial results that exclude certain expenses. These as-if financial results do not conform to GAAP, the rules and guidelines used by accountants in the preparation of financial statements.

You can also obtain information by listening to the company's conference calls when they announce quarterly or annual earnings and other matters.

## Financial Statements

As discussed in Chapter 4, financial statements indicate the status of a company's operations and performance. After analyzing these statements, analysts render their investment recommendations for the company's stock. Any perceived long-term changes in a company's earnings have an effect on the company's dividends and stock price. If earnings are expected to be greater than the expectations on Wall Street, more investors will want to buy the company's stock, pushing prices up. Similarly, if that company's earnings fall short of expectations, investors might sell its stock if they perceive this trend to be a long-term one, putting downward pressure on the stock price. A steady increase in the company's earnings also raises the expectation of increases in dividends, which often contributes to rising stock prices. The opposite is true with decreased earnings.

Forecasting whether companies will meet their expected sales and earnings projections is not an easy task, and you should consider a number of other factors in addition to financial analysis.

Many investors do not have the time or inclination to study a company's financial strengths and weaknesses. If you are one of those people, you can choose from many sources of published information, such as Standard & Poor's or Value Line's tear sheets, in addition to brokerage reports.

For many investors, however, the starting point for investing in a company is the company's financial statements, found in its annual and 10-K report, both filed with the SEC. Annual financial statements are audited by independent CPAs (certified public accountants) and are distributed to shareholders and other interested parties. The annual report contains four financial statements: income statement, balance sheet, statement of changes in retained earnings, and statement of changes in cash.

Financial statements provide the data for an analysis of the company's financial position and also assess its strengths and weaknesses. The relative financial position of the company's standings in relation to its past data and to other companies in the same industry provides a more meaningful picture than merely looking at one set of financial statements in isolation. The company's strengths and weaknesses can become more apparent through ratio analysis.

## COMPETITIVE ANALYSIS

Whether a company can achieve its sales and earnings objectives depends in part on how it competes within its industry. Industry sales and earnings may be growing, but if the company is not competitive enough, it may not capture a large enough portion of the increasing sales in the industry.

How a company competes in an industry depends on many factors:

- The resources the company has in relation to its competitors.
- The company's range of products versus the competition's.
- The level of success of the company's existing range of products.

- The company's level of innovation in its introduction of new products.
- The company's ability to diversify into new markets.
- The strength of the company's competitors.

You should consider these factors when determining the relative strength of a company in an industry.

## Quality of Management

Another factor to consider is the quality of management. Access to a company's management is often difficult for financial analysts and virtually impossible for the general investing public. The most you can do to determine the quality of management is to look at the company's history and read financial newspapers for stories about management. For example, a high turnover rate for top and middle management indicates that all is not well in a company. A company with an effective management is generally assumed to be more successful in meeting its sales and earnings objectives than a poorly managed company.

Exxon, for example, managed to consistently increase its earnings, even during periods of declining oil prices. In addition, Exxon faced a negative climate in the early 1990s because of the *Exxon Valdez* oil spill. Exxon's management was not deterred, sticking to their original investment objectives, which were projects with high returns. This strategy supported their profits, in contrast to the frivolous investments made by many of the other oil companies during the same period.

How CEOs are paid in relation to the company's stock performance tells much about the management. The stock price of Cisco Systems declined by 31 percent in 2002, while the CEO's compensation declined by 67 percent in that same year. These circumstances were certainly not the same at many other companies, including Kmart, JDS Uniphase, Quest, and World Com. Even when their stock prices declined significantly, the CEOs and members of top management rewarded themselves with additional salaries and bonuses.

The Internet has made gaining access to information about companies and management a little easier for individual investors. If you want more information, the first stop is the company's home page on the Web. At the Exxon Mobil website www.exxonmobil .com, for example, you can read about the company's sales strategies and how it is positioning itself for the future. Investors can also read the company's annual and quarterly reports. Read the Management Discussion section to assess any future trends or investments. For 2012, Exxon-Mobil has commingled the "management discussion" into various other sectors of the report.

You can also e-mail questions to the investor relations staff of companies you are interested in. The speed and quality of their replies will tell much about how management views its shareholders.

## FUNDAMENTAL ANALYSIS

Fundamental analysis uses a company's financial statements to determine its value with regard to its potential growth in earnings. Fundamental analysts use projected forecasts of the economy to focus on industries that are expected to generate increased sales and earnings. Companies within those industries are evaluated to determine which stocks to buy.

The financial statements provide the basis for ratio analysis, which assists in determining a company's strengths and weaknesses. Ratio analysis uses a company's financial information to predict whether it will meet its future projections of earnings. Although ratio analysis is simple to compute, its projections and extrapolations can become complex. Ratio analysis is a tool that can assist you in your selection of stocks. From financial ratio analysis, you can assess a company's past and present financial strengths. Then, armed with this information, you can project trends by using one of the five groups of ratios:

- *Liquidity ratios* illustrate the ease with which assets are converted into cash to cover short-term liabilities.

- *Activity ratios* show how quickly the assets flow through the company.
- *Profitability ratios* measure a company's performance.
- *Leverage ratios* indicate a company's level of debt.
- *Common-stock related ratios* relate share price information.

Table 8.1 provides a list of the different ratios in each of these groups to use to evaluate a company's strengths and weaknesses.

## Liquidity

Liquidity is defined as assets that are easily convertible into cash or a large position in cash. Although liquidity is of greater concern to a company's creditors, this is a starting point for a potential investor in a company's common stock. Liquidity indicates the ease (or difficulty) with which a company can pay off its current obligations (debts) as they come due.

The *current ratio* is a measure of a company's ability to meet its current obligations. It is computed by dividing the current assets by current liabilities. The current ratio shows the coverage of the company's current liabilities by its current assets.

A company's current assets generally should exceed its current liabilities, so that if its current assets decline, it can still pay off its liabilities. A low current ratio might indicate weakness because the company might not be able to borrow additional funds, or sell assets, to raise enough cash to meet its current liabilities. Yet there are always exceptions to a low current ratio. Exxon Mobil, one of the strongest companies in the oil industry, has had its current ratio fall below 1 in some years. However, Exxon Mobil has always had the capacity to borrow on a short-term basis to pay off its current obligations. In those years, the notes to the Exxon Mobil financial statements showed that the company had unused lines of short-term financing with its banks and could issue commercial paper. Potential investors should always read the footnotes, which contain additional information that provides more insight into the figures on the financial statements.

**TABLE 8.1**

Framework to Evaluate Common Stock

| Company Name | Year | Year | Year | Year | Year | Year | Year | Year | Year |
|---|---|---|---|---|---|---|---|---|---|
| Current Ratio = $\dfrac{\text{Current Assets}}{\text{Current Liabilities}}$ | | | | | | | | | |
| Quick Ratio = $\dfrac{\text{Current Assets} - \text{Inventory}}{\text{Current Liabilities}}$ | | | | | | | | | |
| Acc. Rec. Turnover = $\dfrac{\text{Credit Sales}}{\text{Acc. Rec.}}$ | | | | | | | | | |
| Inv. Turnover = $\dfrac{\text{Cost of Goods Sold}}{\text{Inventory}}$ | | | | | | | | | |
| Gross Profit = $\dfrac{\text{Cost of Goods Sold}}{\text{Sales}}$ | | | | | | | | | |
| Operating Profit = $\dfrac{\text{EBIT}}{\text{Sales}}$ | | | | | | | | | |
| Net Profit = $\dfrac{\text{Net Income}}{\text{Sales}}$ | | | | | | | | | |
| Return on Equity = $\dfrac{\text{Net Income}}{\text{Equity}}$ | | | | | | | | | |

| | |
|---|---|
| Return on Common Equity $= \dfrac{\text{Net Income} - \text{Preferred Dividends}}{\text{Equity} - \text{Preferred Stock}}$ | |
| Debt Ratio $= \dfrac{\text{Total Liabilities}}{\text{Total Assets}}$ | |
| Coverage Ratio $= \dfrac{\text{EBIT}}{\text{Interest Expense}}$ | |
| P/E Ratio $= \dfrac{\text{Market Price of the Stock}}{\text{Earnings per share}}$ | |
| EPS $= \dfrac{\text{Net Income} - \text{Preferred Stock}}{\text{\# of shares outstanding}}$ | |
| Dividend Yield $= \dfrac{\text{Dividend}}{\text{Price of Stock}}$ | |
| Dividend Payout Ratio $= \dfrac{\text{DPS}}{\text{EPS}}$ | |
| Book Value $= \dfrac{\text{Shareholders' Equity}}{\text{\# shares outstanding}}$ | |
| Price/Sales Ratio $= \dfrac{\text{Price per share}}{\text{Sales per share}}$ | |
| P/E to Growth Ratio $= \dfrac{\text{P/E Ratio}}{\text{Growth Rate}}$ | |
| Cash Flow | |

Moreover, you should not look at a ratio for one period in isolation. By examining past current ratios, you can establish a trend and more easily see whether the most recent current ratio has deteriorated, stayed the same, or improved over this period. What might be the norm for one industry might not hold for another. Utility companies tend to have current ratios of less than 1:1, but the quality of their accounts receivable is so good that virtually all of the accounts receivable are converted into cash. (Most people pay their utility bills; otherwise they find themselves without power.) Creditors of utility companies are therefore not as concerned with the low current ratios. Similarly, Exxon's liquidity was not significantly different from the rest of the oil industry, which suggests that this industry typically has current ratios of around 1:1 or less of current assets to current liabilities.

The current ratio of Cliffs Natural Resources is computed as follows, based on the information obtained from the balance sheet in Exhibit 5.1:

$$\text{Current ratio} = \text{Current assets/current liabilities}$$
$$\text{Current ratio 2011} = \$1{,}790.7 / \$1{,}493.3 = 1.2$$
$$\text{Current ratio 2010} = \$2{,}583.7 / \$1{,}028.7 = 2.51$$

The current ratio in 2011 indicates that Cliffs Natural has $1.20 in current assets for every $1 in current liabilities. Liquidity declined in 2011 from 2010, when the current ratio was $2.51 of current assets for every $1 in current liabilities. The decline in the current ratio in 2011 was primarily due to a significant decrease in cash and an increase in current liabilities over the previous year.

The *quick ratio* is a more refined measure of liquidity as it excludes inventory, which is typically the slowest current asset to be converted into cash, from the current assets in the calculation. The quick ratio is always less than the current ratio unless the company has no inventory. The quick ratio indicates the degree of coverage of the current liabilities from cash and other more liquid assets. A low quick ratio indicates that the company might have difficulty in paying off its current liabilities as they become due. However, this statement might not always be true because many other factors influence a company's ability to pay off current debts:

- Its capability to raise additional funds, long-term or short-term.
- The willingness of its creditors to roll over its debt.
- The rate at which current assets such as accounts receivable and inventory turn over into cash.

The quick ratio for Cliffs Natural for 2011 and 2010 is calculated as follows:

Quick ratio 2011 = (Current assets − inventory) / current liabilities
= ($1,790.7 − 475.7)/ $1,493.3
= 0.88

Quick ratio 2010 = (Current assets − inventory) /current liabilities
= ($2,583.7 − 269.2)/ $1,028.7
= 2.25

The quick ratio of 2.25 in 2010 indicates good coverage of quickly converting current assets into cash to cover current liabilities. However, the drop in the quick ratio to 0.88 in 2011 indicates that Cliffs Natural might have some difficulty in meeting its current liabilities as they fall due without having to resort to additional borrowing.

## Activity Ratios

Activity ratios measure how quickly a company can convert some of its accounts into cash. This type of ratio measures how effectively management is using its assets.

*Accounts receivable turnover* indicates the number of times within a period a company turns over its credit sales into cash.

This ratio gives an indication of how successful a company is in collecting its accounts receivable. This ratio is computed by dividing accounts receivable into annual credit sales:

The larger the accounts receivable turn over, the faster the company turns over its credit sales into cash. For example, an accounts receivable turnover of 17 indicates that sales turn over into cash every 21 days (365/17), or 0.7 times a month (12/17).

Accounts receivable turnover for Cliffs Natural for 2011 and 2010 is calculated as follows, using figures from the company's balance sheet and income statement (exhibits 5.1 and 6.1):

$$
\begin{aligned}
\text{Accounts receivable turnover 2011} &= \text{Credit sales / accounts} \\
&\quad \text{receivable} \\
&= \$6{,}551.7/304.2 \\
&= 21.54
\end{aligned}
$$

$$
\begin{aligned}
\text{Accounts receivable turnover 2010} &= \text{Credit sales/ accounts} \\
&\quad \text{receivable} \\
&= \$4{,}416.8/359.1 \\
&= 12.30
\end{aligned}
$$

Cliffs Natural's accounts receivable turnover increased from 12.30 times in 2010 to 21.54 times in 2011, which translates into an average collection period of 29.67 days (365/12.3) in 2010, and 16.95 days (365/21.54) in 2011. When the average collection period increases, investors should be on their guard.

*Inventory turnover* measures the number of times a company's inventory is replaced within a period, indicating the relative liquidity of inventory. This ratio gives an indication of the effectiveness of the management of inventory.

The higher the inventory turnover, the more rapidly the company is able to turn over its inventory into accounts receivable and cash. For example, an inventory turnover of 7.8 indicates that it takes the average inventory 47 days to turn over (365 days/7.8). If the inventory turnover for the same company increases to 9, the inventory turns over in roughly 41 days (365/9).

Inventory turnover is calculated as follows:

Inventory turnover = cost of goods sold/inventory

Inventory turnover 2011 = $4,105.7/$475.7
$$= 8.63$$
Inventory turnover 2010 = $3,155.6/$269.2
$$= 11.72$$

Inventory turned over more slowly in 2011 (365/8.63) 42 days, whereas in 2010 inventory turned over in 31 days for Cliffs Natural.

With both the accounts receivable turnover and inventory turnover, you do not want to see extremely low values, indicating that the company's cash is tied up for long periods of time. Similarly, extremely high turnover figures indicate poor inventory management, which can lead to stock-outs (not having enough inventory to fill an order) and, therefore, customer dissatisfaction.

*Accounts payable turnover* indicates the promptness with which a company makes its payments to suppliers. This ratio is computed by dividing accounts payable into purchases. If information on purchases is not available, you can use the company's cost of goods sold minus (plus) any decreases (increases) in inventory. The accounts payable ratio indicates the relative ease or difficulty with which a company can pay its bills on time. If the average terms in the industry are net 30 days and a company takes 50 days to pay its bills, you know that many of its bills are not being paid on time. The boxed material discusses how a company can window dress its balance sheet to make the company look more liquid.

---

## HOW A COMPANY CAN IMPROVE ITS FINANCIAL POSITION BY SPRUCING UP ITS BALANCE SHEET AT YEAR-END

Some companies spruce up their balance sheets for their year-end financial statements. Many of the techniques that are used are within accounting and legal limits. One such method is for a company to reduce its working capital through the reduction of inventory levels, accounts receivable, and accounts payable. Working capital is defined as an excess of current assets over current liabilities. If working capital is high, it indicates inefficiency in that resources are tied up in inventory and accounts receivable. Lower levels of working capital are a sign of a company's efficiency and financial strength because less cash is tied up in inventory and accounts receivables.

REL, a London-based consultancy group, looked at the balance sheets of 1,000 companies and found that companies could cut their inventories by shipping more products at year-end. In the quarter following, inventories backed up as customers either returned some of the inventory or cut back on their purchases because they had too many goods in stock.

At the same time, companies worked hard at getting their customers to pay their bills faster before year-end. REL found that companies could reduce their receivables by 2 percent at year-end, only to have them increase by 5 percent in the quarter following.

Companies paid their own bills, thereby reducing their accounts payable at year-end. REL found that accounts payable fell by 7 percent at year-end, only to increase by 12 percent in the next quarter. Assume a company has $50,000 in total current assets and $40,000 in total current liabilities, resulting in a current ratio of 1.25. If the company pays its accounts payable of $10,000 before the end of the accounting year, current assets will be $40,000 and current liabilities $30,000, resulting in an improvement to the current ratio from 1.25 to 1.33.

Any significant reductions in inventory and accounts receivable at year-end should be followed up in subsequent quarters. Answers can often be found in the footnotes and management discussion and analysis sections of the annual report.

Has the company been selling its accounts receivable? Although common among various companies, this can signal that the company is experiencing a cash crunch.

An increase in a company's inventory level is another red flag. Analyze where the increases are: if they are in finished goods, while raw materials have decreased, this is a signal that the company is having trouble selling its goods. On the other hand, if raw materials have increased while finished goods have decreased, it indicates that sales are expanding and the company is gearing up for an increase in sales.[1]

## Profitability

A company's profits are important to investors because these earnings are either retained or paid out in dividends to shareholders, both of which affect the company's stock price. Many different measures of profitability indicate how much the company is earning relative to the base that is used, such as sales, assets, and shareholders' equity. The different profitability ratios are relative measures of the success of the company.

Using sales as a base, you would compare the different measures of earnings on the income statement. Compare the sales for the period with the sales figures for previous years to see whether sales have grown or declined. For example, sales might have increased from the preceding year, yet the company might report a net loss for the year. This situation indicates that expenses have risen significantly. You would then examine the income statement to see whether the additional expenses were nonrecurring (a one-time write-off) or whether increased operating costs were incurred in the normal course of business. In the latter case, you should question management's capability to contain these costs. Establishing a trend of these expenses over a period of time is useful in the evaluation process.

Several profitability ratios use sales as a base: gross profit, operating profit, and net profit.

## Gross Profit Margin

The gross profit margin is the percentage earned on sales after deducting the cost of goods sold. The gross profit margin reflects not only the company's markup on its cost of goods sold but also management's ability to control these costs in relation to sales. The gross profit margin is computed as follows for Cliffs Natural, with figures obtained from Exhibit 6.1:

$$\text{Gross Profit Margin for 2011} = \frac{\text{Sales} - \text{Cost of goods sold}}{\text{Net Sales}}$$
$$= (\$6,551.7 - \$4,105.7)/6,551.7$$
$$= 37.3\%$$

$$\text{Gross Profit Margin for 2010} = \frac{\text{Sales} - \text{Cost of goods sold}}{\text{Net Sales}}$$
$$= (\$4,416.8 - \$3,155.6)/4,416.8$$
$$= 28.5\%$$

Gross profit increased from 28.5 percent in 2010 to 37.3 percent in 2011, primarily because sales increased by a greater margin than the increase in cost of goods sold in 2011. In other words, the markup on the company's cost of goods sold increased in 2011. A decrease in gross profits bears more scrutiny because it might mean that management is unable to control costs and/or increase prices of goods sold.

## Operating Profit Margin

The operating profit margin is the percentage in profit earned on sales from a company's operations. Operating profit is the income from operations (also known as EBIT, earnings before interest and taxes) divided by sales. This profit includes the cost of goods sold and the selling, general, and administrative expenses. This ratio shows the profitability of a company in its normal course of operations and provides a measure of the company's operating efficiency.

$$\text{Operating Profit Margin for Cliffs Natural 2011} = \frac{\text{Operating Profits}}{\text{Net Sales}}$$

$$= \$2{,}348.6/\$6{,}551.7$$

$$= 35.8\%$$

$$\text{Operating Profit Margin for Cliffs Natural 2010} = \frac{\text{Operating Profits}}{\text{Net Sales}}$$

$$= \$1{,}270.2/\$4{,}416.8$$

$$= 28.7\%$$

The operating profit or loss often provides the truest indicator of a company's earning capacity because it excludes nonoperating income and expenses and other one-time gains and losses. For Cliffs Natural, operating profit margins increased from 28.7 percent in 2010 to 35.8 percent in 2011, indicating that operating expenses were kept in check and that the company was able to maintain its gross profit margins.

## Net Profit Margin

The net profit margin is the percentage profit earned on sales after all expenses and income taxes are deducted. The net profit margin includes nonoperating income and expenses such as taxes, interest expense, and extraordinary items. Net profit is calculated as follows:

$$\text{Net Profit Margin for Cliffs Natural 2011} = \frac{\text{Net Income}}{\text{Net Sales}}$$

$$= \$1{,}812.6/\$6{,}551.7$$

$$= 27.6\%$$

$$\text{Net Profit Margin for Cliffs Natural 2010} = \frac{\text{Net Income}}{\text{Net Sales}}$$

$$= \$1{,}019.9/\$4{,}416.8$$

$$= 23\%$$

Cliffs Natural was able to increase its net profit margin from 23 percent to 27.6 percent from 2010 to 2011. The decline in the operating margin from 35.8 percent to 27.6 percent in net profit was as a result of increased interest expenses, increased taxes, and other one-time losses. The increase in interest expenses is a red flag that bears further analysis.

You might not think that calculating all these profit ratios is important because of the emphasis that is usually placed on the net profit margin alone. This belief could be misleading; if tax rates or interest expenses increase, or if some large, extraordinary items occur during the year, a significant change in net profit occurs, even though operating profits have not changed, as was seen with Cliffs Natural in 2011. A company could have a net profit at the same time it posts an operating loss. This situation occurs when a company has tax credits or other one-time gains that convert the operating loss into net income. Similarly, if the net profit margin declines in any period, you would want to determine the reasons for that decline.

Other measures of profitability are the returns on equity, common equity, and the return on investment. These ratios are more specific to common shareholders because they measure the returns on shareholders' invested funds.

## Return on Equity

The return on equity is a measure of the net income a company earns as a percentage of shareholders' equity. This ratio indicates how well management is performing for the stockholders of Cliffs Natural and is calculated as follows, based on information obtained from Exhibits 5.1 and 6.1:

$$\text{Return on Equity on Cliffs Natural for 2011} = \frac{\text{Net Income}}{\text{Shareholders' Equity}}$$
$$= \$1{,}812.6/\$7{,}039.7$$
$$= 25.7\,\%$$

$$\text{Return on Equity on Cliffs Natural for 2010} = \frac{\text{Net Income}}{\text{Shareholders' Equity}}$$
$$= \$1,019.9/\$3,838.7$$
$$= 26.5\%$$

The return on equity is important for shareholders. Debt holders receive a fixed return on their lending; preferred stockholders usually also receive a fixed return, but common shareholders are not provided with promised returns. Common shareholders have claims on residual earnings only after all other sources of financing are paid. Consequently, returns on equity are important to common shareholders.

The return on equity is directly influenced by the amount of debt used to finance the company's assets. If the company does not have any debt, the return on equity would equal the company's return on investment. Because Cliffs Natural has increased its debt financing from 2010 to 2011, the company's return on equity is higher than its return on investment for 2011. Cliffs Natural's return on equity declined slightly from 26.5 percent in 2010 to 25.7 percent in 2011. Cliffs Natural's return on equity should be compared with those of other companies in the same industry.

## Return on Common Equity

The return on common equity is a measure of the return earned by a company on its common shareholders' investment. When a company has preferred stock, the common shareholders might be more concerned with the return attributable to the common equity rather than to the total equity. To determine this return, adjustments are made for the preferred dividends and preferred stock outstanding.

$$\text{Return on Common Equity} = \frac{\text{Net Income} - \text{Preferred Dividends}}{\text{Equity} - \text{Preferred Stock}}$$

Cliffs Natural has not issued any preferred stock, so this ratio cannot be computed.

## Return on Investment

The return on investment is a measure of the return a company earns on its total assets.

This return relates the profits earned by a company to its investment and is computed as follows (figures obtained from Exhibits 5.1 and 6.1 for Cliffs Natural):

$$\text{Return on Investment for Cliffs Natural } 2011 = \frac{\text{Net Income}}{\text{Total assets}}$$
$$= \$1,812.6/\$14,541.7$$
$$= 12.46\%$$

$$\text{Return on Investment for Cliffs Natural } 2010 = \frac{\text{Net income}}{\text{Total assets}}$$
$$= \$1,019.9/\$7,778.2$$
$$= 13.11\%$$

## Leverage Ratios

Leverage is the use of borrowed funds to acquire assets. During periods of rising income, the use of borrowed funds can magnify a company's increases in returns.

Leverage measures the use of debt to finance a company's assets. Although leverage is a major concern for bondholders, who use leverage ratios to determine the level of debt and the servicing of the contractual payments of interest and principal, leverage is also important for common stockholders.

By increasing the use of debt financing, a company can increase its returns to shareholders. Table 8.2 shows how returns for a company can increase through the use of leverage (debt financing). This example illustrates how both the return on equity and the earnings

## TABLE 8.2

Example of the Use of Financial Leverage and Earnings

| Company with No Leverage | | | |
|---|---|---|---|
| **Balance Sheet** | | **Income Statement** | |
| **Assets** | **Liabilities** | Revenues | $1,000 |
| | | Cost of Goods Sold | 600 |
| $1,000 | $ 0 | Gross Profit | 400 |
| | | Expenses | 200 |
| | **Equity** | Earnings before Taxes | 200 |
| | | Taxes 30% | 60 |
| | $ 1,000* | Net Income | 140 |
| $1,000 | $ 1,000 | | |

Return on Equity = 140/1,000 = 14%

Earnings per Share 140/100 = $1.40

*100 shares outstanding

| Company with 50% Leverage | | | |
|---|---|---|---|
| **Balance Sheet** | | **Income Statement** | |
| **Assets** | **Liabilities** | Revenues | $1,000 |
| | | Cost of Goods Sold | 600 |
| $1,000 | $ 500 | Gross Profit | 400 |
| | | Expenses | 200 |
| | **Equity** | Earnings before Interest and Taxes | 200 |
| | $ 500* | | |
| | | Interest {10% × $500} | 50 |
| $1,000 | $ 1,000 | Earnings before Taxes | 150 |
| | | Taxes 30% | 45 |
| | | Net Income | 105 |

Return on Equity = 105/500 = 21%

Earnings per Share = 105/50 = $2.10

*50 shares outstanding

per share can be increased from 14 percent to 21 percent and from $1.40 to $2.10 respectively by increasing the use of debt financing from 0 percent to 50 percent of its total assets.

This increase occurs for two reasons. First, the company can earn more than the 10 percent cost of borrowing. Second, the interest payments are a tax-deductible expense. The federal government bears 30 percent (the tax rate used in this example) of the cost of the interest payments (30 percent of $50, which is $15).

Because the use of debt increases the return to shareholders as well as the earnings per share, why should shareholders be so concerned about the level of debt that a company uses to finance its assets? The answer is that the more debt a company takes on, the greater its financial risk and the cost of servicing its debt. If a downturn in sales takes place, the company might have difficulty making its interest payments. This situation can lead to not only defaulting on a loan and, ultimately, declaring bankruptcy, but also to significantly reducing returns to shareholders and earnings per share. Whenever a company increases the amount of its debt, the costs of raising additional debt issues increase, which means that the company must earn more than the cost of its borrowing or it will not see the benefits of leverage. When the level of debt reaches the point where the earnings on the assets are less than the costs of the debt, the return on equity and the earnings per share will decline.

For common stock investors, a highly leveraged company often indicates great risk and requires a greater rate of return to justify that risk. This increase in the required rate of return could have a negative effect on the share price. The use of leverage increases the value of the stock when the level of debt used is not perceived as adding a great amount of risk to the company.

## What Is the Optimal Level of Leverage?

All companies use different amounts of leverage, and some industries typically use more than others. Industries that require large investments in fixed assets, such as oil companies, airlines, and utilities, use a higher percentage of debt to finance their assets. Banks typically also use large amounts of debt because deposits finance their assets; this leverage results in large fluctuations in the banking industry's earnings whenever slight fluctuations in revenues occur.

When you are considering the leverage of a company, compare it to the typical leverage for that industry. Investors should look at a company's debt and coverage ratios to see the extent of its borrowing and its capability to service that debt.

## Debt Ratio

The debt ratio measures a company's use of debt as a percentage of its total assets.

The debt ratio indicates how much of the financing of the total assets comes from debt.

$$\text{Debt Ratio for Cliffs Natural 2011} = \frac{\text{Total Current and Noncurrent Liabilities}}{\text{Total Assets}}$$
$$= (\$1{,}493.3 + \$6{,}008.7)/\$14{,}541.7$$
$$= 51.5\%$$

$$\text{Debt Ratio for Cliffs Natural 2010} = \frac{\text{Total Current and Noncurrent Liabilities}}{\text{Total Assets}}$$
$$= (\$1{,}028.7 + \$2{,}910.8)/\$7{,}778.2$$
$$= 50.6\%$$

Compare the debt ratio with the average of the industry to get a better feel for the degree and extent of the company's leverage. A company with a large debt ratio becomes increasingly vulnerable if a downturn in sales or the economy occurs, particularly in the latter case if it is a cyclical company. Cliffs Natural's debt ratio is much the same for 2010 and 2011 but is fairly high in that over 50 percent of its assets are financed through debt.

When you examine a company's financial statements, you should always check the footnotes to see whether any debt has been excluded from the balance sheet. If a company does not consolidate its financial subsidiaries into its financial statements, any debt the parent company is responsible for is reported in the footnotes to the financial statements.

## Debt-to-Equity Ratio

The debt-to-equity ratio measures a company's use of debt as a percentage of equity.

The debt-to-equity ratio is computed as follows for Cliffs Natural:

$$\text{Debt-to-Equity Ratio 2011} = \frac{\text{Total Debt}}{\text{Shareholders' Equity}}$$

$$= \$7,502/\$7,039.7$$

$$= 106.5\%$$

$$\text{Debt-to-Equity Ratio 2010} = \frac{\text{Total Debt}}{\text{Shareholders' Equity}}$$

$$= \$3,939.5/\$3,838.7$$

$$= 102.6\%$$

The higher the ratio, the greater the level of financing provided by debt, and the lower the ratio, the greater the level of financing provided by shareholders. This ratio is similar to the total debt ratio and raises a warning sign as to the debt burden faced by the company.

## Coverage Ratios

The coverage ratio is a measure of a company's capability to service its debt commitments (cover its interest payments).

The *times interest earned ratio* measures a company's coverage of its interest payments. It is calculated as follows:

$$\text{Time Interest Earned Ratio for Cliffs 2011} = \frac{\text{Earnings before Interest and Taxes (EBIT)}}{\text{Annual Interest Expense}}$$

$$= \$2,348.6/\$209$$

$$= 11.24 \text{ times}$$

$$\text{Time Interest Earned Ratio for Cliffs 2010} = \frac{\text{Earnings before Interest and Taxes (EBIT)}}{\text{Annual Interest Expense}}$$

$$= \$1,270.2/\$47.7$$

$$= 26.63 \text{ times}$$

Even though EBIT for Cliffs Natural almost doubled from 2010 to 2011, the company's interest expense increased by more than four times, causing the times interest ratio to fall from 26.63 times to 11.24 times. Consequently, a value investor would want to know how much leeway Cliffs Natural has if there is a downturn in earnings before interest and taxes, before it will not have sufficient earnings to cover its interest payments. The margin of safety of the coverage ratio for Cliffs Natural can be computed as follows:

Margin of safety of the coverage ratio = 1 − (1/coverage ratio)

A company with a coverage ratio of 11.24 would have a margin of safety of 91 percent:

$$=1 - (1/11.24) \qquad = \underline{91.1\%}$$

The company's EBIT can fall by only 91.1 percent before the earnings coverage is insufficient to service its debt commitments.

## Common-Stock Price Ratios

Common-stock price ratios relate information about a company's stock price.

### Price/Earnings (P/E) Ratio

The P/E ratio is a measure of how the market prices a company's stock.

The P/E ratio is the most commonly used guide to the relationship between stock prices and earnings and is calculated as follows:

$$\text{Price/Earnings Ratio} = \frac{\text{Market Price of the Stock}}{\text{Earnings per share}}$$

The P/E ratio shows the number of times a stock's price is trading relative to its earnings. The P/E ratios for listed common stocks are published daily in the financial newspapers and on financial websites. For example, the P/E ratio for Cliffs Natural as of January 15, 2013, was 5.81 times ($36.80/$6.33), with a market price of $36.80 per share and trailing earnings per share of $6.33 per share. This number

indicates that shareholders were willing to pay 5.81 times Cliff's earnings for its stock. Put another way, it would take 5.81 years of these
earnings to equal the invested amount ($36.80 per share). P/E ratios
can also be computed on expected future earnings. Cliff's forward
earnings per share are projected to be $3.59 for 2012, resulting in a
forward P/E ratio of 10.25 ($36.80/$3.59).

A company's P/E ratio shows how expensive its stock is
relative to its earnings. Companies with high P/E ratios (higher
than 20, as a general rule) are characteristic of growth companies. Although with the average market multiple around 13 (in
January 2013), a forward P/E ratio of 10 for Cliffs Natural makes
it a value stock.

What becomes apparent is that high P/E ratios indicate high
risk. If the future anticipated growth of high P/E ratio stocks is not
achieved, their stock prices will be punished and their prices will
fall quickly. On the other hand, if growth stocks live up to their
earnings expectations, investors benefit substantially. A low P/E
ratio stock (less than 10) is characteristic of either a mature company with low growth potential or a company that is undervalued
and/or in financial difficulty.

By comparing the P/E ratios of companies with the averages in the industries and the markets, you can get an idea of the
relative value of the stock. For example, the average P/E ratios
for companies on the U.S. stock markets were around 17 times
earnings in September 2006 and around 13 in 2012. During bull
markets, these ratios go up, and during bear markets the average declines (perhaps as low as 6 times earnings, which happened
in 1974).

P/E ratios fluctuate considerably, differing among companies due to many factors, such as growth rates, earnings, and other
financial characteristics.

## Earnings per Share (EPS)

The EPS figure for a company is the amount of reported income
on a per share basis. The earnings per share indicate the amount
of earnings allocated to each share of common stock outstanding.

EPS figures can be used to compare the growth (or lack of growth) in earnings from year to year and to project future growth in earnings.

$$\text{Earnings per Share for Cliffs 2011} = \frac{\text{Net Income} - \text{Preferred Dividends}}{\text{Number of Common Share Outstanding}}$$
$$= \$1{,}619{,}100 / 140{,}234$$
$$= \$11.55$$

$$\text{Earnings per Share for Cliffs 2010} = \frac{\text{Net Income} - \text{Preferred Dividends}}{\text{Number of Common Share Outstanding}}$$
$$= \$1{,}019{,}900 / 135{,}301$$
$$= \$7.54$$

The number of shares outstanding equals the number of shares issued minus the shares the company has bought back, called *treasury stock*. In many cases companies report two sets of earnings per share: regular earnings per share and fully diluted earnings per share.

When companies have convertible bonds, convertible preferred stock, rights, options, and/or warrants, their EPS figures might be diluted because of the increased number of common shares outstanding, if and when these securities are converted into common stock. Companies are then required to disclose their fully diluted EPS figures and their basic earnings per share.

Earnings per share that are increasing steadily because of growth in sales should translate into increasing stock prices. However, earnings per share can also increase when companies buy back their own shares. The number of shares outstanding is then reduced, and if earnings stay the same, the earnings per share increase. Conceivably, earnings per share can increase when sales and earnings decrease if a significant number of shares are bought back. Astute investors examine a company's financial statements to determine whether the increase in earnings per share is caused by a growth in sales and earnings or by stock buybacks. If the latter is true, the result can be a loss of confidence in the stock, which can lead to a decline in the stock price.

Companies with poor fundamentals might try the tactic of buying back their shares to improve their earnings per share and ultimately their stock prices, but this strategy might not work over the long term.

The earnings per share can also be determined as follows:

$$\text{Earnings per Share} = \frac{\text{Market Price of the Stock}}{\text{P/E Ratio}}$$

## Dividends and Dividend Yields

Investors buy stocks for their potential capital gains and/or their dividend payments. Companies either share their profits with their shareholders by paying dividends or retain their earnings and reinvest them in different projects to boost their share prices. Look in the financial newspapers or use the Internet to find the dividend amounts that listed companies pay. Companies generally try to maintain their stated dividend payments even if they suffer declines in earnings. Similarly, an increase in earnings does not always translate into an increase in dividends. Certainly many examples exist in which companies experience increases in earnings that result in increases in dividend payments, but that is not always the case. An imprecise relationship exists between dividends and earnings. Sometimes increases in earnings exceed increases in dividends; at other times increases in dividends exceed increases in earnings. Thus, growth in dividends cannot be interpreted as a sign of a company's financial strength.

Dividends are important because they represent tangible returns to shareholders. In contrast, investors in growth stocks that pay little or no dividends are betting on capital appreciation rather than on current returns.

The dividend yield is a measure of the annual dividends a company pays as a percentage of the market price of the stock. This ratio shows the percentage return that dividends represent relative to the market price of the common stock. For Cliffs Natural Resources the dividend yield as of January 15, 2013, is:

$$\text{Dividend Yield} = \frac{\text{Annual Dividend}}{\text{Market Price of the Stock}}$$

$$= \$2.50/\$36.80$$

$$= 6.79\%$$

In a rising bull market, many investors are nervous about growth stocks that either pay no or low dividends and turn to stocks that yield high dividends. A strategy of buying this type of stock might offer some protection against the fall in stock market prices due to rising interest rates. Dividend yields of many utility companies, real estate investment trusts (REITs), and energy companies might be as high as 4 to 7 percent. High dividend yields are characteristic of a few blue chip companies and the utility companies.

Choosing stocks purely because of their high dividend yields, however, can be risky. Dividends can always be reduced, which generally puts downward pressure on the stock price.

When you are choosing stocks with high dividend yields, you should look at the stocks' earnings to ensure that they are sufficient to support the dividend payments. As a general rule, earnings should be equal to at least 150 percent of the dividend payout.

The *dividend payout ratio* is the percentage of earnings a company pays out to its shareholders in dividends.

$$\text{Dividend Payout Ratio} = \frac{\text{Annual Dividend}}{\text{Earnings per Share}}$$

For Cliffs Natural, the payout ratio as of December 2012 is:

$$= \$2.50/\$3.59$$

$$= 69.6\%$$

In addition to looking at earnings, you should also look at the statement of changes in cash to see the sources and uses of cash. For example, if the major sources of cash come from issuing debt and selling off assets, a company cannot maintain a policy of paying high dividend yields.

Dividends and dividend yields are not good indicators of the intrinsic value of a stock because dividend payments fluctuate considerably over time, creating an imprecise relationship between the growth in dividends and the growth in earnings.

The ratio analysis of Cliffs Natural indicate red flags for investors, and if prices of iron ore continue to fall, value investors should not jump in to this stock.

## PRO FORMA FINANCIAL STATEMENTS

Pro forma financial statements are constructed using projected figures based on assumptions about future sales, income, and cash flow. Pro forma financial statements focus on forecasts of future sales and earnings. These financial statements are not subject to GAAP, even though companies are required to file them with the SEC.

Pro forma statements often exclude certain expenses and charges, sometimes making their projected earnings look more favorable than they truly are. Restructuring charges are typically excluded, while every type of projected gain is included. The lack of standards for earnings also adds to the confusion, making it difficult to compare the pro forma earnings of one company to another in the same industry.

Even though companies may not know the amounts of special restructuring charges that could occur in the future, they should provide more guidance with regard to these special charges and try to quantify them. You should be aware of these shortfalls in your analysis of a company's pro forma statements and not disregard the results of past financial statements as water under the bridge; past statements might still be more accurate than pro forma statements.

## CAN YOU TRUST THE NUMBERS PUT OUT BY MANAGEMENT?

After the Enron, WorldCom, and Global Crossing debacles of "cooking the books," the SEC spent a year reviewing annual reports from the 500 largest companies in the United States and found fault with 350 of the annual reports. The major problem areas were in accounting (the companies did not explain their use of accounting policies and how different interpretations might affect reported profits), revenues (companies did not spell out what they counted as revenue), pensions (companies did not disclose their assumptions on interest rates and how they used them to calculate liabilities on their pension funds), impairments (companies did not disclose how they wrote off their intangible assets), and management discussion (companies failed to analyze industry trends, risks, cash flow, and capital requirements).[2]

This corporate shortfall has been an invitation to lawmakers in Washington, D.C., to step in to regulate and limit the leeway with which corporations can report their numbers. New tougher accounting rules were set. The SEC demanded that companies provide full explanations whenever they deviate from using generally accepted accounting principles.

The Financial Accounting Standards Board put limitations on how companies account for their restructuring costs and have requirements in the works to have companies expense their stock options.[3]

Accounting scandals have occurred since increased regulations were passed by Congress and will probably continue to occur, so you should always be on your guard for warning signs in industries and companies before you invest in their securities. An economy in recession, with declining sales and earnings, seems to provide the right atmosphere for unscrupulous corporate executives to overstate assets and revenues, understate expenses, and hide debt by keeping it off the balance sheets. Similarly, companies that had stellar growth records and were then confronted with slowing sales and earnings also have "fudged" their numbers. Another situation was the Tyco story: growth through aggressive acquisition practices gave the CEO, who suffered from a severe dose of infectious greed, a chance to pay himself enormous amounts, which were hidden in the numbers pertaining to the acquisition of the companies.

How seriously should you take pro forma earnings? Not very seriously, even though they form the basis of analysts' forward projections. Moreover, the track records of analysts were not very good for 2002 and later. Analysts, watching projections for 2002, predicted a recovery in the latter half of the year. They forecasted 16 percent earnings increases in the third quarter and 21 percent in the fourth quarter, which never came about.

# Choosing a Value Stock Portfolio

The previous chapter covered fundamental analysis methods for selecting stocks that are undervalued and the three chapters prior to that analyzed the balance sheet, income statement, and changes in cash flow statement. Armed with that information, you are now ready to construct a portfolio, using an investment style that is suitable for your particular needs and circumstances.

## CHOOSING AN INVESTMENT STYLE

The question that is often asked by investors is: "What types of stocks should I buy?" Should you rush to buy the small-cap growth stocks that have outperformed large-cap growth stocks, or should you look for value stocks? The question relates not only to the investment type but also the size of the company stocks. Some investors feel comfortable investing in going after the winning categories, while the more patient investor is content to invest in the lagging categories, which will rise over time.

Studies have shown that stocks can be classified into categories that have similar patterns of performance and characteristics. In other words, the returns of the stocks within the categories were similar, while the returns of the stocks between the categories were not correlated.[1] In his article, Farrell found four categories for stocks: growth, cyclical, stable, and energy. Other studies measured stocks by their market capitalization or size, which was then translated into small-cap, mid-cap, and large-cap stocks. What portfolio managers found was that they could enhance their performance by moving their money into the different categories of stocks from time to time.

From these categories of stocks two investment styles have emerged: value and growth investing. Table 9.1 illustrates the common styles of equity investing as developed by Morningstar Mutual Funds for mutual fund investing, but it can also be used to determine individual equity portfolio holdings. Investors can use this style box to determine the bulk of their equity investments to suit their investment style, determined by their objectives. Value stocks have different financial characteristics and returns than growth stocks. Value stocks generally have low P/E ratios that are less than their expected growth rates. Growth stocks generally have high P/E ratios and are expected to experience high sales growth for a period of time. A blend includes a mixture of growth and value stocks. The size of the company is measured by market capitalization, which is the market value of its stock multiplied by

**TABLE 9.1**

Types of Equity Styles

|                   | Value | Blend | Growth |
|-------------------|-------|-------|--------|
| Large-Cap Stocks  |       |       |        |
| Mid-Cap Stocks    |       |       |        |
| Small-Cap Stocks  |       |       |        |

Source: Morningstar Mutual Funds

the number of shares outstanding. Small-cap companies are riskier than mid- or large-cap companies, but as the Ibbotson studies showed, the returns over longer periods for small-cap stocks have generally exceeded the returns of large-cap stocks. Small-cap value stocks outperformed large-cap growth stocks quite handily over the two-and-a-half-year period from 2003 to 2005. Consequently, stock picking becomes extremely important for individual portfolios, particularly when the investment style is to time the markets.

Once an investor has identified the equity style that is most comfortable, the value investor can turn back to review Figure 2.2 in Chapter 2 of this book to see which types of stocks should compose her portfolio.

The style box illustrates the choices in terms of investment styles and size of companies. Investors can choose the current winners, which happen to be small-cap value stocks, financial services stocks, and health care stocks as of the year through May 31, 2013, to invest more money. Alternatively, some investors might not want to pay high prices for these types of stocks and instead would look for the quadrants of stocks that have not participated in the recent rally (large-cap and mid-cap growth stocks, for example). Some investors might want to have a combination of growth and value stocks in the different size stocks. This style box can also be used with international stocks.

Research has shown that value and growth stocks do not perform in the same manner within the same time periods. This has been evidenced recently by the spectacular performance of the large-cap growth stocks in the late 1990s, while large-, mid-, and small-cap value stocks underperformed the market. Small-cap value stocks have outperformed large-cap growth stocks since 2000. One investment style (growth versus value) will be dominant at a given point in time. Some investors choose to invest all their funds in the stocks that are performing well and then shift to other investment styles when they perceive that things are about to change. This style of investing would be more conducive to an active management style, as opposed to a passive one, where investors allocate their stocks among the different categories and then hold them for long periods. Active managers are more likely to be market timers and are more inclined to be fully invested in stocks when they perceive the market to be going up. The opposite occurs when they think the market is about to decline; they exit the market. Passive investors tend to stay fully invested in stocks irrespective of the state of the markets.

Ultimately, investors need to decide whether they choose value or growth stocks, and whether they will be active or passive managers of their portfolios. The selection of individual stocks can be made easier if direction is provided through an asset allocation model, which breaks down the different style categories of investment by the asset class. Table 9.2 lists a few examples of the different portfolio possibilities. Investors might invest in a mixture of value and growth stocks, which could be allocated among domestic (U.S) and international stocks. Investors would then decide on the amounts to allocate to the different stock sizes, large, mid, and small cap (example 1).

## TABLE 9.2

### Asset Allocation of Stocks by Style

| Example 1 | | Example 2 | | Example 3 | |
|---|---|---|---|---|---|
| Value/Growth Blend | | Value | | Growth | |
| Value Stocks | | Value Stocks | | Growth Stocks | |
| Large-Cap U.S. stocks | 20% | Large-Cap U.S. stocks | 25% | Large-Cap U.S.stocks | 25% |
| Mid-Cap U.S. stocks | 10% | Mid-Cap U.S. stocks | 15% | Mid-Cap U.S. stocks | 15% |
| Small-Cap U.S. stocks | 10% | Small-Cap U.S. stocks | 10% | Small-cap U.S. stocks | 10% |
| International stocks | 10% | International Large-Cap | 20% | International Large-Cap | 20% |
| Growth Stocks | | International Mid-Cap | 20% | International Mid-Cap | 20% |
| Large-Cap U.S. stocks | 20% | International Small-Cap | 10% | International Small-Cap | 10% |
| Mid-Cap U.S stocks | 10% | | | | |
| Small-Cap U.S. stocks | 10% | | | | |
| International stocks | 10% | | | | |
| Total Portfolio | 100% | Total Portfolio | 100% | Total Portfolio | 100% |

Example 2 illustrates a value stock portfolio, while example 3 is a growth stock portfolio. Diversification within the stock sector of an investor's portfolio offers protection against the downside risk of being fully invested in only one sector, such as large-cap value or growth stocks, for example. If the tide turns against stocks in one sector, investors would be protected by being able to participate in any price improvement in other sectors should the stock market rally become more broad based.

## ACTIVE VERSUS PASSIVE INVESTMENT

Investors who believe in the efficient market hypothesis (stock prices reflect all available information and are always priced correctly, making it difficult to beat the market consistently) would argue on behalf of the passive investment style. If stock prices reflect all relevant information and stocks are always priced at their intrinsic values, it would be difficult for investors to beat the markets over long periods. Consequently, if investors cannot profit from insider information and there are no undervalued stocks, investors have two alternatives: (1) invest in market indices, or (2) choose individual stocks and hold them for long periods. These are known as *buy-hold strategies*.

### Indexing

Value investors who subscribe to *index investing* believe that events affecting companies occur randomly. Therefore, investors have a 50–50 chance of being correct in picking stocks that will go up; hence, their odds of beating the market become more muted. Consequently, these investors are satisfied with the returns of the market and would invest in the stocks that make up the market indices. This strategy can be achieved in the following ways:

- Investing in the individual stocks in the index; for example, the 30 stocks in the Dow Jones Industrial Average. However, investing in the 500 stocks of the S&P 500 Index is not practical for most individual portfolios. Investors could invest more easily in sectors of the S&P 500 Index, like the tech sector, the financial sector, the Nifty Fifty stocks, or in the Dogs of the Dow.

- Investing in index tracking stocks (exchange-traded funds), which underlie the indices. Examples of these are the SPDRs, which track the S&P 500 Index and the sector SPDRs of the S&P 500 Index; the DIAMONDs, which track the Dow Jones Industrial Average; and the Nasdaq 100 tracking stock, which invests in the largest 100 companies in the Nasdaq. These exchange-traded funds tracking indexes are discussed in Chapter 12 on exchange-traded funds.

- Investing in index mutual funds is discussed in Chapter 10.

An examination of the results of index mutual funds versus actively managed mutual funds, as a proxy of passive versus active investing, makes the case for indexing more compelling. Tergesen[2] reported that the average S&P 500 Index mutual fund earned around 18 percent annually over the ten-year period from 1989 to 1999, as compared with 16 percent annually for the actively managed equity mutual funds. This 2 percent annual difference might not seem all that significant, but when the difference is compounded over time, the results point overwhelmingly toward indexing. Over a 10-year period, the compounded returns of index funds exceeded actively managed equity funds by about 80 percent.[3] According to Burton Malkiel, a finance professor at Princeton University, the S&P 500 benchmark index fund outperformed 84 percent of actively managed large-cap funds during the 10-year period from 1993 to 2003.[4] In 2012 actively managed funds did not outperform the market averages, which has prompted many passive investors to invest in total market funds to at least earn close to the average market returns.

There are a number of ways to explain the advantages of indexing over actively managed mutual funds:

1. Actively managed mutual funds may keep some money in cash anticipating a downturn in the market. If this does not materialize, index funds will earn more from their holdings since they are always fully invested.

2.  The annual expense ratios of index funds are considerably lower than those of their actively managed equity mutual fund counterparts. Index funds do not change their holdings unless the stocks in the indices are changed. Actively managed funds can experience high turnovers of their holdings, which means higher transaction costs.

3.  Large-cap stocks, which are followed by many analysts, are probably efficiently priced, which gives the index fund an advantage over the stock picker.

The opportunities for active managers and stock pickers are in the small-cap and international stocks, which may be underfollowed by the analysts. Similarly, in a market downturn, active managers can put limits on the decrease in their funds' stock prices by raising cash or investing in defensive stocks, which might not go down as much as the fixed portfolios of the index funds. That is not to say that actively managed portfolios will not go down in a bear market. These portfolios will go down just like the index funds, but steps can be taken to reduce the amounts of the declines in their values. This can be seen where small-cap equity managers have outpaced the Russell 2000 Index by including some large-cap stocks in their holdings. Other studies confirm that active managers do not consistently outperform indexing.[5]

## Buy and Hold Investing

Besides indexing, the other passive investment strategy for stock pickers is to buy stocks for the long term and hold them, making minimal changes over time. Performance between active and passive strategies is more difficult to evaluate since returns depend on the composition of the stocks in both active and passive portfolios. However, using index funds as the basis for buy and hold investing, the results confirm that active portfolio managers do not outperform the buy and hold strategy. Michael Jensen[6] surveyed 115 mutual fund managers during the period 1945–1964 and found that the average returns of these funds resulted in less than investments in a portfolio of T-bills and the market index would have returned.

Market timers often tout the way they were able to success-fully exit the market before a crash and then reenter at a lower point to increase their overall returns. This may be easier said than done. Research done by T. Rowe Price showed that in order to do better than a buy and hold investor, market timers would need to be accu-rate in more than 70 percent of their calls to enter and exit the mar-ket. A study done by Nejat Seyhun covering the period 1963–1993 found that an investor who exited the market for just 1.2 percent of the market's best performing days would have lost out on 95 per-cent of the total returns.[7]

There certainly appears to be a disconnect between the research results as reported from the ivory towers of academia and the com-munications and hype as reported from many on Wall Street. The growth of newsletters forecasting the precise future movements of the markets and how to time them are on the rise, as more investors enter the stock markets hoping to double or treble their money over a short period. As of this writing, the clairvoyant with 100 percent accuracy in calling the markets has yet to emerge. Until such time the odds are stacked against timing the markets; they favor the buy and hold investor.

What becomes apparent is that it is difficult to beat the mar-kets consistently over long periods, regardless of the method. This theory certainly lends support for buy and hold strategies over mar-ket timers. In addition to those reasons already discussed, a couple of reasons put forth for the under-performance of active investing over passive investing are:

- Active trading means higher transaction (commission) costs
- If the holding period for stocks is less than a year, the gains incurred are taxed at higher ordinary federal tax rates than the longer-term holding periods of the buy-hold investors.

## Value versus Growth Investing

Although growth stocks have outperformed value stocks during certain time periods, this trend has not always prevailed over lon-ger periods. For the two-year period from 2003 to 2005, value stocks outperformed growth stocks, giving value stocks the appearance of being overvalued. Yet over longer periods, such as 1991 to 2010, value stocks outperformed growth stocks both in the United States and internationally. Consequently, an investor looking for value might consider buying growth stocks because he would pay a small premium for them. Should investors continue to choose the leadership in the sector that is doing well and ignore the other lagging sectors of the market? It is easier to answer the question for a long investment period, but over the short term it becomes more of a guessing game. The *momentum investing* style is to jump into those stocks that have been going up in price. The major problem with momentum investing is that the turning point can never be accurately predicted. These leadership stocks will eventually become laggards and the rotation will shift into the other sectors of stocks. If one is investing in these leadership stocks at the top of their price cycles, the returns may be not be positive for some time before they come back into favor. Over the long term, investors who have diversified portfolios of stocks among the different sectors (small-, mid-, and large-cap value and growth stocks) will see steadier returns.

An analysis of the stock market substantiates this premise. Over the 30-year period from 1980 to 2010, there were periods during which value stocks outperformed growth stocks, and others during which the opposite occurred (growth stocks outperformed value stocks), as summarized in Table 9.3.

**TABLE 9.3**

Performance of U.S. Stocks over the Period 1980–2010

| Value Stocks Outperform Growth Stocks | Growth Stocks Outperform Value Stocks |
|---|---|
| 1981 | 1980 |
| 1983–1984 | 1982 |
| 1986 | 1985 |
| 1987–1988 | 1987 |
| 1992–1993 | 1989–1991 |
| 1995 | 1992–1994 |
| | 1996–1999 |
| 2000–2010 | |

Which stocks over a long-term period would have returned more to investors? The answer may be surprising. A study done by David Leineweber et al., reported that $1 invested in both value and growth stocks, as followed by the price-to-book value of the S&P 500 Index stocks during the period 1975–1995, would have resulted in $23 for value stocks versus $14 for growth stocks.[8] These results have also been confirmed by studies done on foreign stocks. A study done by Capaul, Rowley, and Sharpe[9] determined that value stocks outperformed growth stocks abroad (France, Germany, Switzerland, Japan, and the United Kingdom) from January 1981 through June 1992. Jeremy Siegel, a professor at the University of Pennsylvania, found that value stocks outperformed growth stocks over the 35-year period between July 1963 and December 1998. Value stocks earned 13.4 percent annually, while growth stocks earned 12 percent annually.[10]

In short, this phenomenon—value stocks outperforming growth stocks over long periods—should have some significance in the choice of stocks for investment portfolios. The evidence shows that winning stocks do not keep their positions over time; they revert to the mean. Similarly, losing stocks do not remain losers over periods of time because they too rise to the average. In other words, the high-flying value stocks of today will not be able to sustain their abnormally high returns and will turn into lower returns, and the low returns of the growth stocks of today will eventually surprise with higher returns.

This phenomenon of returns reverting to the mean over time can be applied to small- and large-cap stocks as well. However, investing in small-cap stocks outperformed large-cap stocks during the periods 1974–1983 and again in 1991–1992. Investing in small- and mid-cap stocks from 1996 to 2000 would have resulted in either below-market or negative returns. Inevitably, though, small-cap stocks outperform large-cap stocks on a risk-adjusted basis over long periods. The second reason to include small-cap stocks in a diversified portfolio is that small-cap stocks have relatively low correlations with large-cap stocks, thereby improving the risk/return statistics in a portfolio.

Adding mid-cap stocks to small- and large-cap stocks in a portfolio reduces the volatility risks and optimizes the stability of returns. Many market timers consider that this style of investing across different sectors weakens the potential returns they could have achieved by moving with the top-performing sectors. Obviously, a diversified portfolio will not gain as much as the strongest performing sector, or fall as much as the weakest-performing sector. The results for market timers depend on their accuracy in timing their calls to move in and out of the different sectors. Your overall choice of whether to be an active or passive investor and your motivation for the choice of equity style ultimately will depend on your outlook of the market and your specific makeup with regard to risk and return.

## HOW TO COMPOSE A VALUE PORTFOLIO

Value investing relies on fundamental analysis to determine when a stock is trading at less than its intrinsic value. This style is the opposite of growth investing, whose investors are willing to chase after stocks that have good growth records and have already risen in value. Value investors are bargain hunters who are looking for companies that have good ideas or products or that have been performing poorly but have good long-term prospects. A good example of value stocks are the iron and steel companies that have declined in price because of the recession in the developed and developing countries. The stocks of these companies are trading at less than eight times their earnings multiples. When the developed nations and China start growing their economies, companies will begin to use more steel and iron, which will move those industries back into expansionary mode. When a sector of stocks has lagged other stock sectors over long periods, the gap eventually narrows, and those laggard sectors will likely outperform others in the future. As previously discussed, this is known as regression to the mean. The flip side of the coin is that stocks that have been outperforming the market will likely revert to the mean and begin to underperform the market at some stage in the future. Thus value investors are always looking for stocks that are considered to be trading below their expected long-term growth rates.

A definition of a value stock is one in which the company's P/E ratio is lower than its earnings growth rate. Cliffs Natural Resources, for example, is considered a value stock in that its 2012 expected earnings growth rate was 19 percent and its 2012 P/E ratio was less than 8. A stock whose P/E ratio exceeds its growth rate is not considered a value stock.

There is not unanimous agreement on the definition of value stocks. Some definitions center on low P/E multiples or those that are below the market multiples. Others focus on low multiples of cash flow, or low price-to-book ratios. The most conservative definition of a value stock is one that has an above average dividend yield. Out of favor stocks are also classified by some as value stocks. For example, when Apple, Google, and other growth stocks fell in value in 2012, many value fund managers bought them as value stocks. Depending, then, on how you define value, many investors come up with different sets of value stocks. Some of the bases for determining value stocks are discussed in greater detail below.

## Price-to-Earnings Ratio

The P/E ratio for a stock is calculated by dividing the current market price of the stock by the earnings per share. This can be done using the past four quarters' earnings, which is known as a *trailing P/E ratio*. Alternatively, the P/E calculation can use expected earnings based on forecasts for the upcoming year. This *future P/E ratio* may be of greater significance to investors because this is an indication of the expectations for the stock in the future.

However, investors should not base their decisions solely on P/E multiples because the type of industry and the capital structure also affect the P/E. Some industries have higher average P/E ratios than others, and it would not necessarily be a meaningful evaluation to compare P/E ratios across industries. For example, pharmaceutical companies have much higher multiples than broker-age company stocks. Comparing Merck, with a trailing P/E around 20, with Goldman Sachs's P/E of 110 would be meaningless. Some industries require much greater investments in property, plant, and equipment than others, which means they are probably much more leveraged in terms of debt. Generally, companies with high debt ratios are much riskier than companies with low debt ratios, and more highly leveraged companies will have lower P/E ratios.

A low P/E ratio is a relative measure. Some investors might consider Merck to be a growth stock with a multiple of 20, while others would consider it to be a value stock, as compared with the high multiples of some of the other stocks on the exchanges.

## Price-to-Book Ratio

This measure compares the market price to the book value. The book value per share is computed as assets minus liabilities divided by the number of outstanding shares. Value investors look for stocks with market values that are below their book values. Benjamin Graham has some guidelines for stock pickers that include buying a company's stock when the stock price is less than two thirds of the book value per share.

There are a number of reasons why a low P/B ratio is not reason enough, by itself, to buy a stock. The book value per share is an accounting measure, and it can be distorted by using different methods within the GAAP, such as the use of accelerated depreciation versus the use of straight line, or LIFO versus FIFO for valuing inventory. The discrepancy between the historical cost of the company's assets and their market values will make the book value per share diverge from the realizable value per share.

## Beta Coefficient

The capital asset pricing model developed by Sharpe, Lintner, and Markowitz links the relationship between risk and the expected return of a stock. The expected rate of return is the risk-free rate plus a risk premium based on the systematic risk of the stock. In this model, the risk of a stock or portfolio is broken down into two parts: systematic, or market risk, and unsystematic, or diversifiable risk. The risk pertaining to the security itself (such as business and financial risks) can be reduced and eliminated through diversification. What remains is systematic risk, which becomes important in the relationship between risk and return. In other words, by combining several different stocks in a portfolio, the unsystematic risk is reduced and all that is left is systematic risk, which is the relationship of a security's price to changes in security prices in the general market. Some stocks go up and down more than the market and other stocks fluctuate less than the market as a whole. Systematic risk is measured by the Greek letter beta. The beta coefficient, a measure of the systematic risk of a stock, links the sensitivity of the stock's rate of return in relation to the rate of return of the market.

The larger the standard deviation of the return of a stock relative to the returns of the market, the greater the risk associated with that stock. The *correlation coefficient* indicates the relative importance of variability. The range of the correlation coefficient is from +1 to −1. If the correlation coefficient is +1, the stock return and the market return move together in a strong correlation. Thus, if the standard deviation of the stock is 15 percent, and the standard deviation of the market is 10 percent with a correlation coefficient of 1, the beta coefficient is 1.5

A correlation coefficient of −1 with a standard deviation of a stock equal to 8 percent and a standard deviation of 10 percent for the market results in a beta of −0.8.

A negative correlation coefficient results in the stock and the market moving in opposite directions. If no relationship exists between the return on the stock and the return on the market, then the correlation coefficient is 0, which results in a beta coefficient of 0, or no market risk.

A stock with a beta coefficient of 1 indicates that if the market rises by 20 percent, the stock price will increase by 20 percent. Similarly, if the market falls by 20 percent, the stock price will also see a 20 percent decline. The market is assumed to have a beta coefficient of 1, which means that this stock is perfectly correlated with the market. A stock with a beta coefficient greater than 1 should produce above average returns in a bull market and below average returns in a bear market. A stock with a beta coefficient of less than 1 is less responsive to market changes. Investors who seek higher returns are willing to assume more risk.

## Selecting a Value Portfolio

The first step is to select a universe of stocks you are interested in. This can be done using the Internet to select and print up financial information on the stocks of interest. You can then narrow the list down to those stocks that conform with your criteria of value, namely the specific P/B and P/E ratios and dividend yields. You can find stock screening tools at various online websites such as www.yahoo.com and www.cnbc.com and use them to plug in criteria for screening different stocks to come up with a list of value stocks (see Table 9.4). These are not recommendations for particular stocks; over time the financial fundamentals for these stocks will change.

The criteria used to determine which categories of stocks to invest in for the early part of 2013 were based on the following:

- Large-cap stocks that had underperformed mid-cap and small-cap stocks by the end of 2012, hence the choice of stocks with greater than $10 billion market cap and with membership in the S& P 500 Index.

- P/E ratio of less than 10, which favors value stocks as the average P/E ratio of stocks was 13.1 as of December 31, 2012

- Return on equity of greater than 15 percent, which favors value stocks whose P/E ratios were less than their growth rates

- Dividend yields of greater than or equal to 3 percent, favoring value stocks

## TABLE 9.4

Value Stocks Based on Fundamental Factors Listed

| Company Name | Symbol | Sector | Price | Market Cap | Beta Coeff | EPS | Estimated EPS | P/E (TTM) |
|---|---|---|---|---|---|---|---|---|
| Chevron | CVX | Integrated Oil | $116.20 | $227.4B | 1.2 | $2.57 | $3.04 | 9.52 |
| ConocoPhillips | COP | Integrated Oil | $ 61.06 | $ 74.1B | 1.4 | $1.44 | $1.44 | 7.53 |
| Intel | INTC | Semiconductors | $ 20.96 | $104.3B | 1.0 | $0.48 | $0.41 | 9.83 |
| Northrop Grumman | NOC | Defense | $ 67.74 | $16.63B | 1.1 | $1.82 | $1.72 | 8.9 |
| Raytheon | RTN | Defense | $ 55.88 | $18.43B | 0.7 | $1.47 | $1.31 | 9.89 |
| Seagate Technology | STX | Computer Hardware | $ 37.25 | $14.06B | 2.7 | $1.45 | $1.27 | 4.9 |

## Reasons for Selecting These Stocks

Using a stock screener on CNBC's website, the list of stocks in Table 9.4 was produced with the following criteria: a dividend yield of greater than 3 percent, return on equity greater than 15 percent, P/E ratio of less than 10, market cap greater than $10B, and company membership in the S&P 500 Index. From this list the fundamental value for each of the stocks was considered. Chevron and ConocoPhillips are among the largest global companies in their sectors. Future growth in supply of basic materials and oil would not keep up with the growth in demand from the emerging economies of China, India, Brazil, and Russia when the world economy begins to grow again. Intel, a leader in the semiconductor industry, an under-loved stock, was trading at or near its 52-week low, with a dividend yield of 4.29 percent. The defense industry has two value stocks that make the list: Northrop Grumman and Raytheon. Northrop Grumman is a leading defense company that provides innovative products, solutions, and systems in unmanned systems and cyber security. Raytheon is the largest missile maker, with back orders of products well into 2014. Both companies can benefit from growth coming from international buyers of their products, even if there is a downturn in orders from the United States due to budget cuts. The computer hardware sector has fallen out of favor because of Hewlett-Packard and Dell's inability to offer up innovative products to compete with the likes of Apple's products, such as the iPad. As a result hard disk manufacturers such as Seagate Technology and Western Digital have been punished unfairly and offer opportunities for investors. Seagate Technology was only trading at 4.9 times its trailing earnings as of January 27, 2013.

Over long periods, earnings drive the growth in stock prices. Look for companies that will be able to sustain increased earnings over long periods of time. Companies with three-year growth rates that were in excess of their P/E ratios were chosen.

The dividend yield is another measure of value. All the stocks selected had dividend yields in excess of 3 percent. Stocks with high dividend yields are attractive to value investors, who can collect the dividends while waiting for capital appreciation.

# CHAPTER 10

# Using Mutual Funds

**M**utual funds have come close to providing the ideal type of investment for millions of people who do not want to manage their own investments. The managers of these funds invest shareholders' money in diversified portfolios of stocks, bonds, and money market instruments. Investors receive shares in these mutual funds related to the size of their investments. Thus, even with a modest investment, an investor owns a share of a diversified portfolio of stocks or bonds. An advantage of this type of investment is that investors— who do not have the time to manage their financial investments or knowledge of the individual financial securities—can invest their money in diversified stock, bond, and money market portfolios of mutual funds. In other words, value investors can choose mutual funds that conform to their style of investing instead of choosing individual stocks, bonds, and money market securities to invest in. However, value investors need to be aware of the strengths and weaknesses of mutual funds before investing in them.

Studies have shown that stock mutual funds have underperformed the market averages over long periods. Research by Standard & Poor's on equity mutual funds found that very few mutual funds consistently outperform the markets. The small number of funds that did consistently perform well had a common theme: low expense ratios. For this reason many investors have turned to exchange-traded funds as a popular investment alternative, which is discussed in Chapter 12.

With so many mutual funds to choose from, investors should be as careful in their selection of mutual funds as they are in investing in individual securities. Three steps can facilitate the choice of which fund to invest in:

1. Understand how these funds work.

2. Determine what the objectives of the funds are and the types of investments they make.

3. Evaluate the fund's performance from their prospectuses and other sources.

## FUNDS AND HOW THEY WORK

The investment company that sponsors a mutual fund sells shares to investors and then invests the funds that are received in a portfolio of securities. By pooling investors' funds, a fund manager can diversify the purchase of different securities, such as stocks for stock funds and bonds for bond funds. The objectives of a fund determine the types of investments chosen. For example, if a stock fund's objective is to provide capital appreciation, the fund invests in growth stocks.

Dividends from stocks in the portfolio are passed through to the fund's shareholders as dividends. An investor who invests $1,000 gets the same rate of return as another investor who invests $100,000 in the same fund, except the latter shareholder receives a dividend that is 100 times greater (proportionate to the share ownership in the fund).

When prices of securities owned by the mutual fund in the portfolio fluctuate, the total value of the fund is affected. Many different factors—such as the intrinsic risk of the types of securities in the portfolio, in addition to economic, market, and political factors— cause these price fluctuations. The fund's objectives are important because they indicate the type and quality of the investments chosen by the fund. From these objectives, investors can better assess the overall risk the fund is willing to take to improve income (return) and capital gains.

Investment companies offer four different types of funds:

- Open-end mutual fund
- Closed-end fund
- Unit Investment trust (UIT)
- Exchange-traded fund (ETF), most of which are sponsored by brokerage firms and banks.

Closed-end funds, unit investment trusts, and ETFs are discussed in Chapters 11 and 12.

## BASIC OPEN-END FUNDS

Open-end funds issue unlimited numbers of shares. Investors can purchase more shares from the mutual fund company and sell them back to the fund company, which means that the number of shares will increase or decrease, respectively. A closed-end fund issues a fixed number of shares; when all the shares are sold, no more are issued. In other words, closed-end funds have fixed capital structures.

Shares are bought in an open-end mutual fund at its *net asset value* (NAV), which is the market value of the fund's assets at the end of each trading day minus any liabilities divided by the number of outstanding shares.

Open-end funds determine the market value of their assets at the end of each trading day. For example, a balanced fund, which invests in both common stocks and bonds, uses the closing prices of the stock and bond holdings for the day to determine market value. The number of shares of each of the stocks and the number of bonds that the fund owns is multiplied by the closing prices. The resulting total of each investment is added together, and any liabilities associated with the fund (such as accrued expenses) are subtracted. The resulting total net assets are divided by the number of shares outstanding in the fund to equal the NAV price per share. Table 10.1 shows how NAV is determined.

**TABLE 10.1**

How the Net Asset Value of a Fund Is Determined

| | | |
|---|---|---|
| Market Value of Stocks and Bonds in the Fund | $100,000,000 | |
| Minus Total Liabilities | −      150,000 | |
| Net Worth | $  99,850,000 | |
| Number of Shares Outstanding | $    7,500,000 | |
| Net Asset Value | $        13.313 | (99,850,000/7,500,000) |

The net asset value changes daily because of market fluctuations of the stock and bond prices in the fund. Net asset values are important because:

1. The NAV is used to determine the value of your holdings in the mutual fund (the number of shares held multiplied by the NAV price per share).

2. The NAV is the price at which new shares are purchased or redeemed.

Net asset values of the different funds are quoted in daily newspapers or on the fund's website.

Mutual funds pay no taxes on income derived from their investments. Under the IRS Tax Code, mutual funds serve as conduits through which income from investments is passed to shareholders in the form of dividends and capital gains or losses. Individual investors pay taxes on income and capital gains distributions from mutual funds.

Shareholders receive monthly and annual statements showing purchases and sales of shares, interest income, dividends, capital gains and losses, and other relevant data that they should retain for tax purposes. In addition, when investing in mutual funds, investors should keep track of the NAV prices of shares purchased and sold. This information is used in the computation of gains and losses when shares are redeemed.

The value of a mutual fund increases when:

- Interest and dividends earned on the fund's investments are passed through to shareholders.

- The fund's management sells investment securities at a profit. The capital gains from the sale are passed through to shareholders. If securities are sold at a loss, the capital loss is offset against the gains of the fund and the net gain or loss is passed through to shareholders.

- The NAV per share increases.

## TYPES OF MUTUAL FUNDS

Investors can invest in stock funds, bond funds, money market funds, hybrid funds, and commodity funds. Table 10.2 shows the different types of equity fund classifications based on investment objectives.

A stock mutual fund specializes in stock investments. Stock funds vary with regard to the types of stocks the funds choose for their portfolios and are guided by the fund's investment objectives. The SEC requires that funds disclose their objectives. For example, a fund might have the objective to seek growth through maximum capital gains. This type of fund would appeal to more aggressive investors who can withstand the risk of loss because of the speculative nature of the stocks of the unseasoned, small companies in which the fund invests.

A conservative equity fund's objectives are geared more toward providing current income than capital growth. This type of fund invests in dividend-paying stocks, which would also provide for capital appreciation, even though that might not be a primary objective. Growth and income funds seek a balance between providing capital gains and providing current income.

Equity funds can also be classified according to investment style, namely, growth or value stocks, or a blend of both. Value stocks have financial characteristics different from growth stocks.

## TABLE 10.2

Types of Equity Mutual Funds

| Fund Type | Objectives |
|---|---|
| Aggressive-growth | Seek maximum capital gains; invest in stocks of companies in new industries and out of favor companies. |
| Growth | Seek an increase in value through capital gains; invest in stocks of growth companies and industries that are more mainstream than those chosen by aggressive growth funds. |
| Growth and income | Seek an increase in value through capital gains and dividend income; invest in stocks of companies with a more consistent track record than those selected for growth and aggressive growth funds. |
| Income equity | Invest in stocks of companies that pay dividends. |
| Index | Invest in securities that replicate the market; for example, S&P 500 Index, Dow Jones Industrial Average. |
| International equity | Invest in stocks of companies outside the United States. |
| Global equity | Invest in stocks of companies both inside and outside the United States. |
| Emerging market | Invest in stocks of companies in developing countries. |
| Sector | Invest in stocks in the sector of the economy stated in the fund's objectives; for example, energy, health care sector, technology, and precious metals. |
| Balanced | Seek to provide value through income and principal conservation; invest in common stocks, preferred stocks, and bonds. |
| Asset allocation | Invest in securities (stocks, bonds, and money market) according to either a fixed or variable formula. |
| Corporate bond | Seek high levels of income. Invest in corporate bond issues. |

| Fund Type | Objectives |
|-----------|------------|
| High-yield bond funds | Seek higher yields by investing in below investment grade bonds (junk bonds). |
| Municipal bond funds | Seek income exempt from federal taxes. Invest in bonds issued by states and local governments. |
| U.S. government bond funds | Invest in different types of government bond securities such as Treasury securities, agency securities, and federally backed mortgage securities. |
| GNMA funds | Invest in Government National Mortgage Association securities and other mortgage-backed securities. |
| Global bond funds | Invest in the bonds of corporations and governments around the world, including the United States. |
| Money market funds | Invest in money market securities with maturities of one year or less. |
| Hedge | Invest in securities (stocks and bonds) and derivative securities to hedge against downturns in the market, interest rate changes, and currency values. |

Value stocks generally pay dividends and have low P/E ratios, while growth stocks have high P/E ratios and the companies tend to have high sales growth rates for a specified period.

Investing in equity funds does not immunize you from the volatility in the markets. In a market downturn, the more speculative stocks in the funds' portfolios generally decline more than established blue chip stocks. Share prices of aggressive funds are therefore much more volatile than share prices of conservative stock funds.

An index fund is a mutual fund that includes a portfolio of securities designed to match the performance of the market as a whole. An index fund tracks an underlying market index and seeks to match the returns of that particular market index. For example, the S&P 500 Index Fund invests in the stocks of the S&P 500 Index.

This strategy does not require active management of the assets in the fund because turnover is low. The stocks are held in the fund until they drop out of the index. Only then are changes made to the fund. The enthusiasm for index funds has spurred growth into other areas, such as mid- and small-cap stocks and emerging markets in Europe, Asia, and the Pacific Rim.

A combined stock and bond fund is called a *balanced fund*. Balanced funds invest in a mixture of stocks and bonds. The equity portion of a fund aims to provide capital growth, and the fixed-income investments provide income for shareholders. The range of percentages allocated to stocks and bonds are stated in the fund's prospectus.

Generally, the riskier the securities held in a fund, the greater the potential return and the greater the potential loss. This statement is true for all types of funds, including stock funds.

Fixed income funds invest primarily in bonds and preferred stocks. Bond funds can invest in taxable bonds such as Treasury securities and U.S. agency bonds. Corporate bond funds also provide taxable income. Tax-free bond funds include municipal bond funds; the interest received on the bonds are exempt from federal taxes and may also be exempt from state and local taxes if issued in that state and locality.

Much has been written about hedge funds since the disaster at Long-Term Capital Management, a Connecticut hedge fund that had to be bailed out by 14 financial institutions. Long-Term Capital Management suffered heavy losses in its positions on Russian bonds because of adverse swings in the prices in the currency markets. Yet, in 2001, the Dow Jones Total Stock Market Index of U.S. stocks declined by 12 percent, while hedge funds gained 4.4 percent, as measured by the CSFB/Tremont Hedge Fund Index.[1] Hedge funds have been the preferred investment for wealthy investors, but they are prone to charging high fees and their investment returns have been erratic. According to indexer Hedge Fund Research, hedge funds earned 33 percent returns since March 2009 as compared to 110 percent returns for the S&P 500 Index. In 2012 hedge funds rose by 4 percent as compared to 15 percent for the S&P 500 Index.[2]

## WHAT IS A HEDGE FUND?

A hedge fund is not a mutual fund. Hedge funds with fewer than 99 investors are *not* required to register with the SEC. Hedge funds cater to wealthy investors who have a significant net worth ($1.5 million) and are willing to invest $1 million or more. With the negative stock market returns in 2001 and 2002, hedge funds attracted large amounts of new capital and a broader-based clientele. Although returns for hedge funds were low (1–2 percent) or flat for 2001, they were nevertheless much better than the double-digit losses posted by most mutual funds for the same period. The reason is that hedge funds can take both long and short positions in stocks, while mutual fund managers can only take long positions. In addition, hedge fund managers can use borrowed money, which can increase their returns. These positive returns resulted in the introduction of mini-hedge funds in 2002, a new investment product offered by Wall Street. This type of fund requires a relatively low investment of $250,000, even though investors still must have significant assets to withstand any potential risk of loss.[3] However, the combination of long and short positions of hedge funds did not perform as well as mutual funds in a rising stock market.

A hedge fund is a specialized open-end fund that allows its manager to take a variety of investment positions in the market to seek higher-than-average potential gains with exposure to greater-than-average risk. U.S. hedge funds, which have been in existence for almost 50 years, typically take the form of limited partnerships. Hedge funds have numerous investment styles, including market-neutral strategies, in addition to high- and low-risk strategies. Hedge funds, because they are not as heavily regulated as mutual funds, do not have the same limits on the types of investments they can make and have less stringent disclosure requirements. Investors are limited in how they can withdraw funds. Many hedge funds allow investors to withdraw money only at the end of the year. Others may only allow investors to withdraw money at the end of the year or at the end of each quarter.[4]

Value investors might want to explore building their own portfolios replicating the hedge fund of interest using low-cost exchange-traded funds (ETFs), thereby avoiding the high fees charged by hedge funds and avoiding any restrictions on withdrawing their money. The first step in a replication strategy is to understand the makeup of the hedge fund portfolio and the forces that drive returns. Generally, a replication strategy tries to avoid the extreme positions in the portfolio (the positions that can lead to enormous gains and losses). By aiming for the middle positions in the hedge fund, the replication strategy avoids the extreme volatility of the performance of the hedge fund and also avoids the high fees charged by hedge funds, typically 2 percent of assets and 20 percent of profits, and avoids the high minimum investment amounts ($250,000 to $1 million).[5] Some of the low-cost ETFs that can be used to replicate the investments made by hedge funds are: the Russell 3000 Index (includes 98 percent of the U.S. stock market), the iShares Russell 3000 Growth Index (ETF), and the Vanguard Russell 3000 ETF.

Before investing in a hedge fund:

- Read the offering documents.

- Evaluate the hedge fund's risk and use of leverage.

- Understand how long your money will be tied up before you can redeem your funds.

- Ask whether there are any side-letter agreements that offer some investors lower fees and other benefits.[6]

- Understand how the hedge fund makes its money and mimic the hedge fund with cheaper investments.[7]

# AN ANALYSIS OF THE PROSPECTUS CAN ASSIST IN THE CHOICE OF A FUND

The best place to learn more about a particular fund is from its prospectus. The SEC requires that investors receive a prospectus before investing or soon afterward. A prospectus is a formal written document listing relevant information about the fund, the fund's goals, the strategies for achieving those goals, securities held by the fund, risk, historical returns, fees charged, and financial data.

A prospectus contains the following information:

- Objectives
- Strategies for achieving the objectives
- Overall risk
- Performance and fees

## Objectives

The objectives define what the fund aims to achieve and the types of investments it will choose to achieve those stated goals. A fund's objectives can be broadly phrased; the most common are:

1. To seek long-term capital appreciation through the growth of the fund's value over a period of time.

2. To seek current income through investments that generate dividends and to preserve investors' principal.

## Strategies

A fund's strategy reveals the steps its manager might take in achieving its objectives. For example, the manager of a stock fund might buy growth or value stocks of companies with a particular size capitalization (small-cap, medium-cap, or large-cap stocks). Thus, a value investor looking for a large-cap value fund can compare the different funds offering these types of securities.

## Overall Risk

A fund's objectives describe the types of securities in which the fund invests, in addition to the risk factors associated with them. The types of securities in which the fund invests outline its overall risk. For example, if a prospectus states that its fund invests in growth securities, you should not be surprised to find that most of the stocks will have high P/E ratios and can include riskier small-cap stocks. Consequently, a decline in growth stock prices would cause investors in this fund to lose money. A fund's investment policies outline the latitude the fund manager has to invest in other types of securities, including options to hedge bets (on the direction of interest rates or the market), and investing in derivative securities to boost the yield of the fund. Many conservative funds, which supposedly only hold blue chip stocks, have occasionally resorted to small-company and offshore stocks to boost their returns. The greater the latitude fund managers have in investing in these other types of securities, the greater the risk.

Another measure of risk is how diversified the fund is. If the fund cannot invest more than 5 percent of its assets in the securities of one company, it is a diversified fund. However, if a fund has no limits, the fund manager can choose to invest in a few securities, which greatly increases the risk of loss if one of those investments declines significantly.

## Performance and Fees

The overall performance of a fund pertains to these concepts:

- Total return
- Expenses

Funds are required by the SEC to provide annualized returns. These returns can be presented in a table or graphically, showing results for one year, five years, and ten years. New funds provide their returns from the date of inception. These returns are presented on a before-tax basis and an after-tax basis, which shows how tax efficient the fund is. Funds also must compare their returns to an appropriate market index.

Many funds can boast they have attained the number-one position in some area of performance at some point during their existence. Note, however, that good past performance might not be indicative of good future performance. Some funds that did well in the past no longer even exist.

Several business magazines track the overall performance records of many mutual funds during up and down markets. These performance results are a better yardstick to use than the advertising messages of the mutual funds themselves. From these publications, you can see how well funds have performed in up markets and how the funds protected their capital during periods of declining prices. New funds do not have track records, meaning that their performance during a period of declining prices might not be available. That is especially true for funds that come into existence during a bull market.

Organizations such as Morningstar (www.morningstar.com) rate a mutual fund's performance relative to other funds with the same investment objectives. However, this rating can be misleading when you are trying to choose a fund. First, the funds might not be comparable, even though they have similar objectives. For example, one fund might have riskier assets than another. Second, past performance might not be a reliable indicator of future performance.

In choosing a fund, you should look at what the fund invests in (as much as can be determined), and then try to determine the volatility in terms of up and down markets.

## Total Return

Yield is a measure of the fund's dividend distribution over a 30-day period. It is only one aspect of the fund's total return, however. Mutual funds pass on to shareholders any gains or losses, which can increase or decrease the fund's total return. Another factor that affects total return is the fluctuation in NAV. When the share price increases by 6 percent, it effectively increases the total return by an additional 6 percent. Similarly, a decline in the NAV price of a fund

**TABLE 10.3**

How the Total Return on a Fund Is Determined

| The total return of a mutual fund includes the following three components: |
| --- |
| Dividends and capital gains or losses |
| Changes in net asset value |
| Dividends (interest) on reinvested dividends |

decreases the total return. This concept explains why funds with positive yields can have negative total returns.

Interest on reinvested dividends is another factor that might be included in the total return. When dividends paid out by a fund are reinvested to buy more shares, the yield earned on these reinvested shares boosts the overall return on the invested capital.

## Expenses

Expenses are a key factor in differentiating the performances of different funds. By painstakingly looking for funds with the highest yields, you are looking at only half the picture. The fund with the highest yield might also be the one that charges the highest expenses, which could put that fund behind some lower-cost funds with lower yields. Fees reduce total returns earned by funds. You cannot count on future performance projections unless the fees and expenses charged by mutual funds are fairly consistent. A mutual fund prospectus has a separate table with a breakdown of expenses. This table typically shows the different charges paid for either directly by shareholders or out of shareholders' earnings in the fund: load charges, redemption fees, shareholder accounting costs, 12b-1 fees, distribution costs, and other expenses.

The mutual fund industry has been criticized for its proliferation of fees and charges. Granted, these are all disclosed by the mutual funds, but you need to know where to look to find the less obvious ones.

## Load Funds versus No-Load Funds

A no-load fund is one whose shares are sold without a sales charge. In other words, you do not pay any fees to buy or sell shares in that fund. With an investment of $10,000 in a no-load fund, every cent of the $10,000 is used to buy shares in the fund. No-load funds sell directly to investors at the NAV per share.

A load fund's shares are sold to investors at a price that includes a sales commission. The selling or offer price exceeds the NAV. These fees can be quite substantial, ranging to as much as 8.5 percent of the purchase prices of the shares. The amount of the sales (load) charge per share can be determined by deducting the NAV price from the offer price. Table 10.4 illustrates how to determine the effective load charge of a fund. Some funds give quantity discounts on their loads to investors who buy shares in large blocks. For example, a sales load might be 5 percent for amounts less than $100,000, 4.25 percent for investments between $100,000 to $200,000, and 3.5 percent for amounts in excess of $200,000. Investors buying load funds need to determine whether a load is also charged on reinvested dividends.

Funds can also charge a *back-load* or exit fee, which affects investors selling shares in the fund. A back-load is a fee charged when shareholders sell their shares. The back-load can be a straight percentage, or the percentage can decline the longer the shares have been held in the fund. For example, if you sell $10,000 in a mutual fund with a 3 percent redemption fee, you only receive $9,700 $(10,000 - [0.03 \times 10,000])$.

The ultimate effect of a load charge is to reduce the total return. The effect is felt more keenly if the fund is held for a short time. For example, if a fund has a return of 6 percent and charges a 4 percent load to buy into the fund, your total return for the year is sharply reduced. If you must pay a back-load to exit a fund, this charge could be even more expensive than a front-end load when the share price has increased. This is because the load percentage is calculated on a larger amount.

You should not be fooled by funds that tout themselves as no-load funds but assess fees by other names that come right out of

How to Determine the Effective Load Charge

A mutual fund quotes its load charge as a percentage of its offer price, which understates the real charge paid by investors. For example, a mutual fund with a load charge of 5% and the NAV of the fund is quoted in the newspapers at $25 per share. The load is based on the offer price, which is determined as follows:

$$\text{Offer price} = \frac{\text{Net Asset Value}}{(1 - \text{load percent})}$$

$$= \frac{25}{(1 - .05)}$$

$$= \$26.32$$

The investor pays a load fee of $1.32 per share ($26.32 − $25.00), which is a 5% charge of the offer price. However, this load charge as a percentage of the net asset value is higher than 5%.

$$\text{Effective load charge} = \frac{\text{Load charge}}{\text{Net asset value}}$$

$$= \frac{\$1.32}{25.00}$$

$$= 5.28\%$$

investors' pockets, just like loads. Their uses are to defray some of the costs of opening accounts or buying stocks for the fund's portfolio. The fees vary from 1 to 3 percent among the different fund groups. From an investor's point of view, the lofty purpose of these fees should not matter. They reduce the amount of the investment.

Why, then, do so many people invest in load funds when these commissions eat away so much of their returns? Some possible answers are:

- Investors do not want to make decisions about which funds to invest in, so they leave them to their brokers or financial planners.

- Brokers and financial planners earn their living from selling investments from which they are paid commissions. These investments include only load funds and funds that pay commissions out of 12b-1 fees. These funds are promoted as the best ones to buy.

- No-load funds and funds that do not pay commissions to brokers and financial planners are not promoted or sold by brokers and financial planners.

No evidence exists to support the opinions expressed by many brokers and financial planners that load funds outperform no-load funds. According to a study on the long-term performance of mutual funds, there was no statistical difference between the performance of no-load funds and load funds over a ten-year period.[8] However, after adjusting for sales commissions, investors would have been better off with no-load funds.

A 12b-1 fee is a charge a mutual fund can take from investment assets to cover marketing and distribution expenses. A 12b-1 fee is less obvious than a load. This type of fee, assessed annually, can be steep when added to a load fee. Many no-load funds boast the absence of sales commissions and then tack on 12b-1 fees, which resemble hidden loads. A 1 percent 12b-1 fee might not sound like much, but it results in $100 per year less in your pocket on a $10,000 mutual fund investment.

In addition to the above-mentioned charges, funds have *management fees*, which are paid to the people who administer the fund's portfolio of investments. These fees can range from a 0.5 to 2 percent of assets. High management fees also take a toll on an investor's total return.

All fees bear watching because they reduce yields and total returns. Critics of the mutual fund industry have cultivated a sense of awareness regarding the proliferation of these charges. Indeed, do not be deceived by funds that claim to be what they are not. Lowering or eliminating front-end loads doesn't mean that a fund cannot add fees somewhere else. Many new funds waive some of their fees. Check to see whether and when these waivers are set to expire or whether they can be revoked.

A fund has to disclose its fees. You can find management fees, 12b-1 fees, redemption fees (back-loads), and any other fees charged somewhere in the fund's prospectus.

## Selected per Share Data and Ratios

Table 10.5 summarizes a typical fund's performance over the periods shown, information that can be found in the fund's prospectus or annual report. Although the selected per share data vary in detail from fund to fund, the format is essentially the same.

The Investment Activities section in Table 10.5 shows the amount of investment income earned on the securities held by the fund; this income is passed on to the fund's shareholders. For instance, in 2013 all of the net investment income of $0.37 was distributed to the shareholders (line 4), but in 2012 only $0.30 of the $0.31 of net income was paid out to shareholders. In 2012 the $0.01, which was not distributed to shareholders, increased the NAV (line 7) in the capital changes section. (The capital loss and distribution of gains were reduced by this $0.01, because it was not distributed.)

Capital gains and losses also affect the net asset value. Funds distribute their realized capital gains (line 6), but the unrealized capital gains or losses also increase or decrease the net asset value.

Changes in the NAV from year to year give some idea of the volatility in share price. For instance, for the year 2012 the NAV decreased by $1.01, which is a 9.17 percent decrease. If you invest $10,000 knowing it could decline to $9,082.65, how comfortable would you feel with this investment in the short term?

The portfolio turnover rate gives prospective investors an idea of how actively the investment assets in a fund are traded. A turnover rate of 100 percent indicates that the investment assets are sold an average of once during the year. For example, if a fund holds stocks with a value of $100 million, that means $100 million of stocks are traded once a year, with a 100 percent turnover rate. According to the Vanguard summary report, the Vanguard Equity Income Fund, a large-cap value fund, had a relatively low portfolio turnover rate of 26 percent in 2012. By comparison, the portfolio turnover rate for the Vanguard Growth Equity Fund

## TABLE 10.5

Selected per Share Data and Ratios

|  | 2013 | 2012 | 2011 |
|---|---|---|---|
| **NAV** | | | |
| Beginning of the year | 10.02 | 11.01 | 10.73 |
| **Investment Activities** | | | |
| line 1 Income | .40 | .35 | .55 |
| line 2 Expenses | (.03) | (.04) | (.05) |
| line 3 Net investment income | .37 | .31 | .50 |
| line 4 Distribution of dividends | (.37) | (.30) | (.47) |
| **Capital Changes** | | | |
| line 5 Net realized and unrealized gains (losses) on investments | 1.00 | (.75) | 1.50 |
| line 6 Distributions of realized gains | (.70) | (.25) | (1.25) |
| line 7 Net increase (decrease) to NAV | .30 | (.99) | .28 |
| NAV at beginning of year | 10.02 | 11.01 | 10.73 |
| NAV at end of year | 10.32 | 10.02 | 11.01 |
| Ratio of operating expenses to average net assets | .53% | .56% | .58% |
| Ratio of net investment income to average net assets | .45% | .46% | .84% |
| Portfolio turnover rate | 121% | 135% | 150% |
| Shares outstanding (000) | 10,600 | 8,451 | 6,339 |

was 40 percent during 2012. High portfolio turnover (more than 200 percent) might not necessarily be bad for shareholders in that the fund might be generating high capital gains, but the fund is also generating higher transaction costs when it buys and sells stocks in the portfolio.

High turnover is an indication, however, for shareholders to expect capital gains distributions by the end of the year. In accounting terms the amount of the distribution per share is deducted from the NAV of the shares in the fund.

Index funds have extremely low turnover rates, around 5 percent. The Vanguard 500 Index Fund had a portfolio turnover rate of 4 percent in 2012. The advantages of lower turnover are decreased costs and greater tax efficiency. A fund might also have low turnover because it has been holding low-performing stocks for a long time in the hopes of a turnaround.

The ratio of operating expenses to average net assets is fairly low in the example in table 10.5 (close to half of 1 percent).

You can determine an average total return by considering the three types of return on a mutual fund: dividends distributed, capital gains distributed, and changes in share price, by using the following formula:

$$\text{Average total return} = \frac{\left(\begin{array}{c}\text{Dividend +}\\ \text{Capital gains +}\\ \text{distributions}\end{array}\right) + \dfrac{\text{Ending NAV + Beginning NAV}}{\text{year}}}{\dfrac{\text{Ending NAV + Beginning NAV}}{2}}$$

$$\text{Average total return for 2006} = \frac{(.37 + .70) + \dfrac{[10.32 - 10.02]}{1}}{\dfrac{(10.32 + 10.02)}{2}}$$

$$= 13.50\%$$

This simple 13.5 percent yield indicates that an investor in this fund received double-digit returns mainly because of gains realized and increases in the NAV share price. The more volatile the net asset value of the fund is, the greater the likelihood of unstable returns.

Value investors always want to compare the returns of the mutual funds they are interested in with benchmark funds before they invest. For example, the return of the Vanguard Equity Income Fund, a large-cap value fund, can be compared with the Russell 1000 Value Index for the same period. Similarly, the benchmark for comparison for the Vanguard Growth Equity Fund is the Russell 1000 Growth Index.

## THE RISKS OF MUTUAL FUNDS

The major risk of investing in a mutual fund is the risk of *loss of principal* owing to a decline in net asset value. Many types of risk exist with regard to mutual funds: interest rate risk, market risk, and quality of the securities, to name a few. Rising market interest rates tend to depress both the stock and the bond markets, resulting in a decline in the NAV of stock and bond funds. A decline in market rates of interest has the opposite effect: it results in an appreciation of stock and bond prices and, consequently, the NAV of stock and bond mutual funds.

The *quality* of the securities in which the fund invests determines the volatility of the fund's price swings. Stock funds that invest in small-company and emerging growth stocks see greater upward swings in price during bull markets and greater downward swings during bear markets than conservative income equity funds, which invest in the stocks of larger, more established companies. Some small-cap funds have invested in small-cap stocks of dubious value, which has caused some losses.

With bank failures in the past and the shaky financial status of some savings and loan associations in the United States, investors are naturally concerned about the *risk of insolvency* of mutual funds. A mutual fund can always "go under," but the chance of it happening is small. The key distinction between banks and mutual funds is the way in which mutual funds are set up, which reduces the risk of failure and loss due to fraud.

Mutual funds are typically corporations owned by shareholders. A separate management company is contracted by shareholders to run the fund's daily operations. Although a management company oversees the fund's investments, the company does not have possession of these assets (investments). A custodian, such as a bank, holds the investments. Therefore, if a management company gets into financial trouble, it does not have access to the fund's investments. Yet, even with these checks and balances, the possibility of fraud always exists. The SEC cleared two mutual funds whose prices were quoted in the financial newspapers along with all the other mutual funds, but they turned out to be bogus.

A transfer agent maintains shareholders' accounts and keeps track of shareholders' purchases and redemptions. In addition, management companies carry fidelity bonds, a form of insurance to protect the investments of the fund against malfeasance or fraud perpetrated by its employees.

Along with these safeguards, two other factors differentiate mutual funds from corporations such as banks and savings and loan associations:

- Mutual funds must be able to redeem shares on demand, which means that a portion of its investment assets must be liquid.

- Mutual funds must be able to price their investments at the end of each day, known as *marking to market*. This adjustment of market values of investments at the end of the trading day reflects gains and losses.

For these reasons, mutual funds cannot hide their financial difficulties as easily as banks and savings and loans can.

The SEC regulates mutual funds, but fraudulent operators can always find a way into any industry. Although the risk of fraud is always present, it is no greater in the mutual fund industry than in any other. Above all, you should be aware that you can lose money through purchasing a fund whose investments perform poorly on the markets.

## THE TAX CONSEQUENCES OF BUYING AND SELLING SHARES IN A MUTUAL FUND

Tax reporting on mutual funds can be complicated. At the end of the year, the mutual fund sends to each mutual fund shareholder a Form 1099 showing the amount of dividends and capital gains received during the year. Individual shareholders pay taxes on their dividends and capital gains. When you automatically reinvest your dividends and capital gains in your funds, these amounts need to be added into the cost basis. The cost basis is also affected when you sell shares in the fund.

Suppose you invested $10,000 in a fund two years ago and have reinvested a total of $2,000 in dividends and capital gains in the fund to date. You then sell all shares in the fund and receive $14,000. Your cost basis is $12,000 (not $10,000), and the gain on the sale of the shares is $2,000 ($14,000 − $12,000).

When you sell only a portion of your total shares, the calculation is different and can be tricky. It is further complicated when you actively buy and sell shares as though the fund were a checking account. In fact, many mutual funds encourage you to operate your funds just that way by providing check-writing services. Every time you write a check against a bond or stock fund, a capital gain or loss tax consequence occurs. (This does not include money market funds, which have a stable share price of $1.) These actions can cause a nightmare at tax time and produce extra revenue for your accountant for the additional time spent calculating gains and losses. Consequently, you need to keep records of your mutual fund transactions by saving all the monthly statements showing purchases and sales of shares, dividends, and capital gain distributions.

From these records you can determine the cost basis of shares sold, using an average cost method, the FIFO method, or the specific identification method:

The FIFO method (first-in, first-out) uses the cost of the first shares purchased in the fund as the first to be sold. Table 10.6 illustrates the FIFO method of calculating a capital gain or loss on the partial sale of shares in a mutual fund. The example shows that the earliest shares purchased are the first to be used in the sale of shares. After all the shares of the invested funds are sold, the basis of the dividends and capital gain shares are used to determine any gain or loss. During periods of rising share prices, using this method results in the higher tax liability than the average cost method.

Average cost method is an accounting method in which the average cost per share is determined by dividing the number of shares available into the total cost of the shares in the fund. Several

## TABLE 10.6

Calculation of Gains/Losses on the Sale of Shares

| Summary of Growth and Income Fund | | | | | |
|---|---|---|---|---|---|
| Date | Transaction | Dollar Amount | Share Price | # of Shares | Total # Shares |
| 06/14 | Invest | $15,000 | $10.00 | 1,500 | 1,500 |
| 11/26 | Invest | 4,500 | 9.00 | 500 | 2,000 |
| 11/30 | Redeem (sell) | 18,600 | 12.00 | 1,550 | 450 |
| 12/31 | Dividends | 1,000 | 10.00 | 100 | 550 |
| **To Calculate Gain/Loss on a FIFO Basis** | | | | | |
| Sold | 1,550 shares at | $12.00 per share | **Sale Price** 18,600 | | |
| **Cost Basis** | | | | | |
| 06/14 | 1,500 shares at | $10.00 | $15,000 | | |
| 11/26 | 50 shares at | $9.00 | 450 | | |
| **Total Cost** | | | | 15,450 | |
| **Gain** | | | | 3,150 | |
| **Cost Basis of the Growth and Income Fund after Sale** | | | | | |
| Date | Transaction | Dollar Amount | Share Price | No. of Shares | Total # Shares |
| 11/26 | Invested | $4,050 | 9.00 | 450 | 450 |
| 12/31 | Dividends | 1,000 | 10.00 | 100 | 550 |

funds provide the gains and losses on an average cost basis when investors sell shares. The average cost method allows shareholders to average the cost of the shares in the fund. The average cost basis can get quite complex with additional sales and purchases of shares. Consequently, some funds don't provide average cost data after shareholders redeem shares in the fund.

The specific identification method allows shareholders to identify the specific shares they want to sell. You can minimize your gains by choosing to sell shares with the highest cost basis first. However, to get IRS acceptance of this method, you must specify to the fund in writing which shares are to be sold and must receive a written confirmation of the sale by the fund. If the specific shares are not identified, the IRS assumes the shares sold are the first acquired.

The specific identification method works as follows:

Suppose you buy 100 shares at $7 per share and six months later buy another 100 shares at $14 per share. You decide to sell 100 shares at $20 per share. If you specifically identify the shares bought at $14 per share, the capital gain is $6 per share ($20 −$14). Using the average cost method, the cost basis is $10.50 per share ($2,100/200shares) and the capital gain is $9.50 per share. Using FIFO, the shares sold are those purchased first at $7 per share, resulting in a gain of $13 per share.

If you use the average cost method to sell shares in a fund, you cannot switch to the specific identification method for subsequent sales. This limitation does not preclude that investor from choosing other methods to sell shares in any other funds she owns.

For individual stocks, investors cannot use the average cost method, but specific identification and FIFO methods are acceptable.

To minimize the complexities of computations, you are better off not writing checks on your stock or bond funds for your short-term cash needs. This practice only creates gains or losses. You are better served by investing the money needed for short-term purposes into a money market fund, which alleviates any complex tax calculations.

## Hidden Capital Gains

You have no control over the distribution of hidden capital gains from mutual funds, which can upset careful tax planning. Because investment companies do not pay taxes, all income and capital gains in the fund are passed through to shareholders. If a fund has bought and sold investments at a gain, those gains are passed on to shareholders when the fund distributes its gains. Shareholders are liable for the taxes on these capital gains even if the share price of the fund has dipped below the purchase price of the shares. The following example illustrates this concept.

Suppose you purchase 1,000 shares in a mutual fund at $10 per share. The next day the mutual fund distributes capital gains of $2 per share. The share price declines to $8 per share ($10 minus the $2 capital gain per share). You now have 1,250 shares at a NAV of $8 per share ($2,000 capital gain divided by $8 net asset value equals 250 shares). If you continue to hold the shares until year-end, you are liable for the taxes on the $2,000 distribution of capital gains. If you decide to sell all the shares in the fund when the distribution is made at the NAV of $8 per share, you receive $10,000 and experience a loss of $2,000 ($10,000 in proceeds minus the adjusted cost basis of shares is $12,000). This loss is offset by the capital gain distribution, and no tax consequences occur.

In another scenario, you hold the shares and the share price declines below $8 per share. You are still faced with $2,000 of capital gains, even though the principal is now less than the $10,000 invested. This happened at the end of 2010, when the stock market declined. Investors were saddled with capital gains distributions while their principal diminished because of the decline in their funds' NAV.

New investors should avoid buying into a mutual fund toward the end of the year because they can increase their tax burden from hidden capital gains. Before buying into a fund, investors should investigate whether the fund has accumulated any capital gains distributions that have not been distributed to shareholders. These gains are passed on to shareholders at the end of the year through a capital gains distribution, even if the shareholders did not own the fund when the gains were incurred.

## Hidden Capital Losses

Hidden capital losses have the opposite effect from hidden capital gains. For example, a mutual fund with a NAV of $10 per share at the beginning of the year might accumulate capital losses of $3 per share because of a declining market in which investments are sold at a loss during the year. If you purchased the shares at $10 per share and sell them at $7 per share, you have a capital loss of $3 per share. You can use this loss to offset capital gains or income up to the allowable limit ($3,000 for 2012). However, if you buy shares at $7 per share and then sell them later at $14 per share you have a capital gain of $4, not $7 per share; the fund has accumulated a $3 per share loss, which means that the adjusted cost basis of the shares in the fund is $10 (the capital loss is added to the cost of the shares).

Unrealized capital losses in a mutual fund offer potential tax savings for investors in a fund in the same way that unrealized capital gains offer tax liabilities.

---

## TAX-EFFICIENT INVESTING STRATEGIES

Successful investing requires building a portfolio of securities that can generate healthy after-tax returns for long periods of time. This is more than merely minimizing taxes on dividends received and capital gains. For stock investments, a tax minimization strategy would be to buy stocks that pay dividends and offer the prospects of capital gains because both dividends and long-term capital gains (if held for greater than a year) are taxed at lower rates than interest income. However, since the early 2000s, with the decline in the stock market, there has been a greater focus on dividend-paying stocks, which tend to drop less in price than growth stocks that don't pay dividends. Thus, one approach to a declining stock market is to focus on quality stocks that pay dividends.

Hold appreciated stocks for at least a year to take advantage of the favorable capital gains tax rates. If the stock has appreciated and the future prospects for the stock do not look good, sell the stock even if you have held it for less than a year. It is better to have short-term gains than long-term losses.

If you have stocks with losses and the stocks' future pros-pects are not good, sell them to take the losses. You can use these losses to offset capital gains. In addition, you can use losses exceeding capital gains to offset income up to $3,000 (married filing jointly) or carry the losses forward indefinitely to offset future gains. Timing your gains and losses can reduce the amount of your taxes. If you have large capital losses, you can sell stocks with large capital gains to offset those losses.

## SHOULD YOU INVEST IN INDIVIDUAL SECURITIES OR USE FUNDS?

Stock and bond mutual funds have been popular among investors, and record amounts have been invested in them over the years. The advantages of mutual funds, as stated earlier in this chapter, are the professional management, the diversification, the freedom to invest small amounts of money, and the ease of buying and selling. For many investors, these advantages far outweigh the disadvantages of mutual funds.

Mutual funds might be the most practical way for investors to buy many types of securities, including bonds that sell in high denominations (minimum investments of $50,000) and a diversi-fied portfolio of stocks. The decision of which individual stocks to invest in can be avoided by choosing equity mutual funds.

Diversification achieved by mutual funds minimizes the effect of any unexpected losses from individual stocks in the portfolio. The professional managers of these funds have quicker access to information about the different issues. The managers might react sooner in buying or selling the securities in question.

However, in certain cases a strong argument exists for buy-ing individual securities over mutual funds. The rates of return on individual stocks and bonds are often greater than those earned from mutual funds. This statement is true even for no-load funds because in addition to sales commissions, other fees, such as 12b–1 and operating fees, reduce the returns of mutual funds. By investing in individual securities, you avoid these fees. A study by

Malkiel[9] on the performance of equity mutual funds during the period 1971 through 1991 indicates that on a yearly basis throughout this period, the top-performing funds in one year could easily become under-performing funds in the next year. This phenomenon occurred more in the 1980s than in the 1970s.

If you have a small amount of money to invest, mutual funds are a better alternative. A $2,000 investment in a stock fund buys a fraction of a diversified portfolio of stocks, while in the case of individual securities, that amount might allow for buying only the shares of one equity company. Investing in mutual funds is a good strategy if you do not have enough money to diversify your investments, and do not have the time, expertise, or inclination to select and manage individual securities. In addition, a wide range of funds offers you the opportunity to invest in the types of securities that would be difficult to buy individually.

Table 10.7 compares some characteristics of investing in individual securities versus mutual funds, closed-end funds, and exchange-traded funds.

## TABLE 10.7

Characteristics of Individual Securities versus Mutual Funds

|  | **Individual Securities** | **Mutual Funds** |
|---|---|---|
| Diversification | Achieved only if a large number of securities is purchased | Achieved with a small investment |
| Ease of Buying and Selling | Easy to buy and sell stocks at real time prices during the trading day; more difficult to buy bonds | Easy to buy and sell shares. Trades occur only at the closing price at the end of the day |
| Professional Management | No | Yes |
| Expenses and Costs to Buy and Sell | Brokerage fees to buy and sell | Low to high expenses, depending on fund. |
| Tax Planning | Easier to predict income and plan capital gains and losses | Can upset careful tax planning due to unpredictable distributions of income and capital gains |

# WHAT VALUE INVESTORS SHOULD BE AWARE OF WHEN USING MUTUAL FUNDS

Value investors using mutual funds instead of individual investments still need to research the different mutual funds to find those that provide them with suitable investments.

1. The first step is to determine your objectives: whether you want preservation of capital, regular receipt of interest or dividend payments, or the generation of capital appreciation. If the objectives are preservation of capital, the investment options are mutual money market funds. The major disadvantage of money market mutual funds is the current (2013) near zero rates of interest, which translates into exceptionally low yields in money market funds (around three-tenths of 1 percent). The advantage is that principal invested remains intact, but there may be erosion in purchasing power over time if inflation raises its ugly head. Consequently, many investors may decide to invest their funds in short-term bond funds to earn a greater yield than money market funds, even if there is a risk of losing some principal as a result of inflation and rising interest rates.

   Objectives of investing for steady returns of income would use bond mutual funds, preferred stock, and value common stock funds that pay dividends. However, in February 2013, with interest rates at historic lows, Trim Tabs Investment Research estimated that record amounts of money flowed into U.S. equity mutual funds.[10] Money flowed from bond and money market funds into higher-yielding, dividend-paying equity mutual funds. For value investors such a scenario should raise red flags or danger signals. With all this liquidity flowing into stocks, it is not surprising that the stock market has reached a 13-year high as of February 2013. However, value investors are always looking for investments that provide value and are not trading at historically high prices. The goal is to buy undervalued stocks that present opportunities for increases rather than joining in the bandwagon that is late to the party, after stocks have already run up in price. Blend funds appeal to investors who want a combination of value and growth investments to give both income and capital appreciation.

Objectives of investing for capital appreciation would use equity growth funds and aggressive growth funds. Growth funds invest in growth stocks that may have low dividend yields or stocks that do not pay dividends. Aggressive growth stock funds invest in younger, more speculative companies that do not pay dividends. This latter type of fund is the most volatile in terms of price. Figure 10.1 summarizes investment objectives and the types of funds that are most aligned with these objectives.

2. The second step is to research all the mutual funds in which you are interested, Having determined your investment objectives, examine the prospectus of each mutual

**FIGURE 10.1**

Investor's Objectives and the Different Types of Mutual Funds

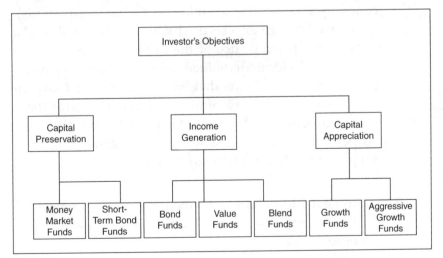

fund. Read carefully the strategy the fund outlines for achieving its stated objectives. Just because the name of the fund is value does not mean that the stocks owned in the fund are all value stocks. The fund manager might use small-cap growth and momentum stocks to boost the fund's performance. Consequently, as a value investor you should study the top holdings of each fund, even though mutual funds do not report their current holdings. The holdings reported by mutual funds are delayed by a financial quarter or as of the last report. If you think that the portfolio has great latitude to invest in riskier securities to obtain the stated objectives, you might consider this fund more risky than similar funds in which portfolio managers do not have this option. Studying the holdings of the fund and comparing them to others allows an investor to choose the fund with the holdings that the investor is most comfortable with. For example, during the financial crisis, some mutual funds held greater percentages of bank stocks, which resulted in the funds with the greater bank holdings declining more in price than other funds. You can also use the Morningstar style box in Chapter 9 (Table 9.1) to determine which equity style you want to invest in (value, blend, or growth, and then the choice of company size, small-cap, mid-cap, or large-cap funds). This style box can also be used with international funds. Look at the performance of the different styles. A value investor looks for undervalued stocks and would be reluctant to buy value funds that have outperformed growth stocks for several years. Similarly, a value investor looking for growth would not invest in growth funds that have outperformed value stocks for several years. You need to keep in mind that growth stock funds can also represent value.

3. Examine the fees charged by the funds you are interested in. Focus on no-load funds with the lowest overall total expense ratios.

4.  Examine the returns of all the funds you are interested in, and do not succumb to the temptation to pick the fund with the largest return for a one-year period. Extend the period to three to five years or longer so that you can see how the fund performed in both up and down markets.

5.  Don't buy mutual funds late in the year; the share price might include capital gains that have already been distributed, and you will end up paying the taxes for someone else's gains. Look at the fund's website for the capital gains distribution of the fund before investing.

# Using Closed-End Funds

**A** closed-end fund issues a fixed number of shares, and when all the shares are sold, no more are issued. Unlike open-end funds, closed-end funds have fixed capital structures. Investors who want to invest in closed-end funds after all the shares are sold (for the first time) have to buy them from shareholders who are willing to sell them in the market. Shares of closed-end funds are listed on stock exchanges and over-the-counter markets, while shares of open-end mutual funds are bought from and sold to the investment company sponsoring the fund. As a result, share prices of closed-end funds are a function of not only their net asset values but also the supply of, and demand for, the stock in the market. The discrepancies in price between market prices and net asset values of closed-end funds present opportunities for value investors.

A *unit investment trust* (UIT) is one type of closed-end fund. A UIT issues a fixed number of shares, which are originally sold by the sponsor of the trust. The proceeds from the sale are used to buy stocks or bonds for the trust, which are held to maturity. Unlike an open-end or closed-end fund, no active trading of the securities in the portfolio takes place. Consequently, no active management of the trust takes place, which should translate into lower management fees, although this is not always the case. A trust has a maturity date, and the proceeds are then returned to the shareholders of the trust.

## TABLE 11.1

Closed-End Funds versus Open-End Funds

| Closed-End Funds | Open-End Funds |
|---|---|
| 1. Issue a fixed number of shares, which are sold to original shareholders. | 1. Issue an unlimited number of shares. |
| 2. Shares (after issue) are traded on the stock exchanges. | 2. Shares (including new shares) may be bought from and sold to the fund. |
| 3. Shares may trade at, above, or below net asset values. | 3. Shares trade at net asset values. |
| 4. Share prices depend not only on the fundamentals, but also on supply and demand for the shares. | 4. Share prices depend on the fundamentals of the assets in the fund. |
| 5. Closed-end funds do not mature. Unit investment trusts do. | 5. Open-end funds do not mature except for zero-coupon bond funds. |

All UITs charge sales commissions, while investors in open-end funds have a choice between the purchase of a fund that does or does not charge a sales commission. Table 11.1 illustrates the differences between open-end and closed-end funds.

## CLOSED-END FUNDS

Closed-end funds have professional managers who assemble and manage the investment portfolios according to the goals and objectives of the funds. Unlike open-end funds, closed-end funds do not trade at their net asset values. Instead, their share prices are based on the supply of, and demand for, their funds and other fundamental factors. Consequently, closed-end funds can trade at premiums or discounts to their net asset values, as shown in Table 11.2. Closed-end fund prices can be obtained from financial newspapers or from websites on the Internet, such as Yahoo, Google, CNBC, and Morningstar.

## TABLE 11.2

Closed-End Fund Premiums and Discounts

| Company | Net Asset Value | Market Price* | Premium/Discount |
|---|---|---|---|
| Gabelli Equity Trust | 6.12 | 6.17 | 0.81% |
| ASA Bermuda Ltd. | 21.09 | 20.26 | −3.93% |

**How to Calculate the Discount or Premium**

$$\textbf{Premium / (Discount)} = \frac{\text{Market Price} - \text{Net Asset Value}}{\text{Net Asset Value}}$$

$$\text{Gabelli Trust} = \frac{6.17 - 6.12}{6.12}$$

Premium $= \underline{0.81\%}$

*Prices as of February 18, 2013

Shares of closed-end funds are bought and sold through brokers. Value investors should be aware of the following facts about the purchase of closed-end funds:

- Brokerage firms underwrite and sell newly issued shares of closed-end funds.

- The brokerage fees on these newly issued shares can be quite high, which erodes the price of the shares when they trade on the market. For example, if a closed-end fund sells 1 million shares at $10 per share and there is a brokerage commission of 7 percent, the fund receives $9.3 million to invest ($700,000 is deducted from the $10 million proceeds). The share price drops in value from the $10 originally paid and trades at a discount to the offer price.

- Another reason not to buy newly issued shares in a closed-end fund is that the portfolio of investments has not yet been constituted, so investors do not know what the investment assets are and, in the case of bond funds, the yields on those investments.

## What Value Investors Should Do Before Investing in Closed-End Funds

Most closed-end funds trade at a discount to their NAV. Consequently, as a value investor, you need to determine the reason why the fund is trading at a discount. The reasons are many (unpopularity of the type of holdings of the fund, uncertainty facing the fund, bad news causing more selling than buying) and you should seek out more information before buying. Even though it is tempting to acquire $1 of assets for less than $1, investors should seek more information from the fund's annual reports and prospectuses before investing.

As pointed out earlier, management fees can be high (1 to 2 percent), which diminish returns. Value investors can do well over long periods of time by investing in closed-end funds at a discount and holding them until their prices trade at premiums to their net asset values.

## UNIT INVESTMENT TRUSTS

UITs are registered investment companies that sell units (shares) of a relatively fixed investment portfolio consisting of bonds or stocks. They have a stated termination date on which the investments either mature or are liquidated. The proceeds are then returned to the unitholders (shareholders). Consequently, these trusts are well suited to bonds, with their streams of income and maturity of principal. With stock unit investment trusts, the stocks are sold at the termination date and the proceeds are returned to the unitholders. The majority of unit investment trusts sold consists of tax-exempt municipal bonds, followed by taxable bond trusts, and then equity (stock) trusts.

UITs are bought through brokers who sponsor their own trusts and through brokerage firms that represent the trusts. If you do not want to hold your trust through maturity, you can sell it back to the sponsor of the trust. The trust sponsors are required by law to buy the shares back at their net asset values, which can be more or less than the amount the investor paid initially. Under certain conditions shares of these trusts can be quite illiquid, particularly for bond trusts when interest rates are rising.

The same caveats apply for buying initial public offerings of UITs as for closed-end funds:

- Investors do not know the composition of the portfolio's investments.

- Investors pay sales charges or loads, which may be as much as 4 to 5 percent higher than the NAV.

In a UIT, the portfolio of investments generally does not change after purchase. In other words, no new securities are bought or sold. Theoretically, therefore, management fees should be lower on UITs than on closed-end funds because the portfolio remains unmanaged. The only time securities are sold in a UIT is generally when a severe decline in the quality of the issues occurs. While no management fees should be incurred on a UIT, that is not the case, and fees can be high.

## REAL ESTATE INVESTMENT TRUSTS (REITS)

A real estate investment trust (REIT) is a fund that buys and manages real estate and mortgages. REITs offer investors the opportunity to invest in real estate without having to own and manage individual properties. REITs were popular during the middle of 1996, when inflation was expected to surge. In 2001–2002, when the stock market declined, investors again turned to REITs as safe-haven investments. When interest rates declined in 2005–2006, REITs were among the top-performing sectors of the stock market. For the 10-year period from 2002 through 2012, returns from the Wilshire US Real Estate Securities Index outperformed the S&P 500 Index.

A REIT is a form of closed-end mutual fund, in that it invests in real estate the proceeds received from the initial sale of shares to shareholders. REITs buy, develop, and manage real estate properties and pass on to shareholders the income from the rent and mortgages in the form of dividends.

REITs do not pay corporate income taxes, but in return they must, by law, distribute 90 percent of their net income to shareholders. Consequently, not much income remains to finance future real estate acquisitions.

The following are three basic types of REITs:

- *Equity REITs* buy, operate, and sell real estate such as hotels, office buildings, apartments, and shopping centers.

- *Mortgage REITs* make construction and mortgage loans available to developers.

- *Hybrid REITs*, a combination of equity and mortgage REITs, buy, develop, and manage real estate and provide financing through mortgage loans. Most hybrid REITs have stronger positions in either equity or debt. Few well-balanced hybrid REITs exist.

The risks are not the same for each type of REIT, so you should evaluate each carefully before investing. Equity REITs generally tend to be less speculative than mortgage REITs, although the risk level depends on the makeup of the assets in the trust. Mortgage REITs lend money to developers, which involve a greater risk. Consequently, shares of mortgage REITs tend to be more volatile than shares of equity REITs, particularly during a recession.

Equity REITs have been the most popular type of REIT recently. They derive their income from rents received from the properties in their portfolios and from increasing property values.

Mortgage REITs are more sensitive than equity REITs to changes in interest rates. The reason is that they hold mortgages whose prices move in the opposite direction of interest rates. Although equity REITs might be less sensitive to changes in interest rates, they too suffer the consequences of rising interest rates. Mortgage REITs generally do well when interest rates fall. Because of the different property holdings in mortgage REITs, they tend to be more income oriented in that their emphasis is on current yields, while equity REITs offer the potential for capital gains in addition to current income. For example, Annaly Capital Management, Inc., a mortgage REIT, paid a dividend yield of 9 percent in the first quarter of 2005, which was a premium dividend rate compared to stock and bond yields.

REITs can either have finite or perpetual lives. Finite-life REITs, also known as FREITs, are self-liquidating. In the case of equity REITs, the properties are sold at the end of a specified period. In mortgage REITs profits are paid to shareholders when the mortgages are paid up.

Little correlation exists in the performance of REITs and the stock market. Consequently, investors should hold a small percentage (no more than 5 percent) of their investment assets in REITs. The box below lists some of the guidelines for buying REITs.

---

### GUIDELINES FOR SELECTING REITs

- Investigate REITs before buying into them. Get the REIT's annual report from a broker or call the REIT directly. You can also get additional information from the National Association of Real Estate Investment Trusts, 1875 I Street N.W. Suite 600, Washington, D.C., 20006.

- Look to see how long the specific REIT has been in business. How long have its managers been in the real estate business and how well do they manage the REIT's assets? How much of a personal stake do its managers have in the REIT? According to Thomas Byrne,[1] insiders should own at least 10% of the stock.

- Look at the REIT's debt level. The greater the level of debt, the greater the risk, because more of the revenue is needed to service the debt. If a downturn in revenue occurs, interest payments become harder to service. Look for REITs with debt-to-equity ratios of less than 50%.[2]

- Don't choose a REIT because it has the highest yield. The higher the yield, the greater the risk. In some cases underwriters raise the yields to hide poor fundamentals.[3]

---

- Select REITs that have low P/B values (1 to −1 or less).

- Check the REIT's dividend record. Be wary of REITs that have recently cut their dividends. Check the source of cash for the payment of dividends. Cash for dividends should come from operations, not from the sale of properties.

- Location is everything in real estate. Look at the locations of the properties in the trust. Avoid REITs that have invested in overbuilt or depressed locations.

*Caveats*

- Avoid REITs that are blind pools. These might be set up by well-known management firms to raise funds to invest in unidentified properties. Before investing in any project, it is important to see what the real estate assets and liabilities in any project are.

- Investors should not invest more than 5% of their total investment portfolio in REITs.

## WHAT ARE THE RISKS OF CLOSED-END MUTUAL FUNDS AND UNIT INVESTMENT TRUSTS?

Both closed-end bond funds and unit investment trusts are subject to interest rate risk. When the market rates of interest increase, generally prices of stock issues held in both the portfolios of unit trusts and closed-end funds decline. This means lower fund share prices. This is a double-edged sword; if there is selling pressure on the fund's shares, the decline in share prices will be even greater than the decline in net asset values. The opposite is true in that if interest rates decline there will be appreciation in the assets and, of course, in the share price. For both closed-end funds and unit investment trusts, there is the risk that share prices will fall way below NAV due to excess selling pressure in the stock markets. Then, of course, the danger arises of not being able to recoup the original price paid for the shares when selling. This is a common phenomenon experienced by closed-end funds and unit investment trusts.

For UIT shareholders there is the added risk of not getting back the full amount of their original investments at maturity. This can be caused by a number of factors. The composition of the trust's assets, commissions, high management fees charged to the trust, and the use of leverage are all factors that can add to the risk of loss of principal. In many cases the managers of UITs and closed-end bond funds charge very generous annual fees, in addition to their up-front commissions on the original sale of the shares. This means that these funds will have to earn spectacular returns in order for the managers to be able to collect their fees without eroding yields significantly. They will also have to rake up some capital gains to be able to recoup the sales commissions in order to return to the shareholders their entire investments at maturity. This explains why many investment trusts use leverage and resort to derivative securities as ways to try to boost their returns.

The types of investments that a fund or trust holds has a marked effect on the NAV as well as the volatility of the share price. Unfortunately for the original shareholders of closed-end bond funds and unit investment trusts, there is no way of knowing the composition of the portfolio investments when they originally subscribe to the shares of the fund/trust. That's because only after the original shareholders invest their money to buy the shares do the managers of the fund or trust buy the investment assets. Thus original shareholders might not be able to evaluate the levels of risk of the assets until the portfolio has been constituted. The composition may include the stocks of highly risky companies. Investors trying to exit the fund or trust at that point might experience losses from the decline in the share price. If there is an exodus of shareholders from UITs and closed-end funds, other shareholders may find it difficult to sell their shares without taking large losses.

## SHOULD YOU INVEST IN INDIVIDUAL SECURITIES OR USE FUNDS?

Stock closed-end funds offer investors the opportunity to invest in diversified portfolios of different sectors in the economy and foreign countries, just as in mutual funds. The advantages of both closed-end funds and mutual funds are the use of professional management, diversification, the freedom to invest small amounts of money, and the ease of buying and selling. For many investors these advantages far outweigh their disadvantages. Decisions about which individual stocks to invest in are avoided by choosing equity mutual funds and closed-end funds.

An advantage of a closed-end fund over a mutual fund is that the former can trade at a discount to its net asset values. This is akin to buying a dollar's worth of assets at less than a dollar. This strategy appeals to value investors who have the patience to wait for the assets to rise in value.

Mutual fund managers can experience liquidity risk from excessive sales of shares by shareholders. Fund managers would have to sell some of their holdings to raise enough cash to be able to redeem the shares sold by shareholders. This does not happen in closed-end funds, allowing their managers to invest in less liquid investments such as real estate and foreign company shares.

Investing in individual stocks and closed-end funds allows investors to choose their purchase and selling prices during the trading day. Mutual fund transactions are enacted at the NAV price as of the close of the trading day. Similarly, there are no minimum investment amounts stipulated with closed-end fund investments, as there are with mutual funds. An investor can buy or sell a single share or in round lots of shares.

However, in certain cases, a strong argument exists for buying individual securities over mutual funds and closed-end funds. Returns on individual stocks could be greater than those earned from mutual funds and closed-end funds due to the fees charged by the funds. This is true even for no-load funds because in place of sales commissions, other fees, such as 12b–1 and management fees, reduce the returns of mutual funds. By investing in individual securities, you avoid these fees. Closed-end funds do not charge 12b–1 fees, but management fees can be high.

Investing in mutual funds and closed-end funds is a good strategy if you do not have enough money to diversify your investments and do not have the time, expertise, or inclination to select and manage individual securities. In addition, a wide range of funds offers you the opportunity to invest in the types of securities that would be difficult to buy individually.

Table 11.3 compares some characteristics of investing in individual securities versus mutual and closed-end funds.

### TABLE 11.3

Characteristics of Individual Securities versus Mutual Funds and Closed-End Funds

| | Individual Securities | Mutual Funds | Closed-End Funds |
|---|---|---|---|
| Diversification | Achieved only if a large number of securities is purchased | Achieved with a small investment | Achieved with a small investment |
| Ease of Buying and Selling | Easy to buy and sell stocks at real-time prices during the trading day; more difficult to buy bonds | Easy to buy and sell shares; trades occur only at the closing price at the end of the day | Easy to buy and sell liquid closed-end funds |
| Professional Management | No | Yes | Yes |
| Expenses and Costs to Buy and Sell | Brokerage fees to buy and sell | Low to high expenses depending on fund. | Low to high expenses depending on fund. |
| Tax Planning | Easier to predict income and plan capital gains and losses | Can upset careful tax planning due to unpredictable distributions of income and capital gains | Can upset careful tax planning due to unpredictable distributions of income and capital gains |

# CHAPTER 12

# Exchange-Traded Funds

**E**xchange-traded funds (ETFs) are baskets of stocks or bonds that track a broad-based index, sector of an index, or stocks in countries. ETFs are similar to closed-end funds in that investors buy these listed shares on the stock exchanges. The predominant listings are on the American Stock Exchange (AMEX). These shares represent ownership in a portfolio of stocks or bonds that track a broad index or sector indices. Investors buy or sell these shares through brokers, just as they do individual stocks. ETFs are priced based on the types of securities they hold, in addition to the supply of and demand for the shares. These shares can be sold short or bought in margin accounts, and they can be traded using market, limit, or stop orders.

The greatest competition to mutual funds has come from exchange-traded funds. ETFs have become popular investment alternatives to mutual funds for many investors who want diversification and low-cost investment options. The typical costs charged to investors in equity ETFs range around 0.4 percent of assets annually, compared with 1.4 percent of assets for the average equity mutual funds, according to Standard and Poor's.[1]

- As of December 2011, there were 1,134 exchange-traded funds in the United States, which have grown in number from 102 in 2001.[2] (www.ici.org)

- ETFs include stocks, bonds, and commodities.

- Inverse ETFs invest in stock, bond, or commodity indices in order to produce the opposite returns of the index.

- Leveraged ETFs seek to magnify the returns of the index tied to the portfolio of securities.

- ETFs are traded on the stock markets, not through investment companies.

There are over 1,134 ETFs to choose from; this number has grown significantly since the first ETF, the S&P Depository Receipts (known as SPDRs), was introduced in 1993. Table 12.1 lists a few of the more popular ETFs traded on the market.

## TABLE 12.1

Some Exchange-Traded Funds

| Name | Ticker Symbol | Category/Index |
|------|---------------|----------------|
| SPDRs | SPY | S&P 500 Index (large-cap) |
| Diamonds | DIA | Dow Jones Industrial Average (large-cap) |
| PowerSharesNasdaq | QQQ | Largest stocks on Nasdaq |
| iShares MSCI EAFE Index | EFA | International Index (large-cap) |
| Semiconductor HOLDRs | SMH | Semiconductor stocks |
| PowerShares Active Real Estate | PSR | Real estate |
| iShares FTSE China 25 Index | FXI | Chinese stocks |
| iShares Lehman TIPS Bond | TLT | Inflation government bonds |

| Name | Ticker Symbol | Category/Index |
|------|--------------|----------------|
| Pharmaceutical HOLDRs | PPH | Pharmaceutical stocks |
| Financial Select Sector | XLF | Financial stocks in S&P 500 Index |
| iShares Russell 2000 | IWN | Small cap stocks in Russell 2000 Index |
| iShares MSCI Spain | EWP | Spanish stocks |

For a complete list of ETFs, visit the following websites:

www.amex.com

www.ishares.com

www.yahoo.com: Click on *Finance* and then click on *ETFs*.

ETFs are the SPDRs (Spiders), which track the S&P 500 Index; Diamonds (ticker symbol DIA), which track the 30 stocks in the Dow Jones Industrial Average; and the Qubes (ticker symbol QQQ), which track ownership in the largest stocks on the Nasdaq. There are numerous ETFs that are specialized in sectors of the broad indices (financial, technology, and industrials, for example), and in foreign stock market indices (iShares, which track the Morgan Stanley Capital International indices—MSCI—for 20 countries and many regions around the world). Visit the AMEX website at www.amex.com for information on the various ETFs listed.

## MORE ABOUT SPDRS, DIAMONDS, AND NASDAQ 100 ETFs

There is a family of ETFs based on the Standard & Poor's 500 Index and its component sectors, including technology, energy, and financials. The SPDR Trust holds shares of all companies in the S&P 500 Index. The purchase of a single share in this trust gives its owner proportionate ownership of the 500 companies in the S&P 500 Index. Several select, specialized SPDRs allow investors to track, for example, the financials in the S&P 500 Index, or the 79 tech stocks in the S&P 500 Index. Investors can also track the utilities, industrials, and five other sectors in the S&P 500 Index. These sector ETFs are traded just like the main SPDR (SPY).

The ETF that tracks the 30 stocks of the Dow Jones Industrial Average is called the Diamond (DIA). The purchase of a single share in this fund gives a buyer proportionate ownership of the 30 Dow Jones Industrial Average stocks.

The ETF that mirrors the 100 largest stocks in the Nasdaq is called a "Qube" (QQQ). The purchase of a single share in this ETF gives its owner a proportionate ownership of these Nasdaq 100 stocks.

The following is a list of some of the features of these ETFs:

- **Trading:** These ETFs are traded on the American Stock Exchange.

- **Approximate Share Price Ratio:** The value of 1 share of a SPDR, Diamond, and Qube ETF in relation to the respective indices tracked are: 1/10th S&P 500 Index for 1 SPY share, 1/100th the value of the DJIA for 1 DIA share.

- **Dividends:** Dividends are paid quarterly (in January, April, July, and October)

- **Risks:** The same risk exists for these ETFs as experienced by individual stocks, namely price fluctuations. There is also the additional risk that the fund may not replicate the exact performance of the underlying index because of expenses incurred by the fund. Ideally the exchange-traded fund should earn the return of the underlying benchmark index minus the total expenses. However, some ETFs underperform their benchmark indices significantly, which is known as the tracking error.

- **Net Asset Value:** The net asset value per ETF is calculated at the close of each business day. The value represents the market value of the stocks in the underlying index, plus any accrued dividends and minus any expenses on a per share basis.

- **Short Selling:** Investors can sell these ETFs short and on a downtick.

Source: American Stock Exchange, www.amex.com.

The description of the net asset value implies that the share price of an ETF can trade above or below its NAV. This discrepancy generally will not occur because of the issuance by the ETF of shares in kind. Whenever a discrepancy in price occurs and an institutional investor wants to exploit this price differential with large blocks of shares (a minimum of 50,000), the ETF trust redeems the shares with the underlying stocks in the index rather than paying cash. The institutional investor then sells the shares of the underlying stocks in the index and not the shares of the ETF to realize the price discrepancy. This concept emphasizes the similarities between open-end mutual funds and ETFs. An ETF buys and sells shares and issues new shares when necessary. However, ETF investors can buy or sell shares at any time during the day on the stock exchanges, whereas transactions involving open-end mutual funds take place only at the end of the day at the closing NAV price. The major difference between an open-end mutual fund and an ETF is that when shareholders in mutual funds sell their shares, the mutual fund might have to sell securities to raise enough cash to pay them, resulting in capital gains or loss transactions. With ETFs, traders buy the shares sold by investors, which leaves the portfolio intact.

## ADVANTAGES AND DISADVANTAGES OF ETFs

Because of the passive management of ETFs, fees and the turnover of securities are low (similar to index mutual funds), which results in low capital gains taxes.

## THE ADVANTAGES AND DISADVANTAGES OF INVESTING IN EXCHANGE TRADED FUNDS

Exchange-traded funds bear similarities to open-end mutual funds, index funds, and closed-end funds. Knowing the advantages and disadvantages of ETFs will help you determine which type of investment is more suited to your needs.

- ETFs offer diversification (similar to mutual funds), but they trade as stocks. Even though the stock prices of ETFs that track the different indices fluctuate when markets are volatile, the effect of the fluctuations on each of the indices might be more muted than in a portfolio of individual stocks.

- ETFs charge low fees and are generally tax efficient, making them similar to index funds.

- ETFs are bought and sold through brokers, just like any other stocks on the market, at real-time price quotes during the day. Mutual funds can only be traded once a day at their closing prices.

- Investors do not need large amounts of money to be able to buy ETFs, which gives them broad exposure to a market index, a sector of the market, or to a foreign country.

- The disadvantage of ETFs is that investors incur commissions to buy and sell shares, while no-load mutual funds charge no transaction fees to buy or sell shares. These transaction costs make it uneconomical for investors who typically invest small amounts of money on a frequent basis.

- ETFs may be too concentrated to share in the gains of their sectors. In 2006 the telecommunications sector had large returns that were not shared by some of the telecommunications sector ETFs.[3]

## SHOULD YOU INVEST IN INDIVIDUAL SECURITIES OR USE ETS OR FUNDS?

The diversification achieved by mutual funds, closed-end funds, and ETFs minimizes the effect of any unexpected losses from individual stocks and bonds in a portfolio. Also professional managers of mutual and closed-end funds might have quicker access to information about the different issues and might react sooner in buying or selling the securities in question. ETFs are similar to index funds and are not actively managed. For investors willing to manage their own portfolios, a strong argument exists for buying individual securities over mutual funds. The rates of return on individual stocks have the potential to be greater than those earned from mutual funds. This is true even for no-load funds because in addition to sales commissions, other fees, such as 12b-1s and operating fees, reduce the returns of mutual funds. By investing in individual securities, you avoid these fees. ETFs generally have lower management fees than mutual funds. However, commissions are charged to buy and sell individual stocks, ETFs, and closed-end funds.

If you have a small amount of money to invest, mutual funds and ETFs are better alternatives. A $2,000 investment in a stock fund buys a fraction of a diversified portfolio of stocks, while for individual securities, this amount might allow for buying only the shares of one equity company. Investing in mutual funds is a good strategy if you do not have enough money to diversify your investments and do not have the time, expertise, or inclination to select and manage individual securities. In addition a wide range of funds offers you the opportunity to invest in the types of securities that would be difficult to buy individually. ETF investors are not hampered by the minimum investment amounts set by mutual funds. Investors can buy a single share of stock in an ETF.

Table 12.2 compares some characteristics of investing in individual securities versus mutual funds, closed-end funds, and exchange-traded funds.

**TABLE 12.2**

Characteristics of Individual Securities versus Mutual Funds, Closed-End Funds, and ETFs

| | Individual Securities | Mutual Funds | Closed-End Funds | ETFs |
|---|---|---|---|---|
| Diversification | Achieved only if a large number of securities is purchased | Achieved with a small investment | Achieved with a small investment | Achieved with a small investment |
| Ease of Buying and Selling | Easy to buy and sell stocks at real-time prices during the trading day; more difficult to buy bonds | Easy to buy and sell shares; trades occur only at the closing price at the end of the day | Easy to buy and sell liquid closed-end funds | Easy to buy and sell ETFs at real-time prices during the day |
| Professional Management | No | Yes | Yes | Replicates a market index. |
| Expenses and Costs to Buy and Sell | Brokerage fees to buy and sell | Low to high expenses depending on fund | Low to high expenses depending on fund | Brokerage fees to buy and sell and low fees |
| Tax Planning | Easier to predict income and plan capital gains and losses | Can upset careful tax planning due to unpredictable distributions of income and capital gains | Can upset careful tax planning due to unpredictable distributions of income and capital gains | More tax efficient than mutual funds |

# WHAT VALUE INVESTORS SHOULD LOOK FOR IN CHOOSING ETFs

Value investors should understand what the exchange-traded fund invests in and whether the fund follows a benchmark index. If, for example, the ETF follows the S&P 500 Index, the returns for this ETF should approximate the returns of the S&P 500 Index minus the expense ratio of the ETF. However, many ETFs lag considerably the returns of their benchmark indices. This discrepancy is referred to as a tracking error. Thus, you do not want to invest in an ETF that lags its underlying index by considerable amounts. Choose an ETF with the lowest tracking error when comparing similar type ETFs.[4] So, for example, if you are considering an emerging market exchange-traded fund, choose the one with the lowest tracking error. Morningstar stated that the iShares MSCI Emerging Market Index Fund (ticker symbol EEM) reduced its tracking error from 2010 to 2011 from 0.52 percent to 0.13 percent.[5] Morningstar provides information on tracking errors, and investors can also compare returns of the funds with their benchmark indices, which can be obtained from the fund's annual reports and prospectuses.

Some reasons tracking errors occur include: fund fees and expenses that diminish returns from the benchmark index; differences between the holdings of securities in the ETF and the benchmark index; cash holdings of the ETF or changes to the holdings of the underlying index; timing differences in the accrual of dividends; market volatility; and the costs involved in complying with existing regulations. Try to determine which of these tracking errors applies to the ETF you are considering.

Investors should also compare the expense ratios of the ETFs they are interested in. The expense ratio comparison is important when choosing between several ETFs tied to the same benchmark index. However, by evaluating the tracking errors of the ETFs you are more or less eliminating the highest expense ratio ETFs from your consideration. Generally, ETFs do not outperform their benchmark indices, so the homework for a value investor is to determine which sectors of the economy will provide the most value.

Beside total returns, fees, and expenses incurred by ETFs, value investors should examine the risk profile of the ETFs they are interested in before purchasing. For example, country ETFs have higher risk profiles than domestic ones. ETFs investing solely in China, for example, face risks specific to China (lack of information about the companies listed in their holdings; political, economic, and social risks; slowdown in economic growth; currency fluctuations; and increased tariff and other trade barriers affecting the growth of Chinese companies). Similarly, a country fund may have a concentration of holdings in a particular sector, making it more vulnerable to losses as a result of adverse occurrences in that sector. This last point begs the question of how diversified a country ETF actually is. If the ETF holds a small number of issues in a concentrated sector of the economy, such a fund is not diversified and has greater sector risk than other ETFs with more sector holdings and greater numbers of issues. Investors can obtain information about an ETF's holdings by going to the fund sponsor's website or from the NYSE or Nasdaq websites. If you cannot find the holdings of the fund, you can also go to the SEC's EDGAR website; ETF sponsors are required to file their information with the SEC.

Another important consideration in choosing an ETF is to look at the overall liquidity of the trading in the fund on the stock exchanges. An ETF that is not actively traded will more than likely have a wide bid-ask spread. A narrow bid-ask spread is indicative of actively traded stocks (ETFs) such as, for example, a bid of $10.00 and an ask price of $10.01, making the bid-ask spread $0.01. Another problem with a thinly or inactively traded ETF is that there are not many buyers or sellers willing to take the other side of a trade, thereby resulting in a significant movement in the stock price of the ETF when a sell order is executed. Liquid actively traded ETFs have many willing buyers and sellers, resulting in either no loss in value or a tiny loss when the ETF is sold. To determine how liquid the ETF is, you can monitor the average daily volume the stock ETF trades in a day. ETFs with higher average daily volume trades will generally have lower bid-ask spreads and will have lower price movements when volume picks up.

Value investors should also watch out for ETFs with high portfolio turnover, which causes higher turnover costs that reduce returns. First Trust Large Cap Growth Opportunities Fund ETF had a turnover ratio of 162 percent compared with the Dow Jones Industrial Average ETF, also a large-cap fund, which had a turnover ratio of 0 percent.[6]

Value investors would probably be attracted to ETFs that have fallen from favor because they hold underlying investments that are being sold on the market. However, value investors should investigate these ETFs very carefully for a number of reasons. First, the ETF industry is in the mature stage of the life cycle, in which ETF sponsors are closing their unprofitable funds. At the end of 2012 there were roughly 1,400 ETFs, but the growth of new ETFs in each of the past years has begun to decline. Consequently, if ETFs are not attracting new investment funds from investors and they are losing money for their sponsors, there is a good chance they could be closed. Value investors should keep this result in mind when they look for ETFs that have come down significantly in price.

Investors should be aware of the risks of the underlying securities held by the ETF, in addition to the other risks mentioned facing ETFs. ETFs holding bonds are subject to interest rate and inflation risk. When interest rates rise there is downward pressure on the prices of existing bonds, which means that ETFs holding bond securities will see their net asset values decline. Inflation also erodes bond prices because bonds are fixed income securities. Consequently, value investors should never buy bond ETFs when interest rates are likely to rise and when inflation is on the increase into the future.

Similarly, investors should understand how leveraged and inverse ETFs work before investing in them. An inverse ETF aims to earn the opposite return of a stock, bond, or commodity index it tracks. Leveraged ETFs can magnify their returns over their benchmark indices by borrowing money to invest in securities and using derivative swaps and futures contracts to earn two or three times the returns of the index. These types of ETFs have unique risks and tend to be more volatile than regular ETFs.

**TABLE 12.3**

Mutual Fund Sector Performance

| Investment Objective | 1-year return%* | 5-year return% |
|---|---|---|
| Large-cap Growth | 13.4 | 1.2 |
| Large-cap Value | 14.6 | −0.6 |
| Mid-cap Growth | 9.3 | 1.5 |
| Mid-cap Value | 14.6 | 2.2 |
| Small-cap Growth | 9.8 | 2.0 |
| Small-cap Value | 13.2 | 3.3 |
| Health/Biotechnology | 23.2 | 6.9 |
| Natural Resources | −0.7 | −2.9 |
| Real Estate | 18.8 | 3.1 |
| International | 11.0 | −4.4 |
| Emerging markets | 8.1 | −3.3 |
| Latin American | 1.5 | −2.9 |
| High-Yield Taxable Bonds | 15.5 | 7.7 |

*1-year though November 30, 2012
Source: Lipper, as quoted in *The Wall Street Journal*, December 3, 2012, R7

Because most ETFs do not outperform their underlying indices, investors should do their homework in choosing the sector ETFs to invest in. Value investors typically look for the sectors and countries that have been out of favor. Table 12.3 lists some of the sectors that recorded the best and worst returns for the one-year and five-year periods ending on November 30, 2012.

It would be hard to see value investors chasing the winning sectors such as Health/Biotechnology and High-Yield Taxable Bonds. The Natural Resources sector looks like it presents value. However, we know from the analysis of Cliffs Natural that this sector has been beaten down, and it will provide value for patient investors when the sector comes back into favor.

ETFs allow investors to feel more comfortable about investing in emerging markets and other specialty areas such as small-cap stocks, bonds, commodities, and leveraged funds, which are more difficult for individual investors to navigate. Value investors who are comfortable investing in individual stocks and bonds will probably do better than using ETFs to invest. However, investors need to spend the time and effort researching the different stocks to build their portfolios.

# Bonds

Those who advocate investing in stocks quote historic returns over 10, 20, and 50 years because stocks have consistently outperformed bonds and other financial investments over these long time periods. However, with shorter time periods, the results can be markedly different. Bonds have invariably outperformed stocks within these shorter time frames, and value investors need to understand the circumstances when bonds traditionally outperform stocks. Historically, bonds have outperformed stocks during recessions, and when interest rates and inflation are rising, short-term bonds have outperformed long-term ones.

The following example illustrates the risk of loss from investing in only one asset class. If you had invested solely in stocks from March 1995 through March 2000, you would have earned spectacular returns purely because the U.S. stock markets reached their all-time highs in March 2000. During that time period, other financial securities such as bonds and money market securities could not match the stellar stock market returns. However, for the following two and a half years, the broad stock market index fell by 50 percent, and technology stocks declined by roughly 80 percent, while bonds earned positive returns. For the next two and a half years, through March 2005, the stock markets increased, but returns came nowhere near the highs of March 2000.[1]

If you were clairvoyant, you would have invested solely in stocks from 1995 to 1999, switched to bonds on January 1, 2000, through 2002, and then switched back to stocks in 2003 through 2004; your returns would have been hard to beat. The problem is that we do not know when we should be fully invested in stocks and when we should switch to bonds. The lessons we can learn from this example are:

- It is virtually impossible to determine how the markets will perform in the future, so we should not have all our eggs in one basket, so to speak, by investing solely in stocks or bonds. We want to minimize the risk of loss.

- The key to minimizing the risk of loss is to invest in different classes of investments whose returns are not correlated, meaning investing in asset classes whose returns do not rise and fall together. When one asset class declines in value, another asset class increases, which minimizes portfolio losses and seeks positive overall returns.[2]

Every investor should be aware of some of the reasons for investing in bonds:

- Investing in a diversified portfolio of stocks, bonds, money market securities, and other asset classes reduces the risk of loss and balances returns due to uncertainties in the markets. Bonds are like an anchor on a ship and act as a buffer when stocks decline.

- Investing in bonds provides financial security because bondholders are paid regular payments of interest and their principal is returned to them when their bonds mature.

- Certain types of bonds provide tax breaks. Municipal bonds are exempt from federal taxes and may also be free from state and local taxes for taxpayers filing in the states and counties where the bonds are issued.

- Bonds can be sold before their maturity dates should bondholders need their money earlier than the stated maturity dates.

- Bonds are less risky than stocks. Treasury bonds are virtually free of credit and default risk, while bonds with high credit ratings seldom default on their interest and principal payments.

- Bond investments preserve and increase capital, in addition to providing the opportunity for capital appreciation (and capital loss).

Despite these good reasons for investing in bonds, many investors overlook them because they do not provide the capital appreciation of stocks. This is true, bonds are not stocks, but bonds can provide you with a lower-risk approach to building a secure nest egg. Consequently, bonds should play a part in virtually every investor's portfolio.

Stock prices are driven by earnings and offer the possibility of growth to a portfolio in the form of dividends and capital appreciation. Bonds provide investors with the opportunity for a predictable stream of income and, generally, the return of capital, making bonds less risky than stocks. Investors can invest in individual bonds or bond mutual funds, closed-end bond funds, or bond exchange-traded funds. When the earnings of a company increases over a period of time, the stock price of the company rises. However, the reactions of bond prices to economic events are mostly different from stock prices. Bond prices generally decrease when news on the economy is good and increase on bad economic news. Consequently, virtually every portfolio needs to be invested in bonds, which leads to the question: How much of your portfolio should be invested in bonds?

An understanding of the characteristics of bonds will provide some answers to this question.

## CHARACTERISTICS OF INDIVIDUAL BONDS

A bond is a negotiable debt security, whereby an issuer borrows money and in return agrees to pay a fixed amount of interest over a specified period of time and pay back the principal amount when the bond matures. *Principal* is the face value (par value) of the bond, generally $1,000 per bond.

A bond is similar to an IOU. Bonds also bear certain similarities to certificates of deposit (CDs) and savings accounts. Investors who deposit money in CDs (or savings accounts) are in effect lending money to banks. The banks pay investors interest on their deposits and then repay the principal when the CDs mature. Similarly, investors in bonds make loans to the issuer (a corporation or government). This process makes them creditors, not owners, as in the case of common stock investors. In return, the issuer regularly pays a specified amount of interest until the bond's maturity date. Virtually all bonds have a maturity date at which time the issuer returns to investors the face value of each bond ($1,000).

The major difference between savings accounts, CDs, and bonds is that investors can sell their bonds on the secondary market to others before the bonds mature. Savings accounts and CDs cannot be sold to other investors (though certificates of deposit in amounts over $100,000 can be sold before maturity, making them negotiable investments). Bonds are negotiable IOUs, unlike savings accounts and most CDs, and the issuers of the bonds pay regular amounts of interest and repay to bondholders the principal at their maturity date. These regular payments of interest make bonds attractive investments to investors seeking fixed amounts of income and the repayment of principal at the maturity date.

All bonds have similar characteristics. A bond has a face value, also known as the par value, which is the amount of the bond that is repaid at maturity. The par value of bonds is almost always $1,000, with a few exceptions. The par value is the amount on which interest is determined. For example, if a bond is bought at issuance for $1,000, the investor bought the bond at its par value. At the bond's maturity date, the investor receives $1,000 per bond held. The maturity date is the date on which the issuer retires the bond and pays the bondholder its par value. Maturity dates for bonds can range from one day to 100 years. Bonds with maturities of one year or less from the date of issuance are referred to as short-term bonds or debt. Bonds with maturities of 1 to 10 years are referred to as intermediate bonds or intermediate notes. Long-term bonds are issues with maturities of longer than 10 years, commonly as many as 30 years. The Walt Disney Company and a few other corporations have issued 100-year bonds, but this is not a common occurrence.

Bonds have two types of maturities. The most common is a *term bond*, in which the bonds of a given issue all mature on the same date. *Serial bonds* will have different maturity dates within the same issue.

The *coupon rate* of a bond determines the amount of annual interest paid by the bond, which is generally stated as a percentage of the face value. If the coupon rate is 5 percent, the issuer of these bonds promises to pay $50 (5 percent times $1,000, the face value) in annual interest on each bond. Many bonds pay interest semiannually. If a bond has a 5 percent coupon rate, paid semiannually, the bondholder receives $25 per bond every six months. Some bonds have adjustable or floating interest rates, which are tied to a particular index. The coupon payments fluctuate based on the underlying index.

A bond's price is affected by the relationship between the coupon rate and market rates of interest. Figure 13.1 illustrates the relationship between bond prices and market rates of interest. Suppose you purchased a bond last year with a 5 percent coupon rate when market rates of interest were 5 percent, and you paid $1,000 per bond. This year, market rates of interest rise to 6 percent. What price would you receive if you tried to sell this bond? Obviously, new investors would not pay $1,000 for a bond yielding 5 percent when they could buy new bonds with current coupon rates of 6 percent for $1,000. Because the new investor would expect to get at least 6 percent, this bond would sell for less than $1,000 (a discount) in order to be competitive with current bonds.

Conversely, if market rates of interest fall below the coupon rate, new investors are willing to pay more than $1,000 (a premium) for this bond. Thus, bond prices are vulnerable to market rates of interest, as well as other factors discussed later in this chapter.

## FIGURE 13.1

Bond Prices and Interest Rates

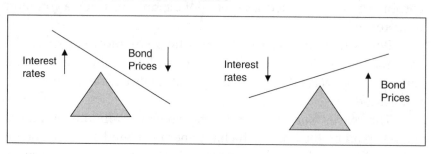

## Bond Prices

Bonds do not necessarily trade at their par values. They may trade above or below their par values. Any bond trading at less than $1,000 is said to be trading at a discount.

For example, Caesars Entertainment Operating bonds, with a coupon rate of 10.75 percent and maturing in the year 2016, traded at a discount, $927.50 per bond on February 27, 2013. Even though the coupon rate is well above current rates of interest, there is uncertainty surrounding the company, causing the bonds to trade at a discount.

Bonds trading at a premium sell for more than $1,000 (par value). RR Donnelly has 6.125 percent bonds maturing in the year 2017 that traded at $1,020 per bond on February 27, 2013. This $20.00 premium is an amount investors were willing to pay in order to receive a 6.125 percent coupon rate for this bond.

## Call Provision

Value investors pay attention to all bond provisions particularly call and refunding provisions. A call provision allows a bond issuer to repurchase a bond at a fixed price prior to its maturity date. Many bonds have call provisions, which allow the issuers of the bonds to redeem them at a specified price before their scheduled maturity dates. After the specific date of redemption, the issuer no longer pays interest on the bonds, forcing holders to relinquish their bonds.

Issuers generally exercise call provisions when market rates of interest fall well below the coupon rate of the bonds. This action deprives bondholders of higher yields on their bonds, although it is advantageous to the issuers who call in bonds with high coupon rates and issue new bonds with lower coupon rates. This strategy lowers the issuer's total borrowing costs. For example, if a corporation issued 10 percent coupon bonds when interest rates were high and rates dropped to 6 percent, it would be advantageous for the issuer to refund the old bonds with new bonds at a lower coupon rate. However, if the bond issue contains a refunding provision, the issuer is prohibited from using the proceeds from a new, lower coupon bond issue to refund a higher coupon bond issue.

An investor in bonds should pay particular attention to a bond issue's call and refunding provisions. There are three types of call provisions:

1. *noncallable* bond is one that the issuer cannot redeem before its maturity. Noncallable bonds offer investors the most protection but have many loopholes. Noncallable bonds have sometimes been called, such as in the case of a fire or act of God, or when a healthy company stops making its interest payments on the bonds; the trustees call the bonds in and the debt is paid off early. Noncallable for life bonds are listed in the dealer's quote sheets as NCL.

2. A *freely callable* bond is a bond that the issuer can call at any time before its maturity. Freely callable bonds offer investors no protection.

3. A *deferred callable* bond is a bond that the issuer cannot call until after a specified period. Deferred callable bonds offer some protection since the bonds cannot be called until after a specified length of time (for example, 5, 10, or 15 years after issue). A bond that is noncallable until 2015 would be listed as NC15 on the dealer's quote sheet.

Because call provisions negatively affect investors, issuers compensate bondholders with a *call price* that is higher than the face value of the bond. The call price is the price an issuer pays to retire bonds called before maturity. The call price is generally equal to the face value plus a *call premium*. The call premium, specified in the call provision, is the amount an issuer adds to the bond's face value.

Callable bonds are generally issued with higher coupon rates than noncallable bonds of similar risk and maturity, to compensate their holders for the risk of having to forfeit their higher yields if the bonds are called. You should check the call provision of a bond issue before buying.

Value investors would be wise to stay away from bonds trading at a premium price that have call provisions; if the bonds are called, investors would not have the time to recoup the premium price paid.

## Put Provision

A put provision allows bondholders to sell their bonds back to the issuer at a specified price (usually at par value) before their maturity date. A put provision in a bond's *indenture*, the legal contract between the issuer of the bonds and the trustees of the bonds, who represent the bondholders, is relatively unusual and is the opposite of a call provision in that the holder makes the decision whether to exercise the put option.

The put provision provides a floor price for the bonds in that issue, in that bondholders know that they can resell their bonds to the issuer at par. This provision gives bondholders protection against rising interest rates and any deterioration in the credit quality of the issue. However, the price for these advantages is higher bond prices. Bonds with put provisions sell at higher prices than comparable bonds without them.

## Sinking Fund Provision

A sinking fund provision allows an issuer to set aside funds for the orderly retirement of the bonds in the issue. In one type of sinking fund, an issuer randomly selects bonds to be retired and then calls them for redemption. After the bonds are called, they no longer earn interest. The other type of sinking fund allows an issuer to make payments to a trustee, who invests the funds. Then the amount accumulated goes toward retiring the bonds at their maturity dates. Issuers can also repurchase their bonds in the bond market and retire them. This practice occurs more frequently when the bonds are trading at a discount. The difference between a call provision and a sinking fund provision is that, with the latter, the issuer does not have to call the bonds in at a premium price.

The significance of a sinking fund provision is twofold:

- It provides some security to bondholders because the issuer in a sinking fund sets aside payments to repay bondholders. Depending on the circumstances, this action could lessen the price volatility of the issue.

- With a random sinking fund plan, bondholders whose bonds are called have their principal repaid before maturity. Thus, the sinking fund provision acts as a ceiling price for the bond issue.

## Secured or Unsecured Bonds

Bonds are issued on either a secured or unsecured basis. A secured bond is backed by the pledge of specific asset as collateral. For secured bonds, bondholders can seize the asset after proceeding to court in the case of a default. Examples of secured bonds are mortgage bonds (bonds secured by real estate), collateral trust bonds (bonds secured by assets owned by the issuer but held in trust by a third party), and equipment trust certificates (bonds secured by equipment). How safe should you feel holding a mortgage bond issued by a utility company that is backed by the collateral of a power plant? During a utility bankruptcy, do bondholders have the expertise to operate the power plant? Or can they sell off the parts on a piecemeal basis? Although the pledging of assets increases the safety of the principal of the bonds, bondholders should hope that the utility company does not default on its interest and principal payments. Generally, investors in bonds should be more concerned with the issuer's ability to service its debt (creditworthiness) rather than with security alone. In case of bankruptcy, pledged property may not be marketable, and it may involve litigation that can be time consuming and costly.

An unsecured bond is backed only by the promise of its issuer to abide by the commitments of the bond issue. The ability of the issuer to pay its fixed interest and repay principal at maturity is based on the issuer's creditworthiness. An issuer of bonds can have several different issues of bonds at any time. These bonds can have different features. When an issuer has many different bonds outstanding, *seniority* becomes important, particularly during bankruptcy, because senior bonds are the first to be repaid. *Junior bonds* are unsecured bonds and, in bankruptcy, bondholders' claims are secondary to secured and senior bonds.

*Debenture* bonds are unsecured bonds issued by corporations. In a bankruptcy, debenture bondholders become general creditors of the company. Consequently, debenture holders assess the earnings power of the company as their primary security, which typically results in only well-established and creditworthy companies issuing debenture bonds. *Subordinated debentures* are bonds whose claims are paid only after the claims of secured bonds and other debenture bonds are honored in a bankruptcy. *Income bonds* are the most junior of all bonds and the riskiest, in that the issuer is only obligated to pay interest when earnings are sufficient to cover its interest payments.

## Bond Indenture

A bond indenture is a legal document specifying the terms of the bond agreement.

Bond securities have similar characteristics, which are summarized below.

- A maturity date: The date on which the bonds in the issue are paid off

- Interest payments: The amount the issuer promises to pay in return for the use of the money that is loaned

- Repayment of principal: The amount the issuer promises to pay back at the maturity date

All bond issues have a master loan agreement, a bond indenture, which contains the information for the issue. The issuer is required to meet all the terms and conditions of the indenture agreement. A failure to meet any of the terms of the indenture, especially the timely payment of interest and repayment of principal, can result in the issuer being in default. The following terms of a bond issue are commonly included in the indenture:

- the amount of the bond issue;
- the coupon rate;
- the frequency of interest payments (annual or semiannual);
- the maturity date;
- the call provision, if any, which allows the issuer of the bonds to call them in and repay them before their maturity dates;
- the refunding provision, if any, which does not allow the issuer to obtain the proceeds from a new debt issue to repay the bondholders of an existing issue before maturity;
- the sinking fund provision, if any, which offers bondholders greater security because the issuer sets aside earnings to retire the issue; and
- the put option, if any, which allows the bondholders to sell the bonds back to the issuer at par value.

## THE RISKS OF INVESTING IN BONDS

Investing in bonds is not without risk, although the degree of risk varies with the type of debt and the issuer. The following list describes the potential risks facing bondholders:

- The interest on the bonds might not be paid (credit and default risk).
- The principal might not be repaid.

- The price of the bond might decline to less than the purchase price before maturity (interest rate risk).

- Interest rates might fall, resulting in less interest income when the proceeds received (interest and principal) are reinvested (reinvestment rate risk).

- Interest rates might rise, causing existing bond prices to decline.

- Inflation might rise, causing an erosion of purchasing power of the interest and principal payments received (inflation risk).

- Bonds may be called before maturity.

You should be aware of how these different types of risk affect bond investments.

Interest rate risk refers to changes in market rates of interest, which have a direct effect on bond prices. The prices of fixed income securities change inversely to the changes in interest rates. During periods of rising interest rates, investors holding fixed-income securities experience losses in the market prices of their bonds because new investors to these bonds want a competitive yield. Similarly, in periods of declining interest rates, the prices of existing fixed-income securities rise. The longer the time to maturity, the greater is the potential interest rate risk. Investors can lessen interest rate risk in a portfolio with different maturities by reducing maturities and staggering their bond investment maturities. As an investor, you minimize interest rate risk if you hold onto your bonds until maturity, but you are also exposed to another risk, namely reinvestment rate risk.

Credit risk (default risk) is the risk that an issuer might be unable to pay their interest and principal payments at their due dates. Credit risk is a function of the creditworthiness of the issuer of debt. Creditworthiness refers to the ability of the issuer to make scheduled interest payments and repay the principal when bonds mature. Credit risk varies with bond issuers. U.S. Treasury issues carry virtually no risk of default because the full faith and credit of the U.S. government guarantees interest and principal payments. U.S. agency debt has a slightly increased risk of default, depending on the financial strength of the issuer. Not all U.S. government agencies have the backing of the U.S. government. Bonds issued by state and local governments depend on the financial health of the particular issuer and their ability to raise revenue. For corporate issuers, credit risks are linked to the strength of the issuing companies' balance sheets, income statements, and earnings capacities. The price of Enron bonds, for example, plummeted when Enron declared bankruptcy. The restructured Enron Corporation settled with its creditors, paying around $0.14 on the dollar. For bondholders, this settlement paid $140 on a $1,000 face value of each bond. Value investors should be aware that not all bonds trading at a discount present real value. Consequently, the first step is to select those bond issues that present value (trading at a discount) and then researching the company's (or government, in the case of agency and municipal securities) ability to earn enough revenue to be able to service the interest payments and pay back the principal at maturity.

Credit rating is a grading of the issuer's ability to service its interest and principal obligations when they become due. Independent ratings services evaluate the credit risk of municipal and corporate bonds. Table 13.1 is a list of credit ratings, ranging from the best credit quality for issuers with the strongest financial status to the lowest ratings for issuers in default. A financially strong company or municipality generally has low business and financial risk.

Moody's and Standard & Poor's (S&P) are two of the best-known ratings agencies, and their ratings are similar, though not identical. Ratings of AAA, AA, A, and BBB from S&P are considered to be investment-grade quality. Bonds with ratings lower than BBB are considered to be junk bonds and are speculative. Because these junk bonds have lower ratings, their issuers are more likely to default on their interest and principal repayments.

These ratings provide only a relative guide to assist potential bond investors because the financial status of an issuer can deteriorate

## TABLE 13.1

Bond Ratings

| Moody's | Standard & Poor's | Interpretation of Ratings |
|---------|-------------------|---------------------------|
| Aaa | AAA | Highest quality obligations |
| Aa | AA | High quality obligations |
| A | A | Bonds that have a strong capacity to repay principal and interest but may be impaired in the future |
| Baa | BBB | Medium grade quality |
| Ba | BB<br>B | Interest and principal that is neither highly protected nor poorly secured. Lower ratings in this category have some speculative characteristics. |
| B<br>Caa<br>Ca | CCC<br>CC<br>C | Speculative bonds with great uncertainty. |
| C | DDD<br>DD<br>D | In default |

over time and result in the bonds being downgraded to a lower rating. A downgrade usually causes a decline in the market price of the bond. The opposite effect occurs when a bond issue is upgraded. The same issuer with many different bond issues outstanding can have different ratings for each issue. You need not be duly alarmed if your bonds are downgraded from AAA to A, for example, because this grade still indicates good quality. However, if an issue is downgraded to lower than BBB, you should consider whether to continue owning that bond.

You can minimize credit risks by buying good quality bonds with ratings of A and above (by S&P), which have a reduced likelihood of default, and by diversifying your investments. In other words, rather than invest all your money in the bonds of one issuer, buy bonds of different issuers in different sectors of the bond market.

Call risk is the risk that a bond issue might be called before its maturity. Bonds with a call provision have call risk. Many corporate and municipal bond issues have call provisions, allowing issuers to repurchase their bonds at a specified (call) price before maturity, which is beneficial to the issuer and detrimental to the investor. Whenever interest rates decline to a few percentage points below the coupon rate of the bond, the issuer more than likely will call in the bonds. The issuer can then reissue new bonds at a lower coupon rate.

Call risk poses a potential loss of principal to the investor whenever bonds are purchased at a premium price that is greater than the call price. You can anticipate the call risk by estimating the level to which interest rates must fall before the issuer would find it worthwhile to call the issue. Callable bonds are not as advantageous as noncallable bonds. Consequently, a callable bond with the same level of risk and comparable features trades at a lower price (higher yield) than a noncallable bond.

To minimize call risk, you should examine the call provisions of the bond and choose bonds that are unlikely to be called. This advice is particularly important if you are contemplating the purchase of bonds that are trading above their par values (at a premium).

*Purchasing power risk* is the risk that inflation will erode the returns from holding bonds. Purchasing power risk is an unexpected change in inflation that diminishes an investor's real rate of return. Purchasing power risk occurs during periods of inflation, which affects bond prices. Because bond interest payments are generally fixed, the value of the payments is affected by inflation. When the rate of inflation rises, bond prices fall because the purchasing power of coupon payments received is reduced. To combat purchasing power risk, you should invest in bonds whose rates of return exceed that of anticipated inflation. If you anticipate inflation in the future, invest in floating rate bonds and Treasury

Inflation-Protected Securities, whose coupon rate adjusts up and down with market interest rates and inflation rates.

Reinvestment rate risk is the risk that payments received from an investment might be reinvested at a lower rate of return. All coupon bonds are subject to reinvestment rate risk. Interest payments received may be reinvested at a lower interest rate than the coupon rate of the bond, particularly if market rates of interest decline or have declined. Zero-coupon bonds, which make no periodic interest payments, have no reinvestment risk.

*Liquidity risk* is the risk of selling an investment at a price that is a significant price concession from the market price. A bondholder who is selling bonds always runs the risk of having to make significant price concessions from the market price. This risk is prevalent for inactively traded bonds, where a large spread occurs between the bid price and the ask price. Thus, if liquidity is important, you should invest in actively traded bonds. Bear in mind that bonds are not liquid investments like money market securities.

## YIELD TYPES AND THE YIELD CURVE

A relationship exists between bond prices and yields, as illustrated in Figure 13.2. When bond yields increase, prices of existing bonds decrease. Similarly, when bond yields decrease, prices of existing bonds increase. A bond's cash flow and an investor's required rate of return or interest rate are two components that are used to determine a bond's price. Four basic types of yields exist, as explained is this section.

### Coupon Yield

The coupon yield is the stated rate return on a bond and is determined when the bond is issued. The coupon yield is the specified amount of interest that the issuer of a bond promises to pay to the bondholder each year. This annual amount of interest may

## FIGURE 13.2

Bond Prices and Yields

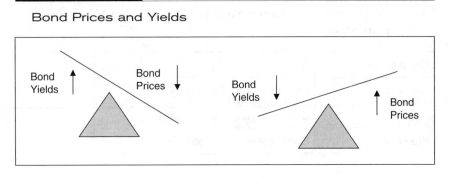

be stated as a percentage of the par value of the bond or as a dollar amount. For instance, a bond with a par value of $1,000 that pays $40 in annual interest has a 4 percent coupon yield. The coupon yield is fixed throughout the lifetime of a bond issue unless it is a variable interest coupon, which fluctuates throughout the lifetime of the bond.

## Current Yield

The current yield is the annual rate of return from a bond based on the income received in relation to the purchase price of the bond. The difference between the coupon yield and the current yield is that the divisor for the current yield is the purchase price of the bond rather than the face value of the bond. The following equation shows how the current yield is determined:

$$\text{Current Yield} = \frac{\text{Coupon Interest Amount}}{\text{Purchase Price of the Bond}}$$

For example, if a bond is purchased at par, $1,000, and the coupon is 5 percent (the interest paid is $50 per year), the current yield is 5 percent (the same as the coupon yield). However, most bonds trade above or below par. For a bond purchased at

## TABLE 13.2

The Relationship between Bond Price, Current Yield, and
Coupon Yield

| Bond price | |
|------------|---|
| Discount | Current yield > Coupon yield |
| Face | Current yield = Coupon yield |
| Premium | Current yield < Coupon yield |

$1,100 with a 5 percent coupon, the current yield is 4.54 percent
(50/1,100).

A relationship exists between bond prices, current yields, and
coupon rates. Bonds trading at a discount to their par values have
current yields that are higher than their coupon rates. Similarly,
bonds trading at a premium to their par values have current yields
that are lower than their coupon rates. Table 13.2 summarizes these
relationships.

For investors who are concerned with high current income,
the current yield is a useful measure of return.

### Yield-to-Maturity

The yield-to-maturity is the annual (discounted) rate of return
earned on a bond held to maturity. The yield-to-maturity is the discount rate calculated by mathematically equaling the cash flows
of the interest payments and principal received with the purchase
price of the bond. This term is also referred to as the internal rate of
return or the expected rate of return of the bond and is the yield in
which most investors in a bond are interested. Table 13.3 illustrates
how you can calculate the yield-to-maturity of a bond using Microsoft Excel software.

The yield-to-maturity is 8.5 percent. If you don't have Microsoft Excel software on your computer, you can use the following

## TABLE 13.3

### Using Microsoft Excel to Compute a Bond's Yield-to-Maturity

The yield-to-maturity of a bond that was purchased for $770.36 and pays a coupon of 5% ($50 annually) with a maturity of 10 years can be solved as follows:

Click on f*, which is on the top row of the toolbar in the Excel spreadsheet program. A list of functions pops up. Highlight *financial* in the box on the left and *rate* in the box on the right, and then click *OK*. A box with five rows in it is displayed:

| | | |
|---|---|---|
| Nper | | Total number of payments |
| PMT | | Enter the interest payments |
| PV | | Enter the purchase price of the bond |
| FV | | Enter the face value of the bond |
| Type | | Enter 0 for payment received at the end of the period |

| | |
|---|---|
| Nper | 10 |
| PMT | 50 |
| PV | −770.31 |
| FV | 1000 |
| Type | 0 |
| Formula result = 0.085 | |

approximation formula to determine the yield-to-maturity (YTM) for the same example:

$$YTM = \frac{\text{Coupon Payment} + \dfrac{1{,}000 - \text{Purchase Price}}{\text{Periods to Maturity}}}{\dfrac{1{,}000 + \text{Purchase Price}}{2}}$$

$$YTM = \frac{50 + \dfrac{1{,}000 - 770.36}{10}}{\dfrac{1{,}000 + 770.36}{2}}$$

$$= 8.24\%$$

Using the approximation formula, the 8.24 percent yield under-states the true yield-to-maturity that is calculated using a computer. The reason is that the approximation formula does not use the time value of money for compounding the coupon payments.

The yield-to-maturity hinges on two assumptions:

- The bonds are held to maturity.

- The interest payments received are reinvested at the same rate as the yield-to-maturity.

If the bond is not held to maturity, you can calculate the internal rate of return of the bond by substituting the sale price of the bond for the maturity value and the period held to the sale date for the period to maturity.

The yield-to-maturity rate assumes that the bondholder reinvests the interest received at the same yield-to-maturity. If this does not occur, the holder's rate of return will differ from the quoted yield-to-maturity rate. For example, if the interest received is spent and not reinvested, the interest does not earn interest; the investor earns much less than the stated yield-to-maturity. Similarly, if the stated yield-to-maturity is 8 percent and the investor reinvests the interest at lesser (or greater) rates, the 8 percent is not achieved. In reality, matching the yield-to-maturity rate for the interest received is difficult because interest rates are constantly changing. The interest received is usually reinvested at different rates from the stated yield-to-maturity rate.

The yield-to-maturity is useful, however, in comparing and evaluating different bonds of varying quality with different coupon rates and prices. For example, by comparing the yield-to-maturity of an AAA rated bond with a BBB rated bond, you can easily see how much the increment in yield would be in choosing the lower-rated bond. You can also see the yield differential between bonds with different maturities.

The relationship between the coupon yield, current yield, yield-to-maturity, and bond price is summarized below:

| Bond price | |
|---|---|
| Discount | Coupon yield < Current yield < Yield-to-maturity |
| Face | Coupon yield = Current yield = Yield-to-maturity |
| Premium | Coupon yield > Current yield > Yield-to-maturity |

## Yield-to-Call

The yield-to-call is the annual rate of return a bondholder receives to the date on which the bond is called. When a bond has a call feature, the bondholder can calculate the yield-to-call by substituting the call price for the maturity price in the equation discussed in the yield-to-maturity section. Both the yield-to-call and the yield-to-maturity should be determined because if the bond is called, the yield-to-call is the yearly total return the bondholder receives on the bond.

## The Yield Curve

The yield curve shows the relationship between bond yields and the term to maturity of bonds with the same level of risk. Figure 13.3 shows the yield curve for U.S. Treasury securities as of June 21, 2000, June 19, 2003, December 31, 2004, June 15, 2007, and March 5, 2013. Yields for the 3-month, 6-month, 2-year, 5-year, 10-year, and 30-year Treasury securities are plotted.

| | 6/21/2000 | 6/19/2003 | 12/31/2004 | 6/15/2007 | 3/5/2013 |
|---|---|---|---|---|---|
| 3-month Treasury bill | 5.63% | 0.82% | 2.28% | 4.773% | 0.12% |
| 6-month Treasury bill | 5.92% | 0.83% | 2.56% | 4.96% | 0.13% |
| 2-year Treasury note | 6.43% | 1.17% | 3.04% | 4.98% | 0.25% |
| 5-year Treasury note | 6.20% | 2.28% | 3.58% | 4.98% | 0.77% |
| 10-year Treasury note | 6.02% | 3.37% | 4.21% | 5.02% | 1.88% |
| 30-year Treasury bond | 5.89% | 4.42% | 5.00% | 5.25% | 3.1% |

**FIGURE 13.3**

Treasuries Yield Curve

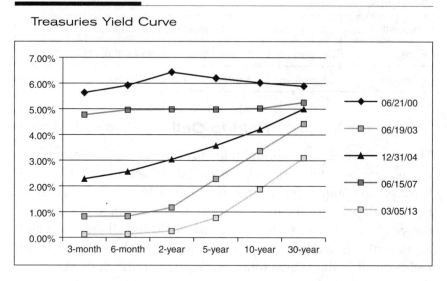

An examination of the yield curve on any particular day gives you a snapshot of the different yields of various maturities for a bond security. Figure 13.3 shows the yield curve for Treasuries, but you can create a yield curve for other bond types, such as municipal bonds, corporate bonds, and agency bonds.

Note the shape of the yield curve for June 21, 2000. It has an upward slope from three months to two years, and then a declining curve for longer maturities through 30 years. This inverted curve is generally atypical. An inverted yield curve indicates that by extending maturities, investors are taking greater risks for smaller returns. Yield curves typically assume four general shapes: rising, flat, falling, and humped, such as the one for June 21, 2000. The most common type is the rising yield curve, as depicted on June 19, 2003, December 31, 2004, and March 5, 2013. You might expect an upward-sloping curve because the longer the maturity, the greater is the bondholder's exposure to risk. For this reason, bond issuers tend to pay more to compensate investors for the risk involved with longer maturities. With interest rates at historic lows, this steeply positive yield curve of 2013 and 2003 points to higher future rates. The December 31, 2004, yield curve shows how yields have increased 18 months later to the yield curve shown in 2007.

On a few occasions, the yield curve has had a downward slope, showing short-term yields exceeding long-term yields. In other words, yields decline as maturities increase. This situation happened in 1979, 1981, and 1982.

The shape of the yield curve changes daily with the changes in yield because of fluctuations in market rates of interest. The yield curve can assist you in choosing which maturities of bonds to buy. Value investors should use the yield curve to determine whether or not bonds should be purchased and then to assist in the decisions of which maturities to invest in. The 2013 yield curve shows the extraordinary low levels of interest rates, which highlight the risks of investing in bonds. The first major risk is that investors in the shorter-term Treasuries are receiving negative yields (yields are less than the rate of inflation, and interest received is also taxed, reducing the already low rates of return to negative returns), and investors in longer maturity bonds are taking more risk by holding 20–30 year bonds with low coupon rates that do not take into account the possibility of increasing future inflation. The second major risk is that interest rates can remain near zero, but there is a good chance that interest rates will eventually rise, causing existing bond prices to decline.

Keep in mind the following generalities about yield curves:

- Most of the time the yield curve is upward sloping, with yields on long-term securities greater than the yields of short-term securities.

- Changes in the yield curve generally take the form of shifts up and down over time. When short-term yields are rising, generally long-term yields also rise. Similarly, when short-term yields are falling, long-term yields also fall.

- During a recession short-term yields fall faster than long-term yields; during a period of economic expansion, short-term yields rise faster than long-term yields.

---

**HOW TO OBTAIN BOND YIELDS TO CONSTRUCT A YIELD CURVE**

Using the Internet, obtain yields for the different Treasury securities to construct a yield curve. Based on the shape of the yield curve, decide whether you should invest in long-term or short-term maturity bonds. You can obtain information from www.treasury.gov/resource-center. On the website's home page you will find a ticker tape that posts the daily prices and yields of Treasury securities.

---

## VALUATION OF BONDS

Bond prices fluctuate because of the relationship between coupon rates, market rates of interest (required rate of return), the bond's creditworthiness, and the length of time to maturity. After bonds are issued, they rarely trade at their par values ($1,000) in the secondary markets because interest rates are always changing. Certain bonds sell at premium prices, while others sell at discounted prices.

The market price of a bond is determined using the bond's coupon payments, the principal repayment, and the investor's required rate of return, as illustrated in Figure 13.4. Using the time value of money, this stream of future interest payments and principal repayment is discounted at the investor's required rate of return or the market rate of interest to its present value in today's dollars.

Most corporate bonds pay interest semiannually, which means that the coupon rate is halved and the length of time to maturity is multiplied by two to convert to six-month periods. Using these modifications, the price of a bond is easily determined using Microsoft Excel.

What is the price of a bond that has a 10 percent coupon rate, pays interest semiannually, and matures in three years? The investor's required rate of return for this bond is 6 percent.

**FIGURE 13.4**

Market Price of a Bond

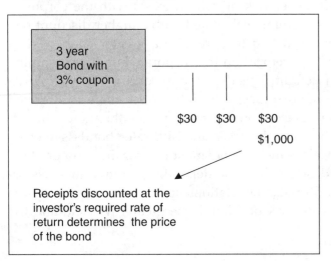

A 10 percent coupon payable semiannually results in a coupon payment of $50 per six-month period, and the 6 percent annual discount rate is halved to 3 percent for six semiannual periods until maturity.

Using Excel to find the price of a bond, click on PV in the right-hand box and enter the data as illustrated:

| | |
|---|---|
| Rate | 0.03 |
| Nper | 6 |
| PMT | 50 |
| FV | 1000 |
| Type | 0 |
| Formula result = 1108.34 | |

The price of the bond is linked to its coupon payment, market rates of interest or investor's required rate of return, risk of the bond, and the length of time to maturity. If you compare the price of a U.S. Treasury note with the same coupon rate and maturity as that of a corporate bond, you will notice that they have different prices. The Treasury note trades at a higher price than the corporate bond because a greater risk of default exists with the corporate bond; the price is therefore calculated with a higher discount rate (or yield-to-maturity). You then require a greater coupon yield (and required rate of return) on the corporate bond for assuming a greater risk of default. This description confirms why an AAA-rated corporate bond trades at a higher price than a BBB-rated corporate bond if the coupon and maturity are the same. The difference in yield between the AAA- and BBB-rated bonds is referred to as the *excess yield*, which issuers must pay for the extra grade of credit risk. Bond prices fluctuate depending on investors' assessments of the bond's risk. The relationships can be summarized this way: the greater the risk of a bond, the greater its yield and the lower its market price.

## WHY BONDS FLUCTUATE IN PRICE

Several factors directly account for fluctuations in bond prices. These factors include the relationships between bond prices, coupon rates, market yields, maturities,[3] and risk assessment. The following axioms illustrate these relationships:

- The coupon rate relative to market rates of interest: when market rates of interest rise and exceed the coupon rate of a bond, the price of the bond will decline in order to relate the current yield to the market rate of interest. When interest rates fall, the price of the bond will rise. The smaller the coupon rate of the bond, the greater will be the fluctuations in price.

  - The length of time to maturity: the longer the maturity, the more volatile the price fluctuations.

  - For a given change in a bond's yield: the longer the maturity of the bond, the greater the magnitude of change in the bond's price.

- For a given change in a bond's yield: the size of the change in the bond's price increases at a diminishing rate the longer the maturity of the bond.

- For a given change in the bond's yield: The magnitude of the bond's price is inversely related to the bond's yield.

- For a given change in a bond's yield: The magnitude of the price increase caused by a decrease in yield is greater than the price decrease caused by an increase in yield.

- Changes in risk assessment by the market: The lesser the quality of the bond, the lower the price, the greater the quality of the bond, the higher the price. The greater the risk of the bond, the more volatile the bond's price fluctuations.

## Interest Rates and Bond Prices

The first reason that bond prices fluctuate has to do with the inverse relationship between bond prices and market rates of interest. When market rates of interest rise, the prices of existing bonds fall; when interest rates fall, prices of existing bonds rise. The extent of this change in bond prices is determined by the coupon rates of the bonds. This relationship between interest rates and the coupon rates of bonds determines whether bonds trade at a discount or at a premium price, as shown below:

- Bonds trade at a **discount** when their coupon rates are lower than market rates of interest.

- When the yield-to-maturity of the bond (ask yield or bid yield) is greater than the coupon rate, the bond generally trades at a **discount**.

- A bond trades at a **premium** when its coupon rate is higher than market rates of interest.

- A bond generally trades at a **premium** when its yield-to-maturity is lower than its coupon rate.

**FIGURE 13.5**

Factors that affect the price of a bond

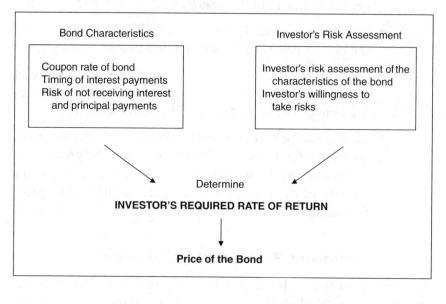

## Interest Rates and Maturity

A second reason for the fluctuations in bond prices is the relationship between interest rates and the length of time to maturity. Some bonds are more sensitive to changes in interest rates than others because of their different maturities. For example, two bonds with the same coupon rate but different maturities react differently to changes in interest rates. Not only is the longer-maturity bond more volatile than the shorter-maturity bond but the magnitude of price changes is also greater for bonds with longer maturities.

Figure 13.5 summarizes some of the major factors that affect bond prices.

# THE PURCHASE PROCESS OF BONDS

Bonds are quoted in hundreds, but trade in thousands. A bond price quote of $86¾ indicates that the bond is trading not at $86.75 but rather at $867.50 per bond.

The bid price is the highest price a buyer will pay for a bond. For example, when someone sells a bond that is quoted at a bid of 94½, the highest amount buyers will offer is $945.00 per bond. The ask price is the lowest price offered by a seller of a bond. For example, an investor buying a bond with a bid of $94½ and an ask price of $94⅝ would pay $946.25 per bond (the lowest price a seller of this bond will accept). The spread is the difference between the bid and the ask prices of the bond, part of which is a commission paid to the broker or dealer. A large spread indicates that the bond is inactively traded.

Bonds are purchased the same way as stocks. Although most bonds are bought and sold through brokerage firms, you can purchase some bonds through banks or directly from their issuers. The different types of purchase orders (market and limit orders) used for stocks also apply to the purchase of bonds. The major difference between buying stocks and bonds is the lack of pricing transparency for bonds. Current price quotes indicating the bid and ask prices for bonds during the trading day are not quoted on the Internet. When you want to buy the stock of a company, you call your broker or search the Web for the current price. You can easily obtain the current bid and ask prices for a stock. Finding the current bid and ask prices for a bond can be difficult, because the bond market is a dealer market, while the same bonds could be offered at different prices. For example, one dealer offered a General Motors bond maturing in 2028 at $867.50 and another dealer asked $900.00 for the same bond.[4] Individual investors are not only unlikely to receive the best prices but also the bid and ask prices of bonds in order to ascertain their spreads.

Although some corporate bonds are listed on the New York and American stock exchanges, the vast majority of bonds are traded in the over-the-counter markets. You can easily find in the daily newspapers the price quotes of bonds that are listed on the exchanges. Figure 13.6 shows examples of a typical corporate and municipal bond listing in the newspapers.

## FIGURE 13.6

### Corporate and municipal bond quotation

#### Corporate Bonds

| Name | Coupon | Maturity | Last Price | Last Yield | Est. Spread |
|------|--------|----------|-----------|-----------|-------------|
| General Motors | 8.375 | Jul 15, 2033 | 101.452 | 8.242 | 346 |

| After the name of the bond, General Motors, is the coupon yield of 8.375%. Bond-holders receive $83.75 in interest each year per bond held until maturity. | This bond matures on July 15, 2033. | The last price Indi-cates that this bond traded at $1014.52 at the close of the preced-ing day Jan. 11, 2005 | The last yield of 8.242% is the percentage yield a bondholder would receive if this bond was bought and held to maturity | The estimated spread is 346 basis points, or 3.46%. The spread is the difference between the bid and ask price |
|---|---|---|---|---|

#### Municipal Bonds

| ISSUE | COUPON | MAT | PRICE | BID YIELD |
|-------|--------|-----|-------|-----------|
| NYC gen oblig bond | 5.00 | 11-01-34 | 101.778 | 4.77 |

| The name of the issuer is New York City New York general obliga-tion bonds. | These bonds pay 5.00% of par ($1000) which is $50.00 per bond per year. | The maturity date is November 1, 2034. | The price of the bond was $1017.78 as of the preceding day. | The bid yield is the percentage yield if the bond was purchased at the bid price and held to maturity. |
|---|---|---|---|---|

## Accrued Interest

An investor who is buying a bond might pay more than its ask price because of the accrued interest on the bond. Accrued inter-est is interest that is owed but not yet paid. It is added to the price of a bond. Although a bond earns interest daily, the issuer of the bond pays out the interest once or twice a year. Therefore, if a bond is purchased between the dates on which the interest is paid, the buyer owes the seller the accrued interest for the number of days the seller owned the bond. The amount of accrued interest is added to the purchase price of the bond. The accrued interest is stated separately on the confirmation statement the brokerage firm sends when the bonds are bought and sold. The following example illustrates how accrued interest is calculated.

Jason bought a bond with a coupon rate of 6 percent payable annually on June 30. He purchased the bond on December 31 of the preceding year. How much must he pay the seller in accrued interest?

Jason owes the seller for the interest accrued from July 1–December 31 (six months of the previous year):

$$\text{Accrued interest} = \text{Length of time the seller owned the bond before interest is paid} \times \text{coupon}$$
$$= 6/12 \times \$60$$
$$= \$30$$

Bonds that are in default and no longer paying interest are said to trade *flat*. Flat bonds do not trade with accrued interest and in the bond quotes in the financial pages of the newspapers have an *f* next to the bond, signifying that it is trading flat.

## WHAT YOU SHOULD REMEMBER ABOUT BONDS BEFORE INVESTING

- Bonds have an element of safety that stocks do not have in that bonds provide a level of steady income.

- Investing in bonds along with stocks and money market securities provide diversification to a portfolio that minimizes the risk of loss.

- When investing in bonds, pay attention to the direction of interest rates and future inflation. If interest rates look like they are going to rise in the future, you will lose part of your principal if you invest in bonds because of the inverse relationship between bond prices and interest rates.

- If inflation is perceived to increase, do not invest in bonds because of the erosion in purchasing power in the interest received and returned principal.

- If you decide to invest in individual bonds when interest rates are likely to rise, you can hold the bonds to maturity and you will receive the face value of the bonds when they mature, and interest payments during the life of the bonds will be lower than newly issued bonds.

- Investing in bond mutual funds when interest rates are rising will result in a loss of principal as net asset values of mutual funds decline as a result of the decline in bond prices.

- If interest rates are perceived to be increasing, investors can limit their losses from bonds by investing in shorter-term maturities.

- In anticipation of a recession, bonds generally do well, as interest rates are expected to decline to help the economy get back on track to growth.

- Bond investments do well when interest rates are declining and there is no inflation on the horizon.

## CHAPTER 14

# Preferred Stock

**P**referred stocks appeal to investors seeking current income due to their higher yields over common stocks. In order to share in the lower federal tax rates on dividends, investors need to make sure that the preferred issues they purchase qualify for the lower tax rates. Convertible preferred stock can earn shareholders capital appreciation should the price of the common stock of the company rise above the conversion price.

## WHAT IS PREFERRED STOCK?

Preferred stock is classified on a balance sheet as equity, but it has many features that resemble debt securities. Equity is defined as capital invested in a company by its owners; debt is capital lent to the corporation that must be repaid. Preferred stock is a hybrid type of security in that it has characteristics resembling both debt and equity. Generally, preferred stocks have a fixed dividend, but owners of preferred stock do not have voting rights. Although preferred stock is classified as equity, preferred stockholders do not have ownership interests in the company. The failure of a company to pay dividends to preferred stockholders does not result in bankruptcy, as it would with the default of interest on bonds. Instead, the company does not pay common stockholders any dividends until the preferred stockholders are paid their dividends. Unlike common stock, the dividend rate on preferred stock is usually fixed. It might be stated as a percentage of the par value of the preferred stock, or as a fixed dollar amount. The par value is a stated value and, hence, a preferred stock issue with $100 par value that has a dividend of 6 percent would pay a dividend of $6 per share (6 percent of $100).

In the event of bankruptcy, the claims of preferred stockholders are senior to the claims of common stock but subordinate to the claims of debtholders on earnings and assets of a company. If a preferred stock issue has a call provision, it may be retired by the company.

## Reasons to Invest in Preferred Stock

The fixed dividend of preferred stock appeals to investors who seek regular payments of income, but in exchange for regular income, preferred stocks do not experience large capital gains (or losses). The downside to a fixed dividend rate is that the price of preferred stock is sensitive to changes in market rates of interest similar to bonds. For example, if you had bought preferred stock for $100 a share that pays a dividend of $4, and market rates of interest subsequently go up to 6 percent, there will be downside pressure on the price of this preferred stock issue. New investors will not want to buy this preferred stock for $100 when the dividend is only $4 (a return of 4 percent, 4/100), when new preferred stock issues return a higher yield. Prices of adjustable-rate preferred stock issues do not fluctuate as much as the prices of fixed rate preferred stock issues with changes in interest rates. Thus, preferred stock is appealing to investors if interest rates remain stable or decrease.

Another advantage to owning preferred stock is the changes to the U.S. tax code enacted in 2003. Dividends from preferred stock are taxed at favorable rates, which are lower than marginal tax rates. However, not all preferred stock issues benefit from this favorable tax treatment. A majority of the preferred stock issues, namely trust preferred stock issues, do not qualify for this favorable tax treatment. These trust preferred stock issues are created by trusts that technically pay interest, and therefore the payments are taxed at the taxpayers' marginal tax rates (which could be as high as 39.6 percent in 2013).

## CHARACTERISTICS OF PREFERRED STOCK

There are a number of characteristics that define preferred stock.

### Multiple Classes of Preferred Stock

Most companies issue one class of common stock, but it is quite common to see companies with more than one series of preferred stock. Table 14.1 illustrates some of the different preferred stock issues of Citigroup Inc., listed on the New York Stock Exchange.

Each class of preferred stock has different features. For example, Citigroup's preferred F series pays a dividend of $2.13 per share, with a yield of 8.24 percent at a closing price of $25.82 per share, and was down $0.12 from the preceding day's closing price. Citigroup has several *noncumulative preferred* stock issues. *Cumulative preferred stock* gives holders the right to receive all missed dividend payments (dividends in arrears) before common shareholders are paid. *Convertible preferred* stock can be converted by holders into a fixed number of shares of common stock of the underlying company. A call provision gives the issuing company the right to call the preferred stock at a specific price (normally a premium over its par value). These issues might also be differentiated in their priority status with regard to claims on assets in the event of bankruptcy.

## TABLE 14.1

Different Preferred Stock Issues of Citigroup Inc.

| Stock | Div | Yld | Close | Net Chg | |
|---|---|---|---|---|---|
| Citigroup pfAA | 2.03 | 6.9 | 29.45 | 0.10 | Noncumulative Preferred Stock |
| Citigroup pfE | 1.59 | 6.3 | 25.26 | −0.14 | Floating rate, Noncumulative Pref |
| Citigroup pfF | 2.13 | 8.2 | 25.82 | −0.12 | Noncumulative Preferred Stock |
| Citigroup pfT | 3.25 | 5.0 | 64.61 | −3.88 | Noncumulative, Convertible Pref |
| Citigroup pfV | 1.78 | 7.0 | 25.28 | −0.15 | Trust Preferred Stock |
| Prices as of March 25, 2013 | | | | | |

## Claims on Income and Assets

Preferred stock has a preference over common stock with regard to claims on both income and assets. Companies are required to pay dividends on preferred stock before they pay dividends to common stockholders. In the event of bankruptcy, preferred stockholders' claims are settled before the claims of common shareholders. This makes preferred stock less risky than common stock but more risky in relation to bonds; bondholders have priority in claims to income and assets over preferred stockholders. Companies must pay the interest on their debt and in the event of a default, bondholders can force the defaulting corporation into bankruptcy, while dividends on preferred stock (and common stock) are declared only at the discretion of the board of directors. In the case of multiple classes of preferred stock, the different issues are prioritized in their claims to income and assets.

## Cumulative Dividend

Many preferred stock issues carry a cumulative feature, which is a provision requiring a company to pay any preferred dividends that have not been paid in full before the company can pay dividends to its common stockholders. In other words, if the company fails to pay dividends to its cumulative preferred stockholders, it will have to pay all the missed dividends before the company can pay any dividends to its common shareholders. A company that fails to pay its dividends is said to be in arrears, which is defined as having outstanding preferred dividends that have not been paid on a cumulative preferred stock issue. Before the company can pay dividends to its common stockholders, it would have to pay the dividends in arrears to its cumulative stockholders first. This cumulative feature protects the rights of the preferred stockholders. A preferred issue that does not have a cumulative feature is called a noncumulative preferred stock. Their dividends do not accumulate if they are not paid.

## Convertible Feature

Some preferred stock issues have a convertible feature that allows holders to exchange their preferred stock for common shares. The conditions and terms of the conversion are set when the preferred stock is first issued. The terms include the conversion ratio, which is the number of common shares the preferred stockholder will get for each preferred share exchanged, and the conversion price of the common stock.

For example, a corporation issues a mandatory convertible preferred stock issue, which will automatically convert on June 15, 2018, into the company's common stock. If the company issues the convertible preferred stock with a par value of $100 and a 4 percent dividend, converting into 4 shares of the common stock when the common stock is trading at $20 per share, the conversion value is $80. If the common stock rises to $30 per share, the conversion value is $120, and the convertible preferred stock will rise in price to reflect the conversion value. If the price of the company's common stock rises above the conversion price before June 15, 2018, holders can convert at their option. The decision to exercise the conversion option depends on three factors:

- The market price of the common stock; it must be greater than the conversion price for the holder to share in capital gains.
- The amount of the preferred dividend.
- The amount of the common dividend.

The conversion feature provides the investor with the possibility of sharing in the capital gains through the appreciation of the common stock, as well as the relative safety of receiving the preferred dividends before conversion. If the preferred dividend is much greater than the common dividend, holders would weigh this into the amount of the appreciation as to whether to hold the preferred or convert to common stock. If, however, the common stock never rises above the conversion value, the convertible preferred stock will continue to be priced based on the dividend yield.

## Call Provision

A preferred stock issue with a call provision entitles the issuing company to repurchase the stock at its option from outstanding preferred stockholders. The call price is generally more than the preferred stock's par value.

The call provision is advantageous to the issuing company and not to the holder of the preferred stock. When market rates of interest decline significantly below the dividend yield of the preferred issue, companies are more likely to exercise the call provision by retiring the issue and replacing it with a new preferred stock issue with a lower dividend yield. Citigroup redeemed for cash all the outstanding shares of its 8.4 cumulative preferred stock Series K at a redemption price of $25 per share plus accrued dividends in

October 2001. In January 2003 Citigroup called in its adjustable rate cumulative preferred stock Series Q and R for a cash price of $25 per share plus accrued dividends.

When a preferred issue is called, the savings to the issuing company represent a loss of income to the preferred stockholders. Thus, not only do preferred stockholders suffer a loss of income when their high-dividend-rate preferred stock issues are called in but the call provision also acts as a ceiling limit on the price appreciation of the preferred stock. When interest rates decline, there is an upward push on the price of high-dividend rate preferred stock issues, but the price of the preferred stock will not rise above the call price. For example, if a preferred stock issue has a call price of $55, potential buyers of the preferred stock would be unlikely to pay more than this amount when interest rates decline significantly. This is because investors who pay more than this ceiling price would lose money if the issue is called.

To entice investors to buy preferred stock issues during periods of high interest rates, companies include a *call protection* feature. This prevents the company from calling the issue for a period of time, generally five years, though this varies. After the call protection period, the issue is callable at the stated call price per share.

## Participating or Nonparticipating

Participating preferred issues allow holders to receive additional dividends (over and above regular dividends) if they are declared by the board of directors. These additional dividends are generally less than the extra amounts paid to common shareholders. The majority of preferred stocks are nonparticipating.

# HOW TO EVALUATE PREFERRED STOCK

Investors invest in preferred stock primarily for the dividend, but dividends can be suspended by the board of directors. Therefore it is important to understand the type of business the company is in, and whether the company can earn enough cash to cover its dividend payments. When you find the preferred stock of a company in which you are interested, read the preferred stock prospectus (usually a 423b prospectus filing).

Most preferred stock issues are rated by agencies such as Standard & Poor's, Moody's, Fitch, or Duff & Phelps. These ratings categories are slightly different from the ratings of bonds. Ratings above B are considered to be investment grade, with AAA being higher than AA and A. Below B are considered to be speculative or junk.

Before investing in preferred stock, compare the yield (dividend divided by the stock price) of the preferred stock with the yield of comparable bonds. The yield of the preferred stock should be higher than the yield of comparable bonds.

Most preferred stock issues do not benefit shareholders from the lower federal tax dividend treatment. Check that the issue you are interested in purchasing qualifies for the favorable tax rate on dividends. If the issue is a preferred trust stock or a derivative, it does not qualify for the lower tax rates on dividend income for investors.

## THE RISKS OF PREFERRED STOCK

There are a number of risks you should consider before investing in preferred stock.

### Risk of Not Receiving Dividends

There are several situations that could occur in which investors would not receive dividends. If the board of directors of a company does not declare dividends for any period, preferred shareholders who hold noncumulative issues will not receive dividends for that period. If the board of directors of that company decides to authorize and declare dividends in later periods, only cumulative preferred shareholders will be paid the dividends that were omitted in the prior period.

Another factor that could preclude preferred shareholders from receiving dividends is if the company has any outstanding junior subordinated debt securities, which prohibit the company from paying dividends. The company could issue additional series of junior subordinated debt securities that prohibit the company from paying dividends, or the company could defer payment of dividends.

Preferred stockholders only receive dividends if the company has the ability to pay them. Unlike debt issues, preferred shareholders have no recourse to make the company pay their dividends, whereas bondholders who do not receive their interest payments when due can start bankruptcy proceedings. The price of preferred stock when dividends are not paid or deferred plummets like a falling knife. Consequently, investors should examine the company's financial statements to determine the company's leverage, its ability to service its debt, and its ability to be cash flow positive, along with investment grade credit ratings of BBB and above.

## Interest Rate Risk

Preferred stock acts similarly to changes in interest rates as bonds. When interest rates in the economy rise, prices of existing preferred stock declines, and when interest rates in the economy declines, prices of preferred stock rise. Assume that you own preferred shares that pay a dividend of 3 percent that currently trades at $25 per share. If market rates of interest rise, and new preferred stock issues are paying dividends of 4 percent, investors will not be willing to pay $25 for the 3 percent preferred stock issue. To be marketable, the price of the 3 percent preferred issue will decline from $25 per share.

In the current (March 2013) low interest rate scenario, investors should be concerned with the possibility of rising interest rates.

## Risk of Inactive Trading of
## Preferred Stock Issues

Some preferred stock issues are thinly traded, which may make it difficult to get in and out of a stock issue at a reasonable price without a large price concession. Consequently, avoid inactively traded or lightly traded preferred stock issues. Stick to those issues that trade above 4,000 shares per day.

## Call Risk

Preferred stock issues could be called prior to their maturity date. Consequently, investors should be cautious when paying a premium for an issue with a call provision. If the issue is called, investors could lose some of their capital.

# TRUST PREFERRED STOCKS

There is very little difference (other than the tax treatment) for investors in whether they invest in a regular stock issue or a trust preferred stock issue, but for issuers there is a considerable difference. Issuers of trust preferred stock issues gain the tax advantages of being able to deduct the interest payments on the subordinated debt, thereby negating the favorable tax treatment on dividends for preferred trust shareholders. Of the Citigroup preferred stock listed in Table 14.1, Citigroup's preferred V series is a trust preferred stock. This is how preferred trust stocks work:

- A bank holding company forms a wholly owned trust that sells the trust preferred stock issue to investors. The proceeds from the sale of the trust preferred stock is used by the trust to purchase the subordinated debt issue of the bank holding company. The terms of the subordinated debt issue and trust preferred stock issue are identical.

- The bank holding company deducts the interest payments on the subordinated debt as well as the dividend

payments from taxes. In order to qualify for the latter, the trust preferred issue must have a cumulative
feature.

- When the financial statements are consolidated, the subordinated debt is eliminated and the trust preferred stock is
shown as "minority interest in equity accounts of consolidated subsidiaries" on the bank holding company balance
sheet.

## Trust Preferred Derivatives

There are different trust preferred issues with different names,
depending on the sponsor or investment bank, each with its
own acronym: MIPS (monthly income preferred shares), TOPrS
(trust originated preferred shares), QUIDS (quarterly income
debt securities), QUIPS (quarterly income preferred shares), and
Corts (corporate-backed trust securities).

The common features of these securities are:

- A par value of $25 instead of the traditional $1,000 par for
a bond

- Listed on the stock exchanges as opposed to the bond
exchanges or OTC

- Pays regular interest

- Most have a maturity date, though there are some issues
that are perpetual, like common stock

- Many have call provisions

Generally these are easier to buy than regular preferred stocks
and bonds, as they are listed on the stock exchanges, where prices
are available, and they do not require as large a capital outlay
as bonds with the lower par value. Table 14.2 lists some of these
securities:

## TABLE 14.2

Trust Preferred Derivative Preferred Stocks

| Stock | Ticker Symbol | Dividend | Yield | Close | Net Change |
|-------|---------------|----------|-------|-------|------------|
| Cort J C Penney | KTP | 1.91 | 7.625% | 17.12 | −0.48 |
| Cabco J C Penney | PFH | 1.91 | 7.625% | 17.32 | −0.28 |

The first of the issues listed is J C Penney's corporate-backed trust securities (Corts), with a coupon of 7.625 percent and a maturity on March 1, 2097. The closing price of this issue as of March 28, 2013, was $17.12, which is a discount to its par value. The rating of this trust preferred issue is the same as the J C Penney 7 5/8 percent bonds in the trust. There is a call provision for this issue that puts a ceiling on the appreciation of the issue when interest rates decline.

J C Penney's corporate asset-backed (Cabco) securities, also issued with a 7.625 percent yield and trading under the ticker symbol PFH, pay a dividend of $1.91 and were trading at $17.32 per share on March 28, 2013. In the early 2000s, J C Penney was not as financially sound as it was in 2006, when it regained some of its retailing momentum, and in the early part of the decade its Cabco securities were listed as junk bonds. J C Penney has lost that retailing momentum in 2013, which is reflected in the prices of its Cort and Cabco securities.

There are some caveats that investors should be aware of:

- Be cautious when paying a premium for an issue with a call provision. If the issue is called, you will receive the par value, $25, or the call price, which means that you can lose some of your capital.

- These companies can suspend their dividends during times of financial hardships.

- Companies with balance sheets that are overleveraged might use this type of security to raise funds. Consequently, you should look for issues with strong credit ratings.

Preferred and trust preferred stock issues appeal to investors seeking income and sacrifice the potential of long-term growth through capital gains.

# CHAPTER 15

# Options, Rights, and Warrants

**O**ptions have many uses and value investors need to be aware of their ramifications in order to be able to use them. For example, the use of options can protect investors' profits by limiting their losses in the likelihood of downturns in the market that can turn profits into losses. In order to do so, however, investors need to familiarize themselves with knowledge about options, and they also need to be aware that money used for options to protect their portfolios can be lost. Consequently, the cost of options should be used with money investors can afford to lose. Other benefits from the use of options, besides the protection of profits, are to reduce risks and increase leverage in portfolios. The following sections discuss what options are and how they can be used. There are many strategies, but because this is an introductory chapter, it points to directions of further use that can be explored. Investors who have the time and inclination to explore the use of options further than on this basic level can use sophisticated strategies to protect profits, limit their risk, and/or increase leverage.

This chapter focuses on options, which are stock derivative investments. A *derivative security* is a financial security that derives its value from another security. Stock derivatives, such as options and futures, are securities that offer investors some of the benefits of stocks without having to own them.

## OPTIONS AND HOW THEY WORK

An *options* contract gives the holder the right to buy or sell shares of a particular common stock at a predetermined price (strike price) on or before a specified date (expiration date). An option is a right, not an obligation, to buy or sell stock at a specified price before or on an expiration date. The strike price is the price at which the holder of the option can buy or sell the stock. An option expires on its expiration date. A stock option is a derivative security because its value depends on the underlying security, which is the common stock of the company. For example, the value of an option to buy or sell Intel stock depends on the market price of Intel stock. Other underlying securities for option contracts besides common stock are stock indices, foreign currencies, U.S. government debt, and commodities.

Options are traded on the Chicago Board Options Exchange (CBOE), as well as on the New York Stock Exchange (NYSE), the American Options Exchange (AOE), the Philadelphia Exchange (PHO), and the Pacific Exchange (PSE). Options can also be traded in the over-the-counter market.

Understanding how options contracts work can provide you with additional tools that can be used successfully in volatile markets. Options are used to speculate on the movement of future stock prices and to reduce the impact of the volatility of stock prices. In some respects, options are similar to futures contracts. One of these similarities is that option holders with a small investment can control a large dollar amount of stock for a limited time. However, the risk of loss is much less for option holders than it is for futures holders.

An options contract gives the owner the right to buy or sell a specified number of common shares (generally 100) of a company at a specified price within a time period.

The two types of contracts to buy and sell stocks are calls and puts. A call option gives the option owner the right to buy shares of the underlying company at a predetermined price (strike price) before expiration, and a put option contract gives the option owner the right to sell shares of the underlying company at the strike price before expiration. The option holder has the right to convert the contract at his/her discretion. It is not an obligation. In other words, holders of the option can exercise the option when it is to their advantage and let the options contract expire if it is not advantageous. There are six items of note in an options contract:

1. The name of the company whose shares can be bought or sold.

2. The number of shares that can be bought or sold, generally 100 shares per contract.

3. The exercise or strike price, which is the stated purchase or sale price of the shares in the contract.

4. The expiration date, which is the date when the option to buy or sell expires.

5. The settlement procedure.

6. The options exercise style.

As in any contract, there are at least two parties: buyers and sellers. The option buyer is also referred to as the option holder, and the seller of the original contract is referred to as the option writer. See Table 15.1 for a summary of the features of options buyers and sellers.

**TABLE 15.1**

Characteristics of Options Contracts for Buyers and Sellers

| Option | Buyer's Obligation | Right | Seller's/Writer's Obligation | Right |
|---|---|---|---|---|
| Call Option | Buys at the option price | Owner can buy the underlying stock at the strike price before expiration from the writer. | Required to sell the underlying stock at the strike price to the buyer, at the buyer's option, before expiration. | Receives the option price. |
| Put Option | Buys at the option price | Owner can sell the underlying stock at the strike price before expiration to the writer. | Required to buy the underlying price stock at the strike price before expiration from the buyer, at the buyer's option. | Receives the option price. |

The settlement procedure is stipulated for stock options, which indicates when delivery of the underlying common stock takes place after the holder exercises the option. There are two basic exercise styles that determine when the option can be exercised. Options on individual stocks can be exercised any time before the expiration date (American style), while stock index options can be exercised only on the expiration date (European style). The expiration date is also important, as it specifies the life of the option. The expiration dates are standardized for options contracts listed on the exchanges. There are three cycles for listed option expirations, and each option is assigned to one of these cycles:

> January cycle: January–April–July–October
>
> February cycle: February–May–August–November
>
> March cycle: March–June–September–December

## How Options Work

The following example illustrates how options contracts work.

Investor A thinks that the stock of Exxon Mobil is going to go up but does not want to invest the large amount required to buy 100 shares. Investor A can buy a call option contract for 100 shares of Exxon with a strike price (or exercise price) of $95 per share. Investor W wrote this contract to sell 100 shares of Exxon stock with a strike price of $95 per share. At the time, Exxon stock was trading around $98 per share. Both investors have different outlooks as to the direction of Exxon's share price. Investor A believes the share price will go up, while Investor W anticipates that the share price is going to decline before the options expire.

Investor W bears the risk of loss if the price of Exxon stock goes up instead of down. If Investor A exercises the option to call in the stock, then Investor W will have to buy Exxon stock at a higher price and deliver it to Investor A. Investor W is compensated for this risk by charging the buyer of the contract an amount of money called a premium or option price. If the premium is $3 per share,

Investor A pays $300 to Investor W to buy the call option contract, giving Investor A the right to buy 100 shares of Exxon stock at $95 per share before the expiration date of the contract.

If the price of Exxon stock rises above $98 per share within the time period before the expiration date, Investor A will profit by exercising the option. Assume that Exxon stock rises to $102 per share before expiration, and Investor A decides to exercise the option. Under the call option terms, Investor A has the right to buy 100 shares of Exxon stock at $95 per share. Investor A pays Investor W $9,500 for 100 shares of Exxon. If Investor W does not have 100 shares of Exxon, he or she would have to buy the stock at $10,200 (100 shares at $102 per share) and transfer it to Investor A.

Investor A paid a total of $9,800: $300 for the option (premium price) plus $9,500 for the stock. The costs for Investor W resulted in a total loss of $400, composed as follows: an outlay of $10,200, which was partially offset by the receipts from Investor A of $9,500 for the stock plus $300 for the option contract. This example is illustrated in Figure 15.1.

**FIGURE 15.1**

How a Call Option Works

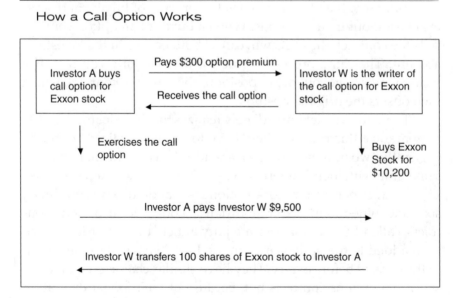

If, on the other hand, the price of Exxon stock declines to $92 and remains at that price throughout the duration of the contract, Investor A will have lost the amount of the contract premium ($300). Thus, the greatest amount that an investor can lose buying an option is the cost of the option contract. The advantage of a call option is that the investor has a high degree of leverage (a small amount of money, $3 per share, which controls a larger sum, $95 per share). The option buyer can also profit from selling the option when there is an increase in the premium price.

Investor W also has some alternatives. If he wants to get out of this contract, he can buy the contract from someone else. The trading of options is greatly facilitated by the Options Clearing Corporation (OCC), which, besides maintaining a liquid marketplace, also keeps track of the options and the positions of each investor.

Buyers and writers of options do not deal directly with one another but instead with the OCC. When an investor buys a contract, the OCC acts as an intermediary, ensuring that the provisions of the contract are fulfilled. When the contract is exercised, the OCC guarantees that the option buyer receives the stock even if the writer defaults on delivery.

Similarly, the OCC facilitates the process of buyers and writers closing out their positions. When a buyer of an option contract sells the contract, the OCC will cancel both entries in the investor's account. The same process is true for a writer of a contract. If a writer wants to get out of her position, she buys the contract, which then offsets the original position.

The astute reader immediately realizes that in order for the OCC to guarantee this process, there have to be standardized contracts. Generally, two options on a stock are introduced to the market at the same time with identical terms except for the strike (exercise) price. The contract period for stock options is standardized with three-, six-, and nine-month expiration dates. Longer-term options contracts, called LEAPS (long-term equity anticipation securities) have been added to the options exchanges. LEAPS have life spans of up to three years before expiry. They have similar characteristics to the short-tem options contracts but, because of their longer expiration periods, have higher premium prices.

## Reading Options Quotes

Newspapers do not list stock options contracts available, so potential investors need to go online to the options exchanges, or financial websites, such as www.yahoofinance.com/options, www.nasdaq /options, and www.quote.com/us/options/, to find the large number of contracts available. Table 15.2 illustrates an example of an actively listed stock option.

The first column in Table 15.2 indicates the name of the option traded, Apple Inc. The month following indicates the expiration, in both cases it is the month of June. The strike price is $235 per share. In the case of the first option, which is a call option, the holder has the right to buy 100 shares of Apple Inc. at $235 per share. In the case of the second option listed, which is a put, denoted by the $p$ following the strike price, the option holder has the right to sell 100 shares of Apple Inc. at $235 per share. The next column shows the sales volume of contracts traded for that day through 1:31 p.m. For the Apple call option contract, there were four contracts traded for the day. The put option had 341 contracts traded up through 1:31 p.m. that day. The last price indicates the price of the last trade of the option ($199.55 per share for the call option and $0.34 per share for the put option). The net change indicates the change in price from the previous day's closing price. There is no change between the current last price for both the call and the put option from the preceding day's closing option prices.

The bid/ask quotes reflect the highest price a buyer is willing to pay for an option and the lowest price a seller is willing to

## TABLE 15.2

Example of One of the Most Active Equity Options

| AAPL stock price as of 3/18/2013 at 1:31 p.m. | | | | | | | | |
|---|---|---|---|---|---|---|---|---|
| Option | Name | Strike Price | Volume | Last Price | Net Change | Bid | Ask | Open Int |
| AAPL | June | 235.00 | 4 | 199.55 | 0.00 | 217.45 | 219.20 | 25 |
| AAPL | June | 235.00 p | 10 | 0.34 | 0.00 | 0.06 | 0.28 | 341 |

sell the option. The bid price of $217.45 per share is the highest price a purchaser of this call option is willing to pay. The ask price of $219.20 per share is the lowest price the seller of this option is willing to accept. An investor buys at the ask price and sells at the bid price. *Open interest* indicates the number of outstanding or open contracts. When an investor buys an options contract to take a new position in the company, it increases the open interest. Similarly, if an investor sells an options contract that he already owns, that investor is closing out a position, and open interest will be decreased by that contract. There are 25 open-interest contracts for the Apple call option and 341 open-interest contracts for the Apple put option.

Different websites provide more comprehensive listings of options and trading information.

---

**OPTIONS WEBSITES AND HOW TO OBTAIN PRICE QUOTES**

Use the Internet to visit the following options exchanges to obtain options price quotes:

www.cboe.com

www.nyse.com/futuresoptions/nyseamex

www.amex.com

www.phlx.com

Using the Chicago Board Options Exchange (www.cboe.com), click on *market quotes* and highlight *delayed options quotes*. The 20-minute delayed quotes are free, as they are with stocks. In the box, enter the stock symbol of the option of interest; for example, *MSFT* for Microsoft, *INTC* for Intel, *PEP* for Pepsi-Cola. Click on all exchanges and list all options and LEAPS. Click on *Submit,* and a list of options for the stock you requested will appear.

## CALL OPTIONS AND HOW TO BENEFIT FROM THEM

A call option gives the holder the right to buy 100 shares of the underlying stock at the exercise or strike price up through the date of expiration of the option. Using the Exxon example cited in the previous section, we can see how buying a call option can be beneficial to an investor.

In return for paying the premium of $300 ($3 premium price times 100 shares), Investor A has the right to buy Exxon shares at $95 per share anytime until the expiration of the option. The downside risk is that the option is not exercised and the investor loses the $300 for the option contract, plus a commission. When buying a call option, the investor puts up a fraction of the cost of the stock in order to participate in the appreciation of the stock if it moves above the strike price of $95 per share. Instead of putting up $9,800 to buy 100 shares of Exxon stock when the market price is $98 per share, she invests $300. Should the stock rise above $98, she can exercise the option and buy the stock at the strike price of $95 per share.

The basic problem is that the stock would have to move up in price above the strike price before the option expires because the option is worth nothing at expiration. It is a wasting asset. There is a time value to the price of an option. The more time before the option expires, the greater is the time value of the option. Similarly, as the option moves closer to its expiration, so the time value of the option decreases in value.

The link to the time value of the option is the underlying price of the stock and the call option's strike price. These relationships affect the *intrinsic value* of the option. The intrinsic value is the difference between the market price of the stock and the strike price. When the market price is greater than the strike price, the call option is said to be *in the money*. In the Exxon example, if the market price of Exxon stock moves up to $99 per share, the intrinsic value of the call option is $4 per share and the option holder can acquire Exxon stock for less than the current price. The value of a call option is greatest when it is in the money. A call option is said to be *out of the money* when the market price of the stock is less than the strike price. *At the money* is when the market price equals the strike price:

**Intrinsic Value of Call Option** = (Market Price of the
Stock − Strike Price)
= ($99 − $95)
= $4 per share

The time until expiration of the option has a direct effect on the valuation of the option. The greater the length of time until expiration, the greater is the chance that the option will be in the money. Thus, an option with a longer time until expiration trades at a higher premium than options approaching expiration.

The option premium price fluctuates depending on two factors:

The underlying price of the stock.

The time left until the expiration of the option.

If Exxon's stock moves up to $100 per share, the intrinsic value of the option rises to $5 per share. This increase in the stock price causes the option to trade for much more than the $3 premium price for which the option was originally sold.

Another course of action for the call buyer is to sell the option for a profit rather than exercising it. The leverage that can be obtained explains why so many investors prefer this course of action. See the example in Table 15.3, which illustrates the benefits of leverage from buying and selling the option rather than buying and selling the stock.

Buying and selling the stock, in scenario one, results in a 20 percent return. This is not to be sneezed at, but compared to buying and selling the option in scenario two, buying and selling the stock comes in as a poor second to a return of 1350 percent. Comparatively, the third scenario, buying and exercising the option, produces the smallest return of 18.3 percent. Moreover, this third alternative also requires the largest outlay of capital ($3,550 versus only $50 for the call option and $3,500 to buy the stock). However,

**TABLE 15.3**

Leverage: Should You Buy and Sell the Option or the Stock?

| | | |
|---|---|---|
| **Stock price $35 Option price $0.5 Strike price $35** | | |
| **Stock price rises to $42 Option premium price increases to $7.25** | | |
| Scenario One: **Buying the Stock** | | |
| Buy 100 shares of the stock at $35 per share | Total Cost | $ 3,500 |
| Sell 100 shares of the stock at $42 per share | Total proceeds | $ 4,200 |
| Profit | | $ 700 |
| Return on Investment 700/3500 | 20% | |
| Scenario Two: **Buying and Selling the Option** | | |
| Buy stock option | Total Cost | $ 50 |
| Sell stock option | Total Proceeds | $ 725 |
| Profit | | $ 675 |
| Return on Investment 675/50 | 1350% | |
| Scenario Three: **Exercise Option** | | |
| Buy stock option | Cost | $ 50 |
| Cost to exercise option at strike price | Cost | 3,500 |
| Total cost | Total | $ 3,550 |
| Sell stock at $42 per share | Total proceeds | $ 4,200 |
| Profit | | $ 650 |
| Return on Investment 650/3550 | 18.3% | |

if the stock price declines to $30 per share, buying the stock at $35 and selling it at $30 results in a $500 loss and a 14.28 percent loss (−500/3500). Buying the stock option and having it expire results in a 100 percent loss on invested capital and a $50 loss of capital. There is no third alternative; the strike price is above the current price, so the option would not be exercised. The maximum loss is the cost of the option, $50. The three profit/loss scenarios are illustrated in Figure 15.2.

## FIGURE 15.2

Profit and Loss from Buying the Stock versus a Call Option

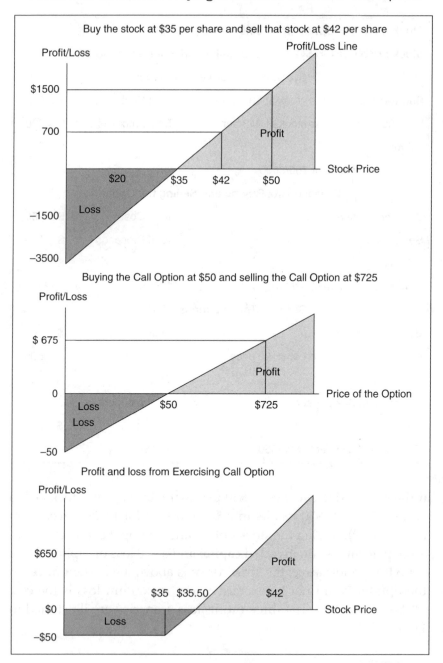

Buying and selling the option not only gives the greatest return on investment but also requires the lowest capital outlay. By buying a call option instead of the stock, the investor invests a small fraction of the cost of the stock. If the stock price rises significantly above the strike price within the period before expiration, the investor can profit by selling or exercising the option. In the latter case, the investor can then sell the stock or hold it for long-term capital appreciation.

The most an investor can lose from buying a call option is the cost of the option. Thus, the downside risk is limited, as opposed to the potential loss in the case of buying the stock. There are many examples of high-flying stocks that have risen to abnormally high prices only to fall back into oblivion, resulting in tremendous losses for those investors who had invested when the stocks were trading at excessively high prices.

## When Calls May Be Used

Call options benefit buyers when the price of the underlying stock rises above the strike or exercise price. The example in the previous section shows that if an investor bought the call option instead of the stock, the greatest percentage return would come from selling the option, due to the concept of leverage. If the market price of the stock declines below the strike price of the option, the most the investor would lose is the option premium.

Call options may also be used as a hedge against an upturn in the price of a stock on a short position. Assume that an investor had sold short 100 shares of Boeing stock when it was $80 per share. When the price of Boeing declines to $69 per share, the investor wants to protect the $11 profit per share against a rise in the price of Merck stock. The investor could buy a call option, which has a strike price of $70 per share. For every $1 increase in Boeing stock above $70 per share, there is a profit on the call option that offsets the loss on the short sale. If, however, Boeing continues to go down in price, the investor has lost only the amount paid to buy the option. This strategy allows an investor to protect profits without having to close out his position.

# PUT OPTIONS AND HOW TO BENEFIT FROM THEM

A put option gives the holder the right to sell 100 shares of the underlying company's stock at the strike price up until the expiration date of the option. This is the opposite of a call option. The put option buyer profits when the price of the underlying stock falls below the strike price. A put option increases in value when the price of the underlying stock declines. Investors buy puts when they are bearish on the stock. The premiums on puts are generally smaller than those on calls for the same stock. This is because more investors are bullish than bearish; hence fewer put options are traded than call options.

## When to Buy Puts

Put options are used to protect existing profits in stocks and limit the extent of capital losses in existing stock positions. Investors profit from buying puts when the price of the underlying stock declines below the exercise or strike price. Rather than selling a stock short when a decline in the stock's price is anticipated, an investor can buy a put option. For example, if an investor is bearish on a stock that is currently trading at $32 per share, a six-month put option with a strike price of $30 could be bought for about $200 (contract for 100 shares). If the stock does go down in price below the strike price, the investor can either exercise the option by selling 100 shares of the stock at the strike price of $30 per share and buying the stock at the lower market price or selling the put option at a profit.

The use of put options limits the risk of loss as compared to short selling, where the risk of loss is open-ended. When selling a stock short, the price of the stock could increase rather than decrease, thereby increasing the amount of money that would be lost. The greatest amount that can be lost with a put option is the premium paid to buy the option.

The put option holder has various alternatives:

- Exercise the option at the strike price using your own shares or buy the shares at a lower price and tender them at exercise.

- Sell the option at a profit.

- If the stock price increases above the strike price, the option expires and the most that can be lost is the amount of the premium paid for the option.

These alternatives are shown below, also illustrating the concept of leverage. Assume that years ago you bought 100 shares of a stock at $30 per share and the stock price is currently $70 per share. You buy a six-month put option on that stock with a strike price of $70 for a premium of $200.

---

### RETURNS FROM BUYING AND EXERCISING PUT OPTIONS OR BUYING AND SELLING PUTS

**Present Situation**

| | |
|---|---|
| Own 100 shares of the stock at a cost basis of | $3,000 |
| | ($30 per share) |
| Buy a 6-month put option with a strike price of $70 per share Premium cost | $200 |

**After 5 months**

Price of the stock declines to $40 per share

A. **Exercise the Put Option using your 100 shares**

| | |
|---|---|
| Exercise the put option (sell the shares at $70 per share) Gross proceeds | $7,000 |
| Tender the shares originally purchased at a cost of | 3,000 |
| Profit | 4,000 |
| Rate of return on investment $4,000/$3200*          125% | |

**B. Exercise the Put Option and buy the shares at the lower price**

| | |
|---|---|
| Sell the shares at $70 per share Gross proceeds | $7,000 |
| Purchase 100 shares at a cost of $40 per share | 4,000 |
|   Profit | 3,000 |

Rate of return on investment $3,000/$4200            71%

**C. Sell the Put Option**

| | |
|---|---|
| Sell the put option $30 per share Gross proceeds | $3,000 |
| Cost to purchase the put option | 200 |
|   Profit | 2,800 |

Rate of return on investment $2,800/200            1,400%

**D. Price of the stock rises to $90 per share at the end of 6 months**

Value of the put option equals 0 at expiration

Loss is $200 or 100 percent of invested capital.

*includes the cost of the option

The put option holder also benefits from leverage in the same manner as for call options. For a small premium, the investor can control the larger dollar value of the stock, as shown by the rate of return of 1,400 percent in alternative C. In alternative A you have protected your existing capital profit against the decline in market price of the stock through the purchase of a put option. If you did not already own the stock or wanted to retain the shares of the stock you originally purchased, you could exercise the option and purchase the shares for a 71 percent return, as shown in alternative B.

As with calls, puts are wasting assets and have no value at expiration. The intrinsic value of the put option is determined by subtracting the market price of the stock from the strike price.

$$\text{The Intrinsic Value of a Put Option} = \text{Strike Price} - \text{Market Price}$$
$$\text{of the Stock}$$

The intrinsic value cannot be less than zero (a negative number) by convention. If an option has no intrinsic value, it is out of the money. When it is profitable to exercise the put option, it is in the money because it has intrinsic value. If the strike price equals the market price of the stock, the option is at the money.

Generally, options are not normally exercised until they are close to expiry because an earlier exercise means throwing away the remaining time value. Another generalization with options (both calls and puts) is that most options are not bought with the intention of exercising them. Instead, they are bought with the intention of selling them.

When an option is in the money, the option holder can sell and receive an amount of money greater than the premium paid, but if the option is exercised, the put holder has to come up with the money to buy the stocks (if they are not already owned), so that they can be sold at the strike price. Transaction costs are incurred in both of these transactions.

The use of a put option can be viewed as an insurance premium to protect profits against a decline in the price of the stock.

## WRITING OPTIONS

Investors can also write or sell options, which provide additional income from the premiums received from the buyers of the option contracts. The upside potential to this strategy for option writers is limited, however, because the most money the writer can make is the amount of the option premium.

There are two ways to write options. The more conservative method is to write covered options. A *covered option* is an option that is written against an underlying stock that is owned, or sold short, by the writer. The writer of the option owns the stock against which the options are written. The second method is the writing of a *naked option*, which is an option written on an underlying stock that is not owned or sold short by the writer.

## Writing Covered Calls

Investors seeking ways to increase income on stocks they already own can write covered calls. Using this strategy works the same way as a call, except that the writer owns the stock. An example illustrates how writing covered calls work.

Suppose an investor has 1,000 shares of Citigroup stock that was purchased some time back at $25 per share. Citigroup is selling around $48 per share. Instead of selling the stock outright, the investor can write call options on Citigroup. If the investor writes 10 call contracts of 100 shares per contract with a strike price of $50 at a premium of $2 per share ($2,000 for 10 contracts) with expiration in September, she will receive $2,000 minus commissions. If Citigroup's stock price never goes above $50 per share before the expiration of the contracts, the buyer will not exercise the call and the writer ends up with an additional $2,000 (minus commissions on the options contracts).

If the stock price rises above $50 per share, the buyer exercises the call and buys the stock for $50 per share. The writer makes a profit of $27 per share ($50 minus the $25 cost of the shares plus the $2 per share premium). This is the maximum profit the writer will get from the covered call option, even if Citigroup rises to $100 per share. This additional appreciation will be lost because the writer must surrender the stock at the strike price of $50.

Summing up, a covered call limits the appreciation the writer can realize. Therefore, it is a good idea to write covered calls on the stocks you think won't rise or fall very much in price. The other side of the coin is that if the stock falls significantly in price during the option period, the writer will lose money if she eventually sells the stock at the low price. The call buyer will not exercise the call because the market price of the stock will be cheaper than the strike price.

## Writing Naked Calls

Writing a naked call on a stock is more risky than writing a covered call because of the potential for unlimited losses. A naked call is when the writer does not own the underlying stock, which would limit the losses if the stock rocketed up in price. For example, assume that a writer writes a naked call on Citigroup stock for which the writer receives a premium of $2 per share with a strike price of $50 per share. If Citigroup rises dramatically in price to $90 per share and the option buyer exercises the call, the writer will be left with a large loss. The writer receives $50 per share (the strike price) plus the premium price of $2 per share, but he would also have to pay $90 per share to buy the stock to deliver to the buyer. Of course, if the writer anticipates the rise in price, he would have bought Citigroup stock earlier at a lower price or bought back the option to close out his position.

Writers of naked (or uncovered) options, calls, and puts must deposit the required margins with their brokerage firms, but writers of covered options need not deposit any money with their brokerage firms.

Investors can profit from writing naked calls on stocks whose prices either decline or remain relatively flat below the strike price for calls.

### Writing Covered Puts

A put is the opposite position to a call. The writer of a covered put sells short the underlying stock and receives a premium for the covered put. If the option is exercised, the writer would buy back the stock at the strike price and use the shares to close out his short position. The use of writing covered put options is rare because if the writer sells the stock short, the writer expects the stock to go down in price. If the stock goes up in price, it would not benefit the writer by writing a covered put because the option would not be exercised and she would have to buy back the stock at a higher price to close out the short sale.

### Writing Naked Puts

The writer of a put option expects the stock to rise or at best not fall in price. If the put writer does not own the underlying stock, the contract is a naked or uncovered put, which necessitates that the writer deposits an amount of money with the brokerage firm for the required margin. Without owning the underlying stocks, the potential loss is not cushioned if the price of the stock falls rapidly.

For example, if an investor writes a naked put on Citigroup when the market price is at $45 per share with a strike price of $45 and receives a $2 premium per share, the writer has the same loss potential as owning the shares. If the shares decline in price, the writer would lose money. If Citigroup shares fall to $40 per share, the writer would have to buy the stock at $45 at exercise, resulting in a loss of $300 ($4500 -$4000 + $200). The most that can be lost is $43 per share (the price of the stock up to $45 per share if Citigroup declines to $0 before expiration minus the option premium $2 per share). If the price of Citigroup's stock rises above $45 per share, the put option will not be exercised and the maximum profit the writer will make is $200. The profit/loss in this example is illustrated graphically in Figure 15.3.

## FIGURE 15.3

Profit and Loss from Writing a Naked Put on Citigroup Stock

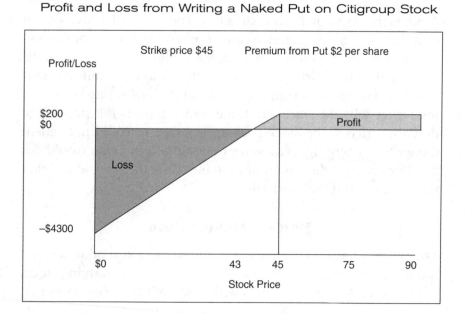

**SHOULD YOU INVEST IN STOCKS OR OPTIONS?**

*The Advantages of Options*

- Options allow investors to speculate on the future direction of the price of a stock by investing a relatively small amount of money.

- Investors can use options as insurance to hedge against large losses from adverse changes in stock prices.

- Writing options provides a source of income for investors.

- The losses from buying options are limited to the amount of the premium.

*The Disadvantages of Options*

- Options are wasting assets in that they have short lives (up to nine months). LEAPs have longer lives.

- If the price of the stock does not reach or go beyond the strike price, the option investor loses money.

- Although options can be used to produce relatively large percentage profits from the small amounts invested, you need to be aware that commissions tend to be high on a percentage basis.

Table 15.4 summarizes the potential profits and losses for the different ownership positions in stocks and options.

# THE USE OF A COMBINATION OF PUTS AND CALLS

As investors get more sophisticated in their use of options, there are situations in which a combination of puts and calls can be combined for profit opportunities. A *straddle* is the purchase (or sale) of

## TABLE 15.4

Summary of Profit and Loss Potential

| | |
|---|---|
| Purchase common stock | Unlimited gain. Maximum loss is the cost of the stock. |
| Purchase call option | Unlimited gain. Maximum loss is the cost of the option. |
| Purchase a put option | Maximum gain is the strike price minus the cost of the option. Maximum loss is the cost of the put option. |
| Write a call option | Maximum gain is the premium received on the option. Maximum loss (limited to no more than the cost of the stock minus the premium). |
| Write a put option | Maximum gain is the premium received on the option. Maximum loss is the strike price minus the premium received from the option. |
| Sell stock short | Maximum gain is the price of the stock. Unlimited loss |
| Covered call | Maximum gain is the strike price minus the cost of the shares plus the premium received on the option. Maximum loss is the price paid for the stock. |
| Write a naked put option | Maximum gain is the premium received on the option. Maximum loss is the price of the stock falling to $0 minus the premium received on the option. |

a put and a call with the same strike price and the same expiration date, whereas a *spread* is the purchase or sale of a combination of put and call options contracts with different strike prices.

## Using a Straddle

The following example illustrates how an investor can profit from using a straddle. Suppose an investor is interested in buying some oil stocks. With an economic slowdown in Europe and Asia, an investor is not sure whether the price of oil will go up or down from its current price.

Consequently, instead of buying oil stocks, the investor could buy a combination call and put option on an oil stock. Options on

Exxon, whose stock was trading at $89 per share, can be bought as follows:

- $2 ³/₈ ($237.50 per contract) for a January call with a strike price of $90.
- $2 ³/₈ ($237.50 per contract) for a January put with a strike price of $90.

The total cost of this straddle is $475.00 ($237.50 + $237.50) plus commissions, which means that the greatest potential loss is limited to this cost if Exxon stock does not rise above $94 ¾ or below $85 ¼ per share in the next six months before expiration.

If the price of oil goes up, oil stocks could jump in price. Assume that Exxon stock goes up to $98 per share: the call option could be sold around $800 ($8 multiplied by 100 shares), resulting in a profit for the investor. If, on the other hand, American oil comes into the worldwide supply causing a glut of oil, oil stock prices could fall. If Exxon stock falls to $83 per share, the put option could be sold for around $7 per share, resulting in a profit from selling this option.

If Exxon stock trades above $94.75 or below $85.25, the investor profits from selling the call or put options, respectively. If Exxon trades within the $85.25 to $94.75 range, the investor loses money on the straddle. The amount of the loss depends on the price of Exxon stock. For example, if the investor sold the call option when Exxon stock was trading at $93.50, the option could be sold around $3.50, or $350 per contract. The loss would then be $125 (the cost of the straddle options, $475, minus the proceeds received from the sale of the option, $350). Commissions increase the loss further.

To profit from this straddle, the price of the underlying stock has to move considerably in either direction, upward or downward.

## Using a Spread

An investor can use a spread strategy, which is the purchase and sale of different options with different strike prices and expiration dates. For example, an investor could take both a long and a short position in two different options on the same stock.

## USE OF A SPREAD

Stock price of a company $43
6-month call option with a strike price of $40 with a premium cost of $4 per share ($400 per contract)
3-month call option with a strike price of $45 with a premium cost of $2 per share ($200 per contract)

### Strategy

| | |
|---|---|
| Buy the call option with a strike price of $40 per share | Cost ($400) |
| Write (sell) the call option with a strike price of $45 per share Premium receipt | <u>200</u> |
| Net Outlay | $200 |

The maximum profit if the stock rises above $45 is $300 from this combination. The investor exercises the call and pays $40 per share and then tenders the shares, receiving $45 per share when the call option with the strike price of $45 is exercised. This results in a profit of $300 ($500 minus the $200 net outlay for option premium). The maximum loss is $200 if the stock price falls below $45 per share.

There are a number of different spreads that can be used to hedge positions that limit potential losses and potential profits. You can use the Internet to obtain information on option prices to test your straddle and spread strategies before you invest. The boxed information below illustrates how to use Yahoo's Website.

## WEB EXERCISE

Go to www.yahoofinance.com/options. Enter stock symbols you are interested in following. Pull up a detailed view of these stocks. Click on *options,* found beneath the chart. Use the options quotes to test your straddle and spread strategies.

## How to Use Stock Index Options

Stock index options allow investors to take long and short positions on the market without having to buy or sell short the stocks that make up the index. A stock index option is a put or call written on a market index. Options are offered on most of the major stock market indices, namely, the S&P 500 Index, the Dow Jones Industrial Average, the Nasdaq 100 Index, and the Russell 2000 Index. Settlement for stock index options is in cash rather than stocks. For example, if a call option for the S&P 500 Index has a strike price of $1,050, the holder has the option of buying the index for cash for $105,000 (100 × 1,050) at expiration. If the S&P 500 Index increases above the strike price plus the cost of the option, the holder will make some money. If you think the market is going to decline, you can buy a put option.

With stock index options you can track the markets without having to buy or sell the stocks. The Dow Jones Industrial Average consists of 30 blue chip stocks, the S&P 500 Index consists of 500 large-cap stocks, the Nasdaq 100 tracks the 100 largest stocks on the Nasdaq, and the Russell 2000 consists of 2,000 small-cap stocks. These broad-based stock index options are actively traded primarily on the Chicago Board Options Exchange. Options on stock indices are valued and trade in the same way as options on individual stocks with the notable exceptions that settlement is made in cash for the former.

The use of stock index options can assist individual investors with large stock portfolios to hedge against potential losses. If the investor does not want to sell holdings of appreciated stocks in the portfolio, the investor can protect these gains by buying stock index put options. If the market declines, the stock index puts will rise in value, which will offset the losses on the individual stocks. Instead, if the investor wrote call options on the stock index resembling the portfolio, the value of the options would decline if the market declined. The stocks in the portfolio would lose value, but this loss would be offset by the premiums received from writing the call options.

## RIGHTS

Rights have some similar features to stock options, particularly call options. Stock rights are issued to existing shareholders on a stated date. A right, also known as a preemptive right, is an option allowing a shareholder to buy additional shares of new stock of the company at a specified price within a specified time period before the shares are offered to the public. A right allows a current share-holder to buy more common stock of the company in advance of the public at a discounted price (subscription price). If a corpora-tion has a preemptive rights clause in its charter of incorporation, it must give its existing shareholders the opportunity to maintain their proportionate ownership percentages in the company when the corporation issues new shares to be sold.

Generally, each share of stock receives one right. Thus, if an exist-ing shareholder owned 10,000 shares of common stock, he would receive 10,000 rights with a rights offering. The board of directors determines the number of rights needed to buy each new share.

For example, if a company has 200,000 shares outstanding and wants to raise $750,000 from the sale of new equity at a subscrip-tion price of $15 per share, it will need to issue 50,000 new shares ($750,000/$15). The number of rights needed to buy each new share of common stock is 4, calculated as follows:

$$\text{Number of Rights to Buy a New Share} = \frac{\text{Number of Shares Outstanding}}{\text{Number of New Shares Offered}}$$

$$= \frac{200,000}{50,000}$$

$$= 4$$

These rights give existing shareholders the opportunity to main-tain their same proportionate ownership in the company after the new issue of common stock. If a shareholder has 20,000 shares before the new issue, with a 10 percent ownership of the company (20,000/200,000), the rights offering of the new shares will entitle this shareholder the right to buy 5,000 new shares (20,000 rights/4 rights per share). After the new share issue, this shareholder will have the opportunity to retain her 10 percent share of ownership in the company (25,000/250,000).

To be eligible to buy these additional shares at the subscription price, the common stock of the company must be owned as of the record date set by the board of directors. Most rights offerings have a short period of time (between two and six weeks) for existing shareholders to either subscribe to the new shares or sell the rights. It is during this period that the stock is said to be trading *cum rights*, where the value of the right is included in the market price of the stock. After a specified date, known as the *ex-rights date*, stock transactions do not include the rights. Theoretically, the stock price goes down after this date, when the rights trade separately.

Rights of the larger companies trade on the stock exchanges, the same as their stocks; those of the smaller companies are traded on the over-the-counter markets, where the stocks of those companies trade.

Like an option, the value of a right depends on the market price of the stock, the subscription price of the right, and the number of rights necessary to buy each new share. The formula to determine the value of the rights before they trade independently of the stock is as follows:

$$\text{Cum Rights Value} = \frac{\text{Market Price of Stock} - \text{Subscription Price}}{\text{Number of Rights to Buy a Share} + 1}$$

For example, a stock whose market price is $20 is offered at a subscription or exercise price of $14 and five rights are needed to purchase each new share; the cum right value is $1.00:

$$\text{Cum rights Value} = \frac{(\$20 - 14)}{5 + 1}$$

$$= \$1$$

After the stock trades ex-rights, its price declines by the value of the right, because rights trade separately from the stock. In this example, the market price of the stock would decline from $20 to $19 per share. Investors who want to buy the rights can purchase them on the market in the same way they can purchase the stock. The ex-rights value is calculated as follows:

$$\text{Ex-rights Value} = \frac{\text{Market Price of Stock} - \text{Subscription Price}}{\text{Number of Rights Needed to Buy a Share}}$$

$$= \frac{\$19 - 14}{5}$$

$$= \$1.00$$

This happens to be the same price as the cum rights value. In reality, the market value of the right fluctuates as the market price of the stock changes, but it does not deviate very far from its theoretical value (calculated with the formula above).

When the stock price rises, the value of the right also increases, but at a larger percentage rate due to the leverage factor. A two-point increase in the stock causes the right to increase by $0.40, which is a 40 percent increase. Leverage also works in reverse when the price of the stock falls. A small decrease in the price of the stock results in a greater percentage decline in the value of the right.

Rights, like options, can be bought for one of two reasons: either to exercise the rights or to speculate on the rights. This then leads to the question many rights owners ask: When should you sell your rights?

The value of the right is linked to the price of the stock, but owners are also acutely aware of the short period of time before their rights expire. This almost implies that prices of rights may be higher earlier in the subscription period. Theoretically, the closer the expiration date, the greater is the decline in the value of the right.

Rights offer their holders distinct advantages:

- The ability to buy more common stock at a discounted price.

- The ability to maintain their same ownership position in the company when more shares are sold.

- The opportunity to profit from trading the rights.

The disadvantage is that with the short life of the right, the investor needs to act before the right expires.

Bearing this in mind, beginning investors should not plunge into the speculative aspects of trading rights. This should be left for more experienced investors.

## WARRANTS

A warrant is a security that allows its owner to purchase a stated number of shares of common stock at a specified price within a specified time period. A warrant is similar to a long-term option in that it gives the owner the right to buy a stated number of shares of the underlying company's stock at a specific price within a specific period of time. The differences between warrants and options are that with warrants the specified price can be fixed or it can rise at certain intervals, such as every five years, and the company can extend the expiration date.

Warrants have longer lives than options. An option can have a life of nine months or less; warrants extend for years, and some companies have issued perpetual warrants. Generally, there is a waiting period before warrants can be exercised.

Corporations issue warrants as sweeteners with other securities issued by the company. Warrants can be attached to bonds or preferred stocks. In some cases, warrants have been distributed to shareholders in place of stock or cash dividends.

Attaching warrants to a new bond issue or preferred stock issue may make the issue more marketable to potential investors. If the warrants are not detachable, they can be exercised or sold along with the bond or preferred stock (almost like convertible bonds or convertible preferred stock).

If the warrant is detachable, it trades separately on the stock or over-the-counter market. Stock warrants are quoted along with the stocks in the stock markets where their respective company's stocks trade. Investors can follow the prices of the warrants in the stock market sections of the newspapers. With detachable warrants, investors can sell the warrants for a profit and still retain the underlying security (bond or preferred stock).

When a company issues warrants, the purchase price of the stock is generally fixed at a higher price than the market price of the stock at issue. For instance, if a company floats a new bond issue with detachable warrants that give the holders the right to buy the common stock of the company at $25 per share when the market price of the stock is only $15 per share, the warrants have no intrinsic value. However, if the market price of the stock rises to $32 per share, the warrant has a value of $7 {($32 − $25) × 1}.

Value of a warrant = (Market price of stock − Exercise price) × number of shares purchased with the warrant

If the market price of the stock never rises to the strike price of the warrant during its life, the warrant is not exercised and expires.

If the market price of the warrant is $8, the premium on the warrant is $1 ($8 − $7).
Premium = Market price of the warrant – Value of the warrant

The major advantage of warrants over options is that warrants have longer lives. Warrants do well when stock prices are rising, but investors should still be selective about the warrants they buy. If the stock never goes up in price, there is little to no opportunity to profit from buying the warrants. Generally, as with options, warrants should be bought to trade and not to exercise. All brokerage firms have lists of the warrants trading on the markets.

## SHOULD YOU BOTHER WITH OPTIONS, RIGHTS, OR WARRANTS?

The natural inclination of most investors is to question whether they should even bother with using options, which can be relatively complicated. Steven M. Sears wrote that most people lose money using options.[1] Options do have characteristics that make them unattractive to some investors:

- Options contracts have short lives, and investors could lose their entire investment if the stock price does not change in the predicted direction within the time frame.
- Investors could lose their entire investment even if the stock price moves in the predicted direction after the time frame.
- The risk of loss is not limited when selling uncovered calls or puts.

Yet there are a number of reasons for using options:

- Investors can profit from using options without having to invest larger amounts to buy the underlying equity. In other words, investing in options costs a fraction of the cost of buying the stock.
- Returns on invested funds from the use of options is much greater than investing in stocks. The lesson that Michael Schwartz, Oppenheimer's chief options strategist, suggests is that if you double your money, take profits. The example used is that if you purchased a GE April $23 call option for $1 and the stock rises to $25 per share, the option will increase in value to $2, so holders should take their profits and not be greedy.[2]
- The risk of loss is limited to the cost of the premium paid on the option when buying options.
- Mini options were launched on March 18, 2013. They represent 10 shares of stock, as opposed to regular options contracts, which represent 100 shares, with the aim of creating a broader audience for this market.

Understanding what rights and warrants are can assist investors in determining a course of action when faced with having to make decisions about them.

# CHAPTER 16

# Portfolio Management and Evaluation

The aim of portfolio management is to assemble individual invest-ment securities in a portfolio that conforms to the investor's level of risk and rate of return. The investor's objectives are the most impor-tant guidelines to managing an investment portfolio. The main types of objectives for a portfolio are preservation of principal, providing income, and/or seeking capital growth. For example, an investor pursuing capital growth for a portfolio might allocate a greater por-tion of the portfolio's assets toward growth stocks, small-cap stocks, and real estate, leaving a small part of the portfolio in assets seek-ing principal preservation and income generation. From time to time the investor should evaluate the performance of the portfolio with regard to risk and return as to whether the portfolio is meeting his or her investment objectives.

An investor seeking income with some capital growth from a portfolio would allocate a greater portion of the portfolio to bonds, along with some stock investments. For example, a total portfolio amount of $600,000 might be invested in the following manner: $500,000 in bonds yielding 3.5 percent, which would generate income of $17,500 per year, and $100,000 in 3 percent dividend-yielding stocks, which would bring in an additional $3,000 in income per year. By investing a small percentage of the portfolio in stocks rather than

100 percent in bonds, this investor is seeking potential capital growth to the portfolio and also minimizing the total risk. If large-cap stocks increase by 8 percent for the year, the value of the stock portfolio would grow to $108,000, which would more than offset the reduction in income from investing in lower-yielding stocks than bonds.

Investors must be continually aware that not only do their objectives and individual characteristics change over time but that their investments must be monitored due to financial conditions and markets. Companies change, and their securities might no longer fulfill the criteria for which they were purchased. Not all investments in the portfolio realize their projected returns, so investors managing their portfolios might need to sell and replace them with other investments. This does not mean that all or most of the investments in the portfolio should be continuously turned over. Only those investments that are unlikely to achieve the objectives specified should be liquidated.

## ASSET ALLOCATION

Asset allocation is a plan to invest in different classes of assets (types of securities, namely, stocks, bonds, and money market funds) so that the capital invested is protected against adverse factors in the market. This, in essence, is the opposite of an investor putting all his eggs in one basket.

Diversification is an important balancing tool in a portfolio. For example, a portfolio might have investments in different asset classes according to a well-balanced asset allocation plan, but all the stocks and bonds might be invested in the investments of companies in the same economic sector, which would not insulate the portfolio from the risk of loss. By investing in the stocks of different companies in various sectors of the economy and different types of bonds, the portfolio would be better insulated against the risk of loss.

The risk of loss has been spread over a number of securities. Increasing the number of stocks and bonds held in a portfolio decreases the volatility. However, by increasing the number of stocks and bonds held in a portfolio, investors are also reducing the potential performance of that portfolio. Diversification seeks a balance between the risk-return trade-off. The return on a portfolio is dependent on the types of investments held in it.

Classifying some of the different types of investments on a continuum of risk, common stocks are considered to be the most risky (in terms of variability in share price), followed by long-term bonds, with the shorter maturities on the low-risk end. Bear in mind that there are many other types of investments, which are riskier than common stocks, such as commodities and futures contracts. Similarly, there is a great variation of quality among common stocks. The common stocks of the well-established blue chip companies are considered to be less risky than the bonds of highly leveraged companies with suspect balance sheets. With interest rates currently near zero, even good-quality bonds exceed the risk of dividend-paying and blue chip stocks, making this a dilemma for investors looking for relative safety of principal and income generation.

Common stocks are considered to be the most risky due to the volatility of stock prices. However, over long periods of time, where the ups and downs of the stock market can be averaged out, stocks have provided higher returns. Common stocks provide the growth in a portfolio and should be included among the investment assets to accomplish the long-term growth goals. The percentage allocated to common stocks depends on the investor's objectives and personal characteristics. A retired widow who is dependent on the income generated from the investments in the portfolio may not have a large percentage of common stocks in her portfolio. However, if the portfolio generates more than a sufficient level of income for the widow's current needs, a small portion of the portfolio could be invested in common stocks to provide some growth for later years.

There isn't a rigid formula for asset allocation. Rather, it is a good idea to think about the concept as a guideline when investing money. Some investors might tilt toward an aggressive portfolio, while others require a conservative portfolio. The mix of investment assets depends primarily on the levels of risk investors are willing to take and their time horizons. The percentage allocated to the different types of assets can always be changed depending on circumstances. As individual circumstances change, so will the investor's objectives. If emphasis shifts, for example, to greater income generation and preservation of capital from capital growth, the percentage of the investments in the portfolio can be changed accordingly. The most important aspect of investing is having an asset allocation plan, which signifies the broad mix of assets to strive for. Once these broad categories are determined, the individual assets are purchased. When considering the different types of securities to choose for a portfolio, investors should weigh the characteristics of the type of investments, along with the risks to assist them in their overall choice.

Investors need to revisit their asset allocation mix from time to time to determine whether to rebalance their mix or realign it to their investment objectives. The frequency with which the asset allocation plan is rebalanced also depends on the investor's portfolio management investment style. A passive investment style suggests leaving the portfolio alone for periods of time and only changing when absolutely necessary. In other words, buying and holding the investments without regard for most, if not all, the superficial factors that affect investments in a portfolio. An active portfolio investment style involves changing investment assets within the portfolio whenever external circumstances have the potential to influence performance. The management of bond portfolios is very different from the management of stock portfolios. Individual bonds provide regular flows of income and have fixed lives, while stocks do not mature, might not provide regular flows of income if the stocks do not pay dividends, and do not have maturity dates, which means uncertainty with regard to future stock prices. Consequently, there is a greater emphasis on stock selection (buying those stocks that will appreciate the most) in the management of stock portfolios.

Table 16.1 illustrates the need for rebalancing a portfolio. If the investor's objectives and personal characteristics have not changed after a year, the asset allocation mix should be realigned to the original mix. Both advantages and disadvantages arise from rebalancing a portfolio. The advantages are:

- The relative weighting of the portfolio assets are aligned with the individual's objectives, personal characteristics, risk tolerance, and rate of return.

- The risk of loss is reduced by selling appreciated assets to realize capital gains.

The disadvantages of rebalancing a portfolio are:

- Rebalancing a portfolio incurs trading costs (commissions) and possibly additional advisory fees.
- Investors run the potential risk of loss that comes from selling the winners in the portfolio to buy more of the losing assets.
- Selling securities involves tax implications in taxable accounts

**TABLE 16.1**

Rebalancing a Portfolio

1. **Begin with an asset allocation plan.**

   The investor started with the asset allocation illustrated in Figure 16.1.

   **FIGURE 16.1**

   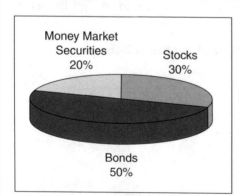

2. **Revisit the asset allocation plan after a period of time.**

   A year later, with the rapid appreciation of the equity portfolio, the asset allocation mix has changed to the percentages shown in Figure 16.2.

**FIGURE 16.2**

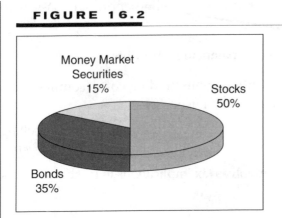

3. **If necessary, rebalance the portfolio.**

   The investor needs to determine whether this new asset allocation mix is consistent with his objectives, personal circumstances, and risk tolerance. With the appreciation of the equity assets, the new equity mix is now 50 percent of the total portfolio value and the bond mix has dropped from 50 to 35 percent. This may not be suitable for an investor who relies more on income-generating assets than growth assets. Rebalancing requires selling off some stocks and buying more bonds with the proceeds in order to realign the asset allocation mix.

4. **Proposed asset allocation plan after rebalancing.**

**FIGURE 16.3**

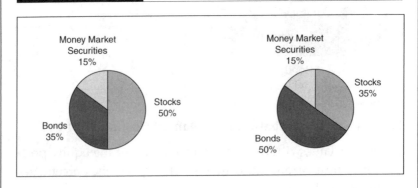

| Current Asset Allocation Mix | | Proposed Asset Allocation Mix | |
| --- | --- | --- | --- |
| Money Market Securities 45,000 | 15% | Money Market Securities | 15% |
| Money market mutual Fund | $ 45,000 | Money Market Mutual Funds | $ 45,000 |
| Stocks | 50% | Stocks | 35% |
| Large Cap Stocks | $150,000 | Large Cap Stocks | $ 52,500 |
| Bonds | 35% | Mid Cap Stocks | $ 52,500 |
| Individual Bonds | $105,000 | Bonds | 50% |
| | | Intermediate Term Municipal Bonds | $ 50,000 |
| | | Long-Term Treasury Bonds | $ 25,000 |
| | | Intermediate Term Agency Bonds | $ 35,000 |
| | | AAA Corporate Bonds | $ 40,000 |
| Total | $300,000 | Total | $300,000 |
| Before Tax Return | 5.10% | Before Tax Return | 6.15% |
| After Tax Return | 3.15% | After Tax Return | 4.5% |
| Risk (Standard Deviation) | 9.00% | Risk (Standard Deviation) | 7.65% |

The most important aspect of investing is having an asset allocation plan that signifies the broad mix of assets to strive for. Once these broad categories are determined, the individual assets are purchased.

## ASSET ALLOCATION MODELS FOR DIFFERENT INVESTMENT OBJECTIVES

A conservative portfolio is one in which the investment goals are to preserve capital, allowing for some growth to the portfolio. The weighting is geared toward high-quality bonds and some common stocks for growth.

**FIGURE 16.4**

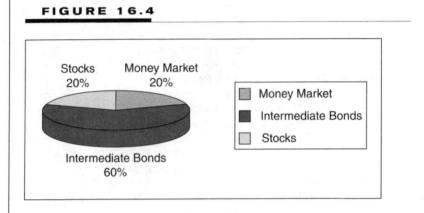

A balanced portfolio has a larger percentage allocated to common stocks, which provides capital growth, as well as keeping a large percentage of assets in fixed income securities, which provide the income for the portfolio.

**FIGURE 16.5**

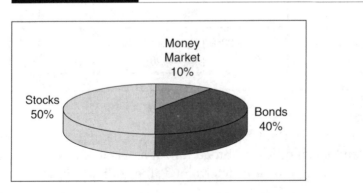

An aggressive portfolio is overweighted in common stocks in order to provide capital growth without any regard for generating income for the portfolio.

**FIGURE 16.6**

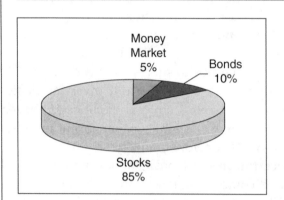

The allocation plan of a young couple, both professionals who are not dependent on income from their investments and are investing for long-term growth, could break down their stock investments into the categories shown in the figure. This is a second example of an aggressive portfolio allocation.

**FIGURE 16.7**

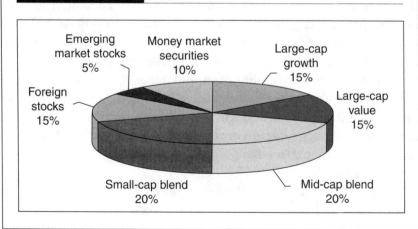

# SELECTION OF INDIVIDUAL INVESTMENTS

In order to match your objectives with specific investments, you need to identify the characteristics of the different investments and their risks. Funds for immediate needs and emergency purposes should be liquid; in other words, able to be converted easily into cash without incurring a loss in principal. Such investments are money market mutual funds, checking accounts, and savings accounts. These are readily convertible into cash. By increasing the time horizon from immediate needs to short-term needs, investors could increase marginally their rates of return by investing in certificates of deposit, Treasury bills, and commercial paper. However, of these, only Treasury bills are marketable, meaning that they can be sold on the secondary market before maturity.

Savings accounts, certificates of deposit, money market mutual funds, Treasury bills, and commercial paper provide some taxable income and are liquid but do not offer the possibilities of capital gains or losses. Although investors might not lose any of their principal by investing in this group of investments, there is a risk that the returns from these investments might not keep up with inflation, particularly with the current low rates of interest.

The financing of intermediate-term objectives, which stretch several years into the future—the purchase of a car, house, or appliance, and the funding of a child's education—requires investments that generate income and the return of principal. These investments need to produce a greater rate of return than a savings account or short-term money market securities. Short- to intermediate-term bonds offer increased rates of return over money market securities, as well as the possibility of capital gains or losses if the investor needs the money before maturity. Although investors receive increased rates of return from intermediate-term securities over money market securities, investors need to be aware that their principal invested in intermediate-term bonds are not as liquid as short-term securities.

An investment plan to finance a child's education in five years requires a relatively safe investment, which would not include investing in stocks. Most people would not gamble with the money earmarked for their children's education in the event of a declining stock market when the money would be needed.

Long-term objectives, such as saving for retirement or for an infant's college education in 18 years, require investments that offer long-term growth prospects, as well as greater long-term returns. Stocks provide larger long-term returns than bonds or money market securities, but stock prices are more volatile. The level of risk that can be withstood on stock investments depends on the individual investor's circumstances.

A more conservative long-term portfolio might consist of long-term bonds, blue chip stocks, and conservative growth stocks. The emphasis of this strategy is to invest in good-quality bonds and the stocks of established companies that pay dividends and offer the prospect of steady growth over a long period of time. Securities offering capital growth are important even for conservative portfolios in order to provide some cover against any potential erosion in future purchasing power from inflation.

A growth-oriented part of a portfolio seeks the generation of long-term capital gains and the monetary growth in value of the stocks in the portfolio. A more speculative portfolio, in which an investor can absorb greater levels of risk to strive for greater growth and returns, would include growth stocks, stocks of emerging companies, foreign stocks, emerging market stocks, convertible bonds, junk bonds, real estate, options, commodities, and futures. Bear in mind that including the last three types of investments— options, commodities, and futures—is not an endorsement that these securities should play a major role in a portfolio. For a speculative investor who understands the nuances of these investments, these securities could account for no more than 5 percent of the total portfolio. The other assets mentioned offer investors the opportunity for large gains, but the risk of loss is also greater. Foreign bonds and stocks should also be considered, but investors should do their homework first so that they understand the risks fully. International mutual funds might be more helpful to spread some of the risks, although in the short term there is always currency risk when investing in off-shore investments. Over the long term, however, exchange fluctuations tend to even out and are not a significant factor.

Figure 16.8 outlines the continuum for the choice of stocks within the range of value and growth. Where the investor feels most comfortable in concentrating her investments will vary on the level of acceptable risk and the time frame for holding investments. Some investors might stick with a portfolio composed of 100 percent value stocks and others could stick with a blend of growth and value stocks, while active investors might include a portfolio of 100 percent growth stocks. Investors who are not comfortable buying individual bonds and stocks could choose mutual funds, exchange-traded funds, or closed-end funds within these styles. Investors willing to make their own investment decisions on individual securities can eliminate the fees and expenses charged by mutual funds and closed-end funds. When considering the different types of securities to choose for a portfolio, investors should weigh the characteristics of the type of investment along with the risks. (See Table 16.2 for a summary of the strategies to reduce the different types of risks.)

## FIGURE 16.8

Value-Growth Continuum

| 100% Value<br>0% Growth | 80% Value<br>20% Growth | 60% Value<br>40% Growth | 40% Value<br>60% Growth | 20% Value<br>80% Growth | 0% Value<br>100% Growth |
|---|---|---|---|---|---|
| Value<br>Stocks | Dividend-Paying<br>Stocks | Economically<br>Sensitive stocks | Growth at a<br>Reasonable price | Growth<br>Stocks | Momentum<br>Stocks |

Long Investment Holding Period                          Short Investment Holding Period

**TABLE 16.2**

Summary of Strategies to Manage Risk

| Investment | Risk | Strategy |
|---|---|---|
| Common Stock | Market Risk | Invest for a long period of time |
| | Financial Risk | Diversification: Invest in companies with low leverage |
| | Interest Rate Risk | Active or passive strategy, depending on the investor's time horizon |
| | Declining Market Rates of Interest | Increase the percentage of the portfolio allocated to stocks |
| | Increasing Market Rates of Interest | Decrease the percentage of the portfolio allocated to stocks |
| | Credit Risk | Invest in good-quality stocks |
| | Purchasing Power Risk | Requires active portfolio management: Invest in stocks that (when inflation increases) will weather the effects of inflation better, such as gold, oil, and commodity stocks |

As mentioned throughout this book, diversification reduces risk without decreasing returns. A portfolio should include at least 12 to 15 stocks in order to lessen the risk of loss. In other words, an investment in one company should not account for more than 10 percent of your portfolio. If that investment declines significantly, you would be limiting the total amount of your loss to at most 10 percent of your portfolio. One method of building a portfolio is to invest equal amounts to different stocks. For example, if you want to invest in 20 stocks, the amount invested in each stock would be 5 percent of your total capital. However, you might identify some of those stocks that have the potential to perform better with lower risk, and you would want to allocate greater amounts to them and lesser amounts to stocks that might not be as attractive.

Investors who assume that the stock markets are efficient strive to build portfolios that are well diversified with risks and returns that match those of the market. In order to earn returns that are greater than those of the market, investors would need to invest in securities with higher risks than the market indices. Passive investment strategies of matching market returns involve indexing and long-term buy-and-hold investing strategies.

Investors who think they can beat the market averages are more likely to choose their own stocks and are also likely to have shorter holding periods for their stocks, namely growth stocks. Market timers buy and sell stocks as market trends and economic factors change, and these types of investors would not necessarily include value stocks. Some industries are more sensitive to the economy than others. As previously mentioned, industries that move in the same direction as the economy are referred to as cyclical industries. The sales and earnings of these companies are generally aligned with the economic cycle. The stage in the business cycle of the economy becomes important to the timing of the investments in these cyclical companies. For example, you would not want to invest in the stocks of automobile companies at the peak of an economic expansion because their stock prices would be at their upper limits and they would face a downturn in earnings when the economy slows down. During a period of economic expansion, the stock prices of cyclical companies traditionally increase; during a recession, the prices decline. Cyclical companies are in industries such as automobiles, building and construction, aluminum, steel, chemicals, and lumber. Because these stocks are sensitive to changes in economic activity, investors should time their purchases of cyclical stocks to the early phases of an expansionary period.

Coming out of a recession, financial stocks tend to do well because of lower interest rates, whereas in the expansionary phase, stocks of consumer durable goods companies are the ones to buy. During a recession consumers delay purchases of automobiles, large appliances, and houses. Cyclical stocks fluctuate with the state of the economy and are always hit hard by rising interest rates. Into an expansionary cycle, capital goods companies benefit from increased sales in the business sector, which result in an increase in the demand for raw materials and commodities. Stable industries include health care stocks, beverage stocks, food retailers, food companies, consumer services, and household nondurables.

This pattern is typical in most business cycles, but exceptions always exist. During the recession of 2000 to 2002, for example, auto companies saw sales of cars rise significantly because of the sales and marketing incentive programs, including 0-percent financing and considerable price discounts. This increase improved auto companies' sales but did not improve their profits. By timing stock purchases in these different industries, investors might be able to improve their returns.

Anticipating changes in interest rates could prompt investors to reallocate the types of investments in their portfolios. If higher rates of interest are anticipated, an investor has a number of different options. Profits might be taken by selling stocks that have appreciated, or the investor might decide to sell stocks in the interest-sensitive industries, such as financial stocks, cyclical sector stocks in the automotive and home- building industries, and utility stocks. Some investors might buy stocks in the pharmaceutical and food industries, which tend to weather the effects of higher market interest rates better than other sectors of the economy. Other investors might decide to hold their existing stocks but not invest any new money in the stock market until interest rates start to level off. True market timers might liquidate their entire stock positions and wait on the sidelines for more favorable conditions.

Purchasing power risk or inflation hurts all financial investments to some degree or another. However, traditionally, returns on stocks tend to outperform those of bonds and money market securities during low to moderate rates of inflation. Mining stocks, such as gold and platinum, and aluminum stocks have been good hedges against inflation.

Even a passively managed portfolio should be examined at various intervals with regard to returns on different investments, as well as the changing economic conditions. Not all investments achieve their anticipated returns, and if they turn out to be poor performers, they might need to be liquidated.

Investors who do not have the knowledge and skills to manage their portfolios might turn to professional advisors. Financial planners and accountants offer advice on the planning and management of portfolios. For investors who do not wish to be involved in the management of their assets, there are professional money managers and trust departments of various institutions. Their fees are often a stated percentage of the total dollar amount of the portfolio, which often requires that the portfolio be substantial in dollar terms.

The key to long-term successful investing is to allocate investments into bonds, stocks, and money market securities suited to the investor's particular objectives and circumstances.

# NOTES

## CHAPTER 1—VALUE INVESTING: WHAT IT IS AND WHAT IT IS NOT

1. Cheyney, John M., and Edward A. Moses. *Fundamentals of Investments*. St. Paul, MN: West, 1992, 19.

2. Mattich, Alen. "Asset Class: Market Timing Makes a Comeback." *Wall Street Journal Online*, March 14, 2003.

3. Veverka, Mark. "Why Intel Deserves Another Look." *Barron's*, May 28, 2012, 15–16.

4. Veverka, 15.

5. Veverka, 16.

6. Veverka, 15.

7. Faerber, Esme. *All About Stocks, 3rd Ed.* New York: McGraw-Hill, 2008.

8. Tan, Kopin. "Who Wins, Who Loses." *Barron's*, July 2, 2012, 16.

## CHAPTER 2—ARE YOU A VALUE INVESTOR?

1. Levisohn, Ben. "Why 'Value' Stocks Lag." *Wall Street Journal*, May 26–27, 2012, B9.

2. Levisohn, B9.

3. Jakab, Spencer. "Idea of a Dividend Bubble Has Some Pop." *Wall Street Journal*, June 8, 2012, C1.

4. Jakab, C1.

5.  Coggin, Daniel T., Frank J. Fabozzi, and Robert D. Arnott. *Handbook of Equity Style Management, 2nd Ed.* New Hope, PA: Frank Fabozzi Associates, 1997.

6.  Capaul, C., I. Rowley, and W. Sharpe. "International Value and Growth Stock Returns." *Financial Analysts Journal*, January–February 1993.

7.  Tam, Pu-Wing, and Patrick McGeeham. "Finding the 'Value' in Value Funds." *Wall Street Journal*, April 16, 1999, C1, C19.

8.  Levisohn, B9.

9.  Ibid.

10. Jakab, C1.

11. Faerber, Esme. *All About Stocks, 3rd Ed.* New York: McGraw-Hill, 2008, 301–303.

12. Ibid.

13. Jakab, C1.

14. Hough, Jack. "Where to Find Dividends That Grow." *Barron's*, October 22, 2012, 26.

## CHAPTER 6—THE INCOME STATEMENT

1.  Ray, Tiernan. "Intel: Building on Otellini's Legacy." *Barron's*, November 26, 2012, 16.

## CHAPTER 7—STATEMENT OF CHANGES IN CASH

1.  Faerber, Esme. *All About Stocks, 3rd Ed.* New York: McGraw-Hill, 2008, 132.

2.  Hoens, Thomas W., and Keith B. Foley. "Cash Is King in Bond Analysis." Fitch Investor Service, Special Report, January 10, 1994.

3.  Equity investments are not common items of CFAR, but in Enron's case these expenditures were large.

4.  Hoens, Thomas W. Personal conversation, March 26, 2003.

5.  Ibid.

## CHAPTER 8—FUNDAMENTAL ANALYSIS

1.  Brown, Ken. "How to Spot the Dirt in Rosy Annual Reports." *Wall Street Journal*, February 14, 2003, C1, C3.

2.  McNamee, Mike. "Annual Reports: Still Not Enough Candor," *Business Week*, March 24, 2003, 74.

3.  Henry, David, and Robert Berner. "Ouch! Real Numbers," *Business Week*, March 24, 2003, 72–73.

## CHAPTER 9—CHOOSING A VALUE STOCK PORTFOLIO

1. Farrell, James L., Jr. "Homogeneous Stock Groupings: Implications for Portfolio Management," *Financial Analysts Journal*, May–June 1975, 50–62.

2. Tergesen, Anne. "With Index Funds, Who Needs Gurus?" *Business Week*, January 18, 1999, 108–110.

3. Ibid.

4. Farrell, Christopher. "Why Index Funds Can't Be Beat," *Business Week Online*, November 14, 2003.

5. Martin, Larry L. "The Evolution of Passive versus Active Equity Management," *Journal of Investing*, spring 1993, 17–20.

6. Jensen, Michael C. "The Performance of Mutual Funds in the period 1945–1964," *Journal of Finance*, May 1968, 389–416.

7. Strong, Robert A. *Practical Investment Management*. Cincinnati, OH: South-Western College Publishing, 1998, 363.

8. Coggin, Daniel T., Frank J. Fabozzi, and Robert D. Arnott. *Handbook of Equity Style Management, 2nd Ed.* New Hope, PA: Frank Fabozzi Associates, 1997.

9. Capaul, C., I. Rowley, and W. Sharpe. "International Value and Growth Stock Returns," *Financial Analysts' Journal*, January–February 1993.

10. Tam, Pu-Wing, and Patrick McGeeham. "Finding the 'Value' in Value Funds," *Wall Street Journal*, April 16, 1999, C1, C19.

## CHAPTER 10—USING MUTUAL FUNDS

1. Clements, Jonathan. "Wall Street's Latest: Mini-Hedge Funds." *Wall Street Journal*, March 26, 2002, C1.

2. Light, Joe. "Build Your Own Hedge Fund." *Wall Street Journal*, December 15–16, 2012, B7, B10.

3. Clements, C1.

4. Scholl, Jaye, and Andrew Bary. "A Lousy New Year." *Barron's*, October 12, 1998, 19.

5. Light, B10.

6. Maxey, Daisy. "At Hedge Funds, Study Exit Guidelines." *The Wall Street Journal*, September 23, 2006, B4.

7. Light, B7.

8. Kuhle, James L. and Ralph A Pope. "A Comprehensive Long-Term Performance Analysis of Load vs. No-Load Mutual Funds." *Journal of Financial and Strategic Decisions*, summer 2000, volume 13, number 2, 1–11.

9.   Malkiel, Burton G. "Returns from Investing in Equity Mutual Funds 1971–1991." *Journal of Finance* 50, June 1995, 549–572.

10.  Jakab, Spencer. "Why Stock-Fund Data Deserve Respect." *Wall Street Journal*, February 11, 2013, C1.

## CHAPTER 11—USING CLOSED-END FUNDS

1.   Byrne, Thomas C. "Beyond Yield." *Individual Investor,* July, 1994, 32.
2.   Ibid.
3.   Zuckerman, Lawrence. "A Look Under the Hood at Realty Stocks." *New York Times,* July 16, 1994, 35.

## CHAPTER 12—EXCHANGE-TRADED FUNDS

1.   Young, Lauren. "ETFs: What the Buzz Is About." *Business Week,* March 1, 2004, 124–126.
2.   www.ici.org/research
3.   Salisbury, Ian. "Telecom Gains Often Elude ETFs." *Wall Street Journal,* November 22, 2006, C11.
4.   Coleman, Murray. "Tracking ETFs with Fewer Errors." *Wall Street Journal,* January 11, 2013, www.WSJ.com.
5.   Ibid.
6.   Prestbo, John A. "Beware Turnover Costs on Index Funds." *Wall Street Journal,* December 3, 2012, R8.

## CHAPTER 13—BONDS

1.   Faerber, Esme. *All About Bonds, Bond Mutual Funds, and Bond ETFs.* New York: McGraw-Hill, 2009, 2.
2.   Faerber, 2009, 2–3.
3.   Malkiel, Burton C. "Expectations, Bond Prices, and the Term Structure of Interest Rates." *Quarterly Journal of Economics,* May 1962, 197–218.
4.   Norris, Floyd. "Putting Sticker Prices on Corporate Bonds." *New York Times,* June 27, 2003, C1.

## CHAPTER 15—OPTIONS, RIGHTS, AND WARRANTS

1.   Sears, Steven M. "The Five Rules of Options Trading." *Barron's,* April 1, 2013, 33.
2.   Ibid.

# INDEX